Making Doctors

EXPLORATIONS IN ANTHROPOLOGY
A University College London Series

Series Editors: Barbara Bender, John Gledhill and Bruce Kapferer

Pnina Werbner, *The Migration Process: Capital, Gifts and Offerings among Pakistanis in Britain*

Joel S. Kahn, *Constituting the Minangkabau: Peasants, Culture, and Modernity in Colonial Indonesia*

Gisli Pálsson, *Beyond Boundaries: Understanding, Translation and Anthropological Discourse*

Stephen Nugent, *Amazonian Caboclo Society*

Barbara Bender, *Landscape: Politics and Perspectives*

Christopher Tilley (ed.), *Interpretative Archaeology*

Ernest S. Burch Jr and Linda J. Ellanna (eds), *Key Issues in Hunter-Gatherer Research*

Daniel Miller, *Modernity – An Ethnographic Approach: Dualism and Mass Consumption in Trinidad*

Robert Pool, *Dialogue and the Interpretation of Illness: Conversations in a Cameroon Village*

Cécile Barraud, Daniel de Coppet, André Iteanu and Raymond Jamous (eds), *Of Relations and the Dead: Four Societies Viewed from the Angle of their Exchanges*

Christopher Tilley, *A Phenomenology of Landscape: Places, Paths and Monuments*

Victoria Goddard, Josep Llobera and Cris Shore (eds), *The Anthropology of Europe: Identity and Boundaries in Conflict*

Pat Caplan (ed.), *Understanding Disputes: The Politics of Argument*

Daniel de Coppet and André Iteanu (ed.), *Society and Cosmos: Their Interrelations or Their Coalescence in Melanesia*

Alisdair Rogers and Steven Vertovec (eds), *The Urban Context: Ethnicity, Social Networks and situational Analysis*

Saskia Kersenboom, *Word, Sound, Image: The Life of the Tamil Text*

Daniel de Coppet and André Iteanu (eds), *Cosmos and Society in Oceania*

Roy Ellen and Katsuyoshi Fukui, *Redefining Nature: Ecology, Culture and Domestication*

William Washabaugh, *Flamenco: Passion, Politics and Popular Culture*

Bernard Juillerat, *Children of the Blood: Society, Reproduction and Imaginary Representations in New Guinea*

Karsten Paerregaard, *Linking Separate Worlds: Urban Migrants and Rural Lives in Peru*

Nicole Rodriguez Toulis, *Believing Identity: Pentecostalism and the Mediation of Jamaican Ethnicity and Gender in England*

Jerome R. Mintz, *Carnival Song and Society: Gossip, Sexuality and Creativity in Andalusia*

Neil Jarman, *Material Conflicts: Parades and Visual Displays in Northern Ireland*

Gary Armstrong and Richard Giulianotti, *Entering the Field: Perspectives on World Football*

Deborah Reed-Danahay, *Auto/Ethnography: Rewriting the Self and the Social*

Marianne Elisabeth Lien, *Marketing and Modernity*

R.D. Grillo and R.L. Stirrat (eds), *Discourses of Development: Anthropological Perspectives*

Making Doctors

An Institutional Apprenticeship

Simon Sinclair

Oxford • New York

First published in 1997 by
Berg
Editorial offices:
150 Cowley Road, Oxford, OX4 1JJ, UK
70 Washington Square South, New York, NY 10012, USA

Berg is an imprint of Oxford International Publishers Ltd.

Library of Congress Cataloging-in-Publication Data

A catalogue record for this book is available from the Library of Congress.

British Library Cataloguing-in-Publication Data

A catalogue record for this book is available from the British Library.

ISBN 1 85973 950 4 (Cloth)
1 85973 955 5 (Paper)

Typeset by JS Typesetting, Wellingborough, Northants.
Printed in the United Kingdom by WBC Book Manufacturers, Bridgend, Mid Glamorgan.

For MA

Contents

Acknowledgements

This book evolved from research undertaken in the Department of Anthropology at the London School of Economics and Political Science, for which I received an ESRC grant for three years. I sought and received help from a large number of people, before, during, and after fieldwork. While most are named below, there are no doubt others, whom, for one reason or another, are not: to these I apologise. The variety of such assistance was enormous, ranging from brief telephone calls to lengthy discussions.

I should like to thank Dr Isobel Allen, Professor Paul Atkinson, Mr Chris Bulstrode, Professor Bill Bynum, Kieran Coonan QC, Dr Chris Evans, Dr Jenny Firth-Cozens, Professor Ronnie Frankenburg, Dr Madeleine Ganley, Dr Graham Gibbs, Professor Conrad Harris, Dr Tim Healey, Dr Tim Horder, Dr Tony Hope, Professor Liam Hudson, Dr Helen Kennerley, Professor Roland Littlewood, Professor Chris McManus, Professor Marshall Marinker, Isabel Menzies-Lyth, Lesley Millard, the late Dr Clare Vaughan, Dr Andrew Powell, Mr Peter Riddell, Dr Anthony Ryle, Dr Alan Shrank and Susan Spindler.

At University College London Medical School I should like to record my particular thanks to Dr David Brenton (without whose help my fieldwork in the teaching hospital would have been impossible), as well as thanking Dr Peter Abrahams, Dr John Betteridge, Dr Gerald Bevan, Professor Geoffrey Burnstock, Dr Brenda Cross, Dr Chris Dean, Mr Tim Davidson, Dr Charles Engel, Professor John Foreman, Dr Frances Lefford, Dr Arthur Miller, Dr Elizabeth Murray, Professor James Malone-Lee, Professor Stanton Newman, Dr Elizabeth Paice, Professor John Pattison, the late Professor John Pegington, Dr Diana Sanders, Dr Graham Scambler, Professor Irving Taylor, Dr Angela Towle, Professor John Wyllie, Dr Lucy Yardley and the administrative staff at the Medical School (especially Gwen Austin, Suzy Nichols and Gaynor Jones) and other officials of UCL. I should, of course, also like to thank the medical students and housemen among whom I worked, particularly the officers of the Students' Union and the various official and unofficial teams that granted me temporary membership. I am indebted to Christopher Bellew for the generous provision of a room in London to live in for the year's fieldwork.

For help given while writing this book, I should like to thank Professor Peter Loizos and Professor Johnny Parry and the members of the seminar group at the LSE, and, for several helpful comments, my examiners Dr Sophie Day and Dr Gilbert Lewis, as well as Dr Julie Bland, Dr David Gellner, Dr Peter Jarrett and Sarah Newell. Finally here, I should record my great indebtedness to the late Dr Phil Strong, to whose encouragement and advice I owe so much.

The range of my acknowledgements to those who, in one way or another, have influenced what follows, should itself indicate my great dependence on others' co-operation in writing this book; responsibility for it, however, remains mine alone.

I am also grateful to UCL External Affairs and to Michele Minto of the Wellcome Centre Medical Photographic Library for help with the illustrations, and to those at Berg Publishers. The chapter headings in verse are taken from: "The 'Eathen" (Chapters 2 and 9), "A School Song" (Chapter 3), and the Chapter Heading to "Thrown Away" in *Plain Tales From The Hills* (Chapter 10), all in *The Definitive Edition of Rudyard Kipling's Verse* (Hodder and Stoughton 1966), by permission of A. P. Watt Ltd. on behalf of The National Trust; "What I Never Saw" by Timothy Corsellis (Chapters 4 and 5) in *The Voice of War* (Penguin 1996) – the editors, the Salamander Oasis Trust, endeavoured to contact the holder of copyright; "Naming Of Parts" (Chapters 6 and 8) in Henry Reed's *Collected Poems* edited by Jon Stallworthy (Oxford University Press 1991), by permission of Oxford University Press; "Strange Meeting" (Chapter 7) in *The Collected Poems of Wilfred Owen* edited by C. Day Lewis, copyright © 1963 by Chatto & Windus Ltd, with acknowledgements to the editor's Estate and by permission of New Directions Publishing Corporation; and "Sonnet: Books" (Chapter 11) in *The Collected Ewart 1933–1980: Poems by Gavin Ewart* (Hutchinson 1980), by permission of Margo Ewart.

Chapter 1

Introduction

> One might say that the learning of the medical role consists of a separation, almost an alienation, of the student from the lay medical world; a passing through the mirror so that one looks out on the world from behind it, and sees things in mirror writing.
>
> Everett Hughes (1984: 399)

A General Introduction to Basic Medical Training

This book is principally an account of 'passing through the mirror', in Hughes' famous phrase. It deals with the basic medical training in a London teaching hospital as it was in 1993/4, when the structure of training in most medical schools in England had remained fundamentally unchanged for the last 150 years or so. In outline, the traditional training (both here and in the United States, where it has been broadly similar) has three structural levels. The first consists of two preclinical years; this is followed here by three years' clinical training; and the third level (known as internship in the US) is the pre-registration year of General Clinical Training, when newly qualified doctors work as House Officers, usually for six months in Medicine and six months in Surgery. Such uniformity and stability has great advantages for anyone such as myself; studies of the traditional form of training, whether in this country or the United States, remain pertinent even though published many years ago.

It should be noted that the word 'medicine' is used in two different ways: as a branch or segment of the profession, often, as above, in opposition to Surgery, and as another name for the medical profession itself. This ambiguity is found in common usage and, to avoid confusion, in what follows I shall indicate the segment of the profession as I have above, by giving it a capital letter. It should also be noted that the process I describe may be referred to both as 'medical education' and as 'medical training': medical schools have been independently granted both graduating and licensing functions, and these two functions, of education and training, are inextricably confused (see McManus 1995). The university degree (MB BS at London University, for example) is also a preliminary licence to practise medicine and, most unusually for university degrees, is unclassed; you either pass or fail, you are either provisionally registered or you are not. While the educative function is now to some extent provided by the optional B.Sc., usually taken between the preclinical and clinical courses, there seems no doubt that the compulsory course is rightly called a training, and I shall continue to refer to it as this throughout.

My account regards medical training very much on its own, largely unaffected by the wider world; the voices of patients, for example, are rarely heard. This reflects the profession's real autonomy. Of course, any profession has, and must have, its own expertise, its own knowledge and skills; but, in addition to modern Western medicine's spectacular technical and scientific advances, medicine also owes its own pre-eminent success to its ethical commitments and their proclaimed affinity with lay aspirations. Freidson (1970) suggests that this combination has conserved the profession's right to continued self-regulation and the independence of its practitioners from review, whether by the lay public (either by patients or the general population) or by professional colleagues; practitioners are accountable only to the profession itself. It also seems to have conserved the profession's right to train its future members in its own way, and this has tended to be the way that its senior members were themselves trained. Questions have been raised about both the justification for and the effect of such autonomy. Freidson does not deny the huge advances of specialist scientific knowledge about disease and its treatment, but reckons that such advances may actually have impeded the social modes of doctors' application of that knowledge for the benefit of patients. His prescription for bringing professional practice more in line with patients' wishes has several features: much wider recruitment; the dismantling of self-sufficient teaching institutions; the encouragement of regular interaction between different sorts of doctors, particularly between those working in hospital and those in the community (where, he notes, the former might learn from the latter about the non-scientific aspects of practice in treating patients' illness); and finally, regular review of practice in the light of both professional and lay standards. Given the stability of the traditional training, and assuming that, to take best effect, any such reforms should be introduced in these formative training years, it should be no great surprise that these features are hardly to be found there, and, where they are, they make little impression.

There have, of course, been minor changes; some of these are the result of internal professional reviews, which all focus on the expressed function of medical schools, which is to produce doctors. Seemingly endless reports, whether governmental, professional or educational, from local studies of small groups of students upwards, and from Royal Commissions and the General Medical Council (GMC) downwards, have all noted the overwhelming burden of facts that medical students have to learn, particularly in the preclinical years; the rate at which these reports are being produced seems to have increased recently, partly as a result of the recent reforms of the National Health Service. Among these reforms are the amalgamation of previously independent medical schools, and their association with other institutions of higher education. The GMC's report *Tomorrow's Doctors*, published in 1993, perhaps together with the problems posed by these large new institutions, has been used to propose more radical plans for changing the method of training; many reformers advocate the 'Problem-Based Learning' method, started in McMaster in Canada, and now found, for example, at Harvard (see Boud and Feletti 1991; Tosteson 1994), and some medical schools are reported as doing away with the preclinical and clinical divide altogether. It is therefore possible (though I will argue highly unlikely) that I was conducting 'salvage anthropology' in recording the dying moments of a traditional form of professional training.

My description of medical training is unusual in two respects, geographical and ethnographic. First, it appears to be the first anthropological or sociological study of basic medical training in England. Medical anthropology has recently been alluded to as anthropology's 'London', a busy centre for debate about important social, political, existential, and epistemological matters (Good 1994: 5). It may be so; but London itself is by no means a well-trodden site for the study of medical training or practice. The majority of such studies come from the US and not from this country, let alone London; the only major ethnographic account of medical training here is from Edinburgh (Atkinson 1981).

Perhaps London's current and historical importance, its central position for medicine (with its Royal Colleges and its concentration of medical schools so close to the seat of government), which would appear to make it such an obvious site, have in fact made London less an open field than a closed city.

Second, these studies of medical training have tended to concentrate both on specific levels of training (usually either the preclinical and clinical years together or the pre-registration year on its own) or on specific matters (such as the 'uncertainty' experienced by students). I discuss some results of this tendency at greater length in the next chapter; here I wish to indicate the advantages of trying (with whatever degree of success) to fill a large ethnographic gap by providing a more comprehensive account of the basic training. My main point is simple: that it is only through such an account that the way the training collectively transforms individuals can be fully understood. This, in turn, allows a greater understanding of another kind of report which describes the effect of training on students' mental well-being.

Earlier reports of this nature (see, for example, Schwartz *et al.* 1978) were concerned with what was described as the transition of students' initial idealism, through training, to a position of disillusionment or cynicism. More recent ones tend to use the psychologically derived and medically approved concepts of anxiety, depression and stress. In three recent studies from this country (Firth 1986; Firth-Cozens 1987 and 1990), surprising rates of mental illness were found among those being trained for a profession that itself treats illness: 31.2 per cent of second-year clinical students were emotionally disturbed (compared to 9.7 per cent in young unemployed people); 28 per cent of House Officers were found to be depressed at a level that indicated treatment; and 46 per cent of women House Officers were later found to be depressed at such a level (compared to 14.9 per cent of a community sample of women in London). The significant numbers of medical students who drink a great deal of alcohol were also noted.

Further, it is likely to be highly relevant that, while longer-qualified doctors are (like members of other professions) physically healthier than average, their rates of mental illness (particularly of depression and alcoholism) and of death from causes that may reasonably be considered to have a significant psychological aetiology (suicide, poisoning and cirrhosis of the liver) are not only higher than average, but higher than those of members of other professions except dentists (BMA 1993: 15–28). While I discuss these matters more fully towards the end of the book, I should here state that, given the similarities between the types of illness found among those training for the profession and doctors themselves, it seems not only a parsimonious but a probable conclusion that the process of becoming a doctor somehow renders people more constitutionally liable to psychological problems (whether these tend to be more situationally related, as the three studies of training might indicate, or more general, as the high rates of morbidity and mortality from such cases among longer-qualified doctors might suggest).

The Nature of the Book and my Place in it

This is not a personal account of medical training, such as those written by students and doctors (apparently only in the US) and given titles that reflect both their tenor and the irony central to medicine: among these are, *A Not Entirely Benign Procedure* (Klass 1987), *To Do No Harm* (Reilly 1987), and *Gentle Vengeance* (LeBaron 1981). In another such personal account, *Becoming a Doctor*, Konner, an anthropologist before he became a doctor, says that he might have written at least two other sorts of book (1987: xiii–xiv). The first could have been a Hollywood 'docudrama', with some of the quality of television medical fiction. And certainly the general public's appetite for both written and televised fictional and documentary portrayals of medical life seems insatiable. What is perhaps surprising is medical students' and junior doctors' own avid consumption of such theatrical accounts of their theatrical world – the television series 'Cardiac Arrest' and 'Casualty' seemed to be particular favourites during my fieldwork.

The second book might have been a 'dry social-science' account of socialisation into the cultural world of medicine. This would have included a review of the literature on the sociology of the professions, details of the profession's social structure with some theoretical foundation for interpreting it, and an analysis, cast in appropriate psychologese, of the personality changes of the typical medical student; there would also have been a profusion of diagrams. This is not altogether a bad outline of my book, though I hope it is not too 'dry': there are some pictures and, in effect, only one diagram, and I have generally tried to make it accessible to non-specialist social scientists. But I beg leave to doubt Konner's assertion that he 'could have done all that' at the same time as being a student. Indeed, he undermines this claim himself by the omission from his narrative of the preclinical years, so overloaded with having to learn facts so quickly forgotten, and of the year as an intern, so overloaded with work. In fact he seems to withdraw this claim later, saying, 'Anthropological participant observation both permits and requires an ultimate detachment to which I cannot in this case pretend.'

Whether Konner is right about the nature of participant observation or not, I cannot pretend an ultimate detachment either. But I think it possible that my situation, the reverse of Konner's, in that I trained as a doctor before studying anthropology, may make detachment a little easier for me; after all, I have had some years to consider these matters. Further, I did not have to learn all those facts again to pass preclinical exams and continue in medical school; my performance and attendance during the clinical training was not assessed and graded, grades that would themselves be considered if I had had to apply for a House Officer's post; and my attachment to House Officers was as and when I wanted it, unlike their own required regular daily and nightly presence, again with continuous assessment of their performance.

I do not appear much in the ethnographic sections of the book; yet it is mine, and my own position in relation to its subject should be made clear. To start with, I decided to do medicine while studying classics at school, for a combination of reasons that I recall: to learn more, not to have to make any more decisions for some years, and to become a doctor, believing that I would be doing both interesting and worthwhile work while earning a reasonable income in a secure job. My early plan to become a psychiatrist was dented by the sort of Psychology I studied at university and was completely lost sight of during my clinical training. After house jobs, I was not sure what to do; Surgery was out of the question, but I found the practice of Medicine unsympathetic. I left for Nepal, where I worked as a doctor for three years, before returning to specialist training in Psychiatry. During the years of my training, I became familiar with the sorts of psychological difficulties that students and junior doctors face. Latterly, I was working part-time, on what some consultants still referred to as the 'Married Women's Scheme'; I decided to use the time made available to study anthropology, also part-time. When a doctorate became a possibility, the question was whether to go abroad to do fieldwork (with Nepal the obvious site) or to use the opportunity to study what was of rather more personal relevance, the practice of medicine in this country and, in particular, the nature of the basic training in medical schools. In the end, I reasoned that it was a little presumptuous to try to understand what other people did before I understood what I had been doing myself.

Fieldwork and the Institution

The practical business of gaining access to a medical school gave immediate reminders of some central features of the institution. My first attempt to be allowed to work with students in a dissecting room (for I was already clear about the central position of Anatomy) failed: at the first school I approached, my proposals and methods were not specific enough for the anatomists, who also feared that my presence might upset the students. My second attempt, again originally through personal contacts, benefited from the previous reminder of the difference between natural and social sciences, and I was accepted to work in the dissecting room at University College London Medical School (UCLMS).

This school, spread over various sites mostly in the very centre of London, was recently formed by the amalgamation of the University College Hospital Medical School (UCH) and the Middlesex Medical School in 1987. Originally founded itself as the University of London in 1828, University College later became only one constituent college, but perhaps always the predominant one, of the University. Medicine was, from the first, one of the principal courses taught there, and University College Hospital, opened in 1834, was the first purpose-built teaching hospital in London. University College London (UCL) is now an internationally renowned institution, and many famous scientists, both past and present, are associated with it. The Middlesex Hospital was established in 1745, and its own medical school in 1835. The two hospitals (and medical schools) merged just prior to the 'Tomlinson Report' (1992); this report was commissioned by the Secretaries of State for Health and Education to consider health service provision in London in relation to medical education and research, in the context of the reformed NHS. The further merger of UCLMS with another medical school and teaching hospital, the Royal Free, was recommended in the Tomlinson Report, and this was being discussed and planned during my fieldwork. The fate of previously independent schools in such amalgamations has been deplored by many; in the formation of UCLMS, for example, it was generally considered that the Middlesex had been to a great extent swallowed up. Its more intimate culture (due to its smaller numbers of students and its strictly medical identity) had been lost within the larger conglomerate. This may have partly been due to another of the Report's recommendations, that the merged London medical schools should all (bar one) become faculties of medicine within the multi-faculty colleges of London University, with 'strong basic science'; UCH obviously had this link already in its close association with UCL, while the Middlesex did not.

Acceptance of my proposal to study in the UCLMS dissecting room was accompanied by an insistence that I use a questionnaire – this was seen as the only way to draw valid conclusions, as well as being necessary to control for differences among students. After this condition was granted by me (privately, most unwillingly) and the head of the academic department's acceptance given, other doors opened easily within the preclinical school; once I was in, there seemed no obstacles to participant observation. My negotiations to work with clinical students provoked a contrary insistence that I did not use questionnaires, as this might interfere with another such study of clinical students. I was therefore again reminded of the conventional agreement about the importance placed on 'objective' forms of investigation and also of the complete separation between preclinical and clinical training, which here placed me in an institutional 'double-bind': this I resolved by preparing a specimen questionnaire but taking it no further. Similar objections were also raised about my status: if I were not medically qualified, I would not understand what was going on; but, because I was, I would understand perfectly well, and might therefore be critical of teaching, again possibly upsetting the students and doctors. After these theoretical objections were overcome, and agreement was given by the clinical school authorities, arrangements to work with clinical students involved further negotiation on my behalf with individual consultants; in particular, no surgeon would at first agree to allow me to join their students. Consultants were not bound, it seemed, by the school's agreement, and my further acceptance was up to them individually – an indication of their personal power. But, as preclinically, specific acceptance by a few consultants led to a more general one, and I could go unchallenged round the hospital, identified as a student by wearing a short white coat. It then became possible to arrange fieldwork at the third level of training, by 'shadowing' House Officers working for consultants whose students I had previously associated with.

Nearly all students knew who I was; some doctors did too, but others, some even working with the consultants who had accepted me, did not. I felt no need to introduce myself to them, and students also usually withheld their knowledge of my identity from them: perhaps because such personal knowledge constituted the only sort of knowledge that was theirs alone; perhaps because I was 'one of them', and no longer a doctor myself; perhaps because of the hope that amusing and possibly embarrassing situations might arise, as they of course occasionally did. Among students I only encountered one episode of real hostility (which I describe) during a year of their transient friendship.

I spent just over a year doing fieldwork at UCLMS, among first- and second-year preclinical students, among first- and third-year clinical students, and among House Officers (both in the teaching hospital and at a local non-teaching hospital), so covering five out of the six compulsory years of training. I had originally planned to live in London during the week and to return home at weekends; I abandoned this plan after two weeks, having become increasingly unhappy at being separated from my family and fully aware of the power of the institution to supplant it. This meant that, while I was able to continue the fieldwork (which I sincerely doubt I could have otherwise), there were some areas of institutional life (parts of what I define below as the 'unofficial backstage') that were not open to me. They would only have been to someone who was prepared, as I was not, actually to live in the institution; I can only describe some of the many friendships and liaisons, and antipathies and enmities, that no doubt existed. Further, as I emphasise in Chapter 5, there is no doubt that my own obvious identity as a white male (with my own experience of medical training) has skewed my account; the policy of perfection to investigate this gendered institution would have been to have had a woman co-worker.

Some Comments on Methods and Analysis

Given the importance that I will attach to the acquisition of medical language, I should say something about my methods of recording what I heard. I did not use tape-recorders; this was partly because of the method's obtrusiveness and lengthy analysis, partly because of the broad scope and limited time of the research, and partly because, in a sense, my own medical training meant there was no need. Further, in some teaching settings (most obviously, in lecture theatres), the audience is expected to write; here there was little difficulty in recording what was said, and my lecture notes are my field notes. In other such settings, notably on ward rounds, the reverse was the case: students, as I describe later, are positively instructed not to write. The impossibility of my writing here was made up for by its cause: the peculiarities of the oral teaching in these settings make what is spoken memorable. Particular agonistic exchanges were therefore fairly easily remembered and written down soon afterwards. At the third level, House Officers need to write a great deal, and I could do so too. As regards conversations outside teaching settings, the introduction of a pen and note-pad was in some circumstances quite acceptable, in others unthinkable. Perhaps the most important test of my general, rather than specific, accuracy will be whether others who have learnt the various languages necessary during medical training find fault with what I have written or not.

The form the book takes has been largely determined by the theoretical analysis in the next chapter. The notion of 'practice' itself allows the combination of functionalist and interactionist approaches; it also provides a framework for understanding the stability of the system and the educational and psychological problems referred to above, as well as a structure for the book itself. That analysis indicates the need for historical background, which is provided in Chapter 3. It should be pointed out that professional censure of doctors who study the history of medicine is usually only lifted when those doctors have retired; otherwise it is held to be a waste of their training. This attitude is quite consistent with medicine's own view of itself as developing and applying scientific discoveries, the more recent the better; the profession looks backwards only for support for its present and future endeavours.

The form of analysis also allows the ethnography (which forms the bulk of the book) to correlate roughly with the three distinct levels of medical training. This begins in Chapter 4, after some discussion about those who enter medical training. Chapters 5, 6 and 7 are concerned with the preclinical years (describing, respectively, the 'unofficial' stages, the 'official' stages, and then a strange mixture of the two, the practice of anatomical dissection); Chapter 8 describes the clinical years and Chapter 9 the pre-registration year. In Chapter 10, I attempt to explain the psychological effects of training and in the last chapter I offer some brief comments about the nature of training and its stability.

There is no doubt that much of my analysis and argument is, in anthropological terms, broadly structural and functional, both socially and cognitively. There are two reasons for this. First, these forms of argument are based on the ancient Anatomical Method of associating structure and function, a method central to the initial and continuing strength of the medical profession (just as its social and cognitive applications have been to anthropology), and are therefore likely to be highly relevant to the institution. Second, one of the well-known problems with social structural-functionalism, its inability to explain social change, can here be reversed; the remarkable stability of the structure of medical training over the last 150 years, when so much else has changed, can be directly related to its function of making doctors. An associated point follows: while Western anthropologists working at home are encouraged to 'exoticise the familiar', they may also be warned, as I was, about the dangers of 'spurious exoticism', of using anthropological concepts derived from studying non-Western peoples. While I personally have no doubt that there are similarities between medical training and other forms of initiation found elsewhere (the Maasai seem to me to be particularly relevant), I have avoided such comparative exercises; where I use anthropological concepts, I shall demonstrate their authors' indications that they are general principles.

Chapter 2

Deriving Medical Dispositions

> The young recruit is 'aughty – 'e draf's from Gawd knows where;
> They bid 'im show 'is stockin's and lay 'is mattress square.
> 'E calls it bloomin' nonsense – 'e doesn't know, no more –
> And then up comes 'is company an' kicks 'im round the floor!
>
> Rudyard Kipling

In principle, the training of medical students is no different from many other systems of training, in that untrained neophytes are transformed into more or less competent practitioners. The two fundamental aspects of those undergoing medical training are implicit in the very term usually used to describe them, 'medical students'. By definition, these raw recruits will in time become full members of the profession, but equally, to be made doctors, they must first be taught and must learn. It has been pointed out (Atkinson 1983: 230–1; Bloom 1971: 97–9) that this distinction between medical students as emergent professional colleagues and as segregated subordinates has given rise to two different approaches to studying the processes of transformation, and that this distinction is typified by the titles of the first two major studies. As *The Student-Physician*, the title given by Merton and his colleagues to their account of Cornell (Merton *et al.* 1957) implies, it takes a functionalist view of the relatively orderly transmission of professional knowledge, skills and values to students in training by trained doctors; these professional attributes are found in the formal or 'manifest' curriculum, and tested in examinations. On the other hand, Becker and his colleagues' interactionist account of training at Kansas (Becker *et al.* 1961) is based mostly on fieldwork with medical students and, as its title *Boys in White* indicates, describes students as a lowly but self-contained group learning the informal or 'hidden' curriculum to help themselves and each other get through medical school any way they can. Both of these studies of students were followed by two of the next level of training, internship, which took the same two lines: Mumford's (1970) after Merton, and Miller's (1970) after Becker. So not only does each of these four early studies concentrate on one or other of the two fundamental aspects of students' and interns' ambiguous professional status, but they all maintain the distinction between students and interns themselves. While both the ambiguity and discontinuity focused on by these studies may reflect important features of medical training, none of them by themselves can provide a full account of the process of being made a doctor. This is the main purpose of my book.

But I shall derive the theoretical framework for my account from one of these early studies, *Boys in White*, and the nature of this classic study provides the reason for my doing so. Becker and his three colleagues did two years' fieldwork among medical students, so basing their account on a remarkable eight researcher-years' data. Their data should therefore be accorded the greatest importance, though their insistence that they were only studying a relatively autonomous student culture should not. Their assumption that their conclusions can refer only to student culture and not to any more general medical culture seriously overestimates the disjunction between students and interns (and indeed more senior doctors), and their assumption that student culture is autonomous seriously underplays students' own recognition of their necessary conformity to the institutional demands made of them. It would anyway be most odd if medical students, even on their own, spent their preclinical and clinical years learning ways of thinking and acting that had little or no connection to their subsequent training as interns and to their practice as doctors. But before refashioning Becker's results (I shall hereafter refer to these collective authors by the first-named) to provide my own analytic framework, which will be applicable to the whole of medical culture, some coherent way of relating the approach of *Boys in White* to other studies of training must be established.

Redefining the Institution

Atkinson (1983: 230–1) has strongly criticised Becker's emphasis on the immediate and situational features of the settings students find themselves in, with its further implications that the medical school is almost equivalent to those physically closed 'total institutions' described by Goffman (1991 [1961]) in *Asylums*, and that students are in a very similar position to such institutions' inmates. There are two consequences of this: first, that too much attention is paid to the 'hidden' rather than the 'manifest' curriculum (the explicit transmission of official knowledge); Atkinson's own study, *The Clinical Experience* (1981), concentrates on students' official teaching in their first clinical year, mostly in Medicine. Another critic, Bosk, who studied the way senior surgeons assess their juniors (including interns) for promotion, describes Becker's focus as resulting in a lack of interest in the 'informal-internal' methods of social control (1979: 18–20). The second consequence, Atkinson considers, is that the undoubtedly segmented nature of the profession (in the major differences between the specialties of Medicine and Surgery, for example, let alone those found in other clinical specialties that students are taught) has been passed over in favour of the assumed homogeneity of the teaching institution.

There is a real problem here. In line with the sociological view that professions exercise highly specialised monopolies approved by the State, Larson (1977: 15) has suggested that professions develop an 'exclusive cognitive identity', necessary for first the creation and then the exploitation of the professionally monopolised market. Such a distinctive and exclusive cognitive identity enables any profession to convert its specialised knowledge and skills into social and economic rewards. But to achieve such an exclusive professional cognitive identity, something like a total institution must be hypothesised; for how else, theoretically, could such an exclusive, and therefore identifiable and relatively invariant, cognitive base be inculcated in students and doctors? The solution to this problem is twofold: the nature of a total institution must both be conceptually enlarged and also ordered to accommodate both the criticisms and the work of such authors as Atkinson and Bosk.

Total institutions such as asylums are institutions distinguished by closure, rationalisation of everyday living and disciplinary control (which lead to 'them' and 'us' divisions between staff and inmates), with other features such as degrading admission rituals. Medical schools would fall into Goffman's fourth group of 'institutions purportedly established the better to pursue some workmanlike task and justifying themselves only on these instrumental grounds' (1991: 17). But, as Atkinson has pointed out, medical schools' functional task of producing doctors is not carried out solely within a particular physically closed environment, and the training also involves different segments of the profession. The training institution is therefore broader and more conceptual than those Goffman originally described; although I shall show that the medical school can indeed act as an institution in the sense of a physically bounded space, it is less in terms of space and more in terms of time spent within the conceptually bounded and cognitively limited organisation of the profession itself that students' institutional life should be seen. Their unceasing need to work for unceasing examinations set by different professional segments will ultimately result in professional cognitive membership of the institution of which they are an inmate (that is, the profession of medicine), a passage and a membership that may exclude the lay world just as surely as asylum walls.

How can this enlarged concept of the institution now be ordered to accommodate the work of the sociologists of medicine referred to above? The way that I have chosen to do this involves the use of another well-known analytic concept of Goffman's, that of the extended metaphor of the theatre applied to the everyday social stage (originally proposed in *The Presentation of Self in Everyday Life* (1990 [1959]) and elaborated in other works). In particular, Goffman notes the importance of the audience to the nature of the presentation of the self, of the co-operative team that composes the role-players, and, as the counterpart to the stage of the front region (or frontstage), where different social roles are played, the backstage, where impressions made frontstage are both constructed and contradicted. Given the new concept of the institution, Goffman's theatrical analysis indicates that the medical school's official function of producing doctors is frontstage work of teachers teaching the 'manifest' curriculum, a stage on which students also appear when they attend lectures and clinical teaching and take exams. Students also do official work backstage, where there are no official staff as audience (in libraries, at home and on the hospital wards). These two very different areas can be used to make sense of the criticisms of Becker noted above: his fieldwork among students took place mainly on the official backstage, as did Miller's among interns. On the other hand, Atkinson's study of clinical teaching and Bosk's study of surgeons took place mainly on the official frontstage, as did Mumford's of interns.

But what about students' time apart from their official work? Broadhead (1983) describes their private lives as being 'inundated' by the institution. So some other well-known aspects of students' existence and medical school life (such as the students' bar, the large numbers of clubs, the playing fields and their own dramatic performances) also fall within the institution, even though they are not part of the school's official function to produce doctors. They may therefore be defined as unofficial. Here again, though, frontstage and backstage exist: an example of unofficial frontstage activity is the 1st XV representing the medical school in playing rugby football, and the unofficial backstage is where preparations for such unofficial frontstage performances are made, and where activities unrelated either to these or to official work take place. The way these institutional areas relate may be shown in a diagram (see Figure 1). It should be noted that the only accounts which cover all four institutional areas (and may include the non-medical offstage) are those that follow students throughout their training; a good example of such longitudinal coverage is the televised account of students at St Mary's (Spindler 1992).

	OFFICIAL	UNOFFICIAL	OFFSTAGE
FRONT STAGE	'Manifest' curriculum — Lectures, Ward Rounds, Exams — Merton *et al.* (1957) Mumford (1970) Bosk (1979) Atkinson (1981)	Games field (e.g. rugby football) Theatrical performances (e.g. Christmas shows)	LAY WORLD
BACK STAGE	'Hidden' curriculum — Libraries, Hospital wards — Becker *et al.* (1961) Miller (1970)	Preparation for unofficial frontstage activities Students' Bar — Broadhead (1983)	

Figure 1. The institution in terms of 'stages', indicating the nature of these areas and the location of various sociological studies referred to in the text. A heavy line shows the boundary of the institution; time is also spent on the non-medical 'offstage'.

Perspectives, Schemas and Dispositions

In *Boys in White*, Becker derives what he calls 'perspectives' from among preclinical and clinical students, basing these principally on what students said and did, unprompted, in each other's presence (on the official backstage, in my terms). A perspective is defined as a 'co-ordinated set of ideas and actions a person uses in dealing with some problematic situation, to refer to a person's ordinary way of thinking and feeling about and acting in such a situation'. Perspectives, then, have an active as well as a cognitive component. They are also collective and shared; in this respect, as well as in that of having a practical component, perspectives are different from attitudes, which are usually thought of as individual cognitive attributes. Further, perspectives are situationally specific, so differentiating them from values, which are 'ordinarily thought of as being generalized and abstract, capable of being applied to a great variety of situations' (1961: 34–7). Consistently with this, Becker is (as I have said) insistent that he is only dealing with medical student culture, and that his perspectives are limited to that culture (1961: 316). Despite his insistence, I should reaffirm my view that, although Becker's perspectives need adjusting, they are to be found throughout medical culture.

Very briefly, Becker considers that students arrive at medical school with a Long-range perspective (that medicine is hard but worthwhile work); faced with the huge quantity of work expected of them in the preclinical years, their Initial perspective (of wanting to learn everything) changes, through the Provisional (the recognition that the Initial perspective cannot be practically carried out), to the Final perspective (of working economically, in ways that will enable them to pass exams). In the clinical years, when students see patients, they learn more perspectives: the strangely named Academic one (that their teachers can humiliate them and stop them passing exams, and so must be accommodated to), and that of Student Co-operation (that students need to share out clinical work amongst themselves). All these perspectives (apart from the Long-range one that they arrive with) are said to be the product of the autonomous student culture. As clinical students, they also learn two perspectives derived from medical culture, that of Clinical Experience (a desirable quality gained from 'seeing' patients) and that of Responsibility (a desirable attribute, archetypally found in the surgeon holding his patient's life in his hands, and so gained by having patients and doing medical things to them).

Becker is concerned to emphasise the concreteness of student perspectives, an emphasis that is both a consequence of his method of study in concentrating on what students said and did and of students' own tendency to concretise thought into action; Becker's perspectives are in fact the set of concrete actions that students agree should be taken in specific circumstances. Students' tendency to concretise is described, for example, in Becker's discussion about the transformation of students' original idealism found in the Long-range perspective: 'When they leave medical school it [idealism] again comes to the fore, but now it has a more specific character, consisting of concrete ideas about how certain problems of medical practice are to be faced' (1961: 430). These concrete actions have then been grouped by Becker into slightly less concrete categories, which, with two exceptions, have been given new abstract names (only the two said to derive from medical culture, Clinical Experience and Responsibility, are terms in general medical use). He has in fact used an 'abstract for concrete' form of synechdochal substitution, the same method as that of Lévi-Strauss for unravelling the thought of people who tend to represent an abstract quality by something concrete that possesses it (see Sperber 1979: 22–6). So Becker's definition of perspectives as combinations of actions and dispositions to act is itself some evidence of the concretisation that goes on in medical school (this is comparable to what happens in medical language, which I describe later – linguistically, words are concretised into things). Given this concretising tendency, recognised and to some extent reversed by Becker, is it possible to reverse it further and so perhaps uncover less limiting analytic concepts? There are two ways of doing so, one psychological and the other anthropological.

Perspectives and Schemas

Cognitive psychologists use an analytic term very similar to that of Becker's perspective, that of the 'schema'. The term describes 'those [mental] structures that integrate and attach meaning to events. The content of the schemas may deal with personal relationships, such as attitudes towards the self or others, or impersonal categories (e.g. inanimate objects). These objects may be concrete (a chair) or abstract (my country).' Not only do these schemas have cognitive, emotional and behavioural aspects, but the mental relationships they define may also be manifest in the body's parallel physical comportment (Beck *et al.* 1990: 32, 40). And clinical psychologists apply the psychological principles of schemas to individuals' problems, principally by investigating and then altering the cognitions and behaviour (psychological terms equivalent to the ideas and actions found in perspectives) of patients, using so-called cognitive–behavioural therapy. The way in which schemas deal with personal relationships has also been extended to include what are known as inverse reciprocal aspects. So, for example, at the same time that a child learns his own relationship to his father, he also learns his father's relationship to him, and learning his own role fully also involves knowledge of his father's. As this example suggests, the infantile origins of such patterns of roles and their reciprocals is stressed in the type of treatment derived from this theory, called cognitive–analytic therapy (see Ryle 1990: 98). (Ryle is, like Beck, concerned with individuals' own difficulties and, in cognitive–analytic therapy, patterns of adult relationship are the particular focus of attention, for clarification before alteration.)

The characteristics of a psychological schema described above might usefully be illustrated by an example: let me describe a 'School' schema that might be used by a schoolchild. This is the psychological and active aspect of his connectedness to school, and, among other things, applies to the sort of work he is likely to do there. He very soon has an idea of what lies before him on each schoolday (in terms of sitting down and listening in lessons, let us say, and doing homework) and will be surprised if this does not turn out to be the case. This schema allows time to be categorised (into term-time and holidays), for example, and people (into school-friends and not school-friends); it also encompasses personal relationships with other schoolchildren and teachers. In this context, the implication of inverse reciprocal relationships is that the schoolchild, in knowing how he is treated by a teacher, will also know how the teacher treats him (how the teacher is likely to react in the event of the child's being cheeky, for example); there may also be similarities in the way that he sees his teacher and his father treating him. So the concept of schema (as applied to individuals) provides an organising mental structure with several facets; it acts as a cognitive category (attaching both cognitive and emotional meaning to events), has physical parallels in the body, directs (though does not determine) action, and organises personal relationships (which also have inverse aspects).

I have so far only described schemas' applicability to the psychology of individuals. While their use as social, rather than personal, constructs, was developed by Kelly (1955) to allow the bridge to be made between idiographic and nomothetic mental representations, this extension is more limited to the psychological than is suitable for anthropological analysis; it is elsewhere that I now look for even further extensions to the concept of the perspective.

Bourdieu's Concepts of 'Dispositions' and 'Habitus'

The account of psychological schemas and their physical manifestation above is strongly echoed in the sociology of Bourdieu. His work is often difficult to understand, principally because of the language he uses (see Jenkins 1992: 162–72 for a discussion of this) and his reluctance to acknowledge and argue with other writers. But there is no doubt that his concepts of 'dispositions' and 'habitus' are useful here, in that they further extend the attributes of the schema to include social aspects. Dispositions are in fact very similar to schemas in organising thought and action: in Bourdieu's tortuous words, they are

> structured structures predisposed to function as structuring structures, that is, as principles of the generation and structuring of practices and representations which can be objectively 'regulated' and 'regular' without in any way being the product of obedience to rules, objectively adapted to their goals without presupposing a conscious aiming at ends or an express mastery of the operations necessary to attain them and, being all this, collectively orchestrated without being the product of the orchestrating action of a conductor (Bourdieu 1977: 72).

The habitus is the collectively created sum of infinitely variable (though organised) mental and physical manifestations of dispositions, as embodied in individual people. So, while the constituent dispositions of a group of people may be the same, the way in which each individual practises them is different, depending on each individual's own experience and 'style'.

The question arises as to whether habitus and dispositions, derived from consideration of the oral, non-literate culture of the Kabyle in Algeria, are applicable to the literate, bureaucratic culture of a medical school. Bourdieu is quite clear that, both in situations where there is formal teaching and where there is not, many of the most vital ways of thinking and acting are transmitted from practice to practice simply through contact of the one who is learning with the one who is teaching (1992: 222–3). He also specifically mentions Goffman's institutions, which seek to produce a 'new man', as places where the physical 'hexis', the sum of the patterned bodily postures of dispositions, is inculcated. As I shall show later, the process of the inculcation of such body techniques in medical students is partly enabled by the materially referential language of medicine, which actually precludes explicit discussion of so many aspects of becoming a doctor and which also makes students acutely aware (though, after a while, hardly conscious) of the non-verbal communication of their teachers in terms of bodily deportment and their own spatial groupings.

There is, though, more to becoming a member of a society than such unspoken learning; there are also explicit exercises that allow practical skills to be learnt.

> Between apprenticeship through simple familiarization, in which the apprentice insensibly and unconsciously acquires the principles of the 'art' and the art of living – including those which are not known to the producer of the practices or works imitated, and, at the other extreme, explicit and express transmission by precept and prescription, every society provides for *structural exercises* tending to transmit this or that form of practical mastery (Bourdieu 1977: 88; original emphasis).

By these exercises Bourdieu means the riddles and ritual contests among the Kabyle, which test the 'sense of ritual language', and games that, in the mode of 'let's pretend', make children develop strategies for winning them, strategies involving the appreciation of both sides of the personal relationships involved. Dispositions also lead to the structuring of external space and to the organisation of buildings within it, which in turn structure the dispositions; such surroundings Bourdieu later calls 'fields' (1992: 66–8). These surroundings, like dispositions and their sum, the habitus, are historical and gendered products. I shall derive the historical origins of medical dispositions in the next chapter.

To show what Bourdieu's concepts of 'habitus' and 'disposition' add to the psychological schema, the example of the individual child's 'School' schema would be extended to the general 'School' disposition of schoolchildren in a given school. These children share an idea of what school is like in general terms, knowing what is expected of them all; their individual differences will be very small compared to their communal understandings which they have, to a great extent, 'picked up' in various ways without being taught explicitly, either by teachers or other children. But, in the classroom, there are also explicit tasks (in the form of tests and examinations, for example) with equally explicit rules, which have to be mastered. Children will come to learn a new language, some of it just 'picked up' like whatever the words describe, some of it explicitly spelt out and taught by teachers. And the settings that children find themselves in (the typical classroom, with desks facing one way, for example) are associated with, and to some extent direct, the nature of their existence within the School disposition itself; further, these physical surroundings have historical origins, which may be uncovered.

Bourdieu's embodied dispositions that structure internal mental space, lead to action, encompass relationships and their inverse relationships, and together make up the habitus are very similar to psychological schemas. What Bourdieu has added is their historical development, and their capacity to structure (and be structured by) external space and its physical shape; these provide the basis for social as well as personal analysis. Bourdieu's study is mainly of the adult practice of dispositions, rather than of their inculcation. He is therefore less attentive to the actual processes of transformation, including the changing emphases on different dispositions at different times and places (so obvious at different levels of medical training), and on the emotion and the language associated with dispositions. In the context of medical training, the ritual language is important (as are other, more general, forms of communication) in the combined constituent dispositions of the medical habitus, and structural exercises are to be found in the seemingly endless examinations and assessments that students must pass in order to pass on to the next period of training. And a specialist language must form part of any professional cognitive identity; in medicine, all the examinations that medical students must pass are written or spoken in specialised scientific language. Learning the knowledge to pass exams is dependent on learning the language in which that knowledge is expressed and, indeed, exams are just as much tests of the use of the language that medical knowledge is expressed in as of the knowledge itself.

Professional Cognitive Exclusiveness and Language

According to Merton (1957: 71), 'like other occupations, medicine has its own distinctive vocabulary, and like the vocabularies of other occupations, this one is often described derisively as jargon by outsiders and described appreciatively as technical terminology by insiders'. Merton's first point, that medical language is distinctive, I think massively understates the importance of language in medical training, by the use of which all assessments, written or spoken, are made; the language learnt by students is therefore far better analysed along the lines that social identity is in large part established and maintained through language (Gumperz and Cook-Gumperz 1982: 1–21). Merton's second point, that medical language is technical, needs expanding to emphasise the often-made point that it is based on science, principally the 'hard' sciences of objective knowledge on which the signal success of the medical profession is itself largely based.

One of the most important things about scientific language is, as Ziman (1991) states, that it should be unambiguous, and should therefore lead to what he calls 'consensibility' (that everyone understands what is said) so that they can either agree or disagree with it. Such lack of ambiguity is associated with the other scientific aim of 'consensuality', that an overwhelming majority of competent well-informed scientists should accept without serious doubt a well-established general body of scientific fact. Both aims depend on science's expression in an unambiguous public language; in the search for perfect precision and overwhelming certitude, written scientific communications become 'formalised statements in which technical terms that have been previously defined with the maximum rigour are bound together in unambiguous syntactical arrangements implying complete logical necessity' (1991: 13). A further interesting consequence is that such 'objective' language promotes greater intersubjectivity, leading indeed to an element of unspoken communion.

My purpose here is not to discuss whether Ziman's view of language is or can be correct, but simply to describe scientists' view of their use of language in order to make my subsequent account more understandable. It is important, though, to note that the scientists' view involves what I. A. Richards (1965: 11) has called 'the Proper Meaning Superstition', that every word has a stable, right and proper meaning, and that metaphor is regarded only as 'a sort of happy extra trick with words' (1965: 90), rather than language's constitutive form, as Johnson (1987), for example, has also argued. It is interesting to note that Bentham, influential in so many ways in establishing the current system of medical training, wrote an early work on metaphor that appears to anticipate much of Johnson's work. Bentham's categorisation of 'entities' into 'real' and 'fictitious' allowed him to observe that 'almost all names employed in speaking of the phenomena of the mind are names of fictitious entities' and that 'to language, then – to language alone – it is that fictitious entities owe their existence; their impossible, yet indispensable existence' (see Ogden 1932 for both Bentham's original work and a commentary). At any rate, a consequence of scientists' deliberate but unselfconscious creation of a precise and materially referential scientific language is that it is actually quite easy to recover the 'root metaphors' they use, as Martin (1987, 1992 and 1994) has shown in her recovery of the metaphors of economic production and warfare in medical accounts of human reproduction and of the immune system.

In addition to the qualities of scientific communication mentioned by Ziman, there are other aspects to communication at all levels of medical training (and indeed at all levels of medicine) that need stressing. These are those of instrumental and moral purpose. It is not enough for doctors to be able to communicate unambiguously, as scientists do – the ultimate aim of medical communication is, put simply, to do good (however such idealistic aims are disguised), just as the practice of medicine is shot through with this aim. As Good (1994: 86) puts it, in criticising the lack of awareness of this moral aim of medicine in Foucault's account of the hospital and medical practice (as well as in much of medical anthropology), 'it is precisely the conjoining of the physiological and soteriological that is central to medicine as a modern institution'. In medical language and its uses, therefore, there are two strands, the scientific and the moral.

The moral aim of medical action is often expressed among students by disparagement of the military, which is, for them, the antithesis of medicine; it is described as hierarchical and hide-bound by tradition but, above all, being concerned with causing death and not, as they hold medicine is, with preserving life. But, whatever students say, the similarities between medicine and the military are strong, not just in the warlike echoes of the centrally important hospital 'wards' and medical 'rounds', for example, but also in the nature of the institutionalised training. Though mine is not a comparative account, I occasionally allude to such similarities (and differences) and, to underline this general similarity, I have chosen chapter headings mostly related to the military; and these are in poetic form to emphasise, by contrast, the scientific language medical students learn.

From Becker's Perspectives to my Dispositions

I propose, in the following chapters, to describe in detail the creation of an exclusive medical habitus (which incorporates a professional cognitive identity). So, having expanded Becker's concept of perspectives through psychological schemas to Bourdieu's dispositions, I now discuss the constituent dispositions of the medical habitus, deriving them from Becker's perspectives. In doing this, I am obviously deliberately disregarding Becker's statement that he was only studying student culture; as I argued above, he has seriously underestimated the power of his observations. It will also become clear that these dispositions vary in prominence at the three different levels of training on the four stages of the institution. When I derive my general professional dispositions, I shall dignify them by a capital letter, as does Becker his perspectives.

The Disposition of Co-operation

The first perspective to attend to is that of Student Co-operation. Becker, in accordance with his definition of perspectives as situationally specific, locates this firmly in the clinical years. But, as the definition of perspectives as collectively agreed thoughts and courses of action suggests, all his perspectives (excepting only the personal Long-range perspective that individual freshmen arrive with) were collectively held by students. Here there is a paradox: for students must have somehow co-operated to reach the perspective of Student Co-operation itself. Such co-operation is logically antecedent to all perspectives, and must therefore be the fundamental mode of existence of medical students, overriding all others. The new disposition of Co-operation should in fact be seen as the paramount disposition throughout the years of training and, given my view that Becker was not just studying student culture, it is therefore also the paramount general professional disposition.

This disposition of Co-operation, paramount in that it is through its practice that other dispositions are taught and learnt, has much in common with Victor Turner's notion of 'communitas' developed in his study of ritual initiation of Ndembu neophytes in the segregated liminal phase of their transformative *rites de passage*. Communitas is described as neophytes' sense of shared existence; within it, they develop an intense egalitarianism, associated with their humiliation and stripping of social attributes by their instructors (1974: 81). Liminality is a zone where classifications of man's relationships to society, nature and culture are made, and these classifications are not only cognitive categories, as they incite men to action too (1974: 114–16). And Turner, like Bourdieu for Kabyle society, finds Goffman's institutions a highly satisfactory parallel for closed Ndembu society. The difficulties experienced by medical students, in their liminal stage on the way to status elevation, are well known to outsiders in terms of the hard work they have to do; but outsiders are rarely aware of the 'teaching by humiliation' that still has a prominent place in students' experience. The levelling that Turner describes takes place away from public view, not only socially but (as I shall show) also cognitively, in students' application to themselves of the reductionist knowledge they have to learn. The material base of Co-operation (for, in medical culture, one must always look for such concrete manifestations of abstract ideas) is found in the important place that teams of all sorts have in medical school, real teams that give rise to the professionally omnipresent structural metaphor of 'the team'.

But, despite their similarity in engendering communitas, there is an important difference between total institutions and closed societies: this is that, whereas Ndembu neophytes will eventually become fully accredited members of society, inmates of institutions like asylums, with their permanent 'them and us' distinction, will never become members of staff. Given this difference, there is likely to be another aspect to communitas in situations like that of medical schools (and, indeed, of the Ndembu themselves): that of rivalry between neophytes in their passage through the stages of initiation. Turner in fact mentions this opposite mode of relationship to communitas which, like it, lies in the liminal phase; he refers to the Hobbesian 'war of all against all' (1974: 119), though he does not pursue this theme. So, while I have argued that my medical disposition of Co-operation has some important similarities with communitas, it also has the important difference that its inverse, Competition, is integral to it. Co-operation will vary proportionately in relation to two factors: it is increased by the presence of a common adversary and decreased by the potential for individual advantage. For example, Competition to get into medical school is individually keenly experienced; once there, Co-operation takes over as the predominant disposition. Later, Competition reappears, at first against outsiders, but increasingly against each other, as I shall also show.

The Dispositions of Idealism, Status and Knowledge

The two main features of Becker's Long-range perspective are that, 'Medicine is the best of all professions' and that 'we want to help people . . . upholding medical ideals' (1961: 72–3). Now not only does Becker himself discuss at length the changes in idealism held by students (1961: 420–33) but, as noted in Chapter 1, the idealism and subsequent disillusionment of medical students has been the subject of considerable research: Idealism must therefore become a separate disposition. It is important to remember that Idealism, while collectively held, is originally a personal disposition; I shall show how its professional nature is developed. The disposition of Idealism is matched by another new one found in the first feature of the Long-range perspective, that of Status. The disposition of Status emphasises separately the functional primacy of the purpose of going to medical school, which is to become a doctor, with all its implications for title, social status, income and power; even as students, the adjective 'medical' differentiates them from all other students, as I have said.

Becker defines his perspective of Clinical Experience as referring to the actual clinical experience of dealing with patients and disease, and a major part of its meaning lies in its implied polarity with 'book learning' (1961: 231). Though he goes on to describe various ways in which 'experience' and 'book learning' differ from each other, and though his Initial, Provisional and Final perspectives are all related to students' different approaches to dealing with their huge amount of book work, a different perspective covering 'book learning' does not exist, and it should. For not only is there such internal evidence from Becker's own material that a disposition to do with 'book learning' is necessary, but the contrast between clinical experience and knowledge learnt from books and other publications is one that has received attention from many other commentators on medical training and doctors (see Atkinson 1981, 1984, 1994; Bosk 1979; Fox 1957; Freidson 1970). I shall call the disposition covering this area of book learning, rather unadventurously, Knowledge. Its polar opposite, Clinical Experience, I shall rename the disposition of Experience, removing Becker's qualifying adjective, which appears to locate it only in the clinical years and above. The important perspective of Responsibility I shall leave unchanged as the disposition of Responsibility.

Consideration of Becker's Academic perspective ('The [teaching] faculty can stop you passing . . . can humiliate you . . . and must therefore be appeased' (1961: 279–80) does make it seem very oddly named; humiliation is not generally thought of as an aspect of academic work. But what Becker is in fact describing is the way clinical students are taught and their response to it (1961: 274); his singling out of this method of teaching alone (without, for example, finding an equivalent perspective in the preclinical years) is understandable because of the method's singularity, which I describe in detail later. But, as all perspectives (bar the Long-range) have to be learnt and, therefore, to some extent taught, it is both confusing and unnecessary to have a separate perspective here. Though there is another element in the Academic perspective (that of appeasement) that I shall refer to later in this discussion, I shall therefore do away with this perspective entirely in my medical dispositions.

Conflict and Resolution: The Economic Disposition

Becker's perspectives of Clinical Experience (gained by 'seeing' patients) and Responsibility (gained by 'having' patients and doing medical things to them) indicate that these are qualities valued by students (1961: 242, 254–5). In the same way, the dispositions that I have introduced (Idealism, Status and Knowledge) are to do with qualities. Idealism is present on admission to medical school; Status is also granted to some degree on admission and fully on qualification or registration; Knowledge is acquired throughout training.

The Initial, Provisional and Final, and the Student Co-operation and the Academic perspectives, however, are different from the five listed above, in that they are less to do with qualities and more with methods or ways of thinking and acting: 'We want to learn everything . . . – but how?' (Initial); 'We will study in the most effective and economical ways' (Provisional); 'We select the important things to study by finding out what the [teaching] faculty wants us to know. This is the way to pass examinations and get through school' (Final); 'Students should co-operate as far as possible to make school assignments more convenient to carry out, in learning medical information and procedures, and in helping fellow students avoid making a bad impression on the faculty' (Student Co-operation); and 'the medical student must be sensitive to faculty demands and modify his behaviour' (Academic) (1961: 94, 111, 163, 299–300, 279–80). This difference suggests that those perspectives to do with method are associated with ways of acquiring those perspectives (or dispositions) to do with quality. That these different qualities may conflict with each other and lead to different methods, is indicated by consideration of the Initial, Provisional and Final perspectives. These may be seen as different attempts made by preclinical students to resolve the three-cornered conflict between their own Idealism (found in the Initial perspective) and acquiring Knowledge, and hence higher Status. The Final resolution of this conflict is in fact an economic approach to learning Knowledge, limiting such book learning to what needs to be known to pass exams. I take the Provisional perspective simply as evidence of this conflict (and therefore find no need for it as a separate disposition), and shall rename the Final perspective the Economic disposition to indicate the form the final resolution of that conflict takes.

That conflicts occur elsewhere is also evident in Becker's own material. For example, the second element of the Academic perspective, which is held to be present only in the clinical years, is appeasement; this may be seen as the resolution of another conflict between Idealism and Status, but this time over the matter of gaining Experience. This conflict was in fact explained to Becker quite clearly, after a faculty member had done something which the students resented very much, although they were not prepared to make a fuss about it. One student explained their inaction in these words: 'We've spent too much time getting this far to start being crusaders about something like that . . . We have too much invested to throw it all away. . . We can't afford to have ideals like that while we're here' (1961: 281). The student's account of 'spending' time, having too much 'invested' and not being able to 'afford' Idealism (referred to in 'crusaders' and 'ideals') strongly suggests that the Economic disposition was used to resolve this conflict too.

But Becker does not describe the development of his Final perspective (my Economic disposition) as the result of a conflict between perspectives. The likely explanations for this are, first, that, by locating perspectives at either the preclinical or clinical levels of training, they are separated in his analysis (even though they are not separated in fact); second, that perspectives do not appear to conflict, as they are defined as situationally specific and located in different physical settings.

Temporal and Spatial Location Hides Inter-perspective Conflict

The first point is easy to show using students' 'book learning', which is in fact what the Initial, Provisional and Final perspectives (all found in the preclinical years) refer to, as I explained above. But Becker himself points out that clinical students must continue their 'book learning': 'They are still presented with bulky texts and fact-filled lectures and must decide which of the multitude of facts they might learn they should try to incorporate into what the faculty refers to as their "fund of information" . . . In general, the perspective developed on similar situations during the preclinical years . . . persists in the clinical years' (1961: 221). This is not presented as creating any kind of difficulty for the students who also have to acquire Clinical Experience during those years, despite the very different nature of these qualities. Again, there is a strong suggestion here that Becker's temporal location of perspectives is misplaced and, conversely, it is likely that all dispositions can be found at all stages of medical training, though with varying emphasis.

The second point is that conflict may also have been hidden by Becker's precise location of perspectives in accordance with his definition of them as situationally specific, such as Clinical Experience on hospital wards. Again, if Experience is a general professional disposition, this cannot be the case. The explanation for this problem is related to Bourdieu's notion of dispositions' both giving rise to and being reinforced by associated physical settings, or fields; though dispositions may be strongly associated with particular settings, people's practice of such embodied dispositions is not limited to such settings. So, while Experience both structures and is structured by the spatial arrangement of doctors, students and patients on the wards, it is found as a collective disposition in individual students in other settings too; for Becker, though, perspectives are so strongly situationally located that there can be no conflict between them. So, by concentrating on settings rather than on the same students in different settings, Becker may have missed the accommodation that students have to make as they move from one setting to another; I shall argue later that such moves also hide such conflicts from students themselves.

The association of dispositions with particular settings or fields, and the power of the archetypal dispositional setting to minimise conflict, is found in a consideration of Becker's account of the Emergency Room [Casualty], which is so important both historically and currently to medical schools. The Academic perspective (the singular method of teaching and learning Clinical Experience, as discussed above) was widespread throughout the usual clinical settings that students found themselves in, with one significant exception: Casualty. While Becker's suggestion (1961: 293) that attendings [consultants] were very rarely present in Casualty is no doubt important as part of the explanation for this, there are other, much more significant ways in which Casualty is unusual. For, as Atkinson (1981: 72–91) has shown, the 'hot' medicine taught in Casualty (that is, medical action directed towards an acutely ill patient who needs immediate treatment) is entirely different from the 'cold' medicine of normal teaching on the wards (where patients await treatment, are in the process of receiving it or are recovering from it). 'Hot' medicine is marked by its immediacy, when neither patient nor student has had the chance to rehearse the history and the whole business is less stage-managed, and medical action must often be taken there and then. So, for students, it is in Casualty where Responsibility is exercised (that is, taking real medical action directed at 'hot' patients, instead of the hypothetical action directed at 'cold' patients that is taught on ward rounds); it is in Casualty that students may take a useful part in this action as a member of the medical 'team' rather than merely as a student ready to be taught by senior doctors. The fact that the Academic perspective was not found in Casualty does nothing more than demonstrate how importantly different the setting of Casualty is from all other clinical settings.

Medical Roles in the Theatrical Settings of Medical Practice

Such intimate associations between dispositions and their structured physical environment lead back to Goffman's social theatre. And his use of the ready-made range of extended metaphors related to the theatre seems particularly powerful in the prominent and quite clearly theatrical settings in medical training; once again in medicine, the abstract is made concrete. The lecture theatre and the operating theatre are the most obvious of these dramatic settings, even though their precursor the anatomy theatre (see Chapter 3) is no longer central; the dramatic properties of ward rounds, with their stage management and the setting that follows along with the performers, has been noted (Atkinson 1981: 52, 81); and then, of course, there are medical students' own dramatic representations in Christmas shows and the like.

Not surprisingly, Goffman's statement (1990: 78) that 'All the world is, of course, not a stage, but the crucial ways in which it isn't are not easy to specify' has led to criticism that he takes account only of appearances. It is clear however that he is using theatrical metaphors as a way of understanding what people do, rather than claiming that everything we do is simply an 'act' (see Burns (1992: 106–39) for a discussion of such criticisms of Goffman). For, however obvious the theatrical settings in actual medical practice are, there is no suggestion that the personally vital matters, sometimes of life and death, being attended to there are faked, or that, after a bad performance, one can simply go back and do it again better. Though rehearsals are possible, performances are real.

The theatrical settings of medicine also lead on to the sociological concept of 'roles'; despite Bourdieu's distaste for this concept (1977: 2), it is quite consonant with his idea of the consequence of the encounter between embodied history (the player, interpreting his individual role by the practice of collectively held dispositions) and objectified history (the field, or setting). Some of these theatrical aspects noted by Goffman have already been mentioned: the importance of the audience, the co-operative team of players and the differences between frontstage and backstage. In Goffman's later work, he also notes the lack of 'visual respect' found in performances – the performer or presenter becomes 'an object that can be looked at in the round and without offence' by the audience – and other features of dramatic settings, such as the 'ecologically' open spoken interaction (in which participants do not face each other directly, so the audience can see into the encounter), the taking of turns to talk, and an elevation of tone and elocutionary manner (1974: 124, 138–44). All these are features I shall identify later, particularly on ward rounds.

Now, though, I wish to draw two conclusions: first, that specific theatrical settings (the lecture theatre, for example, where Knowledge is taught) promote the learning of particular social roles (with all their cognitive and non-cognitive aspects), interpreted with special stress laid on one or more particular dispositions. Second, that the institutional strength of these roles may have several outcomes, two of which I will mention here because I shall describe them later. First, an individual playing different roles when in front of different audiences or in different settings will thereby embody contradictory qualities, and this may result in a personally experienced or socially recognised 'role conflict'. And second, the lack of congruence between a personally envisaged role and an actual one, due to the difference between the prototypical (and therefore formal and idealised) idea of a role and the actual performance, may result in 'role distance', actions which 'effectively convey some disdainful detachment of the performer from the role he is performing' (Goffman 1961: 85–91, 110).

Dispositions in Becker's and Others' Work

In this last section of this chapter, I shall validate the dispositions that I have derived from Becker's perspectives, first by analysing some more of his material to show their use as cognitive categories, and, I hope, their superiority over Becker's perspectives. Then I shall consider, only in summary, aspects of Miller's and Bosk's work to show that dispositions can be used to analyse medical training at the level of interns (rather than just at that of students) to indicate the likelihood of my proposition that these are indeed general professional dispositions. In doing this, I shall also show, as I have suggested above, the stress that different dispositions receive in different institutional settings.

Clinical Students Use Dispositions to Categorise Patients

When Becker describes the way students view patients (1961: 313–40), he finds that, while most such views can be associated with the perspectives of student culture, some cannot; these he attributes to other less-defined perspectives from lay culture and medical culture, as well as to a 'hazy' perspective from student culture. I hope to show by some examples that these patients can be more aptly categorised using my dispositions, and that these vague ideas of medical, lay and student culture can be done away with. In other words, I contend that my dispositions are both analytically more powerful than Becker's perspectives and have the other advantages of rigour and parsimony. It should be remembered that the notion of dispositions implies not just that they can be used as categories, but that such categories also imply relationships with patients.

Some patients are categorised just as well by dispositions as perspectives: 'crocks', for example, are patients with no identifiable pathology and for whom nothing medical can be done. Such patients are viewed negatively through the perspectives of Clinical Experience and Responsibility, and through the dispositions of Experience and Responsibility (as well as of Status, as they are not 'proper' patients). An example of patients who fit better into dispositional categories are 'pleasant' and 'co-operative' patients, placed by Becker in a general and unspecified aspect of medical culture; these are better classified under Co-operation. On the other hand, 'difficult' patients with no respect for doctors' authority are intensely resented not only by physicians but especially by students because of their own ambiguous Status. These patients are again said to be viewed negatively through some vague perspective from medical culture; they fit much more aptly into the dispositional categories of denying medical Status and refusing Co-operation.

Conversely, using dispositional categories does away with Becker's inexplicit catch-all perspectives. For example, the ill-assorted group of patients that are said to be seen negatively under a 'general medical culture' perspective includes psychiatric and paediatric patients. Students dislike both groups of patients for the same reasons: that they are uncooperative and difficult to examine and are likely to provoke 'scenes' that students would rather avoid. These patients again fit more neatly and accurately into the negative dispositional categories of Co-operation and Experience (because they are difficult to examine); the difficulty that students and doctors have with psychiatric patients and Psychiatry will be found again in later chapters. And the 'hazier case for the argument that students draw on student culture in forming their views of patients when we consider their idea that patients should not take up a student's time without giving him something worthwhile in return' is not hazy at all when the Economic dispositional category is used.

Students Use Dispositions to Categorise Medical Specialties

When Becker describes clinical students considering what direction their career will take when they become doctors by their understanding of different medical specialties (or segments), he is insistent that they do not use perspectives but what he calls 'criteria', which can only be speculative and hypothetical (1961: 368). This insistence is again really rather odd, because students might be expected to use the perspectives that they have created together during their preclinical and clinical years (let alone the perspectives derived from medical culture) to think about their future medical career. I think that Becker has, once again, seriously underestimated the power of his data.

And, once again, as detailed re-allocation would be tiresome, I select some examples to show how much more analytically useful dispositions are. For example, the criterion of a specialty's having great prestige with the public and/or with medical colleagues is clearly consonant with Status; the criterion of a specialty that allows a doctor relationships with patients that are close and have no depressing or unpleasant aspects fits fairly neatly into a mixture of Co-operation and Idealism; and the criterion of having great intellectual breadth seems to be the equivalent of Knowledge. Three other criteria (those of making an adequate amount of money, having convenient working hours and involving not too much hard work, and requiring a long residency) can be collapsed into the Economic disposition, with its emphasis not now on the acquisition of Knowledge or Experience or Responsibility, but on money and conditions of work in relation to Status within varying lengths of time.

It is also interesting to see how the different branches of medicine are seen by students, now using dispositions and not criteria to analyse their views. Internal medicine (that is, the hospital specialty of Medicine) is positively distinguished by Knowledge. While Surgery is seen negatively on this disposition, it scores highly on Responsibility (because of the obvious medical action involved) and as regards Status, and, in Economic terms, the long surgical training is offset by large final financial rewards. Paediatrics is badly off Economically with long hours, and from the point of view of patient Co-operation; it scores highly, though, on Idealism, the need to be the kind of person who likes children being seen as very important. Neurology is seen as the most taxing as regards Knowledge, but with no Responsibility (as neurologists can seldom do anything for their patients); Dermatology is seen as a soft option, good Economically with short hours and good pay, but with no Responsibility and very low Status.

There are therefore two sorts of hierarchy. The first is among dispositions: Responsibility is highest for Becker's students, Knowledge less so, and Idealism least important. Economically, the longer-term results (in Surgery, for example) seem to be approved, rather than the 'get rich quick' aspect of Dermatology. The resultant combination of these hierarchically ranked dispositional categories is given composite expression in a second hierarchy, the degree of Status accorded to the specialties. These are thus ranked by students: Surgery, Medicine, Neurology, Paediatrics, and last Dermatology. Given my premiss that dispositions are found in general medical culture, it is not surprising that the hierarchical Status of these different specialties is very similar to that taught by medical staff to the students I worked with (see Chapter 8); it is a great pity that Becker did not ask students their views of Psychiatry, though this would presumably have been coloured by American attitudes. This exercise also shows that Atkinson's second criticism of Becker's work, noted above, that the segmentation of the profession has been overlooked because of the assumed homogeneity of the institution, has been overturned by the derivation of dispositions. For, now, not only does the general understanding of different segments of the profession form part of students' appreciation of the medical world, but such understanding itself comes from the general professional dispositions students acquire through practice.

Junior and Senior Doctors Practise Dispositions

Lastly, I briefly analyse Miller's study of interns, noted as being very similar to Becker's (in that it concentrates on official backstage work) and compare it to Bosk's study as it relates to interns (a study which is concerned with the official frontstage). While doctors in both studies practise dispositions, the emphasis is placed on them differently in a way that I shall also show in my ethnography.

Miller's interns, the most junior of those with official medical Status, at first approach their work, now involving the novel exercise of Responsibility (as well as the continued acquisition of Experience and Knowledge), with the Idealistic aim of 'doing it all'. They soon find, however, that the large amount of work, as well as their need to negotiate for Co-operation with other professional groups like nurses, makes this impossible, and the pursuit of Knowledge is abandoned – a consequence accepted by senior doctors. Interns also develop what Miller (who was clearly not working among surgeons) calls the Operating perspective, very similar to Becker's Final perspective and therefore to my Economic disposition. So, just as Becker's preclinical students developed the Economic disposition as a consequence of the conflict of Idealism and Status over Knowledge, Miller's interns have done so because of the conflict of the same dispositions over Responsibility.

Bosk's junior surgeons must, like Miller's interns, be able to Co-operate with nurses and make patients Co-operate with them. They must also show Idealistic enthusiasm for their work to their seniors and appear to sacrifice any Economic practicalities about their use of time and energy. The junior surgeons' relationship with their superordinates is based on the former's respect for the latter's

Status (based in turn on their Responsibility, Experience and, sometimes, Knowledge); only when junior surgeons are promoted does Co-operation between them and their superordinates develop. There is, then, an important difference between Miller's and Bosk's account of interns; the former's study of their backstage work indicates the importance there of Co-operation and Economy, while Bosk's study of their official frontstage stresses that such Economic practicalities (which Bosk makes clear exist) must be dissimulated by Idealism in front of their superordinates.

Bosk (1976: 36–7) also describes junior surgeons potentially committing four sorts of surgical error in their attendings' eyes, which I introduce here because I shall refer to some of these concepts in my own ethnography. The two most serious errors are the 'normative error' and the 'quasi-normative error'. An intern commits the first when he puts his own needs above those of patient care; he thus causes a fundamental breach in role between surgeon and patient, clearly by abdicating his Responsibility for the patient, though, equally clearly, he is also blamed for transgressing his own low Status. Such errors are fairly constant between different attendings and the services (firms) they had. The most serious error is the 'quasi-normative', when the intern has acted as if he were an attending himself and ignored the attending's own directions; here the intern has not just overstepped a normative role, again based on their relative Status, but also acted beyond the proper limits of his personal relationship with the attending. These errors vary between services, as they depend on the idiosyncrasies of attendings. Such 'quasi-normative' errors and practices will be described later in relation to the personal certainty of senior doctors. But my main task here has been to try to show that my dispositions, derived from Becker's students' perspectives, can also be used to analyse the work of sociologists studying junior and senior doctors, providing evidence that these are indeed general professional dispositions.

Chapter 3

Dispositions and the Profession Historically

'Let us now praise famous men' –
Men of little showing –
For their work continueth,
And their work continueth,
Broad and deep continueth,
  Greater than their knowing!

Rudyard Kipling

Personal Apprenticeship and the Corporations

It is customary to state that there were, historically, three separate categories of qualified medical practitioner in England: these were the three estates of the learned profession (physicians), the craft (surgeons) and the trade (apothecaries), each with its own corporation based in London: the Royal College of Physicians, the Royal College of Surgeons and the Society of Apothecaries. The Royal College of Physicians of London was incorporated in 1518. Surgeons had joined barbers as a guild in 1540 to form the Barber-Surgeons' Company of the City of London; the surgeons broke the association in 1745, and the Royal College of Surgeons of London was incorporated in 1800. Apothecaries were originally general shopkeepers; they separated from the Mystery of Grocers (the Grocers' Company of the City of London) in 1617, being granted a royal charter as the Society of Apothecaries of London.

The method of entry to these three separate all-male corporations was different. The practice of physic was restricted to men with university degrees; only graduates of Oxford or Cambridge (who were therefore Anglicans) could become Fellows, while physicians with Scottish or Irish medical degrees might hold the Licence. Unlike physicians, surgeons and apothecaries were not university men but learnt their skills by apprenticeship; their training was necessarily practical. The legal, internally regulated and mutually exclusive systems of membership of the three London-based medical estates were geographically limited; in the rest of the country, the corporations held little sway even over those officially under their aegis.

Indeed, the large majority of practitioners outside London were surgeon-apothecaries who combined aspects of these three forms of practice; in 1783, there were 2,607 surgeon-apothecaries, 363 physicians, and only 89 surgeons and 105 apothecaries (Lane 1985). The basic principles of apprenticeship of all sorts (laid down in 1563 in the Statute of Artificers, which was unamended till its repeal some 250 years later in 1814) involved binding written contractual arrangements made by parents about sending their child away, sometimes considerable distances, to serve with an apprentice-master. The term of apprenticeship to surgeon-apothecaries was the seven years normal for most occupations throughout the eighteenth century, while the premium was higher than for most, varying from £20 to £200 for a full term. The apprentice learnt how his master conducted his practice (and how to bill patients), as well as guild and personal secrets; at the start no doubt often exploited, with the passing years he was given increasing responsibility for dealing with patients; but in no sense was he in charge of them. For the apprentice, the benefits of the system were that he could not be dismissed during the term of apprenticeship and that, at the end of his term, he had become legally entitled to practise as a surgeon-apothecary, with the possibility of himself becoming a master and, in turn, benefiting from the indentured services of an apprentice. Socially, the system of apprenticeship guaranteed a level of competence in the qualified adult (as demanded by parental, community and cultural expectation, in addition to the master's concern for his own reputation) and also controlled the entry of new recruits, preventing the craft becoming overstocked with too many skilled men; breaches by unqualified persons of the legal requirement of apprenticeship were promptly punished. The ancient system of apprenticeship in upwardly mobile but still separated guilds was well-suited to a stable economy and a static social order. It was, however, quite unsuited to the social changes of the eighteenth century – the huge increase in population and its shift to new industrial centres. The one-to-one master-to-apprentice relationship began to be broken with the weakening of guild control, which specifically forbad masters taking several apprentices.

Towards the end of the eighteenth century, qualified apprentices started to look, in increasing numbers, to further their education. They attended charitable hospitals and private schools at home (particularly in London) and abroad (particularly Paris), where the new classifications of disease based on morbid anatomy, the use of the Anatomical Method for research and the usefulness of dissection for surgical training all emphasised the importance of anatomy.

But the population looked for medical treatment almost anywhere among the advocates of the wide varieties of speculative systems of classification, including the old Galenic theory of the humoral balance of illness and health. Outside the charitable hospitals, the sick had a wide range of therapeutic options. Porter's account (1989) of practitioners of all sorts during the eighteenth century shows that the high levels of illness and the very partial success of pre-modern medicine in alleviating the major lethal and crippling diseases, together with what was in effect a free market for medicine in an expanding economy, together led to a lively and increasing pluralism. The sick exercised acute vigilance in monitoring their own illnesses, actively picking and choosing amongst practitioners, and eager to participate in their own treatment. People not only stocked their houses with the full range of the pharmacopoeia, but looked everywhere for solutions to their problems – to quacks as well as physicians; and, in this open market, sometimes the only difference between the quack or empiric and the physician was the latter's licence to practice. The economic power of patients at large meant that this was a buyer's market, where self-promotion and advertisement could lead to fortunes' being made by both licensed and unlicensed practitioners, but where licence to practice in no sense guaranteed an income.

It should, though, be noted that by far the greater part of medical care in the broadest sense was almost certainly administered by women, in domestic and communal settings. Though this was sometimes market-based, with women charging for their services, it was largely conducted in domestic or community spheres; women learnt their medical methods mostly by experience and oral transmission, though with some access to written sources (Witz 1992: 74–82). Whatever women's access to the new medical markets of the eighteenth century, their market share appears to have been small, and they did not form groups to represent their interests. In the years up to the Medical Act of 1858, women simply do not feature in accounts either of the corporations or of quacks.

What I have been describing above is the transitional period between, in Jewson's terms (1976), Bedside and Hospital Medicine. Bedside Medicine was the previously dominant mode of medical practice, based on the concept of health, and the numerous phenomenological classifications of disease were themselves based on the dominance of the individual patient. This was replaced during the first three or four decades of the eighteenth century by a new sort of medical practice, Hospital Medicine. Hospital Medicine was based on the concept of normality, and on systematic statistical associations being made between external symptoms and internal lesions found at anatomical dissection after death. The relationships of Bedside Medicine are epitomised as those between the sickman as patron, for private fees, and the practitioner as client, very much as Porter describes them above; in Hospital Medicine, the sick poor who were treated there became 'cases', adopting a role of the passive and uncritical patient in the face of incontestable medical knowledge. Jewson's third mode, Laboratory Medicine, said to appear by 1870, though no doubt influential, is irrelevant to my discussion here; the basic features of medical training in England were all in place well before this. While this view of the transition from Bedside to Hospital Medicine no doubt oversimplifies the case, it is one that I shall broadly follow. As a consequence of this change, relationships between medical men were also altered in Hospital Medicine:

> Henceforth the medical investigator was accorded respect on the basis of the authority inherent in his occupational role rather than on the basis of his individually proven worth. The public guarantee of the safety and efficacy of theories and therapies no longer rested upon the patient's approval of their contents, but on the social status of their authors and advocates (Jewson 1976: 235).

So not only did the new knowledge fundamentally alter relationships between patients and doctors, but Hospital Medicine also created new relationships between doctors themselves: between hospital doctors and general practitioners, between senior and junior hospital doctors, and between students and hospital doctors.

The Importance of Anatomy

This new knowledge was based on anatomical dissection. It was anatomy that fundamentally changed the classifications of disease by speculative pathology to those based on the post-mortem

Figure 2. Early dissection: the Professor of Anatomy sits reading from a purely written text above the table with the corpse, which is dissected by an assistant. Mondino's *Anathomia* of 1316 was in manuscript until printed in 1478, when crude woodcuts were added. [Melerstat's illustration on the title-page of the 1493 edition: Wellcome Institute Library, London]

dissection of patients. It is my contention that the three general medical dispositions of Knowledge, Experience and Responsibility discussed in the previous chapter derived from the changes in medical knowledge and practice based on the practice of anatomy.

Knowledge and Experience

The Western tradition of anatomy rested on the Anatomical Method, the inference from anatomy to physiology (based on the assumption that the more one knew of structure, the better one understood function): 'The ultimate goal of anatomy has always been physiology – that is, functional anatomy – and one of the most powerful methodological tools of earlier physiologists was dissection' (Bynum 1973: 445). Since the thirteenth century corpses had been anatomised on the Continent for the purposes of learning the causes of epidemic disease and in cases of suspected poisoning. But Mondino at Bologna, for example, seems to have conducted dissections more to confirm and learn the anatomical accounts of Galen and Avicenna than to test them or make discoveries. The professor, seated above the table, read from the text (by now in Latin), while an assistant dissected the body (see Figure 2); demonstrators pointed out the structures described by these ancient authorities.

Vesalius, at Padua in the first half of the sixteenth century, is usually cited as the anatomist whose published work was based on personal dissection and a scepticism towards Galen's works. And, though Berengario da Carpi was the first to use anatomical illustrations to accompany the text, the developments of perspective by Alberti (Romanyshyn 1989: 38–57) and of much more accurate wood-carving made it possible for readers to link the detailed anatomical drawings found in Vesalius' book *De humani corporis fabrica* (1543) with the Latin text describing the methods and results of dissection (Reiser 1978: 10–15). The anatomical method was further extended by Morgagni (whose *De Sedibus et Causis Morborum* was published in 1761) and others, by relating what was found at post-mortem dissection to the symptoms expressed in life; the new method was, in Bichat's admonition of 1801, quoted by Foucault (1989: 146), to 'Open up a few corpses: you will dissipate at once the darkness that observation alone could not dissipate.'

Foucault describes, in typically oblique language, his own view of the consequence of the new knowledge made available through dissection, a rupture with previous forms of knowledge:

> What is modified in giving place to anatomo-clinical medicine is not, therefore, the mere surface of contact between the knowing subject and the known object; it is the more general arrangement of knowledge that determines the reciprocal positions and the connexion between the one who must know and that which is to be known. The access of the medical gaze into the sick body was not the continuation of a movement of approach that had been developing in a more or less regular fashion since the day when the first doctor cast his somewhat unskilled gaze from afar on the body of the first patient; it was the result of a recasting at the level of epistemic knowledge (*savoir*) itself and not at the level of accumulated, refined, deepened, adjusted knowledge (*connaissance*) (Foucault 1989: 137).

Foucault seems to be saying two things: first, that the relationship between doctor and patient was fundamentally altered by a new sort of knowledge derived from anatomy and, second, that such new epistemic knowledge is personal and acquired particularly by the gaze (*le regard*) of the observer on to previously hidden sights; pre-existing accumulated (and therefore presumably communicable) knowledge, also based on sight, continued to be accumulated in the same way. The first point, already alluded to in the transition from Bedside to Hospital Medicine, I shall expand on later; it is the second that I wish to dispute here. For it is not only vision that is involved in the personal acquisition of knowledge through dissection of a dead body. 'The access of the medical gaze into the sick body' needs a great deal more than just looking: the hand-work of 'chirurgy', cutting through skin and subcutaneous tissues alone, requires touch, particularly, but also smell (and to that extent, taste) and even hearing, as well as sight, even though such work will indeed reveal new vistas to the eyes. But the epistemic knowledge derived from the action of personal dissection is not the consequence of simply looking, any more than Doubting Thomas's lack of belief was dispelled by simply seeing; the common-sense perception of seeing and touching gives rise to a personal certainty through such combined sensory experience.

At about this time another sensory modality, hearing, becomes important. Auenbrugger's diagnostic method of 'percussion' of the chest, described in 1761, was designed to bypass the inconstant and untrustworthy accounts of patients; this was hardly taken up by medical men. What did become common practice relatively quickly after its description by Laennec in 1819 was the use of 'mediate auscultation' (that is, hearing mediated by the stethoscope, rather than by the investigator placing his ear directly on the chest). This, like percussion, gave an account of the different sounds heard in life; the difference between the two methods, and the strength of the latter, was the relation by Laennec of these sounds made during life to pathological findings at post-mortem dissection (Reiser 1978: 23–44). While Foucault later covers other sensory modalities by expansion of the original gaze to a 'gaze that touches, hears, and moreover, not by essence or necessity, sees' (1989: 164), finally he says, 'In any case, the absolute limit and depth of perceptual exploration are always outlined by the clear plane of an at least potential visibility' (1989: 165); in saying this, he has himself lost sight of the personal implications of these new developments. For, as Maulitz describes in connection with the use of the stethoscope, the importation of the French anatomico-pathological tradition into England was

> not simply a matter of knowledge flowing through the funnel of a text tradition. Nor was it simply a question of 'technology transfer' by which the stethoscope was taken to England. The process was rather one in which *experience*, from the dissection table and the hospital wards, flowed through the careers of multitudinous young Englishmen as they made the journey out and back . . . The year in France was, far from a passive period of observation, a veritable *tour de main* (Maulitz 1987: 136; original emphasis).

In other words, there seem to be two new forms of medical knowledge associated with dissection, and not one as Foucault describes. The first (found in the disposition of Knowledge) is public, communally visible (by observing either the dissected flesh itself or pictorial representations of it) and communicable by words (hearing other doctors and scientists speak and reading what they have written); the written and illustrated works of Vesalius are an early example of this form of knowledge. The second form (found in the disposition of Experience) must be personally acquired, as by Vesalius himself (see Figure 3) and by the young Englishmen who learnt how to use a stethoscope. Though Experience may be read about, it is typically transmitted personally through oral

Figure 3. Vesalius of Padua: von Calcar's image of the anatomist as individual acquirer of Experience, from Vesalius' *De humani corporis fabrica libri septem* of 1543. [Wellcome Institute Library, London]

instruction; though associated with sight, it is not typified by sight alone, touch and hearing also contributing significantly. While there are close connections between Experience and Knowledge, and while there is also a tendency for Experience to be converted to Knowledge, these two embodied dispositions are qualitatively different. Looking at the demonstrator's dissection or at pictures of it involves a degree of trust from the spectator, whose inclination to confirm what he sees by touching leads to so many instructions not to do so; only the dissector himself has the personal knowledge of this Experience. But while the basis of Knowledge is its shared visibility, and Experience its personal access, both dispositions involve learning the particular nature of what is to be learnt by training the mind to recognise what the senses convey.

Theatres, Anatomical and Surgical, and Responsible Action

Public anatomies were originally theatrical spectacles that viewers paid to see; tickets for the annual public anatomy were sold at Padua in 1497, apparently before tickets were sold for plays (Hecksher 1958: 28, 32). The tradition of the anatomy demonstration led to the construction of specialised buildings, anatomy theatres, of a circular or semi-circular shape, with tiered levels where observers stood (with rails to lean on) or sat, looking down and in on the dissector and the corpse (see Figure 4). This physical and spatial configuration will recur many times in my account; it has already done so in the previous chapter with Goffman's theatrical metaphors. Here I briefly describe the historical origins of the real theatres of medicine, the anatomy theatre and the operating theatre.

The dead body had been a subject for moral or religious contemplation, for example, by learned physicians or the general public (again see Figure 4); 'the unusual features of the flesh' gradually moved from the sphere of the church to that of medical science and also from public to private, professional spheres (B. Turner 1987: 18–38) as they became the raw material from which both forms of new knowledge, Knowledge and Experience, were hewn. Indeed, as I suggested above, the difference between the two may be related to people with different roles in the anatomy theatre: the spectators can all see and have demonstrated to them (and to that extent know) the result of the dissector's activity; but only the dissector himself has the certain knowledge that comes from the practice of dissection itself.

These theatrical settings, then, led to the acceptance by the audience of what was presented on the stage in its own terms; this involves the audience in the 'willing suspension of disbelief' that Coleridge describes as a prerequisite for participation in artistic endeavours. Anatomy created, from a dead body, those aspects of the body that were intended to be, and so became, the focus of attention: 'The body anatomized as corpse upon the stage of the dissecting table is as much a piece of creative fiction as it is discovered fact' (Romanyshyn 1989: 119), belonging as much to the realm of art as it does to science. But, equally, the power of these new forms of knowledge depended on their apparently natural and uncontentious quality, which itself was taken as the empirical and scientific base of the emerging profession of

Figure 4. The anatomy theatre at Leiden, built in a former church in 1593. Public anatomies were performed in winter, while in summer the theatre became a museum of curiosities. Note the nearly circular tiered stands, directing the male spectators' eyes down and in, and the moral mottoes held by skeletons. [Johannes Cornelis Woudan's *Amphitheatrum Anatomicum Lugduno Batavorum* of 1610; Museum Boerhaave Leiden]

medicine; as Hertz says, 'Every social hierarchy claims to be founded on the nature of things; *phusei ou nomo* [on nature not man-made culture]; it thus accords itself eternity, it escapes change and the attacks of innovators' (1960: 89). At this time, the investigators of the eternal nature of things, the natural body, were all men. Pictures of these public anatomies indicate that not just all the dissectors but all the spectators were male too. And, while the anatomised bodies are of both men and women, it is with a particularly masculine eighteenth-century eye that bodies are pictorially represented (Jordanova 1985) in the visual disposition of Knowledge (see Figure 5). It was also men who pioneered surgical practice, its developments also based on anatomy,

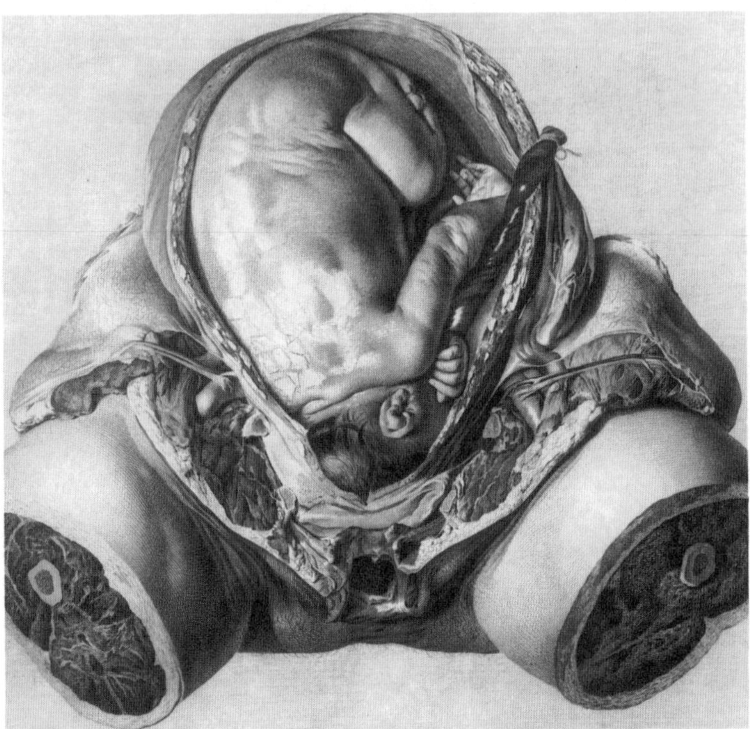

Figure 5. Depiction of dissection: the transformation of personally acquired Experience to publicly available Knowledge in William Hunter's *The Anatomy of the Human Gravid Uterus* of 1774. Note the great detail and the detachment of the specimen both from the rest of the body and from any other context. [Wellcome Institute Library, London]

leading to another new form of medical knowledge found in the disposition of Responsibility.

Anatomy was the basis not only for understanding physiology but, increasingly, also for the practice of Surgery. In the early nineteenth century, 'a more thorough command of normal and pathological anatomy was now at the command of a good surgeon, he had more and better instruments than his predecessors, and operations were now being performed, sometimes with success, that would not have been attempted a century before' (Youngson 1979: 23). And the two major therapeutic advances of the end of the first half of the century, antisepsis and anaesthesia, made surgical operations (while still hazardous) more likely to be successful. Failure was followed by post-mortem examination, allowing technical errors to be identified and subsequently corrected.

The practice of physicians, on the other hand, was relatively unaffected. To be sure, public health was improved by general measures; John Snow, himself a noted anaesthetist, conducted an epidemiological study of a cholera outbreak in Soho, identifying the contaminated Broad Street pump in 1854 (Youngson 1979: 76). But, in England up till 1870 or so, the stagnation of the study of physiology as the scientific base of Medicine was obvious, as was the lack of therapeutic advance in Medicine. This has been attributed to several causes: the powerful anti-vivisectionist lobby; the establishment's commitment to natural theology; national chauvinism (in disregarding the advances made on the Continent, for example, by Bernard in France and Helmholtz in Germany); the power and success of the Anatomical Method, and, particularly, the methods of teaching in medical schools, which relied heavily on anatomy. Medical education at Oxford and Cambridge, the source of most of the members of the Royal College of Physicians, was still heavily classically and mathematically inclined. Physiology at University College was the best England had to offer in the new experimental sciences; but, even there, its hospital medical school was like the others in London: their aims and organisation 'fostered a utilitarian, and correspondingly anatomical conception of physiology'. Medical teaching was there, as elsewhere, in the hands of medical men, whose 'job was to teach and teach in such a way that their students would be able to pass the qualifying examinations of the Royal College of Surgeons or of the Society of Apothecaries' (Geison 1972: 42, 45).

The purpose of this discussion is twofold: first, to stress again the importance of anatomy and, second, to indicate the emergence of one aspect of the disposition of Responsibility – that of action directed towards a patient – which, in the first half of the last century, tended to be surgical action, conducted in the same settings as anatomy in general and post-mortem dissection of patients in particular. Such personal actions and their results, while only partly visible even to well-positioned observers (see Figure 6), become part of a personal repertoire of physical techniques of the performer, who can learn from his actions and improve them. It is only the surgeon who, as an individual, knows what he personally has done and knows the consequences. This leads to another form of certain personal knowledge different from that of

Experience; Experience also involves action (from dissection to auscultation), but it is investigative, not therapeutic, action. Action directed at achieving the practical result of a change beneficial to the patient is the practice of Responsibility, action typified by the surgeon's skill.

Associated with these major changes in knowledge, all divorced in their different ways from the person who, dead or alive, gives rise to such knowledge, is one of language: the common linguistic ground of patients and practitioners found in the first half of the eighteenth century was gradually lost over the course of the second. For example, the Register of the Bristol Infirmary shows the increasing use of standard classifications of disease, with diagnoses based on physical examination of the patients and their dissection after death, in language understandable to other practitioners but not to the patient. There is a swift shift from English to Latin (though one should perhaps note that 'Latin' here includes many words derived from Greek and some even from Arabic (Singer 1959)). In the late 1770s, 70 per cent of diagnoses were in English and 19 per cent in Latin; by 1800, 79 per cent of diagnoses were made in Latin and only 1 per cent were still in English (Fissell 1991).

This change concerns the professional use of a new medical language based on anatomy and the communication of Knowledge through communally visible writing. Knowledge can also, of course, be conveyed through speech, but speech is more important than writing in the personally-based dispositions of Experience and Responsibility, mostly learnt directly from others (and therefore orally). Perhaps not surprisingly in view of the written nature of history, there is no good evidence of the historical origins of the oral form of teaching and learning Experience and Responsibility by Question and Answer that I describe later: Lawrence (1995: 220), for example, talks of up-to-date medical men in the late eighteenth century being able to 'deploy' new specialised anatomical terms, though again she only refers to writing. But, because of the nature of Experience and Responsibility, and the late date of the introduction of written examinations (see below), the oral form of transmission of knowledge is almost certainly of ancient origin. Oral catechisms are still found in induction to religious orders and to Freemasonry.

Figure 6. The Responsible action of Surgery, shown in Thomas Eakins' *The Gross Clinic* of 1875. The privileged spectators are now seated, but clearly in the same almost circular configuration as that in anatomy theatres. The surgeon, Dr Gross of Philadelphia, who 'hated the applause from students as he entered the amphitheatre', is teaching while operating; an assistant makes written notes, while a female figure shields her eyes from the scene (see Brieger 1993). [Jefferson Medical College of Thomas Jefferson University, Philadelphia, PA]

The Hospitals

In London, the hospitals that qualified apprentices attended were mostly of recent origin. In 1718 there were two ancient hospitals, St Bartholemew's (1123) and St Thomas's (1207); during the eighteenth century this number was greatly increased, not only by those hospitals familiar today – Westminster (1719), Guy's (1721), St George's (1733), the London Hospital (1740) and the Middlesex (1745) – but by many other hospitals and dispensaries. While the same expansion was to be found in the provinces, by 1800 there were as many beds in London as there were in the rest of England and Wales – 1500. These new voluntary hospitals were all founded as charities for the sick poor by non-medical people from a mixture of religious, humanitarian and self-interested motives, and run by lay governors, not by doctors. Patients tended to be admitted for a period of rest and care rather than treatment (Abel-Smith 1964: 1–11). The medical attendants (or 'honorary doctors') to hospital patients were volunteers, either receiving no salary at all or a modest honorarium (£40 per year at St Thomas's and Guy's), with their duties limited to a weekly ward round. Surgeons were allowed the privilege of taking pupils or 'dressers' (who had already served their apprenticeship to a surgeon-apothecary, for example) as well as personal apprentices (who were going to become surgeons). The fees arising from teaching were substantial, and the surgeons' material concerns were bound up with this so-called 'firm' system of hospital teaching by which they were, originally, directly paid by each student. But the traditional one-to-one relationship of master to apprentice was breaking down in both directions: masters took on multiple students and students followed multiple masters (Gelfand 1985: 146).

The attractions of London were a consequence of the dominance of the private enterprise system of medical education and the way in which the newly founded hospitals and schools could respond to the demands of the increasing numbers of students; the consequent wide variety of high-quality private teaching available in London is to be contrasted to the more authoritarian and bureaucratic institutions in France, the products of Church and State foundation and administration (Gelfand 1985). And the opportunities for such extra learning were many and varied: there were increasing numbers of medical and scientific societies;

lectures and demonstrations (often anatomical ones given by eminent surgeons) were an established feature of medical life, especially in London (though these might still be open to the general public as well as medical practitioners). Teaching in hospitals was available for further payment, as was attendance there at courses of lectures. The private medical schools were sometimes linked to hospitals; the famous Great Windmill Street school of anatomy run by the brothers John and William Hunter, for example, was unofficially associated with St George's, where John Hunter was an Honorary Surgeon.

The unofficial links between hospitals and private schools were lost as hospitals started to build their own medical schools for lecture courses and demonstrations. New anatomy theatres were built at St Thomas's in 1813 and at Barts in 1822 (Newman 1957: 117); and, at Barts in 1820, there were several hundred surgical students, with just three medical (that is, physicians') students (see Bynum 1994: 48). Students were taught either by the honorary consultants themselves or their appointees, whom students paid directly, just as they paid the same men, the honorary consultants, for teaching on the hospital wards. But with the wealth of alternatives afforded by private teaching, often found cheaper and sometimes better by those purchasing it, it is not immediately clear how the hospitals managed to corner the market in medical training. This seems to have arisen by a combination of the increasing prestige of the individual teachers appointed there (based on their connections with the three corporations) and of restrictive measures favouring the hospitals, passed by the licensing authorities, whose members were usually holders of hospital appointments. An example of this was the ruling by the Royal College of Surgeons in 1822 that it would no longer accept certificates of attendance at summer courses for students wanting to enter for the College diploma. The point of this ruling was that hospitals only ran winter courses, when corpses decomposed more slowly. But a method of preserving corpses had been developed by Joshua Brookes (largely for which he had been made a Fellow of the Royal Society), and, though it smelt like a ham shop, his private anatomy school, running both summer and winter courses, was highly successful. The College ruling, however, was a fatal blow, and his school closed in 1826 (Desmond 1989: 154–65). But cornering the market in medical training was finally accomplished by a cornering of the market in the raw material of professional cognitive exclusiveness itself, in the hospitals' monopolising the raw material of teaching (that is, patients and dead bodies).

The Teaching Hospitals Corner the Market in Corpses and Patients

The need for dead bodies for learning and teaching in hospitals and private schools, as well as for more general scientific purposes, had resulted in a large, free and unregulated market in this new commodity; this is fully described in Richardson's *Death, Dissection and the Destitute* (1989). The 'Paris manner' of providing a cadaver for each student had been introduced to London by William Hunter in 1746; but well before then grave-robbing had become frequent. The private enterprise of anatomy teaching in London continued to keep the prices for bodies much higher there than in Paris (the equivalent of $42 compared to $1.50 in 1815), where a legal, cheap and abundant supply of bodies for State-authorised dissection was available (Maulitz 1987: 142–50). The legal supply of corpses in England was tiny and utterly inadequate to cope with the huge demand; grave-robbing now took place on a grand scale, and worse: in 1828, the bodies of Burke and Hare's murdered victims were found in the dissecting rooms of Dr Knox's private anatomy school in Edinburgh. The surgeon and anatomist, Sir Astley Cooper of Guy's, giving evidence to a parliamentary Select Committee that same year, said, 'there is no person, let his situation in life be what it may, whom, if I were disposed to dissect, I could not obtain'; the Duke of Wellington was buried in four coffins as late as 1852 (Richardson 1989: 63, 322).

Bentham's own attitude to anatomy is well-known; he was himself dissected in 1832, and his Auto-Icon, his articulated, padded and clothed skeleton, is still on public view in University College. He had drafted an Anatomy Bill some years before; but the Act regulating these multitudinous grisly transactions was passed after his death in 1832. The Anatomy Act established a legal secure supply of corpses, a supply particularly important for surgeons, by appropriating the dead bodies of the poor. The Act also worked to the benefit of the hospital anatomy schools. Though the Anatomy Inspector was supposed to allocate bodies both to these schools and their private competitors on the basis of the number of students at each establishment, schools attached to hospitals could always obtain, illegally, the bodies in their own mortuaries, and were anyway not disposed to share them with their competitors. The hospitals also struck deals with parish authorities, who would receive hospital beds for their sick in return for the bodies of their dead. As well as securing the emerging profession's monopoly of the raw material out of which the exclusive cognitive base of modern medicine was originally derived, the Act benefited the teaching hospitals, and private schools soon went out of business.

The honoraries, now called 'consultants', had also managed to gain increasing control over the sort of patients coming into the hospitals, notably by the practice of admitting patients as emergencies through the Casualty Ward, and so bypassing the proper system of admission through governors' tickets. The patients the doctors tended to admit were the acutely ill (and, in particular, the acutely ill for whom some surgical action could be taken); so the hospital's function changed fundamentally from being a place of rest to one of treatment (Abel-Smith 1964: 38–9; Peterson 1978: 175–6). Consultants established the second of the two aspects of the disposition of Responsibility, ownership, by having 'their' patients in 'their' beds; that the majority of patients were surgical is further evidence of the contemporary dominance of Surgery over Medicine in the other aspect of Responsibility, action taken towards a patient. It should be noted that the free treatment of patients in hospital was a continuing source of grievance for general practitioners against hospital consultants, with patients quite wealthy enough to be potential fee-paying customers opting for free hospital care. The division between hospital doctors and general practitioners was one of the significant new relationships between doctors created by Hospital Medicine.

Hospital Medical Schools: The Institutionalisation of Training

The gradual cornering of the market in medical training by the hospitals led to major changes in its organisation. In the previous century, individual apprenticeship had preceded attendance in hospitals or private schools; after that, apprenticeship and attendance were disordered and simultaneous, with the licensing system breaking down. The State had intervened with the

Apothecaries' Act of 1815, which extended the Apothecaries' authority over the whole of England and Wales, and also codified a course of training; that its one innovation, compulsory observation of medical (as opposed to surgical) practice, was effectively overruled by the Apothecaries' examiners in the same year is again evidence of the predominance of Surgery at this time (Lawrence 1991: 51; Peterson 1978: 19–21). The imposition of attendance prescribed by the Apothecaries' Act had an interesting consequence soon after it was enacted. Increasing numbers of applicants had simply satisfied the minimum requirements rather than, as before, having exceeded them: 'the overwhelming impression on the Apothecaries' examiners . . . must have been the appearance of a decided decline in students' initiative and qualifications in the years immediately after the Act went into effect' (Lawrence 1991: 58). This is perhaps the first evidence of the triumph of the principle of Economy in the pursuit of Knowledge and Experience among what may now be called medical students.

New medical schools were soon founded, in London and in large provincial cities, to provide for the large numbers of students. The first prospectus for the new University of London states: 'It is only in large towns that a Medical School can exist. The means of acquiring anatomical knowledge, medical experience, and surgical dexterity, must increase in exact proportion to the town' (Harte and North 1991: 18), presumably because of the need for large supplies of bodies and patients to learn from. As it was later called, University College (which started to give medical lectures in 1828), with its associated hospital (opened in 1834), was the first purpose-instituted teaching hospital, providing fee-paying students with teaching material in the form of non-paying patients. It was to be run on Benthamite principles and with Benthamite aims, and therefore (unlike Oxford and Cambridge) to be cheap, non-sectarian (which meant secular) and enlightened. Its graduates were to reform 'Old Corruption', the corporate establishment devoted to Church and State and staffed through patronage; not surprisingly, legal recognition of University College as a university had been opposed by Oxford and Cambridge and by the medical Royal Colleges. King's College, founded as a Tory counterpart to University College, opened its Medical Department in 1831 and its Hospital in 1839, and Charing Cross and St Mary's followed soon after.

In the University of London's prospectus quoted above, the three qualities of 'anatomical knowledge, medical experience and surgical dexterity' reveal the three new dispositions of Knowledge, Experience and Responsibility, in the order in which they were now to be taught. Attendance at lectures and demonstrations to learn Knowledge now preceded attendance on the wards for the acquisition of Experience. Newman (1957: 219–21) suggests this re-ordering was principally because the previous arrangements' messiness upset the Victorian sense of order. But Bentham himself proposed the view that medicine should only be taught after the basic natural sciences, in accordance with his Chrestomathic principle (1983: 33). Whether because of Bentham's influence or not, the traditional pattern of medical training in England was established.

Knowledge was not taught in a manner derived from the old universities of Oxford and Cambridge, but from Leiden and Edinburgh and the anatomy theatres of the private medical schools, by lecture; in William Wilkins' original plan for University College, the lecture theatre 'for Anatomy, Surgery &c' lies on the first floor, directly above and spatially congruent with another lecture theatre on the ground floor and the anatomy theatre in the basement (see Harte and North 1991: 24–5). All lecture theatres have the shape of Bentham's Chrestomathic school-room, which maximised the Master's economic efficiency (by letting one teach many) in the manner found in private schools, referred to contemptuously by Coleridge as 'Lecture Bazaars'. Bentham's Panopticon principle is also involved in his 'Inspection principle', permitting the Master to supervise large numbers of students:

> By the *Panopticon* principle of construction, security, in this respect [in so far as it is due to inspection by the Master], is *maximized*, and rendered entire: viz., partly by *minimizing* the distance between the situation of the *remotest scholar* and that of the *Master's eye*; partly by giving to the *floor* or *floors* that *inclination*, which, to a certain degree prevents remoter objects from being *eclipsed* by nearer ones; partly by enabling the Master to *see without being seen*, whereby, to those who, at the moment, are unseen by him, it cannot be *known* that they are in this case (Bentham 1983: 106).

And it is, of course, in Bentham's Panopticon principle that Foucault (1991: 195–228) has discerned what he calls 'surveillance'.

But this understanding should also be reversed: if one can see all, all can see one. The reverse, complementary principle (which one might call the Monopticon principle) is found, for example, in the anatomy theatre in Padua, where concentric tiers of observers all look down on the demonstrated dissected corpse, with no suggestion that all these observers can themselves be observed. While I do not dispute the importance of surveillance, it is surprising that Foucault, who (however wrongly, in my view) has raised 'the gaze' to the highest power, should ignore so completely the concentrated gaze of the theatre audience on to a single focus. And, indeed, the historical evidence strongly suggests that he is also wrong to do so: public anatomies had been theatrical spectacles and Boerhaave had lectured in Leiden on medical matters in a similar setting (see Figure 7) long before Bentham crystallised his principles.

At any event, the acquisition of Knowledge so taught was tested in a new way, by written examinations. These were originally introduced in the old universities just before the turn of the century because of the increase in the number of candidates. Not only were examinations to be conducted on paper rather than orally, but there was another novelty, that of 'extemporaneous writing'; the candidate did not know beforehand which questions would be asked, and his answers, set and corrected by impartial examiners, were to be written within a given length of time. The board of examiners for the Society of Apothecaries set written questions for the first time in the 1839–40 session (Carr-Saunders and Wilson 1964: 313–14). During the following years, which the students spent 'walking the wards', Experience was to be acquired. Importance was placed on learning the new methods of examination of the patient by close observation and thorough physical examination, including the use of the stethoscope; it is from these days that the still current serial examination by inspection, palpation, percussion and auscultation arises (Bynum 1994: 33). Methods of examining a student's own examination of a patient must have been introduced to test Experience; but, for reasons given above, it is hard to find any contemporary details of such oral catechism by Question and Answer. It may, however, be just as much a tribute to the stability of this method of examination as to literary tradition, that the surgically-qualified Smollett's account of a surgical *viva* (an oral examination in Surgery) in *Roderick Random*, published in 1748 (Smollett 1930: 110–13), is so similar to

Figure 7. Early lecturing: Boerhaave delivering an oration in the Grand Auditorium at Leiden. Note the pulpit-like construction in which he stands and the spatial configuration of the audience, some seated. The illustration is on the title-page of the published text of Boerhaave's lecture *De comparando certo in physicis* of 1715. [Wellcome Institute Library, London]

Gordon's in *Doctor in the House*, published two hundred years later (Gordon 1955: 135–7).

The new hospital medical schools also brought social changes to these new students. Apprentices had lived with their master and some indentured hospital apprentices had continued to do this; in the early days of the hospital medical schools, students had found lodgings, either alone or with friends, near the hospital. Hospitals were concerned about their students' unruliness and lack of discipline, and began to introduce affiliated 'collegiate' residences, where they could live, dine, and study, supervised more carefully than they could have been in digs. Their new corporate life was further integrated by the formation of clubs and societies of all sorts, from medical societies to sporting clubs and Masonic lodges. It is not clear how far the new collegiality within medical schools was fostered by the governors and teachers, perhaps as part of the general search for status, and how far it was a spontaneous creation of the students themselves, some of whom came from the universities and some from the public schools; though it would be a mistake to imagine that most medical students had been to public schools, it seems to have been a distinct career advantage to have done so (Peterson 1978: 74–84). But features of life in the mid-Victorian public boarding school were certainly introduced: academic competition, which was stimulated by examinations, prizes and scholarships; athletic competition, stimulated by the new team-games of rugby – the oldest rugby club in the world is Guy's Hospital's, founded in 1843 – and association football (instead of uncompetitive field sports); and social competitiveness with the equivalent of the prefect system. In terms of dispositions, Co-operation was introduced into medical schools and, along with it, Competition.

After their years walking the wards, qualified medical men intending to set up in general practice left the hospital; the commonest combination of qualifications was LSA (Licentiate of the Society of Apothecaries) and MRCS (Member of the Royal College of Surgeons). But some stayed on to take up the new posts in hospital. The posts of House Surgeon and House Physician were created in the 1840s and 1850s, their holders selected from previous 'dressers' in Surgery and 'clerks' in Medicine. The post of Registrar, whose job it was to make a written report on all hospital cases, was established first at Guy's in 1853; but many other hospitals introduced it between 1860 and 1880. At the same time, the title of hospital apothecary disappeared; there was now no role for a general practitioner in a large teaching hospital. These new posts were nominally the appointments of the board of lay hospital governors, just as new consultants were in fact (though choice was heavily influenced by existing consultants' recommendations). But, combined with their new control over the patients admitted to hospital, the consultants had also started to control appointments to the new posts available to newly qualified medical men. Perhaps because of the relatively minor patronage involved in such short appointments (of three to six months), perhaps because they reasoned that the consultant staff would choose those who would best reflect on the hospital, governors came to accept the nominations of consultants to these posts (Peterson 1978: 85, 157–65). These junior doctors were delegated Responsibility for their consultants' patients, in an extension of the 'firm' system of teaching.

Medical Status and Links with the State

The pre-eminent success of medicine as a profession is linked to the scientific basis of its knowledge, which I have firmly linked, in turn, to its historical origins in anatomy. Originally, not only medicine relied on anatomy for its authoritative scientific base: both academic and popular enterprises (from theology to social theory to the individual psychology of phrenology) were based, by progressives and conservatives alike, on human and comparative anatomy (Cooter 1984; Desmond 1989; Figlio 1976; Laqueur 1987). But anatomy (and its teaching to medical students) came to be monopolised by the teaching hospitals, by driving private medical schools out of business, and the teaching of anatomy to segregated groups of medical students in fixed theatrical settings promoted the accepted surgical view of the body. In these hospitals a standardised training under professional control was developed, resulting in the nascent profession's 'exclusive cognitive identity' – the argument in this section is based on Larson (1977). In the intensely competitive market for health, the general population's universal but unorganised need for medical services also drove the emerging profession to form itself along monopolistic lines. But these monopolistic tendencies, in turn, compelled the State to intervene in medical men's increasing control of the market. The Apothecaries' Act of 1815, referred to above, is regarded as something of a milestone, marking the watershed between the heyday of unregulated (but not necessarily unqualified) practitioners and the rise of State's involvement with the emerging medical profession. Specifically, the Act stipulated a course of training as a legal requirement for entering the Apothecaries' examinations for a licence to practice, thus providing the population with the assurance that new medical practitioners had reached an approved standard of proficiency.

Of course, links with the State presumably go back as far as the monarch had a medical attendant – it was probably to contain the competition for treating the members of the court that the guilds were first established. And here there is a major difference between the profession of medicine and those of the military, the Church and the law. In a sense, the activities of these other three professions were simply an extension of the monarch (judges acting in his name, the military fighting his battles, churchmen maintaining his spiritual authority) and were bound by personal oath of loyalty to the monarch; there is nothing of the sort to be found among doctors. And, unlike the other three professions, medicine had no head: there was no Archbishop, no Commander-in-Chief, no Lord Chief Justice. The distribution of power, at the same time diffused and concentrated, meant that the State's negotiations with the profession were always difficult.

New associations of medical men formed to achieve professional and economic goals, to prevent competition from druggists, irregulars and other 'unqualified' medical attendants – goals which were ignored or opposed by the corporations; one of these associations was the Provincial Medical and Surgical Association, later the British Medical Association (BMA) (Peterson 1978: 19). The practice of the professional disposition of Competition is evident both in the general Economic drive to monopoly and in the astonishingly virulent and personal attacks made between members of the new associations and the old corporations; Wakley's diatribes on the corporations in his own journal the *Lancet* are astonishing for doctors to read now, after 150 years of professional Co-operation. But continuing Competition between the old corporations themselves, particularly in the lucrative market in licensing to practise, is reflected in the fact that the successful Medical Bill of 1858 was the sixteenth bill to be presented to Parliament since 1806, the previous bills being foiled either behind the scenes or by the parliamentary lobbying of whichever corporations felt most threatened by new proposals.

There is another element involved in the pre-eminence of medicine as a profession, which also involves another disposition in the medical habitus not yet mentioned here. While I have emphasised the monopolistic Economic activities both of the corporations and of the emerging profession in the free market for medical training and treatment, an 'anti-market' component, consonant (if hardly identical) with the prevailing ideology, was also present. This 'mission' of medicine found ample scope in the misery and poverty of the personal consequences of unplanned industrialisation; Engels' indictment of English society, for example, was prepared in terms of unnecessary suffering and death. In terms of dispositions, the corporations' and the new profession's use of Economic methods was associated with Idealism; indeed, however analytically distinct these are, the 'entrepreneurial and vocational dimensions' in the early modern profession appeared fused, as they are in Weber's analysis of the bourgeois economic ethic; such a fusion generates tensions, both for the individual and for the profession as a whole. But even this Idealistic mission must be shown in terms of the demonstrable ability to 'do good', which, in individual terms, was most obviously possible by new surgical activities. Contemporary allusion to the tensions between Idealism and Economy, a theme running through my account, is still to be seen in the Old St Thomas's operating theatre in Southwark (see Figure 8). Above this archetypal official frontstage setting for the practice of Responsibility are the words, *Miseratione Non Mercede* ['For Pity Not Profit'] – for Idealism, not Economy.

Professional medical Status (and with it, intra-professional Co-operation) was fully established by the Medical Act of 1858. A General Medical Council (GMC) was to be formed, composed of medically qualified representatives of the licensing bodies and the universities, with a few nominations by the Privy Council; this was to supervise the activities of what may now be properly called a profession, including medical training. By whichever route medical men had become licensed and however senior they were, in legal terms all medical practitioners registered with the GMC were equal, whether senior honorary consultant or new House Officer. Some of the more surprising routes to licences were abolished, like the MD (Lambeth), which had been in the grant of the Archbishop of Canterbury; but the corporations survived, and power over professional training and licensing was left in the hands of the London élites. There was to be no National Board to give licences to practice (the 'single portal of entry' favoured by

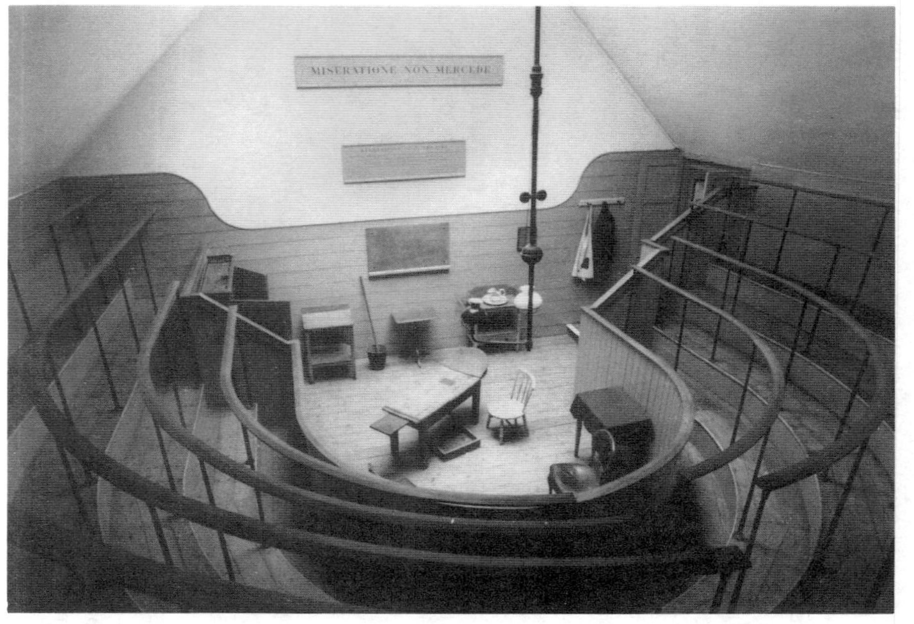

Figure 8. Surgery: Responsibility, Idealism and Economy. The Old St Thomas's operating theatre in the loft of a disused church in Southwark was in use between 1822 and 1842, and is now part of a museum. The semi-circular tiered stands look down and in on the operating table; on the back wall there is a blackboard below the moral motto *Miseratione Non Mercede*. [The Old Operating Theatre, Museum and Herb Garret]

some). And despite the increasing closeness of the new profession to the State, it did not match the older professions' swearing of allegiance to the Crown; its own oath of loyalty is to itself, in the resurrected Hippocratic Oath. The 1858 Act established an impersonal and typically bureaucratic relationship between the new profession and the State, relationship by committee, that of the GMC to the Privy Council. So, while the Act established the profession legally, it ensured the profession's autonomy; and while it united medical practitioners in some ways, it left other functions divided – training in particular. Students were taught at medical schools and usually examined by corporations, organisationally quite distinct from the schools; training was to be supervised by the new GMC, again organisationally quite different. It is perhaps hard at first to understand how the standardised mass-production of the exclusive cognitive identity of newly licensed 'safe' practitioners (which, partly for the protection of the public, the GMC had in effect contracted with the State to supervise) was accomplished. This was no doubt due in great part to the common scientific basis and to the now firmly established sequence and methods of training; but the increasing mobility of teacher–practitioners within the schools must have played a part, as must the fact that (despite the institutional separation of aspects of training), the same person could (and can) be a consultant at a teaching hospital, on a corporation's Board of Examiners, and a member of the GMC.

I have now described, in the context of the emerging medical profession, the historical development of the professional dispositions of medicine I derived in the previous chapter. There are two points that should again be underlined: first, women were totally absent from the various phases I have described. The cult and culture of sensibility arising in the eighteenth century was also gendered; women had weaker but more sensitive nerves, another anatomically-based notion earlier derived by the Oxford proponent of the Anatomical Method, Thomas Willis and his best student of medicine there, John Locke (Barker-Benfield 1992: 3–4). Despite women's innate possession of this capacity, they could educate men with it, moderating and civilising them. In medicine, however, this was not the case. The exclusion of women from the new profession, no doubt partly based on the view of women's easily outraged sensibility, was accomplished by the separation of functions in training (Witz 1992: 83–99). Historically then, the dispositions of medicine are all culturally male; women were *de facto* if not *de jure* excluded from their development.

Second, the new forms of knowledge (Knowledge, Experience and Responsibility) were based on dissection and surgical practice, and all the main social features of medical training are predominantly derived from Surgery in the early years of the last century. This is odd, because the generic name for the profession is 'medicine', and all medical men came to be titled 'Dr' by the end of the last century, surgeons alone retaining their distinction as 'Mr' from the old learned physicians (who had indeed received a doctorate). This apparent contradiction is resolved by considering the strength of the upwards drive for Status, collective and personal; the new profession took its name, and most of its members now took their title, from the most ancient of the corporations and the one still with the highest Status in social terms, even though it lagged behind in professional developments. A further indication of how out of date the Royal College of Physicians was, is provided by the attitudes to its new Licentiate (LRCP); this had been introduced in 1861 in response to the success of the LSA as a licence for general practice. Examination for the LRCP did involve a physical examination of a patient by the candidate, but the observers from the GMC at the LRCP examinations objected to one clinical examination 'because its aim was to test the fitness of a candidate to take a case [that is, to look after a patient] and the visitors thought it should test his ability to discover the nature of the diseases quickly and to apply to it the resources of medicine'. The GMC, as Newman (1957: 203) notes, was 'even then interested in discovering the "safe doctor", not the man who would ultimately be a good doctor'.

The Route to Current Professional Training: A Few Minor Changes

But the 1858 Act had not settled things. In the next thirty years, another twenty-odd bills were proposed, most of them dealing with the unsatisfactory situation that gave the holders of only one licence (such as MRCS, LRCP or LSA) permission to become general practitioners. The passage of all of these bills was prevented (like the ones before the 1858 Act) by the interests affected and the jealousies of the medical corporations. The final entombment of the idea of a 'single portal of entry' with a National Board of examination and registry and the triumph of the professionally unifying idea of the 'safe general practitioner' was accomplished with the Act of 1886, which changed a registrable qualification to qualification in all three subjects of medicine, surgery and midwifery. By the end of the century, most students took the new Conjoint Board examinations, giving them the degree of LRCP MRCS; after 1892, the course was its current five years.

The introduction of the NHS in 1948 not only left untouched the structure found in hospital medical schools, but extended it to the whole country: 'Little thought was given to modifying the traditional teaching hospital structure for the new comprehensive hospital service: it was merely standardized and transposed to all hospitals' (Stevens 1966: 139). Free treatment had always been the case for patients at teaching hospitals, and was now to be found in all NHS hospitals. In 1948, a Ministry of Health memorandum recommended that there was a named consultant in charge of all in-patient beds and out-patient sessions, as was the case at teaching hospitals. The relationships between consultants and patients (the 'ownership' of patients by consultants and their firms, in the disposition of Responsibility) was now the same in all hospitals as it had been in teaching hospitals. In 1950, the authorities decided that the undergraduate curriculum was no longer capable of producing a safe and competent general practitioner; this, and the fact that roughly half all medical graduates would then, as now, become general practitioners, were the reasons given for the introduction (with the Medical Act of 1950) for all graduates of a compulsory pre-registration year as a House Officer in hospital, working for one or more consultants on their firm. The relationships of Hospital Medicine were nationalised.

Over the years since then, changes have in effect been further amplifications of the system of training in place in London by the 1840s, which was based on the historically male professional dispositions. For this reason, I shall henceforward refer to medical students generically as male, and to House Officers as housemen (as they are in fact more commonly known). This should not be thought of in any sense either as a disparagement of women or of housemen, but as a reflection of the attitude of medical culture; indeed, if my referring to either group in these ways appears to cause conflict with any lay understanding of medical training, so much the better.

The traditional training starts with the two preclinical years. During them the student is directed, now as then, to learn medical Knowledge, and is simultaneously taught by several different academic departments. The exponential expansion of the scientific basis of medicine has meant that Neurosciences, Pharmacology, Genetics, Statistics, Sociology and Psychology have been added to the 'big three' of Anatomy, Physiology and Biochemistry. These departments run practical classes, and dissection of dead bodies is usually part of the Anatomy course. There is some continuous assessment during these years, but the main examinations take place at the end of each of the two preclinical years. Students must pass the exams in all subjects to move on to the clinical course, and resitting the exams is now only usually allowed once. An increasing number of students opt, at this point, to take a year to study for an intercalated B.Sc., usually in one of the preclinical academic departments. But the compulsory course continues with the three clinical years.

This takes place to a great extent within the teaching hospital, where students are attached, in rotation, to different firms where Experience is taught. Attending the increasing number of specialist departments had become part of the production of the safe general practitioner through a standard hospital education: 'a new specialism became important, and it was essential for it to be studied, and to make a doctor safe it was necessary that he should know something of so important a new branch of the profession' (Newman 1957: 218). In the first year, Medicine and Surgery are taught in their many different segments (now sometimes with a brief attachment in General Practice), and, in the second, the major specialties of Paediatrics, Psychiatry, Obstetrics and Gynaecology, for some of which students leave the teaching hospital for District General Hospitals elsewhere. In the final clinical year, there is further teaching in the teaching hospital and outside, with an elective period, when students can choose what to do (going abroad, for example, to another hospital). During these years, assessment of students is made after each section of the course; the Final exams always include a clinical examination, while written exams may be taken either at the end of the second or the final clinical year. Success in these exams now results in a university degree (the Royal Colleges, old and new, now confine their attention to the supervision of higher training for their specialties). The student is now 'qualified' to practise but is only 'provisionally' registered with the GMC.

Full registration only follows the pre-registration year of 'general clinical training', usually spent as six months as a houseman on a surgical firm and six on a medical firm. In view of the avowedly educational purposes of these posts, they must be approved by the teaching hospital's associated university, in which the powers to accredit such posts, in teaching and non-teaching hospitals, were vested by the GMC; proof of satisfactory completion of the year is required from the university before full registration. While the nature of these house jobs was originally stated in broad outline, no standards for teaching were mentioned at all, and these have only recently been introduced.

Chapter 4

Medical Status: Getting into Medical School

When I was a civilian I hoped high
Dreamt my future cartwheels in the sky,
Almost forgot to arm myself
Against the boredom and the inefficiency
The petty injustice and the everlasting grudges.
The sacrifice is greater than ever I expected.

Timothy Corsellis

Applicants: Facts and Indications

The Great War emptied the London medical schools, letting in women for the first time in significant numbers. But things settled down again between the wars. The personal selection of students by interview was given more importance than proficiency in examinations, and one London medical school proudly emphasised the result: an influx of those distinguished by three indicators of the public school man, 'high intelligence, outstanding character, and considerable skill at games'. Interhospital rugby, that sport of the public schools, reached its zenith of popularity. At that time, medical students in England tended to be self-financed, much more so than students in other university faculties or medical students in Scotland (Stevens 1966: 57). In 1930, the *British Medical Journal* (*BMJ*) put the cost of the five-year course of medical education at £1,500, of which two-thirds to three-quarters were for maintenance, leaving £85 per year for examination fees, books and so on, as well as tuition (Carr-Saunders and Wilson 1964: 383).

Between the end of the Second World War and the establishment of the NHS, a series of articles (no doubt prompted by the experiences of the war and in anticipation of the NHS) was published in the *BMJ* and the *Lancet* about selection of medical students from the recent rapid increase in applicants. At that time, precise information about numbers was not available for various reasons. In most medical schools there was no last date fixed for receiving applications, and places were filled up as suitable candidates presented themselves. When enough had been selected and a number of reserves chosen no further applications were considered (Smyth 1946). Applicants were usually interviewed by the Dean of the medical school or his representative; these interviews were generally perfunctory, but 'served to exclude those whose unsuitability was conspicuous' (Harris 1948: 317). The numbers of places at each school was small compared to today – about 30 per year at Guy's in 1945, for example (compared to the 200 or so at UCLMS during my fieldwork, to be increased to 300 after the merger with the Royal Free). Among the general increase in applicants, the larger number of women competing for the limited places available to them was noted.

In several of these articles, suggestions were made for new methods of selection from the larger numbers of applicants, an increasing proportion of whom were receiving financial support from the State. In particular, there were comments on the likely usefulness of the new methods of selection of officers for the armed forces developed during the war (partly as a result of pressure from regular officers), variations of which were thought to be potentially useful in selecting students to become doctors in a nationalised health service. These War Office Selection Boards (WSOB) met over several days and, as well as interviews and written investigations, included the 'leaderless groups' that were developed by the ex-tank-commander and psychiatrist Bion and are still used by the Church, the military and the Civil Service today. These selection boards were therefore unlike traditional interviews, when interviewers attached great importance to the impression the candidate made, and relied for their judgements on what was called in WSOB circles the 'magic eye technique'. Concern was also expressed about the psychological difficulties of successful applicants, because of the indications that a problem of great magnitude existed, for which the immediate establishment of student counselling services was advocated. This would provide evidence 'that the educational aim of the university is as much to further the interests of the student in his pursuit of learning as it is to provide the community with a good product' (Millar 1948: 330–1). But this did not happen, any more than the method of interviewing was altered.

For, even though any interview involves psychological methods of some sort, it was pointed out that acceptance of these new forms of selection depended on the acceptance of the discipline of Psychology and its methods (Harris 1948: 317). A leading article in the *Lancet*, 'Selected Seed' (1948: 333–4), appeared to end this flurry of interest in the selection of medical students. It referred to the usual 'need for more facts', but concluded that 'one thing is clear: in the future, as in the past, each university must be free to choose its students according to its lights'. Whether it was this cry for continued medical autonomy from an increasingly State-subsidised training and service that was responsible, and how far medicine's traditional dislike of Psychology played a part, it is impossible to say. At any rate, the methods of selection remain as they were not only before the war, but in the last century, based on evidence of adequate academic aptitude, with or without the impression created at a short interview.

More Recent Information about Applicants and Entrants

Since the establishment of UCCA (now UCAS) as a clearing house for applications to higher education, more precise information about applicants to medical school has been available. The number of students entering medical school climbed slowly for 25 years up till 1985, and is now levelling out at about 4,000 a year (a number controlled by the Higher Education Funding Council for England and Wales (HEFCE), on advice from the Medical Workforce Standing Advisory Committee); numbers of other university entrants have continued to rise. Previously, medical students were by no means renowned for their high academic qualifications; but in the early 1970s there was a sudden increase in high A-level grades among applicants. This change, combined with the limited number of places, has made medicine appear to have an academic cachet matched only by veterinary science; and the high rates of applications to some individual medical schools (for example, there were 20 applicants for every one of the 99 entrants to St Mary's in 1992) seem to indicate that medicine is a very highly sought-after course generally.

But it should be appreciated that, while the ratio of applicants to entrants in some medical schools may be very high, the overall ratio of total applicants to total entrants over the whole UK is not.

The high A-level grades now needed for acceptance appear to have been the result of allowing entry to candidates who did not have A-level Biology, previously an obligatory qualification (as A-level Chemistry still is). Selection from the much larger pool of applicants with 'pure' science A-levels was therefore possible, and numbers of applicants soared; the highest-ever ratio of total applicants to entrants was in 1974, of just over 3:1. From 1973 to 1984, there was a steady rise in entrants' A-level grades; since then, not only has the number of applicants decreased (so that, with the slight increase in places available, the ratio of total applicants to total entrants is now 2:1), but the A-level grades achieved by entrants to medical school have also slightly declined, while the grades of university entrants overall have risen (C. McManus and Lockwood 1992: 128–31). Despite these recent changes, academic achievement (as assessed by grades at A-level) is still the main determinant of entry; the medical profession should be seen to be open to all on the basis of merit.

Other demographic information is available about the sort of people who become students. Most entrants are young; while there are variations between medical schools, the overwhelming majority of new students come straight from school, even though they may have taken a year off after A-levels. In 1981, the overall percentage of 'mature' entrants was 8.3 per cent (I. McManus and Richards 1984: 1203), while at UCLMS it was a matter of great distinction to claim double that figure. The most remarkable change in the past thirty years has been the change in the proportion of women entrants. In 1965, just over 20 per cent of medical school entrants were women; in 1992, 50.5 per cent of applicants and 51.8 per cent of entrants were women. There are no signs of 'topping out' (C. McManus and Lockwood 1992: 135–6; P. Richards 1993: 39), although mathematical modelling suggests that this will occur at about 60 per cent in twenty years' time. There has also been an increase in non-white medical students. When the preliminary screening process for applicants to St George's was computerised in 1987, a formal investigation revealed that the programme was discriminating against women and against those with non-European-sounding surnames. Since then, the proportion of students from ethnic minorities has been monitored; despite continued discrimination, which appears to be still based on foreign surnames (I. McManus *et al.* 1995), the number of entrants from Asian backgrounds has increased so that it now overrepresents their overall numbers in the country, while blacks remain under-represented. Asians constitute 4 per cent of the total population, while 23.6 per cent of applicants and 18.2 per cent of entrants are from this group; the equivalent figures for blacks are 1.7 per cent, 3 per cent and 1 per cent (I. McManus *et al.* 1995). In London schools, the proportion of Asian students is particularly high; in 1992, they constituted 31 per cent of the total entrants (Esmail *et al.* 1995).

There is still some marginal advantage for children of doctors being accepted for medical school: the proportion of entrants with medical parents remains significant at 19.9 per cent overall. But this is not a factor for discriminating against Asians (30 per cent of applicants of Bangladeshi origin having a medical parent, for example) and, equally, there is no discrimination against ethnic minorities based on sex, age, social class, type of school or A-level subjects. The social class of entrants also appears to be stable; the structure reported in 1984 from the Registrar General's social classes I to V was 48.1 per cent, 35.2 per cent, 12.9 per cent, 2.0 per cent and 1.7 per cent, similar to proportions in 1968, giving a similar average social class to that (1.78) of entrants in 1991 (I. McManus and Richards 1984: 1203; I. McManus *et al.* 1995: 498). Here the obvious point to make is that everyone who completes the training will, five years later, achieve the Status of doctor and so will be in Social Class I, as all doctors, like members of other professions, are categorised in this way.

But these are rather lifeless figures. Are there other ways to form an impression of the identity of medical school entrants apart from statistics of this sort? There are two simple ways of doing so: by considering the age at which the decision to do medicine was made, and by considering the nature of A-levels required for application.

Age of Decision to do Medicine

Among medical students a substantial proportion decide to do medicine when very young. Allen's study of the careers of three cohorts of doctors qualifying in 1966, 1976 and 1981 mainly concentrates on the sex differences between doctors. But she is struck by the early age at which some doctors decided to pursue this career, noting that, 'it is unusual for people in later life to say that they always wanted to be a lawyer or a surveyor or a shopkeeper, and most people who say they want to be an engine-driver or policeman at the age of five change their minds by the time they are fifteen. But there seems to be something very different about medicine' (Allen 1988: 47). Of her three cohorts taken together, 17 per cent of the women had decided they wanted to be doctors by the age of 10 and 65 per cent by 15; 10 per cent of men had decided by 10 and 50 per cent by 15. This proportion of these early deciders seems to be changing: 13 per cent of men and 16 per cent of women qualifying in 1966 had decided by the age of 10, but, of the 1981 qualifiers, it was 5 per cent of men and 15 per cent of women. Allen found a fairly consistent pattern within this group of early deciders; the men often had a father or other relative who was a doctor, while the women were more likely to have felt an idealistic desire to help people when they were very young. As another recorder of this phenomenon has noted, 'A youthful decision is generally a more enthusiastic one. Other occupations are seldom considered seriously; doubts about whether a medical career is the right choice are relatively infrequent; and, on entrance into medical school, the chosen profession seems like the only one that could be really satisfying' (Rogoff 1957: 129). My style of research clearly could not give rise to any sort of quantitative conclusions. But there was evidence among medical students of how unsurprising and acceptable it was for medical students to explain to each other (or to me) that their decision to do medicine was made when they were very young indeed, indicating connections between the institutions of the family and the profession.

Some Implications of Making Science A-levels Obligatory

The academic requirements for entry deserve attention not just because of the high grades at A-level needed and the specific requirement of Chemistry (and the consequent need to choose science early), but also because of some implications of the choice of A-levels that applicants make. Perhaps the commonest reason for studying medicine given by applicants (and students) is some version of, 'I was good at science and (or but) I wanted to work with people.' In this common statement is found a general acceptance of C. P. Snow's 'two cultures' and the stereotyped differences between the Artist and the Scientist, no doubt fostered by the early specialisation that is required in English schools (see Hudson 1970), but with an individual rejection of its personal application.

These cultural stereotypes (and their conventional gendering, with Science as masculine, and Arts as feminine) have been corroborated by psychological investigation. In *Contrary Imaginations*, Hudson reported that two very different sorts of psychological test, which he had hoped would cut across the Arts/Science divide, in fact provided one of its best correlates. Schoolboy Science specialists were much better than Artists at standard IQ tests (the many variants of which all have one assumption in common, that there is only one right answer); conversely, Artists were much better at 'open-ended' tests, which are based on the opposite assumption (1974: 56–7). In Hudson's terms, Scientists tended to be 'convergers' and Artists 'divergers'. Convergers and divergers also appeared to think differently. Hudson's prediction was that Scientists (and therefore convergers) would analyse things in terms of their general physical properties and not of particular specific functions, and that Artists (and therefore divergers) would do the reverse. In fact, it was convergers (with practical and outdoor interests, and little interest in the divergers' cultural activities, with the single exception of music) who thought of objects in terms of specific uses, without the divergers' capacity for abstraction. Among other connections, Hudson notes that convergers also tend to approve of social conformity, to be more authoritarian and to display more violence and cruelty in their answers (1974: 68–92).

The point of this discussion is twofold. First, even though some medical schools permit two Arts A-levels in addition, the requirement of all medical schools for applicants to have Chemistry A-level, no doubt because it has come to be seen as the basis of medical science, means that all entrants must have at least the capacity to converge; this capacity is developed during their training, particularly in their acquisition of medical language, with its precise scientific nature. Second, while applicants' most popular combination of other A-levels is Biology and Maths, there is an increasing preference for Maths over Biology, even though studying Biology A-level, irrespective of grade, has been found to be a predictor of the ability to pass medical school exams (whereas Chemistry is not). It seems that it is simply exposure to this subject that makes it easier to comprehend the syllabus (I. McManus and

Richards 1986). The explanation provided is that Biology promotes a particular 'cognitive style', softer and less precise than the 'hard' sciences; another explanation is that Biology's more varied subject-matter makes those who have been taught it more able to integrate the varied subjects of both the preclinical and clinical course, a matter that will recur later.

But the increasing popularity among applicants of Maths, rather than Biology, may be because it is more generally useful (helpful in applying for other science courses) and because good students can expect better grades in Maths than in the more descriptive subject of Biology (P. Richards 1993: 21–2). What is implied by this second, interesting, possibility is that the nature of the subject can affect the predictability of any applicant's results, so that a good candidate in Maths can more reliably be expected to get a good A-level grade than a good candidate in Biology. This is because the nature of the subject, and therefore of the exam, affects the chances of reliably scoring high marks. The difference is related to the difference between Arts and Science subjects; in Maths, there is only one right answer. The Competition for entry encourages applicants to converge. But, however convergently and scientifically trained most applicants are, the most frequent reason given for applying to do medicine is that they 'want to work with people'; that is, in stating their personal Idealism, they reject a purely scientific identity for themselves.

The Similarities and Differences between Students

Trying to categorise entrants to medical school would no doubt result in a series of individual categories; no one is the same as anyone else. But although, sociologically, they are a fairly homogeneous group, I found widely diverse personal reasons for doing medicine among medical students. As discussed above, a substantial minority decided when very young that medicine was their only option, and so no option at all. Another group were the children of doctors (and there may be some overlap between them and the early-deciders). Family influence of varying sorts, from parental expectation to sibling rivalry, was not unusual. The group of late-deciders, and even graduates, were not any less committed to their decision to do medicine (and therefore more doubtful, and perhaps more critical, of the training, though their previous experience may have made them less liable to some of the pressures of medical school); their motivation to change to medicine from another field may indeed have been stronger than school-leavers', perhaps having had to overcome the hurdles of entry qualification (by taking another A-level, for example) and then suffer the financial penalties that any mature student is liable to. Among graduates, then, there was also a mixture of motives, sometimes with parental influence involved in a different form (following the death of a parent, for example); sometimes an earlier wish to do medicine had been reawakened; only occasionally were there severely practical reasons (as with a science graduate who knew that medically qualified scientists got larger research grants).

A large proportion of students are therefore deeply committed to their future profession or, rather, to their Ideal of it. Others are not; in Allen's study, doctors recalled parental pressure to do medicine, the frequent absence of careers advice about medicine or the pressure put on them by the school to do medicine against their will, sometimes to improve the schools' academic record (Allen 1988: 61–5). And I found that some students appeared to be at the medical school as the result almost of a whim, such as one who had told the sixth-form college she was applying to that she wanted to go there because she wanted to do medicine later (this had seemed a good way of getting into the college), or the student who wanted above all to be a vet, but whose A-level grades were not quite good enough for that, and who therefore chose medicine as the next best thing.

Before Application: Anticipatory Socialisation

The average schoolboy or schoolgirl, then, who has decided by the age of (say) fifteen that medicine is a possible career, will choose to study subjects at A-level that fulfil the requirements of most medical schools. These days applicants apply to medical school, as to university, before they have sat A-level exams, and are usually given offers of a place provisional on gaining a stated grade at A-level. They also look around for advice and information both about the profession and about particular medical schools, and the medical schools try to provide this.

The Open Day: Official and Unofficial

UCLMS held an Open Day for first-year sixth-formers, about six months before they would normally apply and therefore a year before they would be interviewed and eighteen months before they would be sitting A-levels. The potential applicants gathered in the preclinical lecture theatre; staff members of the Faculty of Life Sciences and Clinical Sciences (that is, from the preclinical and clinical courses) gave talks about these parts of medical training; the pre-registration year, which is officially and legally part of medical training, and for which the university is also responsible, was not mentioned. The audience heard that the preclinical curriculum was under continuous review and revision, and was moving away from the traditional disciplines of Anatomy, Physiology and Biochemistry towards a more integrated course that followed the recent GMC guidelines of a 'core curriculum'; so, for example, preclinical students would learn how the microphysiological function of the lung is related to the anatomical structure of the thorax (an account involving the Anatomical Method that, in outline, would not have been surprising 150 years before). Along with the set elements of the course, the breadth of opportunity to study other subjects (for example, foreign languages, classics, and life-drawing classes) was stressed. The first year of the clinical course was identified as the foundation of future medical practice; it was then that students acquired basic skills in relating to patients, in examining them and in finding out about their social and psychological aspects – 'Remember: you're not treating a disease, you're treating a person!' The audience was told that students might find the clinical years of training disorganised relative to the preclinical course; this was because, 'Life is disorganised, illness and death are disorganised' and students had to accommodate themselves to the realities of life (and, by implication, death).

The selection procedure was then described, with its academic requirements, and advice was given on filling in the UCAS form. The recommendation by the Deans of medical schools that only five medical schools should be chosen, leaving the other three choices for non-medical courses, was stated. There are, however, no penalties for not doing so (and putting down eight medical schools, for example, or using only five choices, all for medical school). As they could no longer rank their selection of medical schools, applicants were advised to send an accompanying letter to the medical school they most wanted to go to, explaining their preference, 'though I wouldn't recommend that you send every school such a letter!' As well as looking at the A-level predictions, selection of those to interview would be made on applicants' all-round achievements and interests; it was important to mention on the UCAS form things like contacts with the sick, the elderly, and children, in the course of voluntary work, to provide evidence of their attempts to familiarise themselves with the world of medicine. Before questions were taken, the audience were asked for their idea of what proportion of applicants got places in medical schools. They were asked to put their hand up if they thought it was 1 in 50 – none put up their hands; 1 in 20 – about a quarter did; 1 in 10 – rather fewer; 1 in 5 – double that number; 1 in 2 – none. There was a hubbub when they were told that it was actually 1 in 2 (as described above).

The sixth-formers mainly asked questions about getting in, about factors that might affect being called for interview or acceptance (taking a year off, being older, other choices of medical school including Oxford or Cambridge, having a doctor in the family, resitting A-levels): none of these was said to make any difference, though there was a move towards not taking those who resat A-levels. Then details about finances, intercalated B.Sc. degrees, accommodation and opportunities for sports were asked for and given, before the lecture hall had to be cleared for another lecture. Potential applicants were taken off for lunch in the Clubhouse Bar by preclinical students. These were mostly members of teams representing the medical school (see Chapter 5) who had been doing exams and had more to do; they and their friends talked together while also talking to the sixth-formers. Several students were hung over, one with a bright red forehead caused by veins broken from vomiting so vigorously the night before. They talked about the quantity of their work: one preclinical student, in the middle of his first-year exams, said, 'If you did what they [the teachers] said, you'd go mad!'; another asked a friend for the Anatomy Spot Test list from the year before to revise from. The unofficial socialisation of medical students begins some time before their actual entry to the school.

After lunch, the potential applicants reassembled in the lecture theatre and a staff member introduced the President and other

Officers of the Medical Students' Union. Only one question was put at this stage: 'Does being a medical student mean you have no social life?' The answer given was that, though medical students worked harder, they also played harder. A film about UCL was shown, drawing attention to its history (being the first university to teach women), its Great Men and its continuing position at the forefront of scientific research; general remarks about university life followed. At this point, the staff member asked whether there were any further questions; though none were asked, it was clear that many sixth-formers wanted to. The member of staff left the lecture theatre, leaving the floor to the students. The official frontstage presentation was then succeeded by an officially sanctioned unofficial one.

The half-dozen students stood at the front, answering questions as a panel and sometimes providing a sort of impromptu show at the same time; the questions and answers went on for about an hour and a half. Potential applicants asked about the preclinical workload, the nature of clinical work, about electives, about doing an intercalated B.Sc. and about accommodation (the only subject the panel disagreed about). But I shall describe in some detail two questions: first, about dissection – this was the first question asked, and there were no other questions about any other specific aspect of preclinical study; and second, about how to get into medical school, variants of which were by some margin the commonest sort of question asked. The medical students were being asked about the truth behind the official rhetoric.

'What's Dissection Like?' and 'How Do You Get In?'

The first question asked was 'Do people faint in the dissection room?'; answers from the panel were: 'No, never ever', 'Well . . .', 'It's not gruesome at all, it's great!', and 'I've never been the same since!' Questions about this subject recurred:

Q: 'When you do dissection, do you work on any live material?'

Bob [*giving the audience perhaps their first taste of medical irony*]: 'Oh yes! Dissections are done on live people! They're all volunteers!'

Rufus [*answering straightforwardly*]: 'Dissection's done on cadavers, people who have obviously died and left their body to medical science. There's a ceremony at the University Church; you can talk to their relatives there: [*Rufus then acted as if talking to a relative, again clearly ironically.*] "You'll never guess what we did with your mother's ovaries!"'

Bob: 'They're all dead people – or nearly dead! [*Now talking mock ghoulishly*]: Some of them have horrible diseases and mutilations! [*Here there was some horseplay among the panel.*] You just laugh it off!'

Kate [*seriously*]: 'You get out of being squeamish. Believe me, when they put someone's intestines in your hand, you have to! The worst thing is the smell, formalin; but there's no blood. The body I used had been dead three years. The worst is the first time, like the first time in surgery. But they look unrealistic; they don't look like people. It doesn't feel as if you're doing anything to people. And if you do have problems, you can arrange to go round by yourself; people are always willing to help.'

Anatomical dissection had clearly been identified in anticipation by potential applicants as the most unknown and alarming aspect of medical training. This aspect of the course is one that potential medical students devote a considerable amount of preparatory work to, as a specific part of anticipatory socialisation (see Chapter 7). Kate's statement reinforced the need for emotional detachment and indicated that, despite any cultural preconceptions, women can, and should, acquire this.

The next question asked was about interviews and what to say in them, and this subject was returned to again and again. In general, the panel said that interviews assessed your personality to see whether you had 'something else' to offer. The interviewers were interested in your extracurricular life; they wanted a well-rounded person, someone who was going to contribute to college life. In answering these questions, the medical students identified themselves with medical school staff, even when they were not privy to the school's policy. Answers were given in the same way as those to questions about dissection, a combination of fact, personal experience and advice, sometimes jocularly phrased:

Q: 'Do they concentrate on your reasons for wanting to be a doctor?'

Kate: 'No, they recognise that, because they went for interviews themselves.'

Bob: 'I was asked that and I said [*in a tone of mock-piety*]: "Oooh, I want to help people!" [*reverting to a normal delivery*]: Before my mouth had said it, my brain said, "*No! No!*" So they asked, "Why don't you be a personnel manager, then?" and I said, "Well, because you don't get the contact", but all the time I was thinking, "*Shit! Shit! Shit!*"'

Martin: 'You say something like, "I want to do something with science and care for people", or [*Here he did not change his tone.*]: "I just want to be a really ruthless bastard and *not* care for people"!' [*Laughter, from both the panel and from the audience*].

Q: 'What kind of things should you put down for the other three options [on the UCAS form]? Should they be medically related?'

Rufus: 'I'd leave it blank – if you want to do medicine, you want to do medicine! There are so many other courses to choose from. It's just another thing [not choosing a non-medical course] to separate you from the others. If you put down something else, they might question your commitment.'

Rufus again: 'And get your UCCA form in early. Write a storming personal statement!'

Martin: 'Even if you haven't done something, put it down anyway. [*He looked around, mock-furtively.*]: This is all off the record! I put down that I'd done work experience in hospital but I didn't!'

Other students on the panel: 'Aaaah! Now we know!' [*And so on*].

Martin [*returning to the same theme*]: 'I'd just be a cocky son of a bitch!'

Rufus: 'The question is how much you want to be a doctor.'

Deborah [*who had not spoken at all till now, lending her agreement to this final determining point*]: 'It depends how much you want to be a doctor.'

What the students were telling all potential applicants was: if you want to get into medical school, you've got to say the right things, both on paper and at interview; you've got to make it crystal clear on your UCAS form that medicine is the only thing you want to do, and perhaps be prepared to write things down that are untrue in order to demonstrate this. The explicit advice is being given that whatever applicants' motives (which usually include some form of personal Idealism in association with medical Status, in that doctors 'do good'), they should be tempered in applicants' accounts by an Economical approach to the truth in order to demonstrate a more professional Idealism *for* Status. Given the involvement of personal identity in the wish to do medicine and to become a doctor, this advice may come as some surprise; taking it may be the first step made in practice towards achieving this end.

Further anticipatory socialisation for medicine takes place away from the medical school: applicants' intentions and their choice of future career will be discussed and commented on by those at school and home; prospectuses are sent for; arrangements to work at a local hospital are made, along with other activities directed to ensuring an interview; and time and care are spent on the UCAS form (on which the Course Code for medicine, A100, confirms its pre-eminent position) in a way which I now describe.

Written Applications to Medical School

Using data of two sorts – three small books about becoming a medical student: *Learning Medicine 1994* by the then Dean of St Mary's, *Getting into Medical School* by the head of a private tutorial college, and *How to Obtain a Place in Medical School* by a general practitioner (P. Richards 1993; Ruston 1993; Westall 1987) and information from applicants' UCAS forms – I shall show, firstly, that the advice the students gave at the Open Day is repeated and acted on; and secondly, that applicants' possession of the lay form of professional dispositions is looked for and provided.

The need for the 'book learning' of Knowledge is obvious in the academic requirements for application and entry discussed above. Evidence for this, whether as prediction or fact (which is in effect that the applicant has the capacity to be taught, to learn and to be examined) is given first place both by the three books and by the medical school; without this, no applicant is likely to be admitted. A-level grades are the first arbiter, with consequent proof of applicants' possession of some scientific language and convergent thought. Because application usually takes place before A-level results are known, school teachers' reports often emphasise the applicants' eagerness to be taught.

In addition to Knowledge, demonstration of applicants' determination to get into medical school, to achieve the Status of a medical student, is considered essential. This is often couched in terms of 'dedication' or 'commitment' to a career in medicine, often shown by the applicant's visits to local doctors and hospitals. The advice on answering the sample question, 'What have you done to show your commitment to medicine and to the community?' is: 'This should tie in with your UCAS form. Your answer should demonstrate that you do have a genuine interest in helping others. Ideally you should have a track record of regular visits to your local hospital or hospice where you will have worked on the less attractive sides of patient care: bedpans etc.' (Ruston 1993: 19). Advice about this in the interview is: 'Do not hint that your parents have influenced you in your choice of career. Above all, show undivided and strong personal commitment to medicine. Your interviewers will find this hard to resist' (Westall 1987: 27). This advice is not wasted by applicants when writing their UCAS forms, in their descriptions of their fascination with medicine, the early age at which they decided to do it, and their belief that medicine provides an interesting and worthwhile career. They mention their attendance at hospitals and hospices, their talks with doctors to find out more and their attendance at courses designed to inform them about medicine as a career.

On the other hand, as the medical students told potential applicants at the Open Day, personal Idealism is not something to show; the books give more or less vigorously expressed advice that applicants' account of their own Idealism should be highly circumspect. To the typical interview question, 'Why do you want to become a doctor?', applicants are warned, 'Answers that will turn your interviewers' stomachs and may lead to instant rejection are: "I want to heal the sick"; "I want to care for my fellow human beings"'. Instead, 'Start by stressing the importance of aspects that can be taught and, in particular, emphasise the technical qualities that a doctor needs: the ability to carry out a thorough examination, to diagnose accurately and quickly what is wrong and the skill to choose and organise the correct treatment' (Ruston 1993: 18, 20). And again: 'Be especially prepared to give your own frank and honest reply to this question, and especially avoid the hackneyed phrase, "I want to help people." Why not express an interest in anaesthetics or some other subject which appeals to you?' (Westall 1987: 26). The Dean of St Mary's explains: 'A desire to help people is often given as a reason [to consider becoming a doctor]. But do not policemen, porters, and plumbers of sympathetic disposition do that? It is surely not necessary to become a doctor to help people. If more pastoral care is in mind why not become a priest, a social worker, or a school teacher? If a curing edge on caring is the attraction remember that doctors do not always cure. Better perhaps to become a pharmacologist developing new drugs than a jobbing doctor' (P. Richards 1993: 10). Those who have experience of how applicants get into medical school are united on this point. Applicants take this advice, though to do away with their own Idealism altogether (and so to deny this most personal aspect of themselves) may not be possible. They often temper it by combining it with Knowledge, in the combination discussed above of 'being good at science and working with people', evident in this example: 'I hope that a career in medicine will provide both the opportunity of working with and for people, as well as continuing to use scientific knowledge and understanding appropriately.'

An ability to get on with others, often in the structured settings of team games or in communal activities like orchestras (that is, evidence of Co-operation) is explicitly sought by the medical school itself. It is also recommended by the books, often connected to the idea of 'contributing to the life of the school': 'Other activities, such as music, drama, and sport, indicate a willingness and an ability to acquire practical skills and to participate, characteristics useful in life in general but also to a medical school' (P. Richards 1993: 40); the complementary point is also made, that 'Conversely, medical schools are much less interested in applicants whose activities are exclusively solitary or which cannot take place in the medical school environment' (Ruston 1993: 12–13). And applicants provide ample evidence of shared activities, mostly in their accounts of membership of sports teams and enjoyment of sport (football, cricket, rugby, hockey, skiing, ten-pin bowling, and so on) and their membership of bands and orchestras.

I shall emphasise later the disjunction of the medical dispositions of Knowledge, Experience and Responsibility from their lay equivalents. But, as already described, evidence of the lay equivalent of Knowledge ('book learning') is a prerequisite. The lay equivalent of Experience is provided in applicants' accounts of their attempts to find out more about the profession (in the context of showing their commitment, as advised); applicants are highly unlikely to have any clinical Experience, and usually they have to be content with a view from the touchline. The lay equivalent of medical Responsibility is also emphasised by the three books, and applicants also provide evidence of it on their forms: they say they were prefects, Head Girls, form captains, and on school committees; they started conservation groups, ran the school tuck-shop or were sacristans in the chapel. The confidential reports from schoolteachers also comment on these qualities, and may also mention applicants' capacity for Economy ('He is much better organised and is making a determined effort to produce efficient notes and learn from them'). Not surprisingly, applicants themselves, in their need to show unrestrained enthusiasm for their chosen course, do not.

Candidates for interview are selected after assessment of UCAS forms, where the lay form of professional dispositions have been displayed. The guidelines for assessment are similarly informed, the UCLMS 'Notes for Selection Panels' summarising the factors to be considered. First is the academic record (Knowledge), then 'a general impression of suitability', which might be affected by 'lack of motivation' (absent Idealism for Status) or 'signs of instability'; 'evidence of ability to co-operate with others' comes next (clearly Co-operation); 'previous relevant experience, e.g. hospital or laboratory work' is the lay equivalent of Experience, while 'evidence of attempts to inform self about medical career' also indicates Idealism for Status; and 'particular activities where there is evidence they have contributed to the maturity' of the candidate indicate a lay Responsibility. The degree to which applicants can demonstrate these individual attitudes in the written application form affects their chances of being given an interview. The hierarchy of dispositions at this stage is: Knowledge, an Idealistic desire for the Status of medical student, evidence of ability to Co-operate, with relevant Experience and Responsibility. Economy is sometimes mentioned by schoolteachers, the necessity for this being strengthened by the prodigality of some applicants' outside non-academic interests; last, if mentioned at all on the forms, comes personal Idealism.

Interviews for Medical School

All the London medical schools interview short-listed candidates; some provincial schools (Leeds, Manchester, Southampton), all the Scottish schools and Belfast do not. It is to be supposed that the reasons the Dean of St Mary's gave for his own preference for interviewing cover those most commonly held by schools that do so: that interviews provide the opportunity to assess applicants' ability to communicate and to reason, to confirm that they have some idea of the course and profession to which they are applying, and they have chosen medicine themselves 'rather than gravitating into a mould determined by parents and environment' (P. Richards 1993: 46). Though this last reason seems to beg the question of how applicants might make their decision at all, it emphasises the importance of candidates' capacity to state their independence from their family, however untrue this is.

Some advice on interviews has already been described above in the quotations from the three books; these brief events can be prepared for, and indeed rehearsed, beforehand. Dress is stressed: 'Check that your appearance befits that of a future doctor . . . Men would be advised to wear a two-piece suit and dark tie. You are seeking a place to train in what is a conservative and traditional profession' (Westall 1987: 25). Using the correct body-language is emphasised, with practice in answering questions and videoing such rehearsals; a 'big smile and lots of eye contact all round' is recommended at the end of the interview, as is stopping and giving the questioner 'an "Over to you – I'm ready for the next question" look' (Ruston 1993: 30, 31). The only one of these three authors working as a hospital doctor does not offer advice on such matters of appearance and implicit body techniques, which I shall show to be extremely important in medicine.

Interviews: Some General Comments

Interviews at UCLMS are held during the autumn and spring terms, with batches of applicants being interviewed at the same time. These groups were shown round the medical school (the lecture theatre, the common-rooms, the outside of the library and the dissecting room) by preclinical students, who also answered applicants' questions. Within the groups of candidates there is tension between Co-operation and Competition, in that they are all in the same boat, but presumably will not all make it. Candidates nervously rehearse anticipated interview questions together ('Why medicine?'; 'Why UCL?'; 'Why should they choose you rather than anyone else?'), and suggest answers. Then they sit down together in the waiting-room until they are called to be interviewed on their own. At UCLMS, there were two interviewers, one usually being a consultant and the other a member of staff in a preclinical academic department. I attended two series of interviews. Although this was not my intention (rather overstepping the bounds of participant observation, I thought) my presence involved acting as an interviewer myself: I was told by one consultant, 'If you want to find out what happens, the only way of finding out is to do it!' There was no place for an observer. Before candidates were seen, the marking system was confirmed (5 was for the best candidates and meant a definite offer; 4 meant an acceptance; 3½ was equivocal; 3 was a refusal). At this stage, one of the interviewers (commenting on professional Co-operation) remarked how close the grouping of marks normally was and, if they did differ, how discussion brought them closer together rather than separating them further. Then two of the three of us took it in turns to ask questions of the candidates, over a period of about fifteen to twenty minutes each.

The Idealistic Pursuit of Status

Questions asked of candidates were of many sorts, and were sometimes scientific ones, which candidates had been told not to expect and interviewers were told not to ask, as this area was covered by the academic reports. Possession of Knowledge was often of advantage in the interview and good grades were helpful: as a consultant said to one candidate, 'We've got 20 people [final-year clinical students] out of 200 who have failed Surgery [Final exams], who we're desperately trying to pass – they're all repeaters [of A-levels].' Many candidates described a fascination with the workings of the human body and many too showed interest in and enthusiasm for applying the scientific approach of genetics to medicine (an emphasis on this branch of physical science in the latter part of this century that perhaps mirrors that on anatomy in the earlier part of the last one).

As the students at the Open Day had advised, putting down another three alternatives on the UCAS form tended to work against those that did this; it provided evidence that they had thought about failure in their application to medical schools or about alternatives to medicine. In the same way, a candidate's inability to answer a question that I asked occasionally, about what a candidate would do if they failed to get a place at a medical school, was certainly not seen as a problem by the other interviewers. The predicament that applicants were in at interview was explained by a consultant: 'If they don't say that [that they're only considering medicine], then interviewers will say they're not committed!' This draws attention to the importance, known to both candidates and interviewers, of holding the line of commitment to medicine and sticking to it during these interviews, interviews being a rehearsable performance where some pre-ordained lines are known to both interviewers and applicants.

Candidates were, unsurprisingly, often asked questions about why they wanted to do medicine; it was perhaps more surprising that not everyone was asked this. I have described above some of the reasons that medical students (by definition, successful applicants) gave for their doing medicine, which were often related to members of their family; these were very rarely given in answer to this question at interview. Though the few mature candidates had individual answers to this question, those who were applying from school answered in broadly two patterns: 'Ever since I can remember, I've always wanted to do medicine', and 'I was good at science but wanted to work with people.' Sometimes the scientists actually disclaimed an early interest, such as one who said, 'I *haven't* wanted to do medicine since I was so high', holding out his hand two feet above the ground; sometimes they presented medicine as a rational conclusion ('Medicine was the logical choice [of career], as I was good at science and wanted to work with the public'). Despite the advice given about demonstrating personal Idealism, several candidates said, 'It may sound clichéd, but I want to help people.' Another common question was to ask what the qualities of a good doctor are. One candidate answered, 'Stamina, good communication skills, being compassionate and being committed'; afterwards, the consultant commented that the candidate had forgotten to put competence first in the list; the other interviewer joined in, saying, 'It's like the old question: "Would you rather have a good doctor or a nice doctor?"', a question that seems to imply that these qualities are (or can be) mutually exclusive, but that also underlines both the historical purpose of medical training to produce a 'safe' rather than a 'good' doctor, and the unemotional nature of scientific medicine. If candidates had written that they had had experience of medicine, they were usually asked about this; this naturally left the consultants, as being medically qualified, with the edge over the other interviewers, whose own experience did not normally allow them to comment on the candidates' reply to this question. The secondary question was to find out what the candidate had learnt from this experience, a question they were not always well prepared for; again, their answers could really only be judged by the consultants.

At the end of the questions by the interviewers, candidates were always asked if they had any questions. This opportunity to ask questions clearly provides another way in which candidates can impress interviewers, favourably or not. Many candidates turned the opportunity down, saying they had already been told the answers to whatever it was they had had it in mind to ask. On one occasion, the clinical attitude to questions asked by those of lower Status (which I describe in Chapter 7) showed through. A candidate had asked about the possibility of doing computer studies in relation to medicine: without answering this question, the consultant then asked him what he knew about computers and asked him to write out some instructions in two computer languages. After the candidate had left, the consultant commented, 'That'll learn him to ask questions!' What the consultant had done was to use one standard element found in the method of teaching Experience; in response to a question from someone of lower to someone of higher Status, he had simply reversed it.

An understanding that interviews were stressful was shared by interviewer and candidate, and sometimes explicitly referred to by interviewers during interviews. Afterwards, interviewers occasionally commented on candidates' capacity to think under pressure, candidates' good performance at the interview itself being taken as demonstrating their capacity to respond well to stress, essential in a doctor. This view was shared by some medical students, in much the same way that the pressures of preclinical and clinical work are seen as deliberate preparation for the stresses of working as a doctor. But medical students also look for a personal meaning and institutional purpose in interviews: I was talking to two students who had been interviewed on the same day but by different pairs of interviewers, one being asked scientific questions, the other much wider questions about the role of a doctor. Nothing I could say would shake their belief that these questions were deliberately asked of them by their interviewers, so as to ensure a good mix of medical students that year. This tendency to personal involvement and to assume conscious planning by the medical school is, as I shall show, found in other ways among students.

Assessment of Candidates' Suitability

After the candidates had left, the interviewers gave their marks; if, unusually, one interviewer had given a very different mark from the other two, this was amended to bring it more in line with the others' (a Co-operative practice which, as I noted above, was stated before the interviews began). During this discussion, general comments were sometimes made, on the candidates' Responsible reliability, for example ('He wouldn't let us down'), their Idealistic enthusiasm, or their Co-operative capacity (indicated by their potential to contribute to the life of the medical school or by their sense of humour). More personal comments were less acceptable; my deliberately provocative remark that I disliked a candidate's aftershave was met with a raised eyebrow from the consultant. Interviewers tended to concentrate less on personal idiosyncrasies than on general qualities, which they categorise, I have suggested, along the lines of the lay existence of professional dispositions; it is the candidate's ability to present a general compatibility with the institution that is being looked for in these interviews. As one of the three books puts it: 'Remember that applying to a medical school is rather like applying to join a club. The interview panel is like the membership committee. The interviewers will try to find out if your views and approach to life are likely to make you an acceptable colleague in a profession which, to a great extent, depends on team work' (Ruston 1993: 26). Candidates have to demonstrate in their words and physical attitudes that they are, in many ways, already suitable members of the club; emphasis is not placed on difference or argumentativeness, on solitary or broadly cultural pursuits, but on the candidates' presentation of themselves, both on paper and at interview, as Idealistic seekers after Status, with evidence of commitment and internal consistency. And it tends to be the medically qualified consultants, not the other academic interviewers, who have the casting vote.

So the sociologically relatively homogeneous, but individually different, group of successful applicants to medical school is formed by their Competitive Co-operation in conforming to a fairly easily identifiable psychological pattern of lay dispositions recognised by the 'magic-eye' technique. Although these dispositions arose historically when doctors were all men and nearly all white, the rising numbers of women and Asians indicate that, at least on application and at interview, others can demonstrate their possession of these lay equivalents. The importance of applicants' denial, on application and at interview, of both family influence and personal Idealism in their choice of career is stressed beforehand in several ways and is usually acted on, however much Economy with the personal truth this involves.

Chapter 5

Co-operation: Segregation, Teams and the Stage

We sat together as we sat at peace
Bound by no ideal of service
But by a common interest in pornography and a desire to outdrink one another.
War was remote . . .

Timothy Corsellis

In this chapter I discuss the inculcation of some precise aspects of the professional disposition of Co-operation and of its inverse, Competition, among preclinical students on the unofficial front- and backstage settings of the medical school. However integral to its functioning, these settings are not marked by the official purpose of the school of training students to be doctors. Elsewhere I describe the Co-operative activities of what I shall call 'official teams' (the official administrative grouping of students for frontstage work, of preclinical students for dissection, for example, or of clinical students on firms) and 'official-purpose teams' (the backstage groups that students form themselves for managing official work). Here I principally describe what I call 'representative teams', groups which are formed by students for purposes unconnected with the school's official function, but which nevertheless use the school's name and represent it in various ways on the unofficial frontstage, on the games field and the real stage.

There are indicators of significant shifts that have taken place over the years in the medical Status of those performing on this unofficial frontstage. The Christmas pantomime, for example, started at the Middlesex a hundred years ago to entertain patients who were obliged to stay on the wards over Christmas. After the Second World War, it became a more ambitious show in one of the school lecture theatres, attended by doctors and students, but presumably not patients. Now, at UCLMS, though some clinical students and a few hospital staff attend the Christmas show, it is produced almost entirely by and for preclinical students. As well as such historical changes, individual medical schools' own culture may differ in minor ways: I understand that the Christmas pantomime at St George's is still produced by housemen, just as it was at Guy's twenty years ago, when it was written, rehearsed and performed by housemen and junior doctors, who 'took off', with varying degrees of affection, the appearance and mannerisms of the consultants they worked for, who nearly all attended. At Oxford, on the other hand, the pantomime is produced by clinical students, there being no corporate preclinical body of students; they are distributed through the university's constituent colleges. Equally, twenty years ago the Guy's 1st XV, representing the school at rugby, had one consultant and one Senior Registrar playing for it, and there is no reason to suppose this was uncommon. But at one inter-hospital rugby match in 1993, when either of the two doctors known to be playing for St Mary's got the ball, the cry of 'Ringer!' went up from the preclinical UCLMS supporters, indicating that these two were playing under false colours. The UCLMS players in such unofficial frontstage Co-operative enterprises (and indeed their audience) are now almost entirely preclinical students; now, in this school, it is only they who are players on all four institutional stages. So while the Co-operative metaphor of 'the team' is to be found throughout the institution, it is only at its lowest level that the reality is now found.

The point should be made, therefore, that however functional these activities were in the past in promoting intra-professional Co-operative solidarity, the increasing rigidity of the institutional structure may well have made them less so. Another change, that the previously almost entirely white male entrants to medical school have been combined with increasing numbers of women and Asian students, may also mean that these activities have become progressively dysfunctional, alienating rather than incorporating these new contingents. But the unofficial frontstage has remained relatively unchanged, whatever may happen backstage. Here lies a final, important point: my own position as a white male should be borne in mind throughout the ethnography, but especially here. The assortative grouping of preclinical students backstage meant that it was among similar (that is, white male) students that I tended to find myself; it would have required a different ethnographer with a different aim to give a fuller account of unofficial backstage activity among Asian and women students.

Aggregation and Segregation

Having experienced a great sense of Competition to get into medical school, first-year students start their professional aggregation. While it is of course possible for students only to turn up each day to the medical school and the hospital for the work required and to leave immediately afterwards, this is neither publicly approved nor, originally, individually chosen; evidence of potential contribution to the Co-operative life of the school has both been looked for by selectors and volunteered by those selected. While new students' aggregation to the profession is associated with segregation from others, it is their aggregation I describe first.

In Freshers' Week, students are registered (issued with library cards and so on) and teaching starts (including dissection, for which each student has to be licensed by the Home Office). These official administrative aspects of aggregation are accompanied by other events, some also official and arranged by the staff, others clearly unofficial. There is, however, some ambiguity between what is properly official and what is not, and this ambiguity is found in the Introductory Lectures I now describe. I should say that I missed these lecture presentations at the beginning of my own year at the medical school, but attended those at the start of the 1994/5 academic year. I was assured, though, that the ritual nature of the event meant that they were essentially the same.

Official Aggregation: The Introductory Lectures

The official frontstage presentations began with a summons to appear in a lecture theatre, where all new students assembled, completely filling it; latecomers had to sit on the steps down to the front. I was not surprised to see some second-year students there, as their presence at the other Freshers' Week events that they had organised was common. Then, to a taped fanfare of trumpets, the senior members of the Medical School Faculties, in full academic dress, started to process in; at this point, a group of students within the central arc down at the front of the theatre stood up, followed rather unwillingly by the rest. It was only then that I realised that the central group at the front were in fact second-year students, who had planted themselves there to lead the induction of new students into their new Status.

Speeches of introduction and welcome were made by two of the senior members, stressing (in terms clearly related to Idealism and Status) the traditions and innovations of the College and the worthiness of the choice of medicine as a career ('the care of the patient, the cure of the patient if possible; if not, then amelioration of that patient's suffering'); they then left. The Dean of the Life Science Faculty continued with a speech, outlining the differences between school and university and drawing attention to the supportive team of the Faculty administration. This speech ended with the statement, 'It is normal at this stage of the proceedings to say the Hippocratic Oath. Please stand!' While everyone got to their feet, a small transparency of the Hippocratic Oath was projected on to the screen, so small that it was nearly illegible from the back of the theatre. This was recited slowly; at first, everyone tried to follow and read it out loud, but gradually the new students gave up, leaving only the planted claque of second-years at the front to continue the recital to the end. However apposite the Hippocratic Oath is for the purposes of swearing allegiance to their new profession, the group of first-years seemed less to swear themselves in than to be sworn in by the group of second-years, more knowledgeable in the ways of this new world.

The staff then introduced the President of the Student's Union, who outlined the events of Freshers' Week, ending with a clear encouragement to aggregative Co-operation and its association with alcohol: 'Don't think that life at medical school is all about drinking! There's more to it than that but I've forgotten what it is!'; 'The most important thing is: Don't sit in your room! Come down to the Union! Come down and meet us! Social life is an important part of any university course but it's especially important in medicine because it's such a long course.' The official Introductory Lecture was followed immediately by the James Pringle Memorial Lecture.

The President of the Students' Union introduced that year's Lecturer as Dr Roberts from UCH (who had just started as a clinical student and a prominent member of several representative teams). 'Dr Roberts' explained that he'd just got 'off the crash' (a form of words not commonly found in clinical language, but meant to indicate that he'd just got off covering emergencies in the hospital), and that his esteemed colleague, Dr Audley, was delayed in his surgery (an account that might indicate that Dr Audley was a GP, rather than any hospital consultant). It might be noted that 'Dr Roberts'' inaccurate use of clinical language indicates a lack of familiarity with professional practice, a matter I discuss below. Actually, he continued, Dr Audley got absolutely pissed last night. So Dr Roberts made the Union President an honorary doctor, asking the audience to stand while he put a long white coat on her. There followed a mock-serious lecture on the dangers of medical students' life, with warnings about the perils of alcohol and of smoking. Two slides were then shown, the first of the procedure for examining the female breast, and the second of diseased breasts. These were met by the audience with expressions of surprise, horror and disbelief, which turned to laughter. The induction had therefore continued with accounts of medical life (including emergency work, alcohol, sex and the shocking nature of some pathology), all serving to emphasise the nature of the new world of medicine.

A diversion was then caused by the arrival and antics of Dr Roberts' 'psychiatric case' (in fact, another clinical student), who thought he was an elephant, before the lecturer moved on to a description of how to examine the heart. The President interjected to the audience, 'You thought there was no integration here! Wrong! Here we start clinical skills on the very first day!', clearly ironically; the new students will wait for two years before learning clinical skills. Dr Roberts then asked for volunteers; none came forward, so he selected a woman, who came down to the front of the theatre and was given a stethoscope to examine the 'psychiatric patient's' heart. Other new students were similarly selected, a woman to feel the lecturer's femoral pulse in his groin and a man to be examined (he reluctantly removed his shirt to the audience's clapping and cries of 'Off! Off! Off!'). The lecturer told the woman, 'Don't be shy! You can't be shy in medicine!', and the man, 'If you jib out now, you'll always jib!' The lecture ended with some absurd advice about contraception and two more volunteers being requested to mime putting on a condom.

The James Pringle Memorial Lecture, as well as being a parody of an official lecture, introduced further features of medical life:

the importance of medical Status; the shocking nature of some medical experiences; the involuntary exposure and public humiliation experienced by students both at the hands of other students and their teachers; irony; the ludicrousness of Psychiatry; and the central importance of sex (indeed, at some points, the lecture seemed to be little more than a public performance of the children's sex- and role-investigating game of Doctors and Nurses – or Patients). But the Lecture, despite being given by students, was officially sanctioned; the Dean of the Faculty of Life Sciences remained at the front of the theatre all through. I was told that, the previous year, the Dean himself had played a trick on the new students, telling them to turn up at an address in Whitehall to sign the Official Secrets Act. At St Mary's, the equivalent spoof Norfolk Lecture, with all the same elements, is actually given by a consultant (Spindler 1992: 28–9). This indicates an extremely important point about these unofficial aspects of medical school: student culture is not the product of a completely autonomous student body, as Becker considered medical student culture to be. If such activities are not positively endorsed by staff (as they were in the example just given), they are at least tolerated, taking place with the knowledge and, usually, the permission of the medical school authorities.

Unofficial Aggregation: Freshers' Week

New medical students find they are now members of an institution that describes itself quite specifically as an alternative family. At the Introductory Lecture, students had been welcomed to the university and the medical school where, 'You've become part of the family, a very large family, which will nurture you and look after you.' They were also told, if they had any problems, 'Talk to your parents! Your mummies and daddies you've already met. Talk to your subject tutors! Talk to your course tutors!' The 'parents' mentioned arise from the system (also found in other institutions) of allocating a 'mummy' or 'daddy' to each new medical student, to provide a personal contact with a named second-year student. This system is organised internally by students, who have access to the new students' UCAS forms, which contain information about their interests and an accompanying photograph – the confidential reports from the applicants' teachers are on the same form. Allocation of a 'parent' may be made on the basis of shared interests, such as playing a particular sport, or sometimes that of visual attractiveness. While some students find their 'mummies' and 'daddies' extremely helpful, others are 'orphaned at birth'; there is no supervision of these parental contributions. Such pseudo-familial relationships are not limited to support and advice; I was initially taken aback when told that one male student was 'going out with his grandmother'.

The events of Freshers' Week continued, all concerned to promote the incorporation of the new students into a culture that appeared to be dominated by Co-operative shared physical activity, alcohol and sex. This combination is not one that holds attractions for all students, and, indeed, there are no doubt many who find the whole thing utterly abhorrent; this is a point I return to later. One of the events based at the Students' Union Clubhouse was the Freshers' Fair, where all the many medical school clubs had stalls to attract new members. These clubs are run by medical students (and could be said to be autonomous), but a member of staff is often the chairman or president (indicating again that these autonomous activities are officially endorsed). There are currently about sixteen officially recognised clubs, usually forming representative teams for competitive sports (from the all-male Rugby Club to the Women's Water-Polo Club), which receive financial support from the UCL Students' Union. The Medical Society and two other officially recognised clubs representing aspects of medical school life (which are known simply as the Social Account and the DJ [disc jockey] Account) are centrally funded, but in most respects are only administrative branches of the umbrella Medical Students' Society. Two important groups are the MDs (the Manic Depressives, the group that puts on shows written by students, to be distinguished from the Drama Club, which is much smaller and puts on plays written by others) and the Rag (the group that organises Rag Week); these are not registered as clubs because, being of charitable purpose, they receive no monetary grant from the UCL Union and keep their own accounts. The status of some other clubs mentioned in the Freshers' Handbook (such as the Caving Club) is less clear; though apparently in existence, in that medical students do these things together, they do not currently receive financial support. It might be noted that, for many of these clubs, medical students have access to a source of finance which is special to them, the three associations providing legal protection for doctors. The Medical Protection Society was particularly in evidence at UCLMS, in fact sponsoring the whole of Freshers' Week (as well as the Careers Fayre and some club dinners).

In the evening following the Freshers' Fair there was a Boat Trip, when four hundred or so medical students were crammed together on a boat down the Thames, with cheap alcohol and loud music. The next evening there was a lightly rehearsed performance by the MDs, with many actors holding their scripts in front of them; this hardly mattered, so loud was the barracking, but the show took the usual form of occasional shows as a series of sketches, predominantly sexual in nature. Two sketches merit brief mention. The first was a monologue about deaths on the road in Europe, at first delivered in a serious tone. The tone changed with the statement, 'There are not nearly enough! When in Europe, drive on the left, and kill as many Frenchies, Krauts, squareheads, wops, dagoes, spics [and so on] as possible! Do things the British way!' The second was a song, sung by a woman, describing a nurse's sexual encounter with a houseman. Immediately after the song ended, the announcer shouted out, 'The motto is: "Leave your girlfriend behind before you come to college!", an emphasis on segregation from others and aggregation to the school that was greeted with loud applause. The next night there was a three-legged pub crawl and 'Free Beer Games'; these Competitive events, such as drinking a yard of ale, took place in a large room where three Borough of Camden and Islington litter bins stood, lined with plastic bags, provided for players to vomit into. On the following two nights, there were discos, with cheap alcohol advertised. Freshers are left in no doubt about the central role of the bar in medical student culture.

Segregation from Others

New medical students were no different from other students as they joined the diaspora over the country at the beginning of the academic year; students leave home in Cornwall to go to university in York, from Cambridge to Oxford and from Newcastle to London. This migration is not found to the same extent in Scotland, where students tend to stay within Scotland; on the Continent, students tend to go to the university nearest their home, where they may often continue to stay with their families. English students' physical separation from home, where earlier friends may live, such friends' own dispersal to university, and medical students' immersion in an immediately engrossing and different world often result in a general loss of contact with earlier friends. A previous friendship must be very firmly based to survive, and most students lose old friends (and girlfriends and boyfriends, as the announcer indicated at the MDs' show), making new ones among their fellow medical students.

Most medical students live for their first year in a Hall of Residence; these are of varying distances from the medical school and vary in their composition; some accommodate students from different disciplines, some just medical students. During their first two years (and possibly the third, during the B.Sc. year), medical students meet and get to know other students. The nature of the preclinical work, the need for Co-operation in completing it (described in Chapter 6), and the other Co-operative activities of the medical school, however, tend to draw them into the company of other medical students rather than of other non-medical students. The latter start to treat even first-year preclinical students as doctors. Here a male student, who has been at medical school for only five months, describes how he is received by the non-medical students in his Hall of Residence:

> I'm treated differently by the non-medics in hall. Some of them take Ecstasy and have asked me to find out about it for them. The girls let me join in their conversations about contraception and their periods, which they wouldn't do to anyone else. [They say,] 'Oh, you're a medic! You should know!'

Medical students generically are also treated differently by other students, by whom they are recognisable, usually because they go around together in largish groups (which may 'take over' a university bar, for example). In such circumstances, their cohesion was noted by one of the bar staff, who said that, when fights break out, Union officials had to break up fights between other students, but medical students would sort it out among themselves. Medical students are also reckoned to have a better social life, perhaps because of the equal and large numbers of men and women in a year (and, still, the proximity of nurses) and because of their own separate societies and clubs. It is also likely that they spend more money than other students, helped by the greater lenience of bank managers to overdrafts, especially as they near qualification, and their parents' personal financial contributions.

After medical students' third year (whether they do a B.Sc. or go straight on to clinical training), other students whom medical students knew earlier have mainly graduated and may be in employment; by the clinical years, most clinical students are living together, often in a shared house or flat. Medical students may try to reject their stereotyped cohesiveness and go out of their way to get to know other students; this leaves them open to great disappointment, as their work necessarily draws them back into the company of other medical students, however much they regret this. This point was made by Jack, a second-year student, in a spontaneous and heartfelt account of his experience, emphasising not only the loss of friends at home because of the segregation at medical school but also his separation from other students:

> I've just done my exams. I feel totally cynical; all my good intentions have gone. I came into medicine with good intentions, to help people, *not* because I was pushed into it by my parents or because it was 'the thing to do'. I would have been devastated if I hadn't got in [to medical school] – well, I *would* have got in, somewhere, somehow! I come from the lower class; I've had to move into the middle class. I've lost contact with my friends at home; [they say] 'You're a doctor! We can't talk to you!' That 'Cardiac Arrest' – I wonder what I'm letting myself in for, with other people working half the time for double the money, with patients just becoming another exam. I don't understand the exams I've just done. I haven't slept more than half an hour for the past five days. My flatmates are [friends] from hall in the first year, not medics. Now I hate them and they hate me. [He explained that they had a different sort of exams, at different times, and that they led a different life.] Now all my life is at Huntley Street [the medical students' Clubhouse], which I never came to in my first year!

From an institutional point of view, while the medical school is part of the wider college (the few medical schools not yet so integrated will become so) the school maintains a distinct identity, with some buildings used only by the medical school; most importantly it has its own bar (as Jack noted) and playing field. Though these are all ultimately owned by UCL, their use is effectively confined to that by medical students, who constitute about 10 per cent of all students. Further, while there are about 90 student Societies in the University, the medical school Clubs are all subsumed for administrative purposes under the single umbrella Medical School Students' Society (often called the Students' Union), with its own officers. Attempts to integrate the medical school with the university are resisted both by medical students and by some of those who teach them; as well as this resistance to the loss of the medical school's identity, the nature and length of the medical course also prevent integration.

Segregation from the Central Concerns of the Profession

Segregated from their friends and family and other students, medical students are also segregated from their profession. As Ernie, a first-year student, told me in the dissecting room:

> Two interesting things I've noticed. People don't talk about medicine at all, what they're going to be doing; having spent all this time and effort getting here, that's it. What's the other thing? Oh yes. Everyone watches 'Casualty' on Saturday night. In the [my] hall [of residence], there's only a few medics and there they all are . . . You see these people [on the television] going about things, and you know something's going to happen to them; you have to work out what. At the [hospital where I worked as a porter before coming to medical school] the housemen were all used to the sort of injuries people got and they'd spot, when someone was carrying a ladder, say, what was going to happen next [what injury was going to be portrayed].

Preclinical students find it hard to remedy their absence of first-hand experience of the practice of medicine and their ignorance of the profession; few of them have any accurate idea of the structure of the profession and many are quite unaware of the existence of the further professional exams (such as MRCP and FRCS) that await any decision to specialise; but discussion of these matters is likely to betray one's ignorance. Students therefore rely on their own personal experience of medicine, which may have been gained (like Ernie's as a hospital porter) in order to get into medical school, and on the frequent portrayals of medical practice on television. Ernie refers to doctors' habit of seeing things clinically, something other students are not likely to have encountered; his previous contact with numbers of junior doctors is most unusual. Many students therefore use the lay dramatic televised image of professional roles to learn from and perhaps identify with; but there are increasing numbers of medical dramas written by doctors themselves, who take care to make the medical practice represented accurate and up to date (in these series, doctors may refer, for example, to recent papers actually published in the *BMJ*). The general interaction between practice and representation is considerable; but for some preclinical students, the representation may be all they have.

The Consequences of Professional Aggregation and Segregation from Others: Internal Stability and Public Licence

New medical students are therefore in an unusual and ambiguous position: their friends and family and school are likely to consider them to be successful competitors for medical Status, now on their segregated way to acquiring some sort of special and indeed 'sacred' knowledge. But they actually find themselves of the very lowest Status within the hospital medical school, completely divorced from the activities of the hospital itself, and the knowledge they learn is far from sacred (the reductionist account of the workings of the body that students learn by relation to themselves and the world is discussed in Chapter 6). So while medical students exercise officially sanctioned autonomy for their own internal affairs on the unofficial stages, within the profession itself they are on the lowest rung of the professional ladder, at the mercy of incessant exams, which (for all the Student/Staff Committees some of them attend) they are powerless to change; and, of course, they are denied any professional Responsibility for patients.

Now, segregated groups of the young to which their society accords high status and grants licence to run their own affairs tend to conservatism and resistance to culture change (see Musgrove 1964: 132–6, 140). (Though he uses material from non-literate societies such as the Maasai – raising the problem of 'spurious exoticism' – Musgrove is quite explicit about the use of his findings in Western contexts.) I suggest that the traditional social forms found unofficially in the preclinical years are the consequence of the segregation of students both from the public and from professional practice; and that all these social forms (from teams representing the medical school to the more general need to 'get on' with one's two hundred fellows) are concerned with the disposition of Co-operation and Competition, while many also clearly demonstrate the inverse of the professional disposition of Responsibility, public licence. I shall describe three prominent social forms (the Rugby Club, the MDs and Rag Week, which all involve representative teams), before making some more general comments about unofficial life and students' reactions to it.

Unofficial Frontstage Teams

These three representative teams, like most others, meet in the centre of preclinical life, the Clubhouse bar; in the same building are the Students' Union offices, a large room used for meetings of all sorts and the squash courts, as well as smaller rooms used for rehearsals and discos. Here teams meet before and after matches, bags being left quite safely on the floor. It is open at lunchtime as well as in the evening, and food and non-alcoholic drinks are also on sale. Cheques are cashed unquestioningly here, unlike a rather more restrictive bank. Although the Clubhouse bar is one of the UCL bars, it is almost entirely patronised by medical students, many of whom resented the £50,000 recently spent on carpets and new furniture; to them it no longer seemed the bar of the medical school, where you needn't dress up to drop in. But, despite these complaints, it remains the central focus of the medical school, not patrolled by UCL Union officers as other UCL bars are; this responsibility is delegated to the officers of the Medical Students' Society, along with the supervision of the UCL Union rules of ejecting people in line with its policy on sexism and racism. Notices proclaiming these were put up, but both policy and rules are ignored. Despite theoretical integration with the university, practice is segregated. And, even though I have derived a more abstract application of Goffman's original concept of the total institution for my analysis, the physical surroundings of the medical school can in fact act as such a total institution in Goffman's own terms, despite being in the middle of London. While medical students are not physically incarcerated as in a mental hospital or prison, they may choose to sequester themselves within a very small area, centred on the Bar, where all their needs (food, drink, companionship – both male and female – and security) can be met.

Drinking, the Bar and Rugby Songs

Alcohol is associated with medical students by the general public; many medical students themselves show more inclination to support than give the lie to this impression. Celebrations after the frequent assessments and exams are often focused round alcohol, and other events, birthdays for example, are marked in the same way. But drinking need not be connected with specific events; while drinking sessions may simply develop, others are planned, sometimes on a heroic scale, such as doing a round of eighteen pubs, ending up at the '19th Hole', the Clubhouse. Vomiting after (and during) a drinking session is not disapproved of. When I asked why, I was told, 'It shows you were trying', trying, presumably to keep up with others' drinking, a good example of Competitive Co-operation. It might, of course, be tempting to look for other implications, perhaps between home and medical school: at home one sits down to eat, and digest, food eaten together; here, one stands up and drinks alcohol together, with the chance of vomiting accepted.

Indeed, although the general notion of having a drink is associated with having a drink with someone else (that is, of pleasant and social Co-operative drinking), this may turn, among men, into a more formal game of Competitive drinking (see Figure 9). Games like these are based on the premiss that there are rules to be obeyed and that failure to follow them is penalised by having to drink a prescribed measure of alcohol (thus making the infringer of the rules more likely to get drunk, be unable to follow the rules again, and so get drunker). Such drinking games usually take place with the players seated round a table, creating a private space in a public area, where conversation between players is impossible except where this concerns the rules of the game. It is clear that this form of social activity actually precludes any real intimacy, as staying with the group involves complete attention to obeying the rules; speech is confined to the formalised language involved in the game and arguments over the rules.

There are several drinking games, the popularity of each one no doubt dictated by fashion, but all with the common features of Competitive Co-operation. Some are relatively specialised, such as the allocation among a group of students watching a televised game of rugby of the names of the players; when the commentator mentions a player's name, the student to whom that name was

Figure 9. Beer games in the Clubhouse: Competitive Co-operation in a simple drinking game. Each student drinks a pint of beer as quickly as possible, signalling an empty glass by placing it upside-down on his head. The customary circle of students has been opened out to allow the photographer in. [UCL]

allocated is obliged to drink a specified amount of beer. An example of a more general game, also played by non-rugby players, is Fuzzy Duck. The players sit round a table, facing inwards and the game is started by one player saying, 'Fuzzy Duck'. The player on his left repeats, 'Fuzzy Duck', and this continues round the table, with each player repeating the phrase after the person on his right has said it. The direction of play can be reversed by anyone saying, alternatively, 'Does he?'; it is now the turn of the player on his right to answer and the response is, 'Ducky Fuzz', which then goes round the table anticlockwise. The forfeit for failure to respond correctly is to drink, for example, 'three fingers' of beer (as measured by holding three fingers against the side of the glass). Clearly the way is open for incorrect phrases like 'Does he fuck?' and 'Fuck he does.' Another drinking game on the same principle is 'Ooaarr', where the prescribed phrases have to be spoken or shouted with a 'yokel's' accent; the reversal phrase is 'Praaper Jaab [Proper Job]', the anticlockwise phrase 'Oinknargh'. There are also phrases to signify skipping one player, both once and regularly, and of cancelling these new rules, but I don't know them, having never, thankfully, played this game with adepts.

Medical students typically sing in the bars at sports grounds and in the medical school, and in the bus on their way back from sports matches. It is overwhelmingly male students that sing songs, which express both their gender and their medical identity. The UCLMS Rugby Union Football Club produced a small booklet of songs for its own purposes. Among these are several well-known rugby songs, such as 'The Engineer's Song', 'Four and Twenty Virgins', 'The Mayor of Bayswater', 'Dinah' and 'Craven A'. There are others, sung to old tunes or more recent pop songs, with adapted words: 'All I Want Is To Be A Boar' ['All I Want Is A Room Somewhere'], 'All The Nice Girls Love A Candle' ['. . . A Sailor'], 'All My Life I've Been Kissing' ['All My Life I've Been Waiting'], 'Syphilis' ['Yesterday']. And some are mixtures of traditional and new words, such as 'The Wild Rover' and 'Ivan Skavinsky Skavar'. These songs then are mostly either originally sexual in content or, not being so, have been made so; in the second category, the principle that I describe as 'scientising' and 'pathologising' the world (see Chapters 6 and 8) is at work. The admittedly small group of singers are appropriating and 'sexualising' these songs in a culturally crude masculine way.

Two other songs are worth mentioning. The first is a variation of a song sung by soldiers in the Great War ('I Don't Want To Join The Army'), itself a parody of a patriotic recruiting song of 1914 ('On Monday, I Walk Out With A Soldier'). The UCLMS version contains both the original parody with a 'medicalised' verse ('I Don't Want To Go To Mary's') and further verses involving the perennial male fascination with detailing 'the parts of the female body progressively attained during an amorous encounter' (see Palmer 1990: 156). This song, then, keeps alive a national tradition of segregated and institutionalised men. The second song ('The Sexual Life of the Camel') may date back some years, possibly to the last century, because of the internal evidence of well-fashioned verses and, in the fourth verse, of 'recent extensive researches, by Darwin and Huxley and Hall'. It is sung to the tune of the Eton Boating Song, and appears to be the only originally medical song left in the canon. The first verse runs:

> The sexual life of the Camel
> Is stranger than anyone thinks.
> At the height of the mating season
> He tries to bugger the Sphinx.
> But the Sphinx's posterior orifice
> Is blocked by the sands of the Nile
> Which accounts for the hump of the Camel
> And the Sphinx's inscrutable smile.

The Archetypal Co-operative Team: The Rugby Club

I mentioned in Chapter 3 how early in their modern institutional history medical schools were associated with the game of Rugby Union Football or rugger (hereafter rugby, as it is now commonly referred to within the school); the game (see Figure 10) is historically associated with the professional disposition of Co-operation, originating among men without the moderating effect of women's sensibility. Rugby these days is frequently and derisively distinguished by its players from Association Football or soccer (hereafter footy). No doubt more men play footy than rugby at the school, and now women also play footy in the women's footy club (it was estimated that the total pool of rugby players was something like thirty); it is also much easier to play a scratch game of footy in the park, for instance, than it is to play such a game of rugby; and the UCLMS footy team won the Hospitals' Cup in 1994, while the rugby team was knocked out in its first match. But the place of the Rugby Club is much more prominent within the medical school for several reasons: its historical importance; its role in representing the medical school (in distinction to UCL); its obvious solidarity (alone of all clubs, the Rugby Club does not admit women, so rugby players are almost exclusively white, male and middle-class, in the sense that they have mostly been to schools where rugby is played); and its members' notorious practices, their drinking and drinking games, their activities in the bar and their singing of rugby songs.

Given the importance I have accorded the disposition of Co-operation, and given the prominence of this game both historically and currently, consideration of rugby should therefore give some indication of the archetypal nature of Co-operation, though in an extreme form. Bourdieu, indeed, has placed the metaphor of 'a feel for the game' firmly in the centre of his notion of the embodied habitus, and it is of some interest that he himself was a noted rugby player in his youth (Bourdieu and Wacquant 1992: 93 n 40). Though the social similarities between all team games far outweigh their differences (the formation of a Co-operative team playing Competitively, but according to agreed rules, against another team), the distinctions, real and conventional, made between rugby and footy are likely to be significant. So, culturally, footy players are afraid of being hurt (why else do they wear shinpads?); they stop playing when they are hurt, and are known to 'act' hurt when tackled; they may deliberately commit fouls, and they often argue with the referee about the rules; finally, they drink lager (or even shandy tops). Rugby players, on the other hand, drink bitter beer; they play a physically much tougher game, in which reciprocal physical protection and support within the team is necessary, and they only stop playing when they are really hurt; importantly, quite unlike footy players, they do not argue with the referee – and indeed any slowness in obeying the referee's decision, let alone a forthright disagreement, is met with instant penalisation, usually a forfeit of ground; further disagreement may lead to a player's being sent off the field, leaving his team one man short. Playing against another team, then, rugby players are more committed to their teams; they are tougher and more manly, not 'jibbing' or 'whinging'; they not only obey the rules but do not argue with the referee's interpretation of them even when they feel (or know) he is wrong.

Figure 10. An interhospital rugby match: one representative team in Co-operative Competition against another. [UCL]

But these qualities relate to Co-operative Competition against others; within the team itself, Competition, again of an extreme form, is to be found:

> Johnno, a rugby player, was talking to a rugby-playing friend, Fergie, and me about the previous night; he was sitting on a table outside the lecture theatre, after the first lecture of the morning, rather shakily smoking a cigarette. 'It was horrendous', he said. 'There was a kangaroo court. My crime was that I was a fresher and that I had a girlfriend that the chairman wanted to shag; that was what the prosecution was. I had no defence, so I had to "Do The Honours"; they all dipped their knobs into a pint under the table. Then I had to stand on a chair with my knob in it, trousers round my ankles, and then drink it.' Fergie and I, together, made exclamations of disgust.
>
> Johnno: 'Yes! Foreskins back too!'
> Fergie: [*in a spirit of impressed enquiry*] 'Was there much chundering [vomiting]?'
> Johnno: 'There'd been complaints, so we had to line the dustbins with plastic bags, and there were buckets under the table. We just sat at the table drinking till we chundered; we couldn't go to the bogs, because if the Chairman got back before we did, you have to drink again. But if everyone felt like it [vomiting], the Chairman said, "Poor Light!" and we all headed for the window.'

Although this initiation is confined to rugby players, not only footy players but women too may become, in effect, honorary members of the club, following an initiation ritual; this involves kneeling and drinking wine from a breast-shaped mug in a specified time; women are then sung a song, along the lines of, 'Kate, Kate, she's our mate! She knows how to fornicate!' Internally, therefore, the team insists on Co-operative solidarity accomplished by acceptance of public humiliation. The archetypal qualities of this archetypally Co-operative team may be summarised by its series of non-verbal cries expressed when in full throat: 'Waay', a cry of fellow-feeling in greeting or approbation; 'Urgh', an ironical cry of disgust, indicating that no real disgust is felt; 'Wurgh', a cry expressing appreciation of a woman's sexual attractiveness; and 'O-O-Oh', a derisive cry in parody of the female cry of appreciative sympathy, 'O-Oh', dismissing such sympathy as girlish.

The Unofficial Learning of Official Dramatic Roles: The MDs

The second prominent social form is that of explicitly theatrical performances, which are likely to be interesting because of the theoretical and historical importance I have attached to official theatrical settings. The MDs put on two sorts of performance, the annual Christmas shows and occasional performances (which may be annual, such as that in Freshers' Week or Rag Week, or one-off events, such as on the retirement of a popular member of the preclinical staff). The MDs now stands for the Manic Depressives, though this may be a gloss on the original, the Middlesex [Hospital] Dramatic Society. A major role as an actor or in support will result in the student's being awarded an 'MD' (letters recalling a medical doctorate) in much the same way as a rugby player may be awarded his colours.

Unlike the membership of sports teams, where proficiency at the sport is an obvious requirement of membership, membership of the MDs is much wider. The Christmas show is a long production lasting for two hours or so, and running for several days before Christmas; students are needed not only as actors, dancers and scriptwriters, but also for the orchestra, as stagehands and for help with the lighting, props, make-up, and publicity. About 70 male and female medical students, and a few others (mostly nurses), are involved over the three months of preparation and rehearsal, of Co-operation on a grand scale; in the two shows I saw, the few non-whites mostly took singing and dancing roles, rather than acting ones. The occasional shows, however, put together in a few days and running along fairly well-known lines, need only scriptwriters and actors, with lights and sound and a few props; only one non-white student took an acting part in the three of these I saw.

The MDs do not receive direct financial subsidy from the UCL Students' Union. An entrance fee is charged for the occasional shows; this goes towards the MDs' budget for the Christmas show, which has the Idealistic and Economic aim of making money for charity. While tickets are free, money is made from selling advertising space in programmes, which are also sold. These shows raise several thousand pounds each year, which is given to the League of Friends at the Middlesex Hospital. Control of such substantial sums of money is left with the MDs, evidence again of officially sanctioned responsibility (though not professional Responsibility) given to students.

The Christmas shows certainly had a plot, though this was sometimes little more than some tenuous continuity provided between songs, dances and more traditional sketches; they were open to the general public (I cannot say what the reaction was of the few students' parents who came). I attended two of these: the first was generally acknowledged not to have been a success – a lack of success easily explained by its untraditional format, which did not rely on medical settings or jokes at all, and which therefore failed to engage the audience; at the second, the audience reacted both visibly and audibly. The occasional shows take place within the Clubhouse, and no concessions are made to public notions of decency; the public is excluded, and the audience is almost entirely limited to preclinical students, though again with a few members of staff present. These shows consist of a series of sketches, sometimes very brief, and usually involving coarse language. Audience reaction at these shows, usually from members of the Rugby Club (membership of this and the MDs seemed to be mutually exclusive) was sometimes so loud that the actors' words were quite inaudible; for example, a female student's appearance on stage might well prompt a chant (to the tune of the hymn, 'Guide Me, O Thou Great Redeemer', sometimes sung with adapted words at rugby matches) of, 'Get Your Tits Out, Get Your Tits Out For The Boys!'

Many of these sketches involve references to the clinical world, which most of the actors, being in the first and second preclinical years, will have not experienced at first hand at all. There are now few references to specific consultants; even if there were, few of the students would understand them and, even if there were more clinical students in the audience, they would not necessarily appreciate them either, so diverse have the firm attachments become (see Chapter 8) – there are more likely to be references to well-known preclinical students. So students play the roles of generic consultants, housemen, students and patients, reproducing in stylised anticipation the setting and the characters that the actors will soon experience in reality.

I select one short sketch to demonstrate the way in which these sketches of medical life may be seen, aside from the brutal and sexual content, either as exaggerated but broadly accurate representations of, or as critical comments on, the current or past reality of medicine. The 'consultant' introduced himself to the audience and the other players: 'My name is Dr Bastard, Dr Utter

Bastard to you!'; he was approached by a junior doctor on his firm, a woman, who explained how tired she was, working on the wards and working for exams as well. He was apparently sympathetic, but when he asked whether she passed the exam and she told him she had failed, the sketch ended with the consultant simply saying, 'Loser!', in a loud and dismissive tone, to, at first, a rather dismayed silence. Students therefore, as actors or audience or both, come to have an idea of possible roles they may play and also roles that they may have to play against. Though the analogy would be probably be found either incomprehensible or unacceptable to these performers, their personal realisation of roles thought about or anticipated has some similarity with psychodrama; the other purpose of psychodrama, re-enacting already performed roles, is impossible for these inexperienced preclinical students. But the audience, too, while not acting themselves, both learn what a good performance is and what the role of the audience is (mostly critical in occasional shows, mostly appreciative in the Christmas ones).

Some sketches are less easily analysed. Perhaps the most alarming one was the repetition of the introductory words of the television series, 'Cardiac Arrest', which portrayed a fictional group of junior doctors and their experiences. As a contrast to the scenes of heartlessness shown later, each episode started with black-and-white film of children in a playground, with a voice-over saying, in a childish voice, 'When I grow up, I want to be a doctor so I can help people.' The medical school sketch in parody of this started with one player repeating those words, wistfully, to be capped by another, saying loudly, 'When I grow up, I want to be a doctor [*now speaking clearly and forcefully*] so I can shag nurses up the arse!' [*loud cheers, catcalls*]. Is this an affirmation of Idealism by stating its opposite, its transmutation to cynicism, or its complete destruction? Without answering these questions, I think it shows clearly the development of what comes to be recognised as a prevalent linguistic feature of medical life, irony, which I discuss below and elsewhere.

Ambiguous Status: Co-operation in Rag Week

The third social form I describe is the Rag Week, which in fact goes on for several weeks in the Spring Term. It appears to originate from the days when teaching hospitals were independent charitable institutions. There are no members of the Rag, but the organising committee is made up of first- and second-years and, by and large, it is only preclinical students who take part in fund-raising activities, just as it is now mostly preclinical students in the 1st XV and the MDs. As in the MDs, both men and women take part in the Rag, but in the Rag, it is unusual for these not to be white. Its expressed purpose, like that of the Christmas show, is the Idealistic and Economic one of raising money for charity. While it allows students to make some contribution in the same direction as the profession from which they are so segregated, it also has the effect of forming of a number of Co-operative teams. The strength of these dispositions is indicated by the fact that the Rag Week at UCL, with nearly ten times the number of students, normally raises about a tenth of the average £20,000 that UCLMS usually does. The much smaller sum of £5,000 raised by UCLMS in 1994/5, though, may be a straw in the wind of diminishing Co-operation. Rag Week has the air of Saturnalia; official work takes second place to its activities, which may be simply divided into those taking place within the school and those outside it; the first demonstrate students' low Status within the school, the second their high Status outside it. Within the school, the two most obvious features are 'hitting' and the 'Slave Auction'.

Before Rag Week, advertisements appeared on noticeboards and walls offering to 'hit' anyone, with a rate of charges depending on what they were to be hit with (a plate of shaving foam, or with added cold baked beans, or with the further addition of custard). Payment was to a prominent member of several representative teams, who guaranteed the payer's anonymity. Hits usually take place during lectures; the normal quiet murmuring of the students listening to a lecture may grow quieter, as those in the back rows see two or three figures appear, dressed in the 'blues' or 'greens' of the operating theatre, with an American Football helmet on their heads to conceal their identity, carefully holding paper plates on their hands; they move down the aisles of the theatre, signalling to students in the back rows to keep quiet as they approach their victims and surprise them, smearing the contents of the plate on to and over his or her head, before turning and leaving the lecture theatre. During the period of these anonymous 'practical jokes', an expectant atmosphere is engendered, with both enjoyment and fear of public discomfiture if not of individual humiliation. To pay for such vicarious hitting is presumably a material expression of some sort of antipathy; this gives rise to all sorts of suspicion, a suspicion that can only be acted on indirectly by paying, again anonymously, for a 'reverse hit' in which the original vicarious hitter is hit himself. Hits may also be organised, the notice states, on lecturers, although this is only with their permission. The element of surprise and the fear of being targeted was completely absent when the Statistics lecturer was hit: the lecture theatre was, quite abnormally, more than half full from the start; but, even more abnormally, students came into the lecture during the second half hour. The hit fell flat, as the surprise of the attack was absent and its victim a volunteer. But again, this aspect of Rag Week is officially sanctioned.

The Slave Auction was held in the medical school Clubhouse, again attended by preclinical students and a few studying for a B.Sc.; the white male official-purpose team I was with said they might as well go along 'to see those public school types make fools of themselves'. The principle of the Slave Auction is that students volunteer to perform services for anyone who wishes to buy them at auction, the money going to the Rag charities. On to the stage and down the catwalk, came a series of students, usually singly, but occasionally in pairs, while two compères introduced them and described the services they offered, with plenty of verbal and non-verbal sexual innuendo. A lot of this was quite inaudible owing to the noise, fuelled by alcohol, that each new 'slave' was greeted with. Fun was to be had not only in the suggestive patter of the auctioneers but in the absurd and sometimes humiliating costumes and poses that the slaves adopted, and in the tiny sums that each slave attracted (a large St Trinian's girl who would give a spanking attracted £8, for example).

So far, only those who had volunteered for exposure, either as buyers or sellers of services, were exposed. But Tarzan, clad in a loincloth and a girdle of bananas, found no takers until the auctioneer decided that two female students had bought him; with the pressure of the spotlight on them, they were forced up on to the stage, where they were obliged to kneel and eat a banana hanging from Tarzan's waist in simulation of fellatio. It was these 'buyers' who were humiliated.

The finale were two 'Chippendales', men who removed their clothes item by item for sums of money. The Rugby Club put up

£25 for one of them, a rugby player himself, to strip naked; both strippers removed their clothes till they were wearing what I was told are called 'posing pouches'. At this point, there was a call for the captain of the Rugby Club to do a 'Flaming Arsehole'. He was voluntarily joined by another rugby player and they both stripped down to their underwear. The second, while waiting for the rolled-up newspaper to be lit, voluntarily exhibited his genitals; this was no fun, being volunteered. But at this moment, some other rugby players ran up on to the stage and, manhandling the rugby-playing Chippendale, forcibly removed their teammate's pouch and briefly held him up to view, before letting him run off the stage to loud applause. Meanwhile, the newspapers had finally been lit; these were placed between the buttocks and above the boxer shorts of the two rugby players, who then strutted up and down the catwalk in the style of walking peculiar to the Flaming Arsehole, necessary to prevent the burning roll of newspaper from falling out. The strictly segregated session of the Slave Auction involved the humiliation, voluntary and involuntary, both of sellers and buyers of the services offered. In these two internal Rag Week events, the bearers of the dominant unofficial culture humiliate themselves and others, with the tolerance of the school authorities.

Outside the school, it is the Bed-Race and the Scavenger Hunt that are most prominent. The first is not in fact an internally Competitive race between bed-pushing teams, but another way of raising money for charity (though on this occasion it was also used to stimulate students to collect as much individually, in their personal collecting tin, as possible). Three hospital beds were somehow procured and three teams assembled loosely round them. Students were dressed in white coats and operating theatre clothes, some with disposable surgical caps too, and a few men in nurses' uniforms; I was surprised to see the Dean of the Faculty of Life Sciences in one team, wearing a white coat and operating theatre kit. Each bed was pushed round a different circuit of central London by a changing smaller group from each team, while the other members of it spread out, running ahead and behind, calling out the names of the charities and shaking tins at pedestrians and shopkeepers to collect money. The bed was kept moving and the out-runners trotted, with an exhilarating sense of freedom and indeed possession of London, down Gower Street, up Oxford Street (some members taking free rides on buses), and down Regent Street to Trafalgar Square. Here we stopped, with the other two beds; ours was showing signs of strain. Then, with the other two, we carried on along the Strand, settling for quarter of an hour outside the Courts of Justice, where one bed was pushed backwards and forwards over the pedestrian crossing, holding up the traffic so that not just pedestrians but car-drivers too (and particularly cab-drivers, usually generous) could be approached for money; then we went on, further along the Strand, where our bed finally fell apart and, after some discussion ('We can't leave it here, it's NHS property'; 'We can't carry it'; 'We ought to dump it in the river'), was left, fairly tidily, on the pavement near King's College. From here on, the team spread out, now approaching every pedestrian; some members went down on their knees, imploring passers-by to give them money, to buy a Rag Mag. As we strolled through the LSE, one member shouted out the Middlesex rugby supporters' cry, 'Middle', to which the rest of the group bawled, 'Sex'; again, 'Middle!' and 'Sex!'; then, 'Middle! Middle! Middle!' and the group responded, 'Sex! Sex! Sex!' Increasingly separated now, the group returned through Covent Garden in twos and threes to the Clubhouse bar, where individual takings were registered, to be counted later (the sum going towards determining whether the collector would be rewarded for their personal fund-raising by being able to go on a 'free hitch' to Dublin or not).

While, on other occasions, individual collectors were at risk of being caught ('The enemy's the police and the Underground guards'; in the City, one student was asked, 'Don't you know it's an offence to solicit for money in a public place?'), during the Bed Race the group was not so apprehended or criticised; no police stopped us, no bus conductor tried to make a free-rider pay; pedestrians smiled, looked surprised or embarrassed, but were not critical. It was all in a good cause; it was all for charity; it was just medical students. Licence for the purposes of raising money for charity is further exemplified by the contents of the Rag Mag, a collection of stories and jokes of mainly sexual nature; the combination of charity (or Idealism, helping people) and licence (the inverse of Responsibility) makes understandable the at first surprising juxtaposition of advertisements for the Down's Syndrome Association and Spectrum (a charity for medical students to help children with special needs and 'broaden their awareness of disability'), with jokes like:

Q. What do you call a stack of wheelchairs?
A. A vegetable rack.

and a series of 'baby jokes' like:

Q. What's pink, red, silver and walks into walls?
A. A baby with forks in its eyes.

At the end of the Rag Mag was a notice in small print: 'Disclaimer – None of the above filth was intended to be offensive (or funny) it's just something to raise a bit of dosh for charity.' Idealistic Economy excuses the inverse of professional Responsibility.

The Scavenger Hunt took place one night towards the end of Rag Week, perhaps in case 'things went too far' and the whole business was shut down by the authorities, who do not officially endorse it (though they cannot help but know about it). It involves 'scavenging' (that is, stealing) named items – most kudos is given to those who remove objects from other teaching hospitals. For the first time, a list of scavengeable items was produced, in categories arranged by the points that would be awarded for their theft. Traffic cones and beer barrels, for example, scored one point; a fireman and a 'used placenta' scored five; the Minister of Health and the Dean of another London medical school scored 10,000 points; 1,000,000 points would be scored by the theft of Mary's Puffin (a totem belonging to St Mary's Hospital Medical School, said once to have been UCH's) and the London Hospital Medical School 1st XV's rugby kit.

Preclinical students, many who had not been visible in other Rag events, formed small Co-operative but Competitive teams, paid their token entry fee (thus keeping the Scavenger Hunt a Rag Week activity) and set off from outside the Bar. They had been told not to bring back scavenged material to the Rag Office (the previous year the Rag Office was full and the police visited), but bring it back they did, waiting only for points to be awarded before leaving it behind and heading out again into the night. Traffic cones and flashing lights were brought in, firemen arrived in fire-engines, ambulances and post-office vans appeared; someone brought in a wheelchair from UCH and was told, 'Minus points! You don't rob your own hospital!' Two policemen drew up in their car and were ushered into the bar, while their registration plate was removed and brought in for points to be awarded; the team did not manage to screw it back in place before the policemen emerged – this was the best so far. But the teams were urged to go and get something better. They returned with a photo of the 1919 Hospital staff and sheaves of pathology results, dated 1982, from King's College Hospital; with a framed map of the London Hospital and a rugby shirt from Guy's; with Dr Fox, a disc-jockey from Capital Radio; with plaques of the AFC and the Students' Union, and more photos and notices, from St Mary's (the Puffin was at their sports ground in Chobham); and with plans for the Channel Tunnel terminus. But the unofficial winner was a large metal plaque commemorating the opening of the West Wing of St Thomas's Hospital by HM the Queen. All teams had Co-operated to appropriate the outside world, especially the property of other teaching hospitals. It is no doubt the case that, in some circumstances, if caught, these students would have been charged with theft (with no licensed immunity). But there was also a chance that they would have been able to explain and extricate themselves by saying it was a part of Rag Week, just as medical students may find themselves 'let off' the consequences of drunken exploits that attract police attention, on the simple grounds that they are medical students.

To put the internal and the external aspects of Rag Week together: internally, students humiliate themselves and are humiliated, levelling and stripping themselves and each other, literally as well as metaphorically; externally, on the other hand, they assume and are granted public licence because of their charitable purposes. Preclinical students Co-operate for Idealistic and Economic reasons, relying on the inverse of professional Responsibility.

Ambiguous Status and Language: Punning

The points I made at the beginning of this chapter, that now (at any rate at UCLMS) it is only at the preclinical level that all four areas of the institution are present, and that these students are in an ambiguous position (in the gradual process of professional aggregation, but with one foot still in the lay world) are demonstrated by their use of punning. I describe more fully in other chapters students' acquisition of medical language in official frontstage settings, where the stress is on precision and lack of ambiguity; at the interface between the institution and the lay world (found by preclinical students on the unofficial frontstage of the Christmas show and Rag Week), punning is common, using words both to indicate students' separation from the lay world and to medicalise the world (see Figure 11).

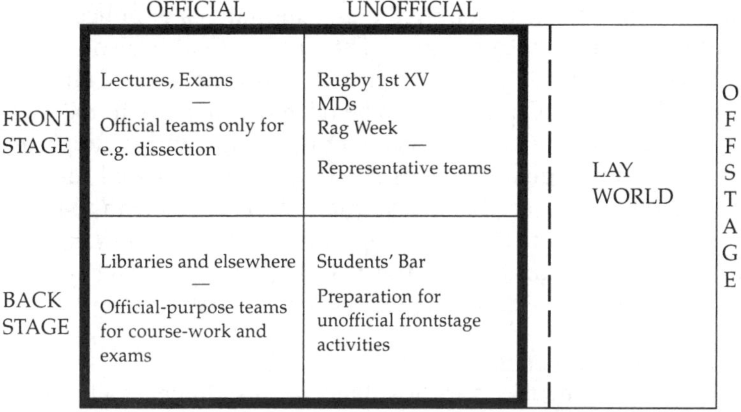

Figure 11. Preclinical students' institution. Preclinical students' ambiguous Status between the institution and the lay world is indicated by the dotted line, and is acknowledged in their punning and medicalising of the lay world in several ways.

Though the shows' dialogues often contain puns involving words' lay and medical meanings, designed to elicit a groan from the audience, the titles of Christmas shows demonstrate this punning very clearly by the transformations of recent lay films or books: for example, 'Lady Chatterley's Liver' ['Lady Chatterley's Lover'] (1960), 'One Threw Up in the Doctors' Mess' ['One Flew Over The Cuckoo's Nest'] (1972), 'Desperately Leaking Lumen' ['Desperately Seeking Susan'] (1985), 'Hannah and Her Cystoscope' ['Hannah and her Sisters'] (1986), 'The Sly Glance at the Glans' ['The Silence of the Lambs'] (1991), 'Ailing Lung 3' ['Alien III'] (1992), 'Thoracic Spark' ['Jurassic Park'] (1993) and 'Polyp Friction' ['Pulp Fiction'] (1994).

In the Rag Mag, the format of Multiple Choice Questionnaires was used, reflecting the way preclinical students' Knowledge is often tested (see Chapter 6), as well as their use by the Church of Scientology nearby in Tottenham Court Road. So, under 'The Church of Histology's Free Personality Test', is the question:

> What is a cell?
> a) The unit of the body.
> b) A place where Charlie spends the night now and again.
> c) Something you need to power your personal stereo/vibrator, etc.

The first answer is obviously the medically correct one, though it is worth noting that by now the lay alternatives (a police cell, a battery) are also both concrete. The same format is also used in the Rag Mag to display students' cultural dislike of Statistics, which I show (in Chapter 6) can be related to this discipline's use of lay words with complex abstract meanings. In the Rag Mag, the concrete language used is not in any sense official medical language, but refers in lay language to excretory and sexual functions; the statistical meanings themselves are mocked. The following questions appear under 'BMS [Basic Medical Sciences] Part I Statistics and Biometry Course Questions':

> 1) Is the distribution normal?
> Yes, unless the subjects are pissed then the distribution is all over the place.
>
> 2) What is the Standard Error?
> Coming too soon.

Medical identity is not necessary to understand these forms of words as puns, though perhaps it is to appreciate the humour arising from the absurd transformations involved, all of which also emphasise the supremacy of the materially referential meaning of words. I was reminded of this supremacy by a rugby player when I explained I was leaving the bar to go and see a play; he simply said, derisively, 'Ha! Culture! Yoghourt!'

Unofficial Backstage Life

In the last section I described the activities of the most prominent representative teams on the unofficial frontstage. I have also indicated that these social forms, arising when medical students were mostly white and male, are nowadays likely to alienate a large proportion of students rather than promote Co-operation. This point was strikingly made at a rugby match when, in the pouring rain, two Asian women students stood huddled together on the touchline, utterly out of place and utterly miserable; they had been persuaded to come to the match, but all they wanted to do was get away as soon as they could. But what I have described is also what is there most prominently to be seen – the televised account of students at St Mary's (see Spindler 1992) deals with almost exactly the same features that I have mentioned.

I must again make it plain that my own colour and sex, and the method and purposes of my investigation, meant that I was both drawn into and tended to concentrate on this sort of activity. No doubt there are also larger unofficial social groups, perhaps of the sort described by Becker in Kansas (1961: 137–52), where the system of fraternity houses had institutionalised these groups; his methods of interview and statistical analysis made conclusions about their constituent members possible. There might well, for example, be a large unofficial group of the sizeable number of Asian students (who are seldom members of representative teams), within which smaller teams form. But only another sort of study by another investigator could answer this question, and give detailed answers to the question of how other medical students reacted to the dominant culture. In particular, the precise reactions of the sizeable proportion of Asian students and those women who did not join in would be important to establish. But I think I can give answers to two questions that might be asked: why the unofficial dominant culture is so dominant, and what others' reaction within the institution appears to be.

The Dominance of the Unofficial Culture: Teams and Official Endorsement

Preclinical students' segregation from others by the length and nature of their course and their social identity is matched by their official aggregation, for example in lecture theatres, where they spend so much of their time. They look to each other for help, forming the official-purpose teams described in Chapter 6, so as not to spend their whole time dealing with the still excessive and conflicting demands made by official work. There is often considerable overlap between these official-purpose teams and unofficial teams like representative teams. Unlike other students, who may choose to spend their free time (the equivalent of medical students' unofficial backstage time) with friends from different disciplines, medical students by and large spend both official and unofficial time with each other. So things get done in medical school by teams, and high status and licensed autonomy promote a tendency to tradition. The main organisers of the unofficial culture, the small team of the officers of the Students' Union, are usually elected on the basis of having already become visible by being prominent members of important representative teams (particularly the MDs), in this way ensuring a degree of continuity of the unofficial culture. But all representative teams, though autonomous, have access to and contact with the medical school staff, who appear to condone, if not endorse, the traditional activities of these teams, even of the Rugby Club. Information gained by students through this route is passed on, accounting for the occasionally accurate output of the 'rumour mill'.

Preclinical students are also told that the profession to which they all aspire works in teams; they may also know that the application form for housemen's posts includes a heading for recording 'University or Medical School Activities'. The teams that I have described in this chapter all Co-operate internally, with Competition being directed externally (though it is difficult to see how some, like the Caving Club, could be significantly Competitive). A purely functional reason for the continued existence and official endorsement of these unofficial teams is that they harness the considerable powers of co-ordination that students possess, directing them both away from the school itself, to outsiders (often other medical schools), and away from the official purpose of the school (the training it provides), to raising money or scoring tries. Competition within the school, however, is not approved of, something I was told very forcibly when I had been to see a production by the Drama Club. I was struck by the contrast between this play (dealing sensitively with adoption, race and parenthood) and the entirely crude approach of the MDs. When I mentioned this contrast, I was quickly told that I had got the wrong idea completely; there was no contrast or competition, intentional or otherwise – the two clubs simply represented different aspects of the medical school. So Co-operation in teams of different sorts is both necessary and encouraged, and there appears to be no obvious mechanism for students to change the unofficial dominant culture.

The Dominance of the Unofficial Culture: The Public Nature of Life

Medical students' cohesiveness in unofficial settings means that what is done and said in official settings is therefore available for unofficial comment and vice versa. Public displays of affection between men and men, women and men, and women and women are common, as is talk about sexual and drinking exploits (when the events of a drunken evening are pieced together and woven into a communally acceptable form over several days). So even within such a large group, it is possible for any student to recognise a good proportion of the two hundred others in his year. Within the segregated institution, then, life is public and individuals are therefore vulnerable. Revelation of personal information about oneself is, on the one hand, both asked for and volunteered (on the principle, I was told, that 'You shouldn't have secrets from your friends') but, on the other, leads to public vulnerability. Information about one's family may be revealed to a few friends (usually only to be dismissed in the general process of social levelling), but may then be circulated quickly within the overlapping groups of all sorts – questions about who was going out with whom could often be answered instantly – and is remembered. One woman's drunken and shouted wish in her first year to be 'shagged by an elephant' was related several times to others in her embarrassed presence at least two years later.

Not surprisingly, then, such personal information is also withheld; I was sitting next to a male student in a lecture with other members of an official-purpose team, when a spider appeared on the desk. He recoiled and quietly asked me to remove it, saying, 'For God's sake don't tell the others or they'll always be putting spiders in my beer and things!' The identity of students as the children of doctors was also sometimes withheld by them; I was present on several occasions when such a revelation or discovery was made among students who had known each other for one or two years. This again emphasises students' levelling tendency; those who are publicly known as doctors' children often keep to their own group. Again, the revelation of his homosexuality by a male student to a female student who had asked him out was privately admired by Fitz, another student, precisely because he knew that this news would get around quickly and irreversibly;

despite his private admiration, Fitz admitted that he talked publicly about 'poofs' in a derogatory manner. The consequence of such public broadcasting of personal knowledge means that, while medical students generally sort things out themselves, the price of such Co-operation for personal difficulties is that personal information often becomes public – a price that may be too high for many.

It is not just 'poofs' that are the subject of derogatory public statements: female students are also the common target of sexist remarks by male students ('That's a nice pair of tits') – but it is only within the medical school that such remarks are, clearly unwillingly, tolerated. Racial stereotypes, too, are not uncommonly voiced aloud or indicated non-verbally, as when an officer of the Students' Union rubbed his nose with his forefinger to a Jew, or a rugby player spread his lips to indicate a black man. An Asian woman student recounted that after a bout of kissing with a rugby player, he told her, 'You'd be great if you weren't black!' Here she acted a double-take to indicate her then amazement, and then added, semi-humorously, 'I'm not black anyway!' Such stereotypes are sometimes voiced by their victims, as when a black student said to his white girlfriend, 'I shouldn't be going out with you! I should be hitting old ladies over the head!' It is not just people that are seen in purely physical terms; I was dismayed when the admittedly not very appealing sauce over some fish I was eating in the Nurses' Home with some male students was described by one as semen (using the unofficial equivalent of what I describe happening officially in Chapter 6 of 'scientising the world').

Students' segregation from the medical profession means that to question in public the unofficial culture in which they find themselves may either lead to public derision or to discussion of medicine in general. Open profession of personal Idealism is not endorsed, and discussion of medicine would reveal either ignorance (an exposure avoided like any other, in view of the public nature of the culture) or knowledge (implying some special access to information, again to be avoided because this would contravene the assumption of equality between students). In Chapter 6 I describe the prevailing hostility to both self-analysis (as found in Psychology) and social analysis (as found in Sociology), where I also indicate the lack of a conceptual vocabulary to talk with, at least officially. While these attitudes (again apparently officially endorsed) partly cause students' lack of interest in analysing their position, it is also no doubt partly attributable to the self-evident and unquestionable nature of the purpose of medical students' training, that is to become a doctor and to do good (however much any such Idealistic motive was expediently qualified at interview and may be satirised publicly). For many students, medical school is what it is and is what it was.

And the physically coarse aspects of the male dominant culture are by no means incongruent either generally with the common interest in sex of people of preclinical students' age, or more specifically with the nature of the reductionist Knowledge that medical students are obliged to learn both preclinically and clinically. There is therefore, both officially and unofficially, both front- and backstage, what might be called a 'corporate corporality'. Nor is the way in which some students humiliate both themselves and other students in theatrical settings a far cry from the position they find themselves in officially, both preclinically and clinically, when their ignorance of their new world is sometimes brutally exposed to an audience of their fellows. The humiliation by levelling and stripping, literal and metaphorical, is found both officially and unofficially.

Individuals' Public Reaction to the Dominant Unofficial Culture

Despite the continued and seemingly unassailable dominance of the unofficial culture I have described, I have made it plain that are many students who take no part in it, finding the whole business foreign, uncongenial and distasteful; but, even for them, it is difficult to resist and impossible to ignore. Though women and non-whites (and the substantial subset of Asian women) are in a difficult position, some white males' own position may be even more problematic, given that they may be expected to conform to the obvious social stereotype. But it seems entirely possible that women's position has been adversely affected by their increasing numbers. Whereas, earlier, the predominantly male medical students tended to go out with student nurses and physiotherapists, who have their own separate professional groups, medical students now go out with each other; indeed, Lydia, a female physiotherapy student, told me that she and her colleagues had been warned off going out with male medical students by a group of female medical students. The traditional association between doctors and nurses has been altered, with future social implications which are difficult to envisage. But the immediate effect is that women medical students find themselves in a predominantly masculine culture which may be deeply offensive. Their (and other students') public reactions to this seem to me to be of several sorts: membership, ambivalence, tolerance, further segregation and rejection. To fight it is impossible; on one occasion, a female student who had remonstrated with a rowdy group of rugby players about their personal and sexist comments left the bar in furious tears. She returned to the fray, where, because she continued her opposition, a cement-filled rugby ball was chained to her leg by the rugby players, who then left.

Membership may be attained by participation, by becoming full members of some representative teams (or honorary members of the Rugby Club, for example), or by joining in the jokes and making them back, which often involves frequent open banter about sex by women themselves. Ambivalence is not uncommon, being partly a member and partly not; Lydia, the physiotherapist, who was a member of the women's footy club, explained to me in the bar that the men's team were actually rather intimidated by them. So, in the bar after matches, 'We let them get on with their male bonding for an hour and a half and then join them.' But it is most important to realise that however a group of male students behave together, individually they may be rather different. Knowledgeable female students put the critical number for a group of male students to behave outrageously to be not four but eight; when I remarked that this was the number of players in a rugby scrum, they smiled. This difference between public and private attitudes, and group and individual ones, indicates that, while men can 'have it both ways', ambivalence also becomes more possible for women, in that they may place more importance on the private individual statements of men. As an illustration of this, Rita, an Asian woman student, told me what I already knew, that there were some students (mostly rugby players) who had no doubt that 'blacks are coming over here, taking our jobs', and that they should be repatriated. During a conversation of this sort when she had taken an opposing view, Rita reported that the rugby players made her an exception, saying, 'You're different! We don't mean you!' After the conversation was over and the group had broken up, they all, individually, came back and told her that they didn't really mean what they'd said. With some reservations, she accepted their private individual recantation.

It is, of course, quite possible to acquire the profession's exclusive cognitive identity and become a doctor without joining any clubs or becoming members of any representative teams; the official training is quite strong enough on its own, with its practically efficient Co-operative teams informing the institution, both in fact and as metaphor, and providing the medium for the development and transformation of other dispositions. Tolerance therefore, perhaps surprisingly, is not an uncommon public response, ignoring the dominant culture in so far as this is possible, making the odd jibe when pushed, and only taking part in activities that are free from it; these, given the pervasive masculine culture, may well take place on the lay offstage. But intense dislike of the extreme form of Co-operation found in the Rugby Club does not necessarily imply the rejection of a more general Co-operation; though personal animosity is by no means uncommon pre-clinically, avoiding confrontation is fairly easy. 'Getting on' with at least some other students is important for official work; you're going to be with the rest of the year-set for some three or four years hence and, however improbable this may seem at times, you're all going to be doctors. Such tolerance shades into further segregation, which appeared to be the response of some Asian students, who are hardly to be seen in the Clubhouse; 'It's not for us', one said. But the merger of the two medical schools means that there is another UCL bar at the old Middlesex Hospital Medical School, where few unofficial activities take place. While this bar is used mainly by clinical students during the day, it is also frequented by Asian students, who are often to be seen at its pool tables, with soft drinks. Complete public rejection is extremely difficult while staying in medical school. One clinical student, whose dislike of the system of medical training she was undergoing was profound, told me that going near the Clubhouse made her feel physically sick; she looked for support from Women In Medicine (a cell-based support group for women doctors), thus further segregating herself from the medical school; but even this was not enough. The only way for her to express her views adequately was actually to leave medical school altogether, even though her academic and clinical achievements were well above average. Dissident students are free to leave the institution, unlike prisoners and asylum inmates.

Chapter 6

Knowledge: Writing, Sight and the Self

> And this you can see is the bolt. The purpose of this
> Is to open the breach, as you can see. We can slide it
> Rapidly backwards and forwards: we call this
> Easing the spring. And rapidly backwards and forwards
> The early bees are assaulting and fumbling the flowers:
> They call it easing the Spring.
>
> Henry Reed

In the last chapter, I described something of the unofficial life of preclinical students. Here I discuss their official work, front- and backstage, work that is predominantly concerned with the 'book learning' of the disposition of Knowledge in their study of the Basic Medical Sciences; these students do not see patients. In view of the changes to this part of the curriculum already made by some medical schools and the changes envisaged by others, I should again draw attention to both the timing and the location of my fieldwork to emphasise that I am describing a traditional form of training; it has been in reaction to such a form that some of the changes in medical education have been made. I should also state that I am only describing the compulsory part of the official preclinical course in basic medical training, and that I am therefore not dealing with students studying for an intercalated B.Sc. (even though this is likely to be in one of the preclinical disciplines).

Lectures: The Audience in the Theatre

For preclinical students, the lecture theatre is still the main setting for the teaching of the huge quantity of material that they will be tested on in exams. Of the organised timetable as set by the different preclinical academic departments, lectures are by some margin the single most common form of teaching, and first- and second-year students each have their own lecture theatre, where nearly all the lectures are given over that year. In 1994, for first-year students, the total organised teaching time was 434 hours, of which lectures took 219 hours (51 per cent) and tutorials 32 (7 per cent); for second-year students, total teaching time was 428 hours, of which lectures took 273 hours (64 per cent) and tutorials 37 (9 per cent). Reduction in the number of hours in the organised timetable, with a view to loosening the curriculum, has been accomplished by reducing both the number of lectures and of practical classes; some disciplines have introduced to their allotted time periods of 'self-directed learning'. Computers are used both as an aid to learning Knowledge and to simulate practical experiments no longer done in reality. The classroom settings of tutorials and, to a lesser extent, practical classes are also places where Knowledge is taught, though these occur much less commonly in terms of frequency and duration (that is, in terms of hours spent there). It is lectures that predominate and lectures that I shall concentrate on.

Students' attendance at lectures varies considerably; there is no compulsion to attend. After their initial attendance at every lecture, students become more discriminating about what lectures they attend. As exams approach, some students will go to lectures more, if only to find out how their colleagues are doing; others less, as working by themselves is found a more efficient use of the time – for them, the need for Economy is now paramount. Some courses have revision lectures, usually well attended. Those attending nearly always carry a bag of some sort for the large amount of paper they use (for making notes from lectures and books) and refer to (the printed material provided by different preclinical disciplines and books themselves).

Up to two hundred students in each preclinical year may spend up to four consecutive hours in the same seat, listening to a series of different lecturers from different disciplines, who talk, usually entirely uninterrupted, for an hour or just less. The familiar internal structure of the lecture theatre is important: students sit in tiered curved rows of seats, with a small ledge, like a desk, in front of them. This configuration naturally draw the eyes of students down and in, to the focal point of the theatre, the central area where the lecturer stands, with its desk, a blackboard behind and a screen above. As was discussed in Chapter 3, two functions of the structure of lecture theatres are that all the students can see the lecturer, and that the lecturer can see all the students. Students in the back rows, though, can see not only the lecturer but also all the other students sitting in front of them, and are furthest from the lecturer; those sitting at the front can only see the lecturer and the screen without turning round and so drawing attention to themselves. Students sit where they like in the theatre, though often, as Becker noted (1961: 140 and diagram), in social groups, for lectures provide an important social meeting-place (and Students' Union elections, Rag Week, and other students matters are sometimes advertised there before lectures start). Friends ask each other if they are going to a lecture or may meet there, either by arrangement or chance. The ideal is to sit with someone you know and like; as first-year students sort themselves out into social groups and teams over the first term, their positions in lectures may change. Broadly, those who expect to stay for the whole lecture sit at the front, while sitting in the back rows means that late entrances and swift exits are possible, and that talking and joking during the lecture is further away from the lecturer's eyes and ears. As a generalisation, let me say that rugby players sit at the back. It is not uncommon for preclinical students to occupy roughly the equivalent seat (down at the front on the left, say) for the whole two years, translating the same seat from the first-year to the second-year lecture theatre.

Perhaps the main way in which students show their appreciation of lectures is by writing. Sometimes lecturers tell students to 'get this down [in writing]', as it is something to learn, sometimes not to; but when either is the case, to write or not is the student's own choice. This simple binary way of classifying students' response in lectures is especially obvious when the lecturer projects on to the screen a slide or overhead with written or drawn material on it. When this is worth noting down in writing, heads move up and down all over the theatre: up to look at the slide above the lecturer's head and down to the sheet of paper on which they write their notes. If there is no written slide, they look at the lecturer and down to their paper to write when this seems, for whatever reason, indicated. Some lecturers provide 'handouts', one or more sheets of paper covering the subjects also covered in the lecture; if this is done before the lecture starts, it may be enough for students to take the handout (or several, for the members of his official-purpose team) and leave, while others may make notes during the lecture on the handout itself. Some students sit in lectures deliberately not taking notes or even attending to what is being said. There are several reasons given for this: that they might learn something there, while they certainly wouldn't if they weren't; that they might miss something if they hadn't come; and that they might at least find out what they have to learn.

Towards the end of the sixty minutes each lecture takes, and certainly if the lecturer runs over time, students start shifting about, gathering their belongings, talking to each other now without bothering to keep quiet, and getting up and going. At the end of a lecture, it is customary for the lecturer to ask if there are any questions – questions during lectures are extremely rare; when students do address the lecturer, it is usually to ask for a slide to be left up a bit longer so they can copy it all down. Afterwards, a few students may go down to the front to talk to the lecturer and ask questions, but most leave straight away. No concessions are made to allow an easy exit from the theatre for the lecturer, who often has to make a gangway through crowds of chatting students.

Students' Role in the Lecture Theatre: Becoming an Audience

It is clear that lecturers give frontstage performances in the explicitly theatrical setting of the lecture theatre. Lecturers control the visual elements of the lecture, which are clearly directed at an observing audience (a lecturer, for example, may refer to the difficulty that 'those of you in the cheap seats [at the back]' might have in seeing the details of projected slides). And lectures are also official performances, part of the medical school's explicit function of training doctors, though this official stage is sometimes invaded by the unofficial world (by the 'hits' of Rag Week described in the previous chapter, for example).

Students spend the majority of time in lectures sitting and listening to the lecturer, looking at him and his visual presentations on the screen, and writing their notes. But during lectures they may also eat, drink, belch (though seldom fart), laugh (or try to make their friends laugh uncontrollably), groan, cheer, read a book or newspaper, doze, stare sightlessly ahead, sit with their head in their arms on the desk, carry on a conversation with a neighbour, applaud one of their number who always comes in late, or get up and leave either noisily or quietly; students respond to the lecturer by behaving in different ways. These ways are very similar to what

Goffman describes as backstage behaviour (1990: 129); but lectures have been identified as official frontstage performances. The way out of this apparent paradox is quite simple: while students are no doubt to some extent constrained and under surveillance (as Foucault states) in the setting or 'field' of these theatres, they are also learning the active role of an audience as they sit looking at the lecturer's presentation (see Figure 12). They can be an unruly audience too, quite capable of making the lecturer inaudible; this is not uncommon during lectures on a culturally disapproved subject, like Sociology, Psychology or Statistics; then their comments are loud ('Rhubarb!' or even 'This is wank!') and loud derogatory remarks about the lecturers are frequent.

New electronic technology has also drawn attention to students' role as audience under surveillance. While all preclinical students attended lectures in one lecture theatre, clinical students attended lectures on two hospital sites, and the two theatres were linked by video cameras. The camera in the first theatre (where the lecturer was) transmitted his image or what he was showing on the screen there on to the screen in the second. Conversely, the camera in the second theatre was used to transmit the image of the students there (as seen from the vacant lecturer's desk) to the screen in the first when, for example, the lecturer asked questions of the students actually in front of him. And, before and between lectures, the screens in both theatres might show the students in the same or the other theatre, as they stood up and stretched and chatted. By linking the 'eyes' of the two theatres, the new technology emphasises the fact that in lecture theatres the audience is also part of the cast.

The Nature of Knowledge

Lectures are monologues by the lecturer, monologues almost entirely composed of connected but unattributed statements in the present tense, which are related to visual images. In these respects, there are great similarities between lectures and the textbooks (and the videos) that students use. I shall not even attempt to try and convey by quotation the huge quantity of such statements that are made in lectures but, in the 492 hours over the two years, it is immense. However scientists produce it on their own backstage (see Gilbert and Mulkay (1984) for an account

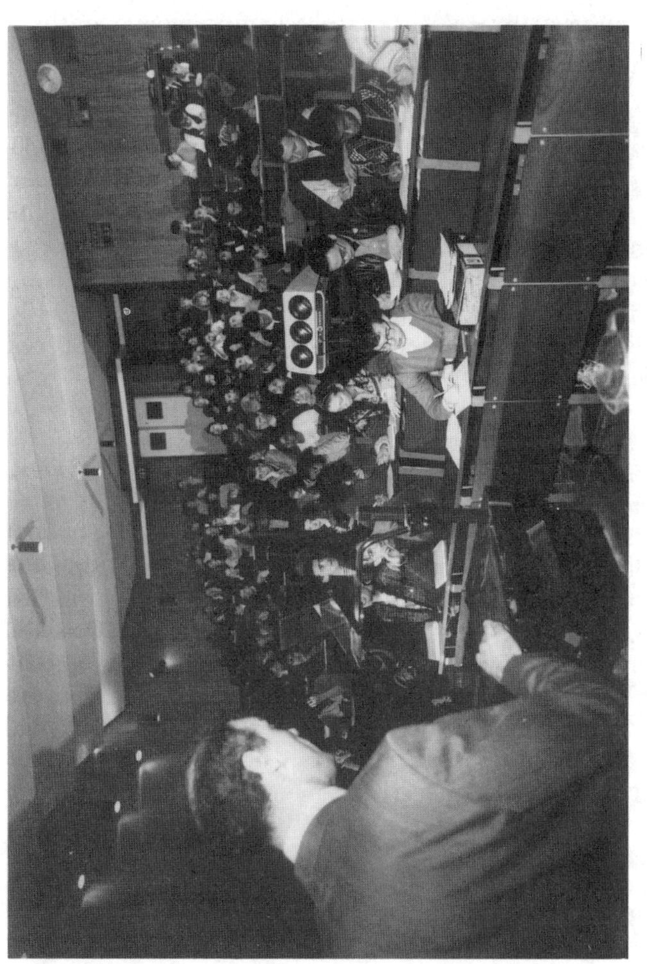

Figure 12. Lecturing: the official frontstage where Knowledge is taught and students learn the role of audience. Note the tiered stands focusing down and in, the equipment for projecting visual images on to the screen, and (even in this relatively posed photo) the tendency for students at the back to be less attentive. [UCL]

of the linguistic differences in 'informal' and 'formal' contexts), the scientific Knowledge so expounded in the present tense is seen as the accumulation of discoveries of scientists, usually unacknowledged, though some famous scientists and doctors are commemorated in eponyms. This Knowledge is defined by Ziman's 'consensuality' as the body of scientific knowledge that a majority of competent scientists agree with, and forms the cognitive basis for preclinical medical study. There is rarely any suggestion that these factual statements are anything more than the results of increasingly successful scientific enquiries into the real natural world of the body, verified by associated images. Whether such images are photographs or diagrams, both hold implications similar to the sort of language in which Knowledge is revealed: that it is timeless and so commonly known that an account of its provenance is unnecessary.

Such 'tenacious assumptions' of Western medicine are based on the scientific culture of 'naturalism', alluded to in the discussion in Chapter 3. Such assumptions rely on the Enlightenment view of nature, with its distinction from the supernatural, from human consciousness, from culture, from society, morality, psychology, and particular time and space (Gordon 1988: 23). And most students share the assumptions underlying proper scientific Knowledge, which (in something more like their own terms) is not a matter of personal opinion but a generalisable, reproducible, apolitical, communally demonstrable (and therefore visible), historically progressive revelation of indisputable and uncontentious objective fact about the real world, expressed in a precise and unambiguous language with material referents. But as students' aim is not to become scientists but to practise as competent doctors, they often make judgements about the Knowledge they are taught in lectures that influence their attendance there. Importance is attached to 'interest', an aspect of Knowledge, but rather more to proleptic clinical 'relevance', which involves their uninformed preclinical ideas of the dispositions of Experience and Responsibility, as yet only known through dissection (see Chapter 7). Their own further personal Idealistic aim, of helping or working with people and becoming a 'good' doctor, originally provides much of their motivation. Statistics lectures were an early casualty on all these criteria, a matter I return to.

Scientific Language: The Languages of Knowledge

To tackle preclinical work, students need to learn the languages of the different academic disciplines in which Knowledge is expressed (a point that is sometimes made explicitly in lectures), and exams in these subjects are to some degree assessments of students' proficiency in each discipline's language. Although doctors are not generally thought of as linguists, the acquisition of the various languages of medicine is a necessary and important part of their training, no doubt helped by the capacity to converge, to find the right answer to any question. As I discussed in Chapter 4, all students have A-level Chemistry; they therefore come to medical school not just with at least one lay language (English) but also with some sort of scientific language, though here there is considerable variation between students in their proficiency; there are students who may have not just a B.Sc. in Biochemistry or Physiology but a Ph.D. in such subjects, while there are a few with the minimum requirement of a Chemistry A-level and no other experience of science at all. Further, there are the children of doctors, who may have been exposed to medical language for years. But it is most unusual for any students to have much more than a smattering of the scientific language of Anatomy, and its terminology has to be learnt from scratch by nearly everyone; this is the discipline that I draw most of my examples from in this section. From now on, I shall indicate words used in scientific and medical language in bold type.

Sometimes these new words can be directly translated from the everyday words for parts of the body in lay language: the collarbone is the **clavicle**, and the shoulder-blade is the **scapula**, and so on. There are other new words that have a specific reference to Anatomy and that have no direct equivalent in lay language, though they are explained in those terms: 'They [these **arteries**] **anastomose**: they join together, they mix up, there is a communication', whereas 'a **plexus** is a mixture of nerves and the plural is **plexuses**'. But there are also words from lay language that have specific anatomical meanings; these concrete applications of lay words often have a meaning quite distinct from their lay one. The concrete nature of anatomical terms is evident in the anatomical use of the words **structure**, **relation** and **reflect**: an **artery**, for example, may be referred to as a **structure**, and its **relations** [its concrete relationships relative to other **structures**] may be defined; **reflecting** the skin means cutting and turning back the skin. An example of another word that is given a new and distinctive concrete meaning is **sympathetic**: 'There are three parts to the **autonomic nervous system** – the **sympathetic**, the **parasympathetic**, and the **enteric**. The **sympathetic nervous system** is responsible for fight or flight.' The **sympathetic nervous system**, then, is a visible and palpable concrete thing. In view of the scientific need for an unambiguous language, the word **sympathetic** is, in scientific and medical contexts, now no longer used in its lay sense but only to refer to this material object. At the same time that students are learning new words, they are also losing old ones.

Derivations may be given for some new words, often from Latin or Greek, which not unnaturally present problems for students. But etymological derivation stops once students have started to learn the uses of the language; besides, the derivation is usually just something else to learn, an extra piece of information that may not only not be helpful (and indeed may be unhelpful), but that is also irrelevant both to passing exams and to medical practice; and by no means all these new words are learnt (being unnecessary to pass exams). But to convey some idea of the number of new words that occur, I give those from one lecture in Neuroanatomy: **thalamus, cingulate, gyrus, pulvinar, internal laminar, calcarine, fissure, dyskinesia, corpus striatum, neostriatum, paleostriatum, substantia nigra, caudate nucleus, putamen, lentiform nucleus, globus pallidus, basal ganglia, limbic system, cingulum, uncus, hippocampus, mamillary bodies, fornix, entorrhinal, pre-frontal cortex, ventro-medial nucleus, internal capsule.**

Now it may seem an over-obvious point to make, that anatomical language is an unambiguous language with concrete referents – how could it be otherwise? But I stress it because of the association of words with things made communally visible by slides in lectures (and individually visible by pictures in books): 'the language learned and the world revealed to the medical gaze are closely linked' (M. Good and B. Good 1989: 307). I describe in Chapter 7 preclinical students' concurrent material dissection of the body, cutting things away in order to reveal other things, both visible to the naked eye and palpable to the fingers, which are therefore incontrovertibly consensible (here I use Ziman's term not just for the language of science but also for its material). In this context, one of Whorf's more determinist views of language, that 'we dissect nature along lines laid down by our native language' (1956: 213) should be modified to state that the natural body is dissected (whether pictorially or in the flesh) along lines laid down by the language of Anatomy; here unambiguous words apply unambiguously to unambiguous things.

I have referred above to students' 'loss' of lay meanings of words in the medical context. I should state more explicitly what I am arguing both here and throughout the rest of the book when I describe medical language. My argument is simply that students and junior doctors, in official frontstage settings (when there is a member of staff or senior doctor present), find it very difficult (if not impossible) to use, in any non-medical sense, words which have both medical and non-medical meanings. I shall also indicate, with students' gradual aggregation to the profession as the institution closes in on them, their increasing difficulty in using such ambiguous words in any setting, medical or lay.

Eponyms and Hearing the Written Language Spoken

Students are also introduced to the practice of using eponyms. In Anatomy, this results in naming parts of the body after people: there is the **pouch of Douglas**, for example, and the **sternal angle** is also called the **angle of Louis**, while, microscopically, there are the **nodes of Ranvier** and **Purkinje fibres**. In other disciplines, there is **Starling's Law**, and the **Krebs cycle**, and so on and so on. As with the eponyms that students will learn in their clinical years, these are almost without exception names of Great Men – students learn, from the possessive descriptions of the scientific basis of medicine, that medicine is a man's world.

Such eponyms, often involving foreign names, bring out another point about these scientific languages: their oral pronunciation. I noted above that students in lectures sometimes gave oddly inadequate reasons for attending lectures in which they did not make notes; there is one good reason for attending (though it is one they may be unaware of), which is to hear the new language spoken out loud, so that reading the language in books and from notes becomes easier. If possible at all, it is extremely difficult to read text where the pronunciation of every other word is unknown. I referred above to what I. A. Richards calls the 'Proper Meaning

Superstition', that there is ideally one right or good use for every word, a view of words found in Ziman's description of technical terms 'that have been defined with the utmost rigour' in scientific communications. But Richards also describes the 'Club Spirit', which makes 'the conduct of language subservient to manners – to the manners of special set of speakers invoked' (1965: 78, 80); the formulation for this would presumably be that there was one right or good pronunciation for every word. He suggests that one important justification for lectures in the Arts is that they ensure that those who attend them will know how to pronounce the names of Italian painters and Greek heroines, so giving protection from the 'awful dangers' of incorrect pronunciation. This point about how to pronounce some Greek or Italian names is actually much more cogent when applied to scientific languages (and particularly anatomical language), in which such a large proportion of the huge number of new words are derived from Greek and Latin. Lectures therefore provide both the names of things and their culturally proper pronunciation; they also provide images of things.

The Visual Referents of Words Spoken in Lectures

The direction of the student audience's eyes is focused centrally, not only on to the lecturer but also on to the large screen behind and above him, where there is nearly always a projected image of one sort or another: 'Of course no medical lecture can be given without slides' (Good 1994: 75). While a blackboard is still always found in lecture theatres, and is used by some lecturers for drawing diagrams during a lecture, this demands considerable skill and preparation, as well as taking up time during the lecture. The blackboard has been almost entirely superseded by slides or overheads projected on to the screen, and is now generally only a peripheral aid occasionally used for spelling new words introduced by the lecturer. Lectures are, in fact, often explanatory running commentaries on the series of slides shown, the link between the spoken and the seen made by the lecturer with a pointer. This fundamental interdependence of visual images and spoken words is highlighted when, for whatever reason (slides are left behind, or the projector broken) the slides can no longer be projected or the link cannot be made between words and pictures (the wooden pointer is not long enough, or the laser pointer does not work); lecturers are then almost at a loss for words.

Slides themselves may take several forms: photographs, diagrams and writing. Written slides are very often brief summaries of the lecture, usually in note form, made by the lecturer himself; nearly all students copy these down. Diagrams are schematic encapsulations of what the lecturer is talking about; they may be pictorial representations of, for example, the **brachial plexus** or the **metabolic pathways** of drugs, and the lecturer explains what is represented in diagrams just as if it were a photographic image. Photographic slides are important as providing evidence for the real existence of scientific entities described by scientific language. But there are different levels of existence: photographs of a whole human body are very rare, and those of a higher order than the individual person or patient are very rare indeed. The series of slides of smaller and smaller things at increasing powers of magnification are all projected on to the same space on the screen: 'a slide at one level is often followed by one just above or just below in this hierarchy, and each level reveals the more basic structure of the next higher order', demonstrating 'underlying mechanisms at an ontologically prior level' (Good 1994: 75–6), if not causation itself.

As well as confirming the reality of concepts, the matter of learning to see (of knowing what there is to be seen, and not being able to see without learning beforehand what is to be seen) is also a major part of lectures, actually forming part of the teaching on the **visual system**: 'the brain's function is to acquire knowledge' and 'the brain invests the world with properties not of the world's own' were taught in Neurophysiology lectures. This, in principle, relativist account of the actively selective and creative nature of perception is not accompanied by any kind of reflexive application to its own understanding of the subject of its enquiry; the scientifically observing eye alone remains neutral and objective. And, as the projection of slides to two hundred students suggests, this factual visual information is communally visible and explicable. Only individuals can make the sort of comment made by a mature student after an Embryology lecture, in which slides of human foetuses at different stages of development were shown: 'I could only see them [the slides] each as personal tragedies for someone.' But he would have to learn the stages of **organ development** shown in these same slides for exams.

Levels of Knowledge and the Certainty of Knowledge

Becker stated that preclinical students identify what is important to study 'by finding out what the faculty wants us to know' (1961: 163); his view is that they find the 'tentative, scientific approach' of their teachers disturbing. In the same way, Fox (1957: 213) claims that the 'experimental point of view' of preclinical teachers is one of the causes of uncertainty that students have to acknowledge and so to tolerate. In his discussion of the matter of 'uncertainty' in medical training, Atkinson is sceptical – in my view, rightly – of this particular sort of uncertainty among students. They tend to dismiss as unscientific subjects where Knowledge is not simply a matter of observable and objective fact. But Atkinson does not mention the degree to which uncertainty is also absent among teachers of disciplines from the natural sciences. There was only one lecture in the 'hard' sciences that I attended in which doubt was cast on the nature of the normally unquestioningly accepted visual evidence; when this lecturer raised the question of whether the slide of the electronmicrograph that he had projected contained many **artefacts** [elements created by the process of investigation rather than revealed by it], many students stopped writing and sat back, muttering their dissatisfaction with this uncertainly stated lecture. Uncertainty about the limits of Knowledge is much more likely to be found among clinical teachers, who favour a different sort of certainty, that based on Experience and Responsibility (see Chapters 8 and 9).

Normally, without suggesting that there is any doubt about the status of the facts involved, preclinical lecturers themselves try to make it clear what Knowledge they expect students to know; this is not just left to them to work out. Indeed, while the certainty of facts is assumed, students are often told about the vast quantity of facts there are to be known, so vast that they could spend the rest of their life studying a subject and not know it, or so vast that it is impossible to convey anything but the briefest summary in the time available (often with the lecturers complaining that their lecture hours have been cut). As a consequence of this huge amount of Knowledge, a level at which student learning should be set is referred to; their teachers tell them what they need to know to pass exams. Lecturers may indicate this level of learning in terms of the likely nature of exam questions generally, with reference to an officially approved textbook. For example, the Anatomy that had to be learnt (or rather, that exams would be set on) was to be found in the master copy of the recommended textbook, held in the Dissecting Room, on the pages that had not been blacked out with ink. Sometimes a specific fact or slide is referred to as relevant to a likely exam question. Conversely, lecturers also point out what is unnecessary for students to know. Here, then, I emphasise again, there is no question about the certainty of Knowledge expressed by lecturers. But what these teachers do not make clear is the precise nature of the exam questions they will ask – this is undoubtedly a real cause of uncertainty (and therefore anxiety) for medical students, as indeed for any students.

Assessments of Knowledge: Examinations

Assessments of one sort or another become an everyday feature of preclinical life. After little more than three months at medical school, students take their first 'professional' exam (that is, an exam where the results make some contribution to the requirements for becoming medically qualified). In their second year, in addition to exams in six composite subjects, there are in-course assessments – there were eleven such pieces of coursework to be completed within the first ten weeks of the spring term; exams in many subjects followed in the summer. Passing each composite subject is necessary to go on to the next year, and formal assessments are overwhelmingly of what students write in exams, as they sit separated at numbered desks. Coursework is of essays, projects or 'written up' practicals, usually finished at home. Knowledge and the language it is expressed in is informally tested in oral settings like tutorials, but oral examinations are now rare; they are found exceptionally in Prize *vivas* or *vivas* after borderline exam performances, but only regularly (as I discuss later) in the Dissecting Room. It is therefore possible (though unlikely for reasons discussed above) to pass assessments of Knowledge without knowing the accepted pronunciation of words; this is not possible in clinical assessments of Experience and Responsibility.

The emphasis placed on the certainty of Knowledge by preclinical teachers is reflected in the way it is assessed and, equally, the way Knowledge is tested determines students' attitudes to it. Written exams are made up of a varying combination of essays, 'short answers', and Multiple Choice Questionnaires (MCQs). The increasing use of MCQs, tests so suitable for convergers, is itself good evidence of the certainty of Knowledge. In these tests, a series of factual statements is provided and the student's task is to put a mark against one of the three options relating to each statement: True, False or Don't Know. The last option does not indicate any uncertainty in the statement itself, but only the student's lack of Knowledge; one of the other alternatives, True or False, is certainly true.

The percentage awarded for each piece of work and exam is officially stated and is known from the first day of the course; 50 per cent is the pass mark. Despite what lecturers occasionally say, it is not the case that there are 'pass or fail' questions (that is, individual questions that, by themselves, students must answer correctly to pass and that, if they answer incorrectly, will fail them). Exams of this sort are marked on the overall score, and these overall scores are then added. There is, though, a further sort of uncertainty to be found among students, which concerns doubt about the way marks for exams are themselves treated to decide who passes and who fails: will a certain percentage (determined by the department or the medical school) fail, or is there a standard criterion, representing an acceptable level of Knowledge, that would make it possible for everyone to pass?

Learning Knowledge

While teaching Knowledge certainly takes place in lectures, it is to be doubted whether much learning of Knowledge goes on there, if only because exams often take place months after the lectures on the subject. In learning Knowledge, as in lectures, the principal body configuration is again sitting at a desk (see Figure 13). This mostly takes place in the similar settings of libraries or at the student's own desk at home, and now also in the congruent setting in front of a computer or video recorder. When working at a desk at home, students get up to stretch, to make a cup of coffee, to find another book or more paper; they may do so in libraries too, and get up and go over to a friend and talk more or less quietly.

In basic medical science textbooks, as in lectures, Knowledge is presented, for the most part, in a series of unattributed statements made in the present tense in one of the languages of the preclinical academic disciplines. The textbook is the written equivalent of the

Figure 13. The library: the official backstage where Knowledge is learnt individually. [UCL]

lecture, and its named author (again, nearly always a man) may be thought of as the lecturer. The most famous of these textbooks is *Gray's Anatomy*, though this is seldom used by students, while other Anatomy textbooks, such as 'Hall–Craggs' and 'Snell' are. Written textbooks, like spoken lectures, are lavishly illustrated with a wealth of photographs, diagrams and short notes found among the text. So textbooks may be thought of as portable written lectures – indeed, there is a series of such textbooks called 'Lecture Notes'. The use of videos combines the same elements found in lectures, those of speech and visible referents. In these, as in 'good' lectures and textbooks, students value clarity, certainty and concision of expression.

I have suggested that hearing the way the new vocabulary is spoken is necessary for reading textbooks and making notes from them, and that, without being able to speak and hear internally such new words, this may be very difficult. Attempts by students to read up a discipline beforehand, in the holidays, are given up for this reason, no doubt among others. In libraries, where students read textbooks and their own lecture notes, the words are mentally articulated or heard (one student told me, 'I just have to look at my lecture notes and I can hear the lecturer') – presumably the reason why silence is usually enjoined there; at home, on the other hand, it is possible to mutter or say words out loud, sometimes with a loud background noise of music.

For some students, apparently blessed with a memory like a camera or tape-recorder, reading a textbook or re-reading their lecture notes is enough to fix the Knowledge expressed there in their mind. But for most, some form of processing is necessary, usually by making one's own notes and diagrams. Making notes from textbooks and from lecture notes represents a synthesis between the student and his lecture notes and/or textbooks. To put this another way, this synthesis involves converting the monologue of the lecture (from notes) and/or the textbook into a dialogue, the upshot of which forms the student's own notes. But in each subject studied in this way, as in lectures, there is very little conflict found in the material used for making notes; where inconsistencies occur, they are an irritation rather than a stimulus to enquiry, though resolution may be found by asking a colleague or occasionally a teacher. So generally the process of making notes is one of selection and compression for the purpose of memorising important facts; it is not one of argument. Such notes are the coded compressed objectification of speech, ready for revision and memorisation for exams. And the writing of notes in such quantities, whether in lectures or during revision, is for oneself. It is generally accepted that other students' notes are of mixed value; to decipher their writing and shorthand abbreviations may be much more trouble than it is worth. Doctors' traditionally illegible writing is not illegible to themselves.

Learning Knowledge by Scientising the Self

Latour (1987: 60) describes readers of scientific literature (what he calls 'fact-writing') as having only three choices: giving up reading, going along with what is written, or working through and re-enacting it through laboratory experiment. Giving up, Latour reckons, is the most common reaction by readers (they are not interested in what is written and so do not read it), and re-enacting the rarest, being so costly. Going along with it, accepting what is written, is the normal outcome; the reader believes the author's claim and, by not disputing it and using it, helps the author turn it into fact. Medical students, of course, cannot give up; their own need to remember these certain scientific facts for exams makes them go along with it, as does the form in which the facts are presented, in connected but unattributed statements in the present tense. But, while going along with it, students also take Latour's third and rarest option, and re-enact it and confirm it in their own bodies. This obviously takes place when they themselves are used as subjects for demonstrations on the official frontstage (in Physiology laboratories, for example; see Figure 14). But there are less obvious methods of relating Knowledge to their bodies and to the outside world, so that their whole world becomes scientised.

While facts are stated in lectures as uncontested statements, they are often couched in theory-laden terms (whether because that is how the lecturer sees things or whether as an aid to memory is often unclear). This is particularly obvious when teleological theory is used: 'The **sympathetic nervous system** is responsible for fight or flight; to remember what it does, all you have to do is think of your ancestors living in a cave and sharing it with a sabre-toothed tiger.' This lecturer's instruction to students to think of their ancestors in a dangerous situation clearly involves thinking

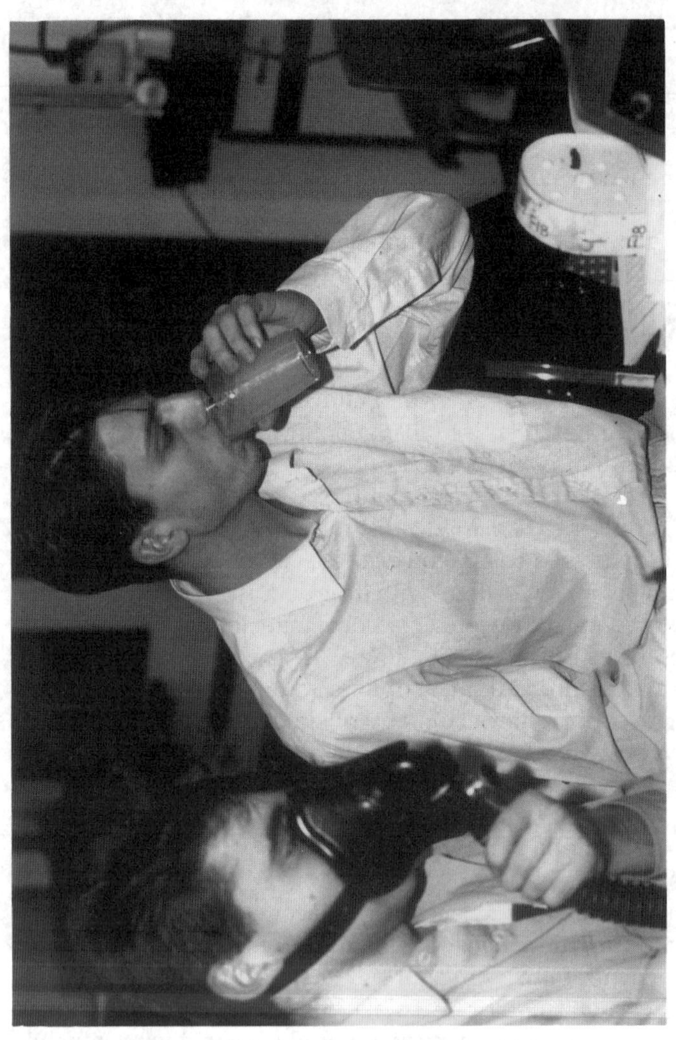

Figure 14. Scientising the self on the official frontstage: two students taking part in a physiology practical, in which they are both experimental subjects and recording scientists. [UCL]

of themselves in one too. The use of students' own bodies is often more explicit: 'Why do we have tendons, rather than muscles at the wrist? **Functionally** they would work just the same. If you remember the leg, the same is true; but if you put all your muscles in your foot, it'd be like running with great boots on – you could run, but not so fast.' Here teleology is couched in terms of the Anatomical Method used to understand the body by relating **structure** and **function**. This ancient system is also referred to even when it is not applicable (in that it doesn't reach the right conclusion, there being no unequivocal **function** for a **structure** like the **frontal sinuses**, for example) or when it runs counter to the facts (the **pectineus** muscle ought, **structurally**, to be supplied by the **obturator** nerve, but, because it lies so close to the **femoral** nerve, 'it can't resist being supplied by it').

So students are encouraged to use the Anatomical Method for learning facts that can be immediately confirmed on their own body. Lecturers also encourage students both to look at such **structures** on themselves ('The next time you have a shower, have a look at your ankles. There's a big blue vein running over the **medial malleolus**') and to feel these **structures** themselves (as a lecturer pointed at a slide of the **central body of the perineum**, he said, 'If you're male *or* female, feel yourselves in the bath tonight.'). The translation of visual Knowledge to such visible and tactile experience differs in an important way from proper medical Experience; the latter is learnt on others, not on oneself. So, although Knowledge is learnt for exams from books and notes and assessed by written exams, it is often confirmed and learnt by relating it to students' own bodies. While this is most obvious in Anatomy, it is by no means confined to it. For example, the fact that **caffeine** suppresses **ADH [Anti-diuretic hormone]** and so increases the rate of **micturition** can be checked individually by students on their own person by noting that they do urinate more than they might expect after drinking a number of cups of coffee.

Preclinical students come to see themselves differently by using their bodies to check or test their memory of facts. Ernie, the student with special insight into the way doctors think because of his work as a hospital porter, described the way he used this method:

> On TV or a film, if someone's hit by a bullet, I work out what it's going to go through. I'm pretty good at **surface anatomy** and

> **markings** on my front but less good at the back; I can do my own front. Sometimes we do it together but not on girls. If someone's chatting a girl up in a pub, I lean over and **percuss** their back. So far, I'm my only really co-operative subject.

In this preclinical stage, Ernie, despite his attempts to use **percussion** (a method of Experience) on others, is limited to his own body for confirmation of Knowledge. He has also drawn attention to the need for his subjects to be Co-operative, a matter that becomes much more important in the clinical years.

Memorising Knowledge by Relating it to the World

While Ernie was using his own body to check out and learn facts, he was also using features of the world beyond, films, to help him revise and memorise Anatomy, an approach to the world that lecturers also promote. Anatomical **structure** and **function** are associated with different features of the outside world, such as people ('If you're a sword swallower, it's not a good thing to get hiccups, because the **oesophagus** is closely **related** to the **left atrium**') and, in a remarkable example, buildings (the ground plan of the tallest building in the world, the Sears-Roebuck Tower in Chicago, was described as identical to the **cross-sectional structure** of three penises). Lay words themselves are also given scientific associations, as mnemonics. So students were taught rhymes ('The **trapez*ium*** [bone] sits at the base of the *thumb*') and word associations ('The **hamate** [bone] has a hook on it; if you still think of being "hooked" as being engaged, the **hamate** is at the base of the ring finger'). Anatomists seem to have taught mnemonics for many years, often using sexual imagery; the changing race and sex of students, together with students' decreasing need to know quite so much, means that such mnemonics are less taught in lectures than in earlier years. As an anatomy demonstrator explained to me in the dissecting room: 'You can't give lectures saying "Ten Zulus Buggered My Cat" for the **branches of the facial nerve supplying the face** [a mnemonic acronym for the **Temporal**, **Zygomatic**, **Buccal**, **Mandibular** and **Cervical** branches]!' But, though 'Ten Zulus' was not taught in lectures, it was taught to groups of students in the dissecting room, as was this mnemonic for the **cranial nerves**: 'Oh! Oh! Oh! To Touch And

Feel Virgin Girls' Vaginas And Hymens' [for the **Olfactory, Optic, Oculomotor, Trochlear, Trigeminal, Abducens, Facial, Vestibulo-cochlear, Glosso-pharyngeal, Vagus, Accessory** and **Hypoglossal** nerves], repeated to me by Dave, a rugby player. Dave also did what many students do, and made up his own mnemonics; his mnemonic for the **branches of the carotid artery** was, '"Organs Please!", Said Timothy's Active Mother, Lovingly Stroking Larry's Super Length.' As well as being acronyms, mnemonics sometimes involve visual images; for example, to remember the fact that **pilocarpine** is a **muscarinic agonist** which crosses the **blood–brain barrier**, another student devised the image of a chunky (**muscular**) **car**, with protective bags (**pillows**), crashing through a barrier. In other words, despite the official frontstage association of scientific things with scientific words, there is a further scientising of lay words in the formation of mnemonics on the official backstage; and, for some students at any rate, such associative scientising of lay words is also heavily associated with sex.

So, whether students learn by function, teleology, self-referral or association with other features of the world including lay language itself, they check out the Knowledge from different disciplines on themselves and associate Knowledge both with their own bodies and with the surrounding world. With official encouragement, they project the science they have to learn on to the world; their whole world becomes scientised, reverberating with scientific illustrations of and associations with the physical body's structure and functions that they are taught. To indicate this scientisation, Eliade's term 'hierophany' (1959: 11), the manifestation to religious man of sacred realities in ordinary things, could be modified to 'sarcophany', the manifestation to medical students of the fragmented scientific natural body in ordinary things. In this way, officially taught preclinical Knowledge therefore promotes what I have called a 'corporate corporality' that is quite consonant with the coarse physicality of the male-dominated unofficial student culture, and, in providing no opposition to it, may appear to lend it further official sanction. This fundamental aspect of official life also results in the 'levelling' of all students to a physical uniformity, being 'stripped' of individual differences. And, although Knowledge is held to be objective and unemotional, when learnt in this way it becomes deeply personal and subjectified (which may in turn account for the powerful erotic charge in libraries used by preclinical students).

Scientising the World: 'Medical Students' Disease'

Preclinical students, I have suggested, are segregated from the central concerns of the profession they have enlisted in, however much they are treated as having medical Status by those outside the profession. One way of trying to overcome this process of subordination is to see what is 'relevant' in what they learn, anticipating the dispositions of Experience and Responsibility. Students' scientising of their own bodies, combined with their desire for clinical relevance, may lead to the alarming symptoms of 'medical student's disease'. Such hypochondria is normally noted among clinical students and various reasons have been produced to account for it: as the outcome of heightened stress and anxiety, or an increased awareness of the clinical manifestations of disease (Atkinson 1981: 21). But both these explanations fail to recognise how far preclinical students use their own bodies for the purposes described above and how far they try to anticipate the clinical relevance of their Knowledge. Both aspects are shown in the following interchange between members of a preclinical official-purpose team, backstage, in the coffee room:

Rhys:	'I've got blood on the paper, just a tiny bit. [*To me:*] What's that?'
SS:	'Piles?'
Rhys:	'How much do you get with **bowel cancer**? A lot? [*After a pause:*] I haven't got piles.'
Josh:	'Why not?'
Rhys:	'I looked it up in the book, the causes of bleeding: cancer, **ulcerative colitis** . . .'
Bob [*contemptuously*]:	'Oh God!'
Josh:	'I think everyone should have a **CT scan** every four months. Or at least age twenty and aged forty.'
Rhys:	'Another thing: I was looking at myself in the mirror – my left bollock's much lower than my right!'
Josh:	'That's *normal*!'
Bob [*disgustedly*]:	'Oh God, here we go again!'
Rhys:	'And my right one's much bigger than my left! [*Laughter.*] I was feeling all this stuff – what else is there, the **vas [deferens]**, what else?'

Josh [*implying that he had had exactly the same concerns*]: 'The **pampiniform plexus** – I went along to my GP. I was really worried.' [*Rhys looks at me, inquiringly.*]

SS: 'If you're worried, I'd go to my GP.'

Rhys: 'Oh no, I'm not going along there! They'd say, "Here comes another hypochondriac medical student!"'

Josh: 'I've got no problems about going – my GP's a dude.'

[*Later, just before the group dispersed:*]

Rhys: 'I wasn't going to come in today. I'm really glad I did! I thought I had cancer and something wrong with my bollocks – now it's all right!'

Rhys had not simply done what he was told to do in lectures, and only confirm the facts of Knowledge on himself; he had worked the other way about, using lay methods of physical examination on himself (rather than the specialised body techniques of Experience on others), and had found what could have been evidence of pathology in his **rectal bleeding** and **testicular asymmetry**; he then used written Knowledge to explain this to himself, with alarming results. But, because he had practised Co-operation and had told his concerns to the other members of his team (and was prepared to put up with their reactions to his revelation, now and in the future), they were able to reassure him that all was normal.

Scientising the Stresses Caused by Preclinical Work

In a more general way, some preclinical students come to understand the stress they undergo in learning and being tested on Knowledge as an important part of the process of becoming a doctor. This may be one way of dealing with their separation from the profession; but it is also entirely logical for them to consider that, in an officially organised course, the absurdities and problems they encounter are actually officially intended too. They may even appear to find official confirmation of this; a first-year preclinical student told me about one difficulty he experienced:

Stan: 'He [a lecturer] said, "Don't take notes in my lectures!" But if you look around you'll see people taking notes. We don't know what we have to know.'

SS: 'But quite often you're told you don't need to know something.'

Stan: 'Yes, I've been told that three times and each time it's been wrong. We did need to know it.'

SS: 'So it's a sort of trap?'

Stan: 'Yes. One of the other teachers told me that, in effect.'

In fact, the whole pressurised business of acquiring and being assessed on Knowledge is seen by some students as a way of testing how they stood up to it, with implications for how they would stand up to the practice of medicine itself. One student had had experience of being trained in the military, to which he likened preclinical training:

> At the time, you don't know what's going on, you're humiliated and so on. As you go up the system, you realise that it's a policy to break you down and then build you up, as you actually take part in it [as a trainer]. There's small groups of eight, then three, with people watching you the whole time, physiologists and psychologists seeing how you react physically and mentally, monitoring you – I've not seen any of this yet, but no doubt it'll come.

But it doesn't; medicine, unlike the military, is not scientifically interested in its recruits' psychological experiences, either their individual *morale* or the *esprit de corps* of their groups. Psychology, as I have already implied and as I shall show further, is a low-Status discipline.

In another example, during a Sociology seminar on 'Stress in the Medical Profession', the talk turned to the personal tutors arranged by the medical school for preclinical students, to help them deal with non-academic problems. Omar said, reflecting the general student attitude, 'It's very much take it or leave it [seeing personal tutors]; personally I hold on to problems and deal with them myself'; but he went on, 'Of course they [the medical school] won't admit it but it [seeing personal tutors] may well be actively discouraged.' While Omar's attribution of the medical school's intent may or may not be accurate (again, the profession's distaste for Psychology may be relevant), substantial numbers of students who held this view about the deliberate nature of the stress they experienced found the use of drugs (both prescribed and otherwise available) perfectly acceptable to deal with it.

In other words, the stress of preclinical training – which has been acknowledged for years to be overloaded with the learning of clinically irrelevant fact well known to be quickly forgotten after exams, and which is consequently being thoroughly overhauled under the authority of the GMC – is itself seen by some students as a deliberate prefiguring of medical practice. Once again, 'medical school culture' is not the autonomous entity defined by Becker, but directly related to medical culture itself by these junior students, who, however desperately, suppose there is an official explanation for their treatment. Conspiracy is preferred to cock-up as an explanation for their position; at least a conspiracy theory assumes that someone is conspiring with them in mind. Soldiers in the Second World War were noted to look on the bright, or orderly, side of things; this was 'indispensable if soldiers were to keep their psychic stability and perform their duties at all'. Disasters occur, 'but people must not be told so, lest the illusion of planning and order be shaken' (Fussell 1990: 19–20).

Dealing with Knowledge

I have so far described some ways in which individual students collectively deal with the huge amount of unchallenged Knowledge in propositional form that they may be tested on in exams. For coursework and passing exams, Co-operation and Economy are practised within the groups I call 'official-purpose teams'.

Official-purpose Teams

Co-operative action takes place with the formation of such teams, smallish groups of from two to about eight students. These teams arise in many and various ways: school-friends or those who went to the same tutorial colleges to resit A-levels may form a nucleus; students may team up because they live in the same hall, play the same games, are the same colour or sex, or are put in the same official tutorial or dissection groups, or because they find themselves always sitting next to each other in lectures. Even failure at exams, which might be thought to break up such teams, promotes their formation; exams are taken at the end of the academic year, and students who fail them have to resit them in September, just before the new year begins. For some of the summer months, the members of the officially designated 'September Club' work together, often forming working relationships that persist into the next year. However created, like-minded official-purpose teams form. Within them, particular interests may be represented, for a diversity of specialisation may be very helpful for dealing with work set by the diverse academic disciplines.

The methods and principles of Economy and Co-operation themselves are also handed down from one year's students to the next, rather than having to be developed by each successive year; such inter-year Co-operation is very clearly present among some official-purpose teams, particularly those with members who are also members of representative teams. For them, Co-operation may have an instrumental aspect, in that taking part in whatever activity the representative team is concerned with takes time and energy, and may therefore seriously impinge on time which might otherwise be spent on individual learning. For others, it is their 'mummies' or 'daddies' that give them their old and now unwanted written material, while the more distanced and individualistic students may even note how stand-offish the year above them is. But, although written material may be passed down by inter-year groups, actual working groups are of students within the same year.

Official-purpose Teams: Exams and Course Work

Within official-purpose teams, old exam papers, specimen MCQ questions, lecture handouts and other useful written material are acquired by their members, from other teams and from more senior students; these are handed round within and between such teams (like the 'house files' kept in fraternity houses in Kansas that Becker (1961: 174) records). Some of these strategies are not officially allowed; removing MCQ papers from exam settings is usually officially forbidden, but it continues. If this is impossible, students may Co-operate and memorise, or even write down, five questions each; this often happens in MCQs that are used as trials. These old, ideal and sample questions are pooled and studied hard by individual members.

A striking example of the way such Co-operation functions was the report of the surprising result of one MCQ exam. Such exams are close-marked by computer on the statistical premiss that the scores achieved by the group of students sitting them are normally distributed along a Gaussian curve, with a single large hump in the middle representing the scores of the majority, those scoring either much more or much less than this being far fewer, and forming the tails of the hump. When the results of this exam were analysed, however, the scores were found to correspond to a binomial distribution (that is, there were two humps rather than one); these represented two different populations of students, those who had seen previous papers on the same subject and those who had not had the advantage of this instance of intra- and inter-year Co-operation.

The real uncertainty of what questions may be asked results in revising for exams by 'question-spotting' (a practice not confined to medical students): guessing what questions the examiners will set, and revising on that basis. This attempt to assume the reciprocal relationship of the one that students normally experience in the disposition of Knowledge involves trying, however successfully or unsuccessfully, to enter the examining teachers' mind. So students may more or less confidently say, 'They won't ask that!' or, with some apprehension, 'They *can't* ask that!' The sorts of consideration assumed to be involved are that such questions have always been asked or, conversely, that they may not have been set for some time. Students also consider that particular emphasis may have been given to certain subjects during lectures or tutorials or even privately (some lecturers are known, rightly or wrongly, for being likely to give broad hints about probable questions). When revising for MCQs, the need to imagine the examiners' intention is important, because of the complete impossibility of any discussion of the question; a single short pencil-stroke in one of the three positions on a card is the only writing allowed for each answer. So, as well as some words acquiring an MCQ-specific meaning ('normally', 'often' and 'frequently' come to have percentage ranges attached to them, for example), the statement may have to be analysed along the lines of 'What are the examiners getting at here?' A few students do not try to enter this sort of imaginary reciprocal relationship at all, preferring one based simply on learning the answers True or False to specimen questions by rote, without even attempting to understand or learn why those were the answers; their subordination is complete.

Co-operation and Economy are also practised by official-purpose teams for coursework (mostly practicals and essays), set especially in Sociology and Psychology (though the fact that these courses were unusual in changing from year to year tended to make inter-year Co-operation impossible). It is by no means uncommon for one member of the team, who is personally interested in the subject, or who may have been delegated this particular task in rotation, to write up his version for circulation to the other members to copy. This interchange of material can give rise to a degree of contempt for its examiners; much enjoyment is had, for example, when different marks are awarded for what is effectively the same piece of work. These marks form part of the calculations made by each student for each subject, as they weigh up the Economics of passing; as Rhys said, 'I've worked out that, if I get 70 per cent on the project and 60 per cent or 70 per cent on the essay with a bit of help from Bob, I only need 28 per cent on the MCQ to pass!'

Co-operation and Economy in General

Most teachers are aware of the existence of Co-operation among students. Some teachers, anticipating their role as examiners, try to foil Economy and Co-operation among students by warning them, for example, that 'suspiciously similar papers will be investigated' and advising them not to concentrate on only a few topics in case of a *viva*; such teachers are disliked. Others state the opposite, that students are not competing with anybody else and that they 'simply have to reach a level [of Knowledge] that we're happy with', as judged by the final mark for the exams in that discipline. But, in general, there is considerable contact between preclinical students and staff, as is shown both by the content of the rumours that circulate (about their teachers' private lives, new marking systems, the plans for the medical school and other official matters) and by their occasional startling accuracy. The official frontstage distance of teachers from students may in some circumstances become much closer, usually for members of representative teams, or in academic settings on the official backstage. Such students are sometimes unpleasantly surprised by their teachers' later insistence on re-establishing a proper distance in official frontstage settings; but most students are aware of the concern that some of their teachers show for them, if only to help them pass that discipline's exams.

For students' official work, as unofficially, Co-operation is the generally preferred mode, and passing exams Economically rather than excelling is the main thing to do, though some individual students hoping for Prizes work very hard. It should be no surprise that it was the Rugby Club that was rumoured to have put up a prize for the student that passed every subject by the minimum margin. Competition, so intensely felt on application to medical school, may seem to disappear almost entirely, though it always lurks, reappearing when it becomes publicly known that an exam is marked so that a certain percentage of students will fail. Sympathy is reserved for those who actually fail, and who therefore fall for a period outside the main group of those who passed. In general, students are generous to those that have done particularly well in exams, congratulating but not envying them (at any rate in public). If such high-scorers are known to be hard workers, they are more likely to be scorned or pitied for 'not having a life'; if they are not so known, they are highly regarded, achievement without apparent effort being the most prized result. This well-known attitude found in many other spheres, derived I dare say from the public schools, which seem to have furnished medical schools with so many of their institutional aspects, may be seen as a statement about Status and its relation, in this case, to Knowledge: 'We are naturally good at something because we are generally naturally superior; if we are not good at something, and have to work hard at it, then the subject (or whatever it is) is of little importance and of low status.' To claim to have done no work also, of course, affords protection in the event of failure.

Ultimately, though, despite the impressive exercise of Co-operation for official work before exams (and sometimes in them, with students deliberately making their papers visible to their neighbours), the way that written exams are approached and taken is individual. Students develop their own different strategies for dealing with MCQs, for example, some answering all the questions, others calculating how many correct answers are needed to pass. It is not uncommon for students who have never failed an exam in their lives before to fail at least one preclinical exam. Levelling experiences like these may come as a great personal shock; but this may be modified, in public at least, according to which discipline's exam was failed: the cultural acceptability of failing specific exams is one way in which preclinical subjects are ranked. For example, it is not only acceptable to fail Statistics, but students may actually congratulate one another on doing so. While some students are actually quite confident at using statistical concepts when applied to their own work (for example, in terms of working out the economics of how they should direct their energies or deciding how many MCQ questions to answer), this confidence is not found in the exam. It is, of course, the only exam where students are required to solve given problems (and can bring in calculators and are provided with tables to do so), rather than remember and restate facts. Other, non-medical students may be brought in to help prepare for Statistics exams – the only time I ever heard of this. As I show below, Statistics is, for medical students, a profoundly non-medical subject.

Combining Different Disciplines

Preclinical Knowledge is organised on the basis of separate university-based academic disciplines, which independently teach and assess students' learning. Some associations between these disciplines have recently been established, under both internal and external pressure, in an attempt to provide students with a more integrated curriculum (so that, for example, Anatomy and Embryology have become Structural and Developmental Biology). But such nominal associations do not break down inter-disciplinary boundaries, which are obvious to seasoned students, and which are maintained by the system of paying different departments according to the time allotted in the curriculum to each department's subject.

The teachers of the preclinical disciplines, though often nationally and sometimes internationally respected, are seldom medically qualified themselves. And, although there is very seldom any internal conflict in the Knowledge that different departments present, there may also be little overlap between the Knowledge presented by different departmental disciplines each with its own identity, purpose and frame of reference. Whatever may be said about the development of an 'integrated' curriculum, it is at the moment predominantly the work of the students to integrate what they are taught and learn, using their own bodies to do so when they can (though even this is not always easy; their own 'physiological' body, for example, may be rather different from their 'anatomical' one). In their effort to integrate their curriculum, students rank disciplines in ways that can be analysed in terms of dispositional categories. So the traditional medical disciplines of Anatomy, Physiology and Biochemistry, with Pharmacology and Pathology, are all seen as proper Knowledge, with clear relevance to Experience and Responsibility. Student attitudes to four other preclinical disciplines (Neuroanatomy, Sociology, Psychology and Statistics) can also be analysed in this sort of way, as well as with reference to their different languages.

Neuroanatomy, Sociology, Psychology and Statistics

Neuroanatomy is generally agreed to be the most difficult preclinical subject. It is held to be very complicated, hard to learn and hard to visualise, but not 'irrelevant', as it constitutes proper Knowledge and is concerned with the guessed-at dispositions of Experience and Responsibility. There are some obvious reasons for its difficulty: as against the rest of the dissected body, the brain is smaller and visually fairly homogeneous; pictures and photographs of neuroanatomical structures need more explanation; students do not dissect a brain, making the process of discovery relatively slow and assimilable, but have it dissected for them by a demonstrator slicing through it; structure is not obviously related to function, there being only one tube, and no pumps, bellows or pulleys. But perhaps more importantly, in view of the importance of vision in Knowledge and students' method of relating Knowledge to themselves, it may be significant that it is very hard in imagination to look at one's own brain (which would mean looking behind one's eyes), especially at the revelation of highly complex three-dimensional **structures** in different (**coronal, sagittal, horizontal**) two-dimensional planes. So most learning of Neuroanatomy is from lectures and books, rather than in relation to oneself (though students are taught that the brain is an information-gathering and information-processing mechanism, in another concordance between official and unofficial approaches to Knowledge). But while Neuroanatomy is generally held to be extremely difficult, though relevant, two other subjects, Sociology and Psychology, are generally not held to be scientific at all.

For, while interesting to some, these subjects are found woolly, not objective, not scientific, and a matter of opinion rather than certain fact. A student said of Sociology, pointing to his foot (the **lower limb** was being studied in Anatomy that term), 'It's non-scientific – there's no meat to it; it's not like *that*! It's not like having a foot; it doesn't matter who tells you about it, who discovered it.' Another said, 'I waited for half an hour [during a Sociology lecture] for a *fact* to write down!' Psychology was criticised along the same lines: 'It's all a matter of opinion.' Unlike Sociology, Psychology is seen to have some potentially relevant aspects, though these are not concentrated on enough: 'Psychology is interesting when she's [the lecturer's] talking about [doctor–patient] interaction, but nothing much else.' Further evidence of this view is found in the substantial numbers of medical students who choose an intercalated B.Sc. in Psychology (though the 'woolliness' of the subject also appeals to those who want an easy year 'as an ordinary student'). And some students found the theoretical discussions about medicine in Psychology helpful; underlining the lack of preclinical contact with or talk about the medical world, one said at the end of a seminar, 'It's nice to talk about what we're doing generally; we don't do it anywhere else. Thanks for the chat.'

But generally these two disciplines are criticised. After a detailed account in a lecture of Milgram's experiments concerned with obedience to authority, one student described Psychology as a pseudo-science, which he justified by saying, 'How could she [the lecturer] say that 100 per cent of us would have turned up the volts in that experiment? Some of us certainly wouldn't!' After an account of another experiment on the same lines involving nurses, and a further one involving psychiatrists, students concluded that all this showed was how stupid nurses were and how unscientific psychiatrists were; they did not comment on the absence of similar experiments from other branches of medicine. Both these disciplines fall far short of providing proper scientific Knowledge, ahistorical and apolitical factual and visible certainty, the universal nature of which can be checked on one's own person. This understanding may have been further prompted by the habit of lecturers in both subjects of identifying their sources by name and date; it may even be that their handwritten overheads (rather than the typed sheets used by those of other departments) lent some further force to this view; and, of course, there were no photographic slides. It may also be relevant that the opposite method to medical students' confirmation of taught Knowledge by their personal bodily experience is used to teach Psychology and Sociology students: such students are encouraged to use their own personal psychological and sociological experience to inform their understanding of what they read, and to convert their personal experience to more general written knowledge.

At any rate, these lecturers' absent medical Status meant that their lay accounts of diseases were mocked, while some students were outraged that they might be trying to assume medical Status; their comparisons of medical students with other groups in subordinate positions were utterly dismissed. But mostly, in another example of the concretisation of thought, these lecturers were held to embody the qualities attributed to their different disciplines. So a Sociology lecturer was described as opinionated (and consequently egocentric) and politically minded, and 'relishing talking about the "proletarianisation" of medicine'. His appearance with an open shirt and a beard, no different from some natural science lecturers', was good hard evidence that his politics were left-wing.

Statistics is above all the subject disliked by students. At first sight, this is perhaps surprising, as it cannot be considered remotely unscientific; indeed Ziman (1991: 13); holds that the language of mathematics is the ultimate step in formalising a language. Nor can Statistics be easily held to be woolly, political, dated or a matter of personal opinion. The usual reasons for dislike are generally held to be located in the person of the lecturer (and it is no doubt difficult to lecture in Statistics to non-mathematicians): he was said to be boring, uninteresting, bad at explaining, not making it relevant, liking numbers [and therefore not liking people], and so on. Again this is a concrete personalised reflection of students' views of the subject itself. But students' dislike of Statistics may also be understood in terms both of its uncertainty and its conceptual nature.

For Statistics is centrally concerned with probability and degrees of certainty, in terms of the confidence attachable to a statement; uncertainty, not the certainty attributed to proper Knowledge, distinguishes it. Again, it is a conceptual subject, dealing not with qualitative physical aspects of individuals, but quantitative attributed aspects of numerical populations; there are few facts to learn (being a method, it has no findings anyway), there are no pictures (only similar diagrams of the Gaussian curve of normal distribution occurred frequently and repetitively) and there are no obvious associations to make in the visible world. There is therefore no chance of individual students' being able to check, memorise or integrate this subject by application to themselves; whereas even the findings of Psychology can be tested out by and on individual students and found wanting. As I have indicated above, there is greater uncertainty involved in the exam, making Co-operative revision impossible. Statistics may also break up a more general sense of Co-operation, as when a lecturer asked how many students present had had a **pneumothorax**, indicating that in two hundred there should be three or so. Statistics, therefore, is not only without medical Status, Knowledge, Experience and Responsibility, but also acts against the disposition of Co-operation.

Different Languages for Different Academic Worlds

In view of what I have written about the scientific languages that students learn, the vocabularies of these three subjects call for comment. Psychology and Sociology, taught after natural sciences in the second preclinical year, use some words without material referents (like 'society', 'socio-economic' and 'rationality', for example). They also use words that have material referents in the natural sciences (like **structure, function** and **relations**); such words have not uncommonly been extracted from their prior use in the natural sciences for use in the social sciences. The consequence for medical students of having to learn words that have material referents in the natural sciences and conceptual meanings in the social sciences is ambiguity – an ambiguity not experienced either by specialist Sociology or Anatomy students; only medical students have to learn to use the vocabularies of both these disciplines. It is therefore perhaps not surprising that, faced with the languages of widely different disciplines, they find the earlier learnt languages of natural science with their material referents much more compelling than those of social science. It is presumably a consequence of the strength of the materially referent meaning of the word **relation** that, in medical language, members of a patient's family are never referred to as 'relations', but always as **relatives** (shortened, backstage, to **rellies**). In addition to the other factors at work to maintain students' general dislike of these two subjects, both the non-referential and the ambiguous nature of the vocabulary may contribute to it. It is also worth noting that the materially referent languages of natural sciences (like Anatomy) are, quite unusually in English, made up of many words derived from Greek and Latin. One of the strengths of English is its range of words derived from classical languages, which are often used as a 'meta-language' for abstract concepts (like the words 'meta-language', 'abstract' and 'concept' themselves); this linguistic strength of English, which allows a parallel, conceptual discourse on material events, may therefore be denied to medical students.

In Statistics, this linguistic feature is even more striking; the non-mathematical language that is used does not have new words with either material or conceptual referents. On the contrary, most are lay words (like 'standard', 'error' and 'distribution') with highly specialised and complex theoretical mathematical meanings; while it was these specific words that were mocked in the Rag Mag (see Chapter 5), nearly all statistical terms have perfectly common lay usages (even though they may have re-entered lay language from the scientific language of Statistics). The linguistic situation in Statistics is therefore the reverse of that found in Anatomy, which has new scientific words relating to things that are found in individuals and that are palpably real; Statistics has scientific meanings for lay words, relating to numerical concepts about groups. As I noted above, Statistics is a profoundly non-medical discipline.

Chapter 7

Strange Meeting: The Dissecting Room

> Yet also there encumbered sleepers groaned,
> Too fast in thought or death to be bestirred.
> Then, as I probed them, one sprang up, and stared.
>
> Wilfred Owen

At the same time as preclinical students are plunged into the settings of unofficial Co-operation and official Knowledge, they also meet in an entirely different setting: the Dissecting Room (the DR). I have pointed out the fundamental importance of anatomy historically in forming the original material base for the cognitive exclusiveness of the profession. And indeed, dissection is still widely seen as the most significant aspect of medical students' segregation from the lay world and aggregation to the medical one. The UCLMS Anatomy department was fed up with being asked by television companies if they could film there, as part of almost any documentary relating to medical training. And for one medically qualified anatomy demonstrator, the relatively recent introduction into the DR of students from other disciplines (such as Physiotherapy) was most upsetting, and indeed almost sacrilegious.

Dissection is anticipated by students long before they get to the DR, as was shown by the questions put by sixth-formers at the Open Day and is emphasised by other ethnographers of the DR (see Hafferty 1991: 53–77; Lella and Pawluch 1988: 128). Indeed, the problems some students may encounter in the DR are also mentioned as creating a way of getting into medical school at the last minute: 'Try telephoning round the deans' offices about 4–5 days after the October term has commenced. By this time, some new students will have already dropped out of the course. Perhaps, because of psychological reasons, they could not face up to the dissection of the cadaver' (Westall 1987: 45–6). But it is not just with a view to surviving a process referred to by doctors and observers alike as a 'rite of passage' that students approach the DR; it also provides them with a place where they can actually do something 'hands-on', however irrelevant this is to most medical practice. The confidential GMC 'Survey of Medical Education Practices' showed that, in 20 of the 25 UK medical schools, students still dissected the whole body, and that more than half the curricular time allocated to Anatomy was spent in 'laboratory or practical work' (GMC 1992b: 11). Despite the large variation in time spent on Anatomy between medical schools, and despite the general reduction in time spent preclinically on practical work, dissection remains an important part of many medical schools' preclinical curriculum.

For all these reasons, the DR has attracted considerable interest, reflecting researchers' various approaches. Becker (1961: 56 n 5), for example, treats students' experience of dissection as they reported it to him, very much as a matter-of-fact business. More recently, Hafferty's *Into The Valley* (1991) contains a fuller discussion of the DR as part of students' exposure to death, criticising Becker's acceptance at face value of what students told him and drawing out some of the gendered emotions present among students. There are also several psychological studies of students' reaction to the experience of dissection (for example, Druce and Johnson 1994) and accounts of the personal importance of dissection (for example, Hellman 1991: 114–23; Ballard's *The Kindness of Women* contains a powerful description of dissection and the concurrent 'scientising' of his girlfriend's body (1991: 77–98)). In nearly all these works, two themes stand out: these are the perhaps rather obvious ones of the variably human nature of the bodies dissected and the tendency of students to see the dead body as their 'first patient'. Though these themes are also present in my account, I am more concerned with the empirical discovery of all the professional dispositions in practice and describing certain features associated with these dispositions.

The DR: Appearance and Organisation

The DR is entered through swing doors; it is light and cool (it was previously the UCH canteen, and bodies are prepared in what were the kitchens). At the entrance, to the left, is a washing area, with a stainless steel trough running round the walls; the taps are pushed on and off with the elbows (as outside operating theatres; here there are also similar scrubbing-brush dispensers). Beyond that is the 'playpen', where students can sit and look at video-computers, its name indicating the inferiority of Knowledge gained there to the Experience and Responsibility gained at the 'tables' on which the bodies lie; this designation also anticipates and recalls the 'table' in an operating theatre.

Tables are arranged within the room at some distance from each other, parallel to the walls. Though some tables are therefore at right angles to others, others are in lines, lines that are irresistibly reminiscent of the lines of beds in a hospital ward; and all tables have a smaller adjustable one-legged table, identical to those over hospital beds. Within the DR, there are skeletons and manikins painted to demonstrate **dermatomes** and **nerve root supplies**, while anatomical pictures and shelves with 'pots' containing anatomical specimens line the walls. There are also closed-circuit television monitors throughout the room; often at the start of a session, an anatomy demonstrator gave an explanatory commentary on the televised images of what students should be looking for during the day's dissection. This televised demonstration with an uninflected spoken account (in effect an impromptu lecture) no doubt also normalises what still has the power to alarm. The day-to-day running of the DR is the responsibility of the two male technicians, while the demonstrators who teach and examine students are both men and women. Some demonstrators are from the Anatomy and Physiotherapy Departments (whom I shall call Dems) but about half the demonstrators are medically qualified (MDems); this distinction is not made explicit either by staff or students, but I shall show it to be important.

Students have to wear a white coat in the DR; with the decrease in practical exercises of all kinds, particularly in laboratories, dissection is by some margin the main occasion for wearing this distinguishing uniform of the scientist and the doctor. Before going into the DR, students must change, hanging up their everyday coats in the locker where their white coats are kept. Coats may be personalised, some with names written or appliquéed on the back, or a skull and crossbones drawn in biro, demonstrating the mixture of official and unofficial, of front- and backstage, that characterises the DR and that I discuss in more detail below. Name badges have also recently been made mandatory because of thefts of electronic equipment from the DR (this also helps the technicians and demonstrators, who try hard to get to know students individually, which is difficult now because of their large numbers). Bags are not allowed in the dissecting room, for the same reason. There are also spoken rules about eating and drinking, which are adhered to (unlike the similar written rules in libraries). Gloves are available for dissection, but not mandatory. Students are under no other restrictions about what they wear in the DR, although those with long hair are advised to tuck it away.

Practising Dispositions: Operation and Symbolism

I have stressed the way that preclinical students are removed from general professional concerns; dissection brings students, quite unusually, into personal contact with doctors in a way not found elsewhere in the preclinical course. Some MDems are GPs and consultants, retired or near retirement; but there is also a tradition that junior doctors who are training to be surgeons may be demonstrators in the DR while they study for the first part (Primary Fellowship or Part I) of the specialist surgical qualification of FRCS, much of which is concerned with Anatomy – there were three such demonstrators during my attendance. While these doctors may teach students what is clinically 'relevant' in Anatomy, their presence in the DR adds to the medical Status acquired by students there. These doctors talk not just about Anatomy but also in an informed way about medical life in general.

Students are allocated to alphabetically ordered groups (or 'official teams') of eight students or so, which are in turn allotted to one table (and therefore one body); the doubling of student numbers in the medical school means that two groups (A and B) share a table and a body, attending alternately at the two dissecting periods a week. The importance of the official team of the dissection group is stressed: in the notes given to each student, the first aim of teaching Anatomy by dissection is 'learning to interact and work as a team', and this aim is reinforced verbally, membership of a dissection group being exactly likened to work in other professional teams, 'like a research team or in hospital on a firm'.

In a short instruction given to a dissection group on the first day, Co-operation within that official team was emphasised and contrasted with Competition, the connection of dissection to medical practice was made explicit, and a common sort of remark about psychiatrists was made:

> The official team of students (to whom I had attached myself) were standing around their table, not sure what to do; they picked up the surgical instruments, read the printed sheets, and looked round the room to see what students at other tables were doing; one lifted a skin flap, others were pressing their fingers on the body, trying to identify **bony landmarks**. Dr Gordon, an MDem who knew my identity, approached the table and said briskly: 'Right, now you start to work as a team! All that competitive stuff you leave behind you with A-levels! All doctors work as a team, even psychiatrists! [*He looked at me and laughed*.] Yesterday I interacted with four other health professionals, for example. One of you reads . . . one of you cuts . . . one of you goes over to the skeleton and answers the questions on the sheet that another of you is looking at; and take it in turns!'

In saying this, Dr Gordon also drew attention to the difference between the written Knowledge of the dissection manual ('one of you reads') and the exercise of Responsibility ('one of you cuts') in the pursuit of Experience. The tensions between Knowledge and Experience are obvious.

Experience and its Difference from Knowledge

As was discussed in Chapter 3, vision is an important part of Experience, but other sensory experiences are also prominent. Although dissection itself is properly carried out with instruments, there are occasions when handling the body is necessary, and students are explicitly encouraged to feel their body. Students were told by a demonstrator, who had exposed the **parietal pleura**, 'Go on, feel it! Don't believe what I say, feel it! I want everyone here to feel it!', and, when an MDem had just asked a student a question, which she had answered correctly, he questioned the basis of her Knowledge by asking, 'How do you know [that]? You haven't felt it!' Vision may indeed be completely absent for the acquisition of Experience, as when students were told in turn to locate the as yet undissected **trachea**, which they could not see, by feeling how springy it was. But the touching and feeling of the body that demonstrators advocate is also practised by students for purposes quite unconnected with precise anatomical Experience, which are more related to an everyday familiarisation with the body's new tactile qualities: they pushed fingers into the lungs (now dissected out) as they were passed round the group; when the head was uncovered, they touched the cheeks, opened the eyelids, and fingered the ear-lobes; and as one male student folded the breasts back over the **thorax** at the end of the session, he gave them a push.

Anatomical dissection is performed in order to reveal the **structures** of the body; over and over again, students are told that they have to know what they are looking for in order to find it, emphasising the link between Knowledge and Experience. But all bodies are different from each other, and some **structures** may be better seen (that is, can be more easily defined, showing a more typical form and appearance) on some bodies than others; the emphasis is on a 'good' example or a 'good' specimen on or in a 'good' body; fat on a body is almost unequivocally 'bad'. Its amorphous substance has to be removed in order to reveal anatomical **structures**; during dissection, fat melts and is dispersed, making gloves slippery and getting on to coats and sometimes the face or hair. The DR staff comment that bodies are rejected for dissection on these grounds: 'We won't have *any* body here! There were some [bodies that we were sent] so fat that no one could have dissected them!' Students also comment on the fatness of 'their' bodies or those on other tables: 'They've got a really good body [on another table]; no fat at all. Their dissection looks as though they've been scraping away for hours!' Reference to the 'goodness' of specimens is also made in Neuroanatomy. A demonstrator had shown, on a video on the closed-circuit television, a 'good' specimen of the brain, where the **tectum** and the **pineal** could be demonstrated clearly. When he came to our table, he said: 'This [our brain] is a poor specimen, I'm afraid. Up till five years ago we used to have good specimens, fresh from the post-mortem room; we slipped them £5. Then *The Sunday Times* got hold of it and, because there was no permission from the **relatives**, it was stopped.' In official terms of Experience, then, good specimens are therefore standard ones, displaying the features described in the written accounts and pictures of Knowledge. But, in the anatomical reality of the flesh, things are different; things are not as they are shown in books or on slides, as demonstrators explain: 'These lungs are an example; you see in the books what they're supposed to be like, but on this body it's not the case. Maybe 20 per cent are variants, maybe more – go and look at other bodies and see.' Students sometimes have trouble identifying **structures** on their body because pictorial representations are so different from what they have in front of them. The difference was commented on when a dissection group was trying to identify an artery, and identification could only be made on the visible and removable presence of blood:

Saeeda [*joking*]: 'They [arteries] should be red [as they are shown in pictures]; these are all yellow, like nerves [in the pictures]!'

Rick [*who had been probing the area with forceps, holding up a small blood clot*]: No, there's some blood in this – look!'

I described in Chapter 6 how students learn to relate their Knowledge to themselves; in the DR, it is also related to others (to 'their' bodies and the skeletons and manikins around the room, as well as to their colleagues). But in the DR, unlike the lecture theatre, the demonstrator can insist on students checking such Knowledge on themselves. An MDem, holding a **bony pelvis** and orienting it to correspond with a student's, pointed out how the position of the **innominate bone** changed in relation to whether the student was sitting or standing, and said, 'That's your "sit-upon". Feel your own **ischial tuberosity**. Feel how the **gluteus maximus** [muscle] slides away when you sit down.' Sometimes, as in lectures, anatomical **structure** and **function** are projected on to the wider world, where objects are used for confirmation and memorisation. In this episode, an MDem was teaching students about the muscles of the arm:

Dr Jolly: 'The **biceps** is called "the waiter's muscle". When a waiter takes a cork out of a bottle, to a right-handed man, is that clockwise or anti-clockwise?' [*He looked at Mack.*]

Mack: 'Clockwise. No, anticlockwise.'

Dr Jolly [*ignoring Mack's incorrectly revised answer by asking another question*]: 'What does a wine-waiter do? He uses **biceps** to turn the corkscrew by **supinating** and to pull the cork by **flexion**. That's why we put screws in clockwise the way we do. So screws would go in a different way only if our **pronators** were more powerful than our **supinators** or we were left-handed, which we're not.'

Once again, these certain facts can be checked on one's own body. Just as the facts of Knowledge are certain, so the usually simultaneously visible and tactile aspects of the body have removed any doubt about the certainty of Experience (see Segal (1987), another ethnographer of the DR). Uncertainty for students is again mainly in terms of what they need to know (to pass exams) or are expected to know (and may therefore be asked about in exams). It should also be clear from the description of Experience so far that, quite unlike the predominantly literate disposition of Knowledge, Experience is mostly an oral disposition, where the correct pronunciation of words (the 'Club Spirit') is provided by MDems who look for it in students, though not with the insistence that is found on the wards. The oral language of Experience is just as precise and unambiguous as the written language of Knowledge, as Dr Gordon spelt out on the first day in the DR, also giving students their first taste of being put 'on the spot' by a question:

Dr Gordon: 'This [Anatomy] is a precise science. [*Looking at a student:*] What does 'love' mean? [*The student looked blank.*] You don't have to answer that; I'm not putting you on the spot. It means a thousand things. But if I say **the contents of the anterior mediastinum**, then everyone knows where I mean. [*Dr Gordon turned to look at me.*] Where did you train? Oxford?'

SS: 'And London.'

Dr Gordon: 'Well, London, India, Africa, **the anterior mediastinum** means the same thing – it's a precise language.'

The Practice of Other Dispositions in the DR

The professional disposition of Responsibility, with its combined elements of ownership and action, is also practised in the DR. As Hafferty and others have pointed out, naming the body is a time-honoured but unofficial act of groups of dissecting students; this both emphasises the previous personhood of the body and diminishes it, by making the body the personal property, that is the Responsibility, of the group. In the second session, discussion took place in the dissection group about what they should call the body ('She's an old woman . . . Mabel? Winifred?'), despite the fact that the still just legible hospital name-tag remained on her left wrist. The ownership of the body is often referred to in terms of 'our' body or parts of it ('Our heart's tiny compared to that one over there').

Students were told in the introductory lecture, 'Some thoughtful and generous people have left their body for you to learn anatomy', enabling them to 'learn to take responsibility for your actions, doing things that may frighten you so the next time you do something frightening, you won't be frightened; you'll have the edge on people who haven't done it – you'll be less anxious in other jobs.' This point was amplified in a conversation in the DR, when a Dem said to two students: 'What we teach is not just the Anatomy . . . [what else we teach is] for example, taking responsibility for someone who's dead, taking responsibility for their [your] own learning . . . I'm told by some of the [medically qualified] demonstrators that people aren't getting the [surgical] jobs if they haven't been to places where they can take this sort of responsibility, where they haven't done things [dissection].' Responsibility has other practical applications too; for example, in their second term, at the end of a Head and Neck dissection period, students were all told over the microphone, 'You are still responsible for taking care that the **thorax** and **abdomen** don't dry out and stay in reasonable condition till the summer.' Responsibility and Co-operation are then both closely linked to Status; in the DR, the official team has collective Responsibility, expressed in terms of both ownership and action, in dissecting 'their' body.

Dissection, the action of Responsibility in the mode of 'let's pretend', is usually carried out with surgical instruments; the second and third aims given in the notes are, 'proper use of surgical instruments; development of spatial skills essential for surgery'. Here another transformation takes place, from a lay to a medical (or more strictly, surgical) manner of using that everyday implement, a pair of scissors. Students were told, 'You may be used to holding scissors with your thumb and forefinger in the holes; we hold them like this, with the thumb and third finger, and the index finger guides the scissors. You might as well get used to using them properly.' Later, a student who had been dissecting, holding scissors like this, was told, 'Now you'll never hold them any other way!' Students are also shown a surgical way of using scissors for dissection, by opening rather than closing them, and of **blunt dissection**, using the back of a **scalpel** blade rather than its sharp edge.

It is dissection (rather than any other DR activities such as reading the dissection manual) that is seen as the main work of the DR; and dissection tends to be taken in turns. So, a student may say, laying down the **forceps** (no longer lay 'tweezers') and **scalpel**, 'I've done my bit', and another, 'I'm fed up with doing all the work!' While students sometimes talk about who dissects, the holder of **scalpel** and **forceps** may be left with them, despite offering them verbally and holding them out; possession of the instruments implies Responsibility. Indeed, anyone who hogs the instruments and won't let anyone else take a turn is criticised, although any student who has made it known that he wants to be a surgeon may be ceded more dissection time by his colleagues to develop these surgical skills. Any negotiation about dissection, whether verbal or not, presupposes what Hafferty (1991: 130–1) found, that dissection is very rarely carried out alone; the critical number of students that I found had to be present before dissection started was three. Visitors to the official team are usually welcomed, provided they obey the rules of membership. One male student belonging to group A came in on group B's day, causing considerable annoyance to at least one member of group B; the interloper took a pair of group B's gloves without asking, interrupted teaching by 'volunteering information' (see below), and showed off by demonstrating with **forceps** what he had learnt earlier in the week. Conversely, infrequent attenders are not criticised on the grounds of not helping with dissection. This is perhaps because there are eight students in each group, too many for all to be actively employed together; but a more important reason may be that, 'students who were not engaged in actual dissection and thus were physically situated outside the area of dissection activity reported a heightened sense of the cadaver as human and therefore more anxiety' (Hafferty 1991: 130).

Because of its previous humanity, many students hold their body in respect; the link is made between their attitude towards the dead body and that towards patients in the future. This Idealistic attitude decreases as the body is dissected and its human integrity dismantled. At the beginning of the term, students were also Idealistic towards dissection itself, and attendance in the DR was originally high. But, throughout the passage of the first term, students' attendance slowly dwindled. However keenly students started the year, determined to honour the body and learn from it as much as they could, as the summer term with its many assessments of Knowledge approaches, numbers in the DR (particularly, it seemed to me, of female students) dropped further, as students turned to their books to study for these written exams. Hafferty, finding a similar reduction in attendance, can relate it only partly to his concept of the body seen as an ambiguous, and therefore upsetting, human referent (1991: 145ff.). His students, though, cited other reasons: the quality of their body (principally how fat it was), the quality of the demonstrators and the nature of the dissection group, as well as finding learning from books more useful – these reasons strongly suggest that the disposition of Economy had triumphed in the DR as well as elsewhere in the preclinical years.

Dissection confers medical Status on students. The body is therefore seen as the reciprocal element in the relationship involved in the disposition of Status, that of patient. Students' families also become associated with such Status. Despite what students were told in the lecture preceding the first dissection period, that all the bodies had been donated, in a conversation in the DR immediately afterwards, Farouk asked: 'Where do they come from? Are they all vagrants?', to which Rick replied, 'Yes.' They were both surprised when Jane said, 'Not all; my mother's given her body to science.' Farouk then asked in horrified tones, 'How *can* she. . . ?' Most of these students showed a similar reaction to the violently negative response Hafferty found given to 'The Question' (whether students would consider leaving their own body for dissection). This finding leads in two interesting directions, back to the family and on to medical life. Students are emphasising the entirely different Status of themselves (and, by association, their families) and their bodies (their first patients), a difference reflected in the stories about students finding they are dissecting a relative, Hafferty's fourth DR story type (1991: 58); the version of the story I heard in the DR was that a Canadian student had found he was dissecting his grandfather. The DR staff also, in effect, lend credence to this form of story and give medical Status to students' families; one said to me, 'The main rule is that they don't find themselves dissecting a **relative**.'

An Unusual Aspect of Dissection: The Body as Food

The DR is well ventilated and, on walking in, it has only a vague, but nevertheless distinctive, smell. Bodies are preserved with a mixture of glycerol, methyl alcohol and formalin; brains are kept in dilute formalin. The distinctive smell of the DR is often commented on by students (though sometimes this is only to point out how mild it is). But, especially after the team has been dissecting for a while, their manipulation of the body, by handling tissues and dispersing fat, and their closeness to it, makes them more aware of the smell: 'It only hits you after a bit'; 'You get it on your hands'; 'It covers up what you were doing last night.'

And it is pervasive, this smell. During my attendance in the DR, my hands smelt of it after dissection, whether I had worn gloves or not. Sharp wafts of it suddenly appeared when I was far away from the DR, sometimes for no obvious reason, sometimes when eating food, notably meat or cheese (meat is obviously similar to the flesh of the body, and cheese no doubt related to its fat). This is an another example of the way that associations made between Knowledge or Experience and the wider world reverberate; the associations between the DR and food are made in the DR, but food encountered in the outside world evokes the DR, producing another element in the medical view of the world. Students also give expression to this unusual, non-anatomical aspect of the body, its similarity with food (no doubt connected with the similar DR stories that Hafferty mentions (1991: 58)). Such comparisons are often made, usually by male students: the body was likened to a piece of meat or tuna; with the yellow fat, to tuna mayonnaise; flakes of bone to almonds; blood clot to black pudding or liver; the brown preserving fluid to scrumpy [cider]. One male student suggested making a cocktail out of blood-stained fluid collecting in the **pleural cavity**, because it looked like tomato juice; he was ticked off by a female colleague for laughing and showing disrespect for the dead, but she smiled. While much of this can easily be attributed to a gendered attitude of an assumed familiarity and a desire to shock, there is a wider association. At first, students may say their appetite disappears in the DR and even imply they feel nauseated; after a few weeks, however, there is general agreement that attendance there promotes hunger. This notion is expressed even by women, as when Saeeda said, taking over the **scalpel** in her right hand and **forceps** in her left, and starting to remove the fat, 'I don't even eat meat!'; later she said, 'Let's see what the others have got up to with their knife and fork!' One female doctor I know said she had dreamt of eating the flesh of the bodies she was dissecting, another that she was conscious, during dissection itself, that eating it was a fantastic, though real, possibility. And there are also material associations with kitchens: plastic food containers for putting dissected material and brains in, rubbish bins with flip-lids for collecting unwanted dissected scraps, old-fashioned wood-handled dish mops used for dabbing preservative over the body and, to hold larger 'wet' specimens for Spot Tests, bakers' trays (stamped 'The Sole Property of Sunblest Bakeries Ltd. who will prosecute for the retention or unauthorised use of this container').

This strong association with food has an interesting theoretical application. As I have shown above, students categorise the body in terms of all professional dispositions. But this is not done in the way that I analysed Becker's students' categorisation of patients in Chapter 2; all bodies (though they are different, some being 'good' specimens, for example) are each categorised by each disposition (rather than psychiatric patients only being unCo-operative and providing no Experience, for example). All bodies are seen in terms of all dispositional categories and, while this was at first in a positive light, with time they are all categorised negatively. This can also be shown using Hafferty's more extensive material, just as I have sketched it out using mine: students no longer found that the Knowledge from books could be related to their dissection, preferring demonstrators' own dissections to learn from, and concluding later that books were better than the body (1991: 144, 145); Experience and Responsibility originally looked for in the DR were later disregarded, dissection finally being held Economically to be a complete waste of time (1991: 144–50, 84); the Idealism of respect for the body was lost to jocular and derogatory names (1991: 85–90) and the Idealism for dissection disappeared as the need for Economy in the use of time took precedence (1991: 145ff.); and, above all, students' violently negative answer to Hafferty's 'The Question' – 'Would you consider donating your body to a medical school to be used as a cadaver?' (1991: 122–6) – indicates the conclusively medical Status of students, now antithetically opposed to that of the body/patient. The dead body is therefore a polysemic symbol. Adding the 'appetitive' aspect of body as food introduces the second pole that Victor Turner (1967: 54) describes for central ritual symbols, the 'orectic' one. Despite the smaller amount of time spent on dissection and the decreasing importance attached to it, for the many students that attend the DR, their body has a central cultural and individual significance. If medical training took place in a totally closed society, with dissection compulsory (as it was until fairly recently), then this analytic line could have been pursued further. As this is no longer the case, the possibility shades into personal psychology, which, although fascinating, forms no part of my account.

And the notion of 'leaving one's body to science' is an odd one, really. No bodies dissected by students in the DR are going to increase general scientific or medical knowledge (though this may still happen as a result of post-mortem examination of patients, now rare); they are all the raw material from which personal Experience is quarried. The gift of one's body to a medical school may, however, be in exchange for treatment received or, perhaps as by Jane's mother, in exchange for the body that her daughter was herself dissecting – I know of another non-medical parent who decided to leave her body for dissection while her son was a preclinical student. This also begs the question of what the students who are given the body do in exchange; certainly these days, when students are hardly obliged to turn up at all in the DR, no resulting contract can be binding. But it may not be too fanciful to think that, in the past, for some students at any rate, the exchange following the gift was that, after taking the gifted body apart in their training, they would spend their lives putting others back together again.

Other Links with Clinical Methods: Question and Answer

I have indicated above similarities between the DR and both operating theatres and hospital wards; students also group themselves round the table as they will do round a patient's bed for ward rounds in their clinical years. But there are other features of the DR which are found elsewhere during the years of training, though they must be looked for among the mixture of dispositions and theatrical settings found in the DR. One of these is the form of teaching and assessment, referred to by Dr Gordon on the first day when he spoke of putting a student 'on the spot'.

Teaching and Assessment: Question and Answer Catechisms

Although there are some clinically relevant anatomical facts that all demonstrators teach, such as where in **relation** to a rib a **chest drain** is inserted, such facts are generally much better known by MDems, while Dems may say they don't understand some medical practice or even disagree with it. Clinical application of what preclinical students learn is eagerly sought by them in their pursuit of 'relevance', and this naturally means that MDems are more eagerly listened to (see Figure 15). MDems also demonstrate and teach in a way that is quite distinctive and is clearly the same as the method used to teach Experience on the wards, though this is unrecognised by these preclinical students, who have no clinical experience.

MDems nearly always stand during a demonstration, and students, copying them, do likewise, while Dems are much more likely to sit down and encourage students to do the same; one MDem, indicating by the direction of his glance a dissection group and a Dem all sitting round a table, said dismissively, 'What are they doing over there? Looks as though they're having a philosophical discussion!' When dissecting a group's body, it is typical for MDems to describe to the group what they are doing; they may also ask members of the group questions (as shown in several interchanges above) in a way that they will become very familiar with as clinical students, the Question and Answer series. The MDem asks the questions, affirming his Status and displaying students' ignorance (which, even now, may be felt as personal moral culpability).

Most Dems, on the other hand, demonstrate and explain without asking questions; if they do ask questions, these are not directed at individuals, and consequently no one is obliged to answer. The group is looser; students' attention is not held, and they may look around the room or even drift away. The straightforward exposition of fact by Dems can be interrupted by students in a way that would be highly unlikely if a MDem were in charge; in Neuroanatomy, where there are few (if any) MDems, students can interrupt Dems with impunity, as Josh did:

> A young Neuroanatomy Dem was holding a brain, demonstrating the anatomical **structures** to an official-purpose team of students.

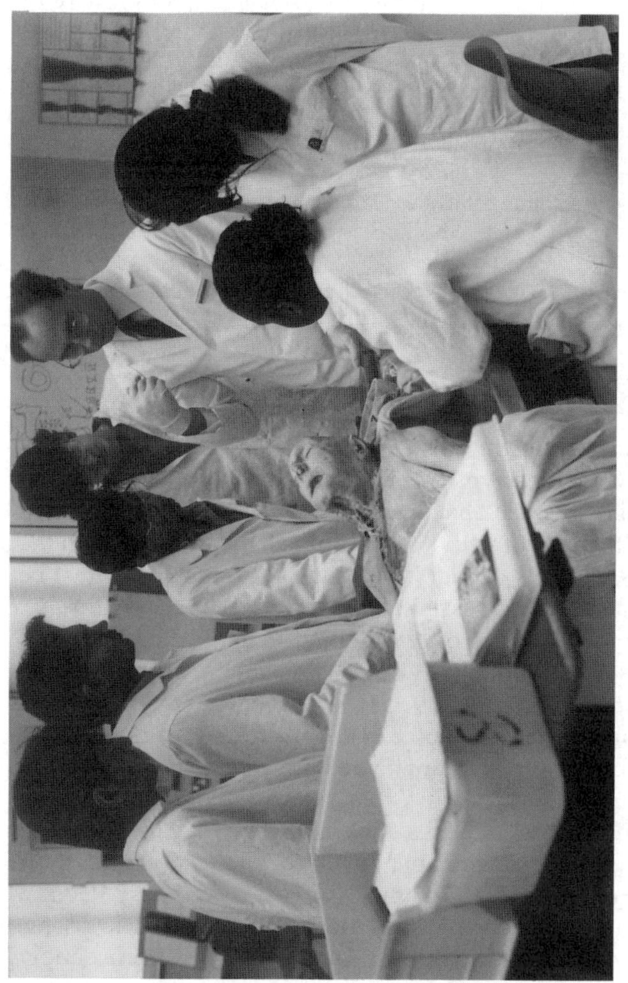

Figure 15. The Dissecting Room. An MDem teaching on the official frontstage; only one student is sitting. There is also only one white student in this group, which strongly suggests that this is an assortative official-purpose, rather than an official, team. [UCL/Loizos]

Dem: 'This is the **frontal area**, which is not well understood . . .'

Josh [*sarcastically, referring to the difficulty that students find with Neuroanatomy*]: 'You mean there are some areas which *are* well understood?'

Dem: '. . . controls personality and **higher functions** . . .'

Josh: 'Like pissing in women's handbags. [*Briefly turning to Dusty, another student, and saying with reference to a personal revelation made by him unofficially:*] That's the bit you're missing, Dusty, take a look at it!'

Dem [*carrying on through this*]: '. . . famous patients, like Phineas Gage, who had an iron bar through his **frontal lobes** . . .'

Josh [*also continuing*]: 'He [Dusty] pisses in handbags even with them!'

The rules of Question and Answer are sometimes explicitly spelt out by MDems. The questions are addressed to an individual student, who is obliged to answer, while no one else should do so: 'Don't answer unless you're being asked; it's much easier [to answer] when you aren't being asked the question. If you're being asked, it all flies out of your head, but that's the way it'll be in the exams.' These exams cannot be preclinical exams; they must be either clinical exams or, possibly, his own Primary Fellowship *viva*. The relation of this form of questioning to clinical practice was also made clear by another MDem: 'Come on, I'm putting you on the spot. You have to make a decision. That's what medicine is all about, making decisions – you can't hang around! And this is the way it's going to be in an exam if you have a *viva* – it'll just be you and me though.'

When students ask MDems questions, they may be answered straightforwardly or, to their surprise, they may find their questions reversed. Cathy, who had just asked an MDem a question, was affronted to be asked the same question back, saying, 'Hey, that's not fair! I asked *you* the question!' The MDem simply replied, 'And now I'm asking you!' Cathy had no further response, but she had learnt another of the rules of Question and Answer, which itself (with its methods of controlling students' speech by interrupting, challenging and ignoring their utterances, and its central use of direct declarations of fact) appears to be a culturally masculine form of verbal interaction. Some of the cultural features of male, as opposed to female, communication that Maltz and Borker (1982) have identified would indicate this: men see questions as requests for information, while women use them to maintain the conversation; men shift abruptly between topics, while women look for continuity; men may ignore previous comments, while women look for their acknowledgement; and men may use overt aggression to organise the conversation, while women interpret this as personally-directed hostility. For these reasons, it seems likely that women students will find the form of spoken interaction of the Question and Answer series so often directed by men much harder to come to terms with, both in the DR and later on ward rounds, than men.

If the MDem has gone round the group with the same question and not got a correct answer, or if he judges the question too hard (perhaps having asked a question he might expect to be asked himself in his Primary Fellowship *viva*), he will answer it himself and follow up with another question, sometimes preceded by a brief explanation. MDems may also make comments on the inadvisability of 'volunteering information'; this implies giving a fuller answer than the question demands, adding statements that are not in answer to a question, or answering a question that another student has been asked. Volunteering information contravenes the conventional Question and Answer series, where questions are put by those of higher medical Status to students they specify (often by simply looking at a student), usually by going round the members of the group in turn, but sometimes picking on a student who is hanging back from the group or trying to avoid the demonstrator's eye. Volunteering information also leaves the student vulnerable to loss of face if the information is wrong or to being asked further questions until he doesn't know the answer. By the method of teaching by Question and Answer, then, Co-operation within official teams is promoted on the official frontstage and, with it, enforced Competition. Within the student team, volunteering information can easily be construed by other students as evidence either of culturally disapproved-of Competitive keenness by currying favour or of Idealism; it is safer to remain silent, unexposed and in line.

Question and Answer series with the full clinical rules are still sometimes to be found in the DR on ordinary days, but they also survive in the official *viva*, now referred to as an 'oral quiz' of official teams, for which grades are given only to check that students are not falling behind; official marks are only given for written MCQs and Short Answers, and Spot Tests. Students find *viva*s unfair, though the unfairness may work to their advantage: Rick was given a B because the examining demonstrator could not remember him getting any answers wrong (even though he was asked only one question); Andy was disgusted with a C, as it was generally agreed within the team that he know more than Rick. But Question and Answer series are much less evident than they were twenty years ago; the DR staff recalled the intense anxiety preclinical students showed before *viva*s, some even vomiting and fainting. Such levels of anxiety are now only found before clinical Finals, at the end of the three clinical years, when the same method of assessment, by oral Question and Answer, is used.

Question and Answer: A Socratic Method?

Talking about *viva*s, Dr Gordon told me: 'The Socratic method is very useful, both for teaching and for finding out what they [the students] don't know.' Other writers also call this method of teaching by questioning Socratic, no doubt following medical practice; Becker, for example, uses this adjective to describe teaching both in the DR and on the wards (1961: 64, 277). I consider that it is quite mistaken to call this method Socratic, unless a revisionist view of the Socratic method (see, for example, Vickers 1988: 83–147) is held by doctors, and this I judge unlikely. For Socrates' method of questioning was usually based on an agreed and explicit ignorance (*agnoia*) of the subject under discussion on the part of both Socrates and his interlocutors, even though Socrates' own professed ignorance was sometimes considered to be falsely assumed (*eironeia*) and has therefore come to be called 'Socratic ignorance' or 'Socratic irony'. In the DR and on the wards where this method of teaching is commonly found, on the other hand, there is no doubt that the questioner knows the answer (which is certainly one of the reasons that he is asking that question), and students are being tested on their possession of it. As is made clear by the biochemical metaphor of 'learning by **osmosis**', usually used in the clinical context of Experience but occasionally heard in the DR, teachers are held to possess medical knowledge of all sorts in **higher concentrations** than students do; this **difference in concentration** will lead to a **passive diffusion** of such knowledge through the **semi-permeable membrane** surrounding the student's brain. In fact, there is a link (not made by Becker, despite his identification of the same method in the DR and on the wards) between these two different settings; in both, the predominant disposition that is taught is Experience, and this oral catechism is the historical form of teaching and assessing Experience.

The similarities between the Anatomy Spot Test for preclinical students and clinical Short Cases are occasionally very striking. Preclinical students are not allowed to touch the numbered anatomical specimens that they have to identify; they hold their hands together behind their back or in front of them, while looking at these specimens from all angles, just as clinical students do when told to 'inspect' patients before examining them in any other way. And, on one occasion, after all the students had done the Spot Test, one senior MDem, a surgeon, asked a junior MDem who was studying for Primary Fellowship, 'Do you want to go round?' (that is, round the anatomical specimens, as if seeing patients on a ward round), as a rehearsal for the *viva* of that exam.

A Strange Mixture of Stages

Hafferty's statement that, 'Lab [the DR] is a very public place, where one's mistakes and successes, strengths and weaknesses, are constantly on stage' (1991: 129) is certainly the case, but needs further comment in relation to my analysis of the theatrical stages found in the institution. In summary, while the DR as an official setting cannot stage the performances of unofficial frontstage teams, a most unusual mixture of the other three areas (official front- and backstage, and unofficial backstage) is to be found there. As a consequence of this, official teams are not necessarily held to (except for *viva*s), and official-purpose teams may take their place. The mixture of areas also leads to a similar mixture of roles, which depend on the particular audience present.

The Unofficial Backstage

As well as asking MDems for help, students may talk to them about medical practice and difficulties associated with it (in terms of extra work beyond contracted hours, the effects of the NHS reforms and administrators' intransigent incomprehension of medical practice, for example) in ways that could be heard in any Doctors' Mess in the country. Students also ask about matters of more immediate concern: their future years as students. An MDem had been asked whether there would be a lot of spare time on the clinical course. Her answer, in clinical language, gave the standard professional (or more strictly in her case, surgical) version of Psychiatry and psychiatric patients, as well as a common version of the professional need to be found 'safe' in professional exams:

> Yes, you do have quite a lot of time in the clinical course; it depends what you're doing . . . Psychiatry was a total waste of time as far as I was concerned; I didn't do any work. In Finals [the Final clinical exams], I was told I needn't examine the patient [physically]. My heart sank; it was a psyche [psychiatric] patient! I muddled through somehow . . . [*She went on to talk more about the Final clinical exams, now five years away from these first-year preclinical students.*] What they [the examiners] really want to be sure is that you're not dangerous. Someone in our year had a surgical patient and was asked about a patient **post-op** with **difficulty in breathing**. What they wanted him to say was that you should remove the stitches from his neck; they tried for about half an hour, but he didn't say it and he failed. He said it was terribly unfair, but it wasn't. He said he hadn't seen a patient with **thyroid surgery**; but that was his fault. Why do they have **stitch-cutters** by the bed? It's something you have to know if you're a House Surgeon.

Now I heard an identical horror story just before my own clinical Finals; it is possible that this had indeed happened recently to the story-teller, though I consider this is unlikely for two reasons: first, on the grounds that it is a well-known 'horror story'; and, second, given this, that (even if the examinee had really been asked this question), the knowledge of this story would have made it likely that he could have answered the examiners' question correctly. So, along with the range of DR stories about dissection, other medical morality stories are told and retold in the DR. This horror story tells of the importance the examiners in Finals attach to candidates showing they are 'not dangerous' (or, in other words, that they are 'safe' and have achieved a basic level of professional competence) and to the fact that in Finals, quite unlike the exams testing Knowledge, there are indeed 'pass or fail' questions.

It is, I suppose, also just possible that the Dem who told me that he had seen people skipping with a length of **small intestine** had indeed done so, though again I doubt it. The point about such stories, however, is not their veracity but, as Hafferty shows, that they create camaraderie by allusions to insiders and outsiders (whether the latter are non-medical people or naive students) and, while they demonstrate the emotional imperviousness expected of students as a consequence of their experience in the DR, within the DR itself 'a shocked emotional response by medical students is portrayed as both reasonable and appropriate' (Hafferty 1991: 58). Such an emotional response is possible because of the rather surprising existence in the DR of the unofficial backstage, as well as the two official stages.

The Different Roles Students Play in the DR

During a dissection session, although students may glance round the room, wander off to another table or move over to the shelves to examine the specimens, they mostly stand or sit around their table looking in and down at the body. By forming an inward-facing circle either round the table or just by themselves, it is possible to exclude other students, and even demonstrators, who cannot reasonably push or elbow their way into such a group; I saw a Professor deliberately excluded in this way by a group of students. Stray students who stand close to such a dissection group, but without forming part of it, may be met by one of the group's turning round with an automatic disapproving and exclusive look. This reaction, I suggest, is connected inversely to the anxiety Hafferty describes (see above) of those outside the active dissection group; for those inside, the self-evident activity of dissection provides the focus, while, for those outside, the whole inner group (including the body on the table) is a performance in which they are not now actually involved and which they are apparently only observing.

Such groupings round the table, while homologous with the configuration of ward rounds (the official frontstage of the clinical years), may or may not form an official frontstage; they most obviously do in *vivas*, when there is a demonstrator using the Question and Answer series and the body on the table constitutes a similar focus to the patient on the bed during ward rounds (see Figure 15). In the absence of a superordinate acting in this mode, the theatrical setting remains but students' activities are no longer constrained. In other words, at any time within the DR, both official and unofficial backstage may be found, as well as the official frontstage. In the DR, owing to the absence of sentient patients, it is possible to take different roles in the same setting and to practise practising them. So one group of students may take entirely unofficial backstage roles in their circle, talking, for example, about what happened the previous night, or about a recent sporting fixture. There may be shouts of laughter from another table where there is no demonstrator (see Figure 16), or where a demonstrator may be taking an official backstage role. But at a third, the presence of a particular demonstrator means that the students there maintain an official frontstage demeanour.

Students in the DR therefore do not have to maintain the front of professional Idealism towards the acquisition of Experience that is engendered among clinical students on ward rounds. They may use their instruments in quite improper ways: Elliot hurling his **scalpel** into the **thoracic cavity**, exclaiming disgustedly, 'Fuck! I don't understand *any* of this!'; Josh, the second-year student doing Neuroanatomy, having asked the other members of the official-purpose team questions about the location of various **structures** in the brain placed before them, finally asking, in frustration, 'And where's the G spot? *There* it is!', plunging his closed **forceps** into the **soft tissue** of the brain. Equally, horseplay, confined in the clinical years to unofficial backstage settings such as the bar and the canteen, is to be found in the DR: when one member of an official-purpose team, in white coat, approached another from behind, saying, as he placed his left hand on the other's back and pushed his head down, 'Right now, this won't hurt if you bend over!', his straight gloved right index finger clearly suggested that he was about to perform a mock **rectal examination** on his friend. And the proper pronunciation of medical words may be mocked too: as two first-year students looked through the Anatomy textbook, one said, 'God, do we have to learn all this?', while the other read out loud from it, deliberately mispronouncing even simple words, saying 'bon-ay' for 'bone'.

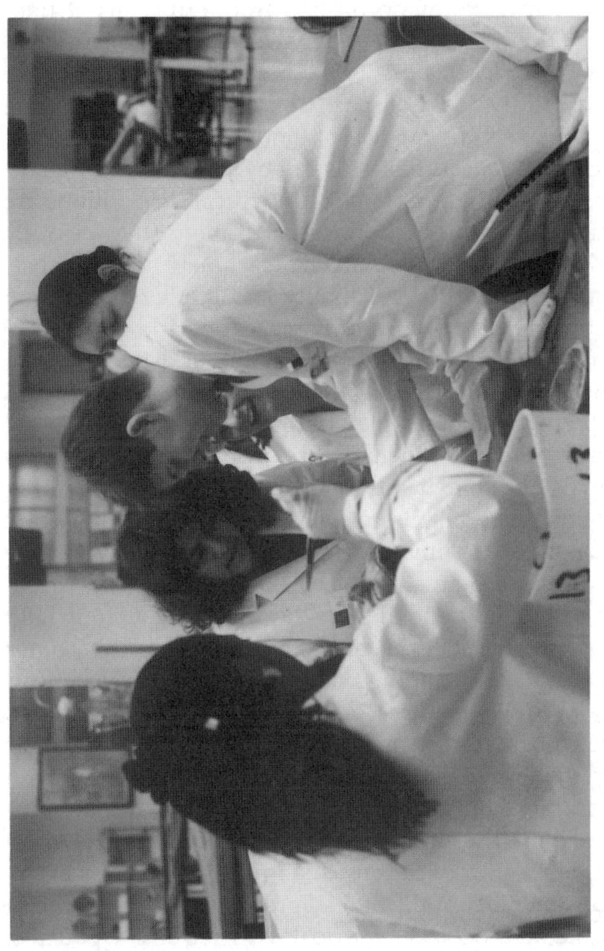

Figure 16. The Dissecting Room: a dissection group without a demonstrator. Students' facial expressions indicate the way that the DR may also provide official and unofficial backstages in addition to the official frontstage shown in Figure 15. Note also how the student sitting bottom right and reading the dissection manual is excluded from the group, showing aspects of the difference between Experience and Knowledge. [UCL/Loizos]

Learning Emotional Attitudes

Hafferty describes gender-stereotyping in the DR on the basis of attribution of emotion; men reacted both positively and negatively to the presence of women, who were said to be more emotional than men. Women were thus protected from criticisms of their emotionality and found themselves 'between a normative rock and a paternalistic hard place' (1991: 140). The demonstrators (whose gender Hafferty oddly does not specify – it seems likely they were not all men) were seen as models of emotional detachment, an attitude not taught but nevertheless learnt by students. Now I have shown that historically all professional medical dispositions are male; the emotional attitudes connected to them (the scientific objectivity of Knowledge, the emotional detachment of Experience, the mature judgement of Responsibility and the harsh cohesion of Co-operation) are also all culturally masculine and opposed to stereotyped female emotion. But the emotional aspects of dispositions can, of course, be learnt by and from women, and practised by them, just as men may find them repugnant.

The final point to make, then, is that, in the varied theatrical settings of the DR, both men and women can practise expressing different emotions. Overall, dissection is held, along the lines of it as a rite of passage, as something to be endured, leaving one stronger and of surer Status. This is evident in students' great interest in who might faint on the first day and the generally held view that after two weeks everyone settles down, and becomes familiar with their body, leaning an elbow on the covered head when looking in to see the dissection of the **thorax**, for example. Equally, those who do not attend the DR are not criticised by their colleagues on the grounds of withholding Co-operation or even missing out on the acquisition of Experience itself, but because they will not acquire the emotional detachment linked to Experience, with its clinical implications. As a regular attender in the DR said about a member of the official group who rarely came: 'I don't understand her. She says she'll do it when it's on live patients, not dead ones, and she'll learn it [Anatomy] all from books. But if they don't do any hands-on stuff, how are they going to cope? If there's blood all over the floor, what'll she do then?'

Despite the emotional detachment learnt in the DR, emotional detachment itself is by no means an unbroken rule there, especially when what Hafferty (1991: 90–5) calls 'the anxiety-provoking human referents' of the body re-emerge, as they did on the first day of the dissection of the Head and Neck. A dissection group had, together, without words being spoken, removed first the formalin-sodden cloth and then the plastic bag covering the head of the body; with the head revealed, they all spoke together: 'That's really freaky!'; 'She's got bristles!'; 'I thought she was a woman!'; 'She is, she's got boobs!' (and the student who said this raised the plastic cover over the body's chest, before saying, 'She hasn't changed sex!'). The students then lifted the head on to a wooden block; they found this surprisingly difficult because the heaviness of the head and its connection to the rest of the body meant that the shoulders too had to be lifted (perhaps this was surprising because the new separate subject, verbally titled 'The Head and Neck', had led them to think they had separated the physical head and neck from the rest of the body too). With the head resting on the block like a pillow, students now spoke in turn:

Misha: 'It's gross! It's disgusting! Oh my God it's gross! I don't want to go anywhere near it!'
Brian: 'You're supposed to be reacting with scientific interest, not "It's gross!"'
Fred to SS: 'Now you know why medical students get sick!'
SS: 'Why?'
Fred: 'It's disturbing, isn't it!'
Misha [*who had moved a little away from the head, picking up a skull from the box of bones nearby and looking at it*]: 'That's someone's skull! It's really weird!'
Tony [*to Misha, clearly daring her to go further than just holding a skull*]: 'Go on, touch it [the head]!'
Misha: 'No way!'

It was certainly Misha, a woman, who expressed revulsion most strongly, but when the head was first revealed they all did; and Fred was prepared to say how disturbing he found it, though he did not (perhaps could not, having no vocabulary) say in what way. In other words, students in the DR can be both alarmed and blasé, practising varying degrees of detachment in front of varying audiences; this applies to women just as much to men, even though women may have to demonstrate more detachment than men in order for this to be fully accepted by their audience.

Chapter 8

Experience: Patients and Ward Rounds

> This is the lower sling swivel. And this
> Is the upper sling swivel, whose use you will see,
> When you are given your slings. And this is the piling swivel,
> Which in your case you have not got.
>
> Henry Reed

This chapter covers students' clinical training. While Knowledge continues to be taught in lectures and learnt as preclinically, the main emphasis for clinical students is on learning the disposition of Experience on the wards of the teaching hospital. This is a different world from the medical school, where, by the end of preclinical students' first day, they had learnt at least one route to their lecture theatre; their other destinations are fairly few and, though spread out, not that difficult to find, if only because large numbers of other students are also on their way there. Clinical students, in much smaller groups, now have to get to know the hospital, its different buildings, and the routes (with short-cuts and dead ends) above and below ground, to wards, to operating theatres, to Out-Patients, and to doctors' and departmental offices. The names of wards (Bedmakers' Ward, CCU [Coronary Care Unit], Jack Hambro, St Philip's Ward and so on) are indicators of the hospital's history, not of their whereabouts. Finding the way, at first, is difficult and based on a known entry (an outside door, the start of a tunnel) to the three-dimensional maze; some students find quicker ways, demonstrating their greater familiarity with their new surroundings. Tunnels slope up and down, level stretches lined with beds, with broken chairs, old filing cabinets and wrecked photocopiers; insulated pipes and leashes of electric cable run the tunnels' length, appearing and disappearing behind panels. A pair of new fire doors give on to newly carpeted corridors, light modern offices and technical equipment, patients sitting in waiting-rooms; through a second set of fire doors, the concrete floor resumes, sloping round unknown masses, a painted yellow line misleading the new student to the kitchens, not to the lifts for the wards.

The wards themselves are all different; on some, the smells are obvious and commented on ('This [geriatric] ward smells worse than the Dissecting Room!'). Students find themselves among the regular staff of the hospital, nurses at their various levels indicated by uniforms, physiotherapists, phlebotomists, nursing auxiliaries, cleaners and porters. With the general loss of preclinical students' contact with student nurses because of the equal numbers of male and female students, even this slight potential for clinical students' being personally recognised is diminished. Nurses may be helpful to students if they have time; but by and large students feel themselves 'a spare part' in the functioning machinery of the hospital, which would carry on unchanged without them.

Clinical students are told that their dress should be 'professional and reasonably conservative'; their hands and fingernails should be clean, as should their short white coat. This emphasises their ambiguous official Status and makes them immediately recognisable; the rare failures of students to wear this institutional uniform are commented on. Its pockets are filled with equipment: a stethoscope (the mark for so long of the doctor, and often a parental present to mark a child's new Status) and sometimes an ophthalmoscope; the pocket-sized *Oxford Handbook of Clinical Medicine*, a note-pad and a pen; there may also be a tourniquet and other various items necessary for taking blood from patients. As in the DR, students learn not to take other possessions (coats, bags and so on) on to the wards; there's nowhere to put them, they're in the way, and they'll get stolen; but, most importantly, they are an encumbrance on the peripatetic ward round.

Official Teams: Firms, Consultants and Patients

For periods of six weeks, clinical students are attached in small groups, usually of six to eight, to different 'firms' (these groups do not have an official name, but they are, in my terms, official teams). Firms, the hierarchical groups of doctors trained or training in one specialty, are headed by consultants who give their names to the firm ('the Lloyd/Jenkins firm', for example). The consultants heading the firms in the teaching hospital were overwhelmingly men, the few women being in Geriatrics and Rheumatology (low-Status branches of Medicine, as I explain later in the chapter). The *UCLMS Clinical Course Student Handbook* states, 'The Consultant to whose team ("Firm") you are assigned is responsible for your teaching', though it is explained that students will also be taught by junior doctors on the firm, Senior Registrars (SRs), registrars and Senior House Officers (SHOs) and House Officers (housemen); it is also made clear that teaching will be 'necessarily interrupted' by emergencies and patients' needs. While interruptions do occur, teaching is much more commonly simply cancelled without notice; teaching Experience is less important than practising Responsibility.

The *Handbook* continues: 'The firm attachments [of Medicine and Surgery] are absolutely basic to clinical training, and provide the opportunity to learn to take [a] history [from] and examine patients.' Students see the patients of the firm's consultants: 'When a patient enters hospital, he or she is placed under the care of a Consultant, who is ultimately responsible for treatment.' So students acquire Experience by taking a history from and examining patients and writing their findings down (so 'clerking' them). These patients are described as 'under' a named consultant or, more commonly, as belonging to a consultant ('Dr Lloyd's patient'). Both terms indicate the ownership that forms one part of the disposition of Responsibility, and it is, of course, only doctors that 'have' patients to teach on. Most firms make it clear that as a general rule all patients coming into hospital under the firm's consultants should be clerked on admission and 'followed' during their stay by one of the attached students. In this way, students are delegated a hypothetical Responsibility for patients, frequently alluded to by doctors' asking the firm group, 'Who's got a patient for us to see?' or, if at the bed of a patient, 'Whose patient is this?' But the huge majority of students' clerkings do not form any part of the treatment that patients receive in hospital and are used solely for the purposes of teaching and assessing students; and it is overwhelmingly not students' written clerking but their oral presentation of clerkings that is used for these purposes. Real Responsibility is only exercised by students in two settings: in Casualty, when the firm is 'On Take' and admitting patients as emergencies, and, in their second clinical year, in Obstetrics.

The great majority of patients clerked by students are, therefore, in Atkinson's terms, 'cold' (that is, patients who no longer present an acute clinical problem and for whom treatment has already been started); they are used to recreate putative 'hot' situations where action (the other component of the disposition of Responsibility) may be discussed in terms of hypothetical Responsibility. Students on a firm are expected to be prepared for the typical teaching ward round by ensuring that all the patients are clerked and can be 'presented' to the doctor, and are therefore expected to Co-operate with each other in allocating such delegated Responsibility. At the end of each firm attachment, students are given a grade (from A to E), on the basis of their performance, both as regards turning up to firm activities (like ward rounds and Out-Patient clinics) and their possession of Experience (increasingly assessed in a sort of clinical exam or *viva* at the end of the firm). Students also know that by Co-operating they can become a 'good' firm, which is likely to give them all a better grade, but that their individual grades are considered when they apply Competitively for house jobs.

Patients

Students are apprehensive about their own new Status when seeing patients. As Roger put it:

> I've never talked to a *patient* before. It could be someone's grandmother or mother or wife . . . I should be able to take a history from them – I've got a book which tells me what questions to ask – but I don't know how to do it . . . I've never failed a test before and I feel I may fail this one . . . Everyone just says, 'You'll get used to it!'

And so they do, but their worry about facing patients is rather less than their worry about facing doctors. This is no doubt partly due to reports from students in the years above about the way doctors, and particularly consultants, may cause them embarrassment on ward rounds and in clinics (Moss and McManus 1992). But students' anxiety about encounters with senior doctors is also related to students' closer professional aggregation; intra-professional relationships are nearly always more important than those with clients (see Larson 1977: 187–9, 236). Bosk has, however, overstated the case when he writes of surgical training that, 'however lamentable the fact, the patient is an exogenous variable falling outside the system of social control' (1979: 25); patients are an integral part of the social control of training – without them, doctors would not exist, let alone consultants and firms.

The ambiguous Status of students as regards patients, as 'student-physicians' in Merton's phrase, is barely acknowledged officially; they are told that, 'Many of them [patients] will treat you in the same way they will a fully trained doctor.' But this is rarely the case and, on ward rounds, the idea that 'in the patient's eyes, you're a doctor' is untenable by anyone (see Atkinson 1981: 48). Ward rounds are by far the most frequent setting for clinical teaching, being therefore the typical official frontstage of the clinical years; students clerk patients on the official backstage, unsupervised by doctors. But even backstage, students themselves may experience discomfort in their ambiguous Status and regard seeing patients as involving 'a bit of a con-trick'. Their ambiguous Status may also lead to patients refusing to see them (and refusing Co-operation), as Peter described:

> Patients are very difficult to find and clerk properly; I had a run of five patients who weren't co-operative, which rather put me off . . . [On a ward round] the consultant asked me if I'd examined a patient. I said, 'No. She wouldn't let me.' He said, 'Well, I asked her today if she'd let me examine her and whether she'd mind if a student did and she said she wouldn't.' I couldn't say to him, 'Yes, but you're a consultant!' Anyway, he told me [on the ward round] to examine her and I did that, though she didn't look too pleased!

It is quite clear that whatever the student–patient relationship is like (and there is no doubt that a few students may strike up a close relationship with some of their patients), the doctor–student relationship is much more important. Students, for example, often find themselves proclaiming their ignorance of diagnosis or treatment to a patient, for fear of revealing something that they don't know whether the doctors want the patient to know or that they have been told not to reveal.

The Nature of Experience

Clerking Patients: History and Examination

Of the two elements of clerking, the history and the examination, the first is officially accorded great importance, students being told that in 60 per cent or 70 per cent of cases the diagnosis can be reached from the history alone. While students are occasionally told to ask a patient questions on a ward round, 'taking the history' is usually done on the official backstage, it being generally assumed that simply asking patients questions is within the student's own competence. Some questions are more 'open' than others, but many are questions that effectively have Yes or No answers. Lists of these questions are, as Roger said, often written in books, and referral to such lists may help students originally as they ask some of the more intrusive questions, such as those involved in 'taking a sexual history'.

Students convert the answers into a highly formalised narrative. This marks another transition for the student, in that he would have described any previous episode of illness (his own or a member of his family's, say) as patients do; he now develops the clinical narrative style. The history as 'given' by the student to the doctor is, in effect, a reconstruction of the patient's experience as if the patient were a doctor; the history starts with a short account of the patient's problem (known as the 'Presenting Complaint') and how the patient first 'presented' to the profession (usually to Casualty or to their GP). This is followed by a more detailed description from the point where the patient first noticed something wrong (the 'History of the Presenting Complaint'), and then goes back to the patient's earlier life, before the numerous closed questions of the 'Systems Review' to check the existence of any other symptoms; the clerking then continues with the physical examination. The important process of converting the patient's account of their illness to a medical narrative of disease has recently been described (see Hunter 1991: 51–68), and I shall not cover it further.

The Experience gained from the second part of the clerking, the physical examination, is even further removed from any previous experience the student may have had as a patient; the student learns privileged practical techniques to investigate someone else's physical state. Such medical Experience is quite different from any patient's own experience, which is usually given no voice at all, a point which was crystallised by an elderly patient:

> On a ward round, we had stopped around the bed of a man in his eighties, a retired professor who had been admitted after a **myocardial infarction** [a heart attack]. The SHO taking the round asked the patient

> if he minded her and the students talking about him and examining him; while he was saying he had no objections, his friend, who had been visiting him, made to leave in view of this. 'Don't go', the patient told his friend, 'And listen: it's very interesting. They treat you as if you're a body and not a soul!' At the end of the round, the doctor thanked the patient, who replied, 'Not at all; glad to have been of help.' He added, expanding on his comment before the round started, 'I'm sure I could arrange at short notice for you to have my body when I'm dead, if you like!'

Patients, then, are bodies, stripped of their social attributes (it was a probably a combination of the patient's age and high lay status and the doctor's youth, gender and low medical Status that kept the patient's friend by his bed). Little consideration is paid to explicit recognition of even observable social aspects of patients; the only possessions of a patient that might warrant mention are medical ones, like a **sputum pot** or a **Salbutamol inhaler**. As a preliminary to gaining Experience, patients also often have to be stripped more literally, as Peter implied, and students have to learn to negotiate with patients before examining them because of the frequent need for patients to undress. This is originally quite embarrassing enough for the student; later they learn the far more personally intrusive techniques involved in **rectal** or **vaginal examinations.**

Learning Experience from physical examination is a matter of learning to recognise what is there to be found, which (as in the DR) means knowing beforehand what you're looking for; this is sometimes put the other way round by doctors: 'If you don't know what you're looking for, it's much more difficult to find it.' Unlike history-taking, the techniques of examination are frequently taught (see Figure 17), and students are urged to practise them again and again, so as to learn to recognise abnormal 'signs' of disease from the normal. Gerry, a first-year clinical student, explained to me how this learning and teaching worked, referring to a recent demonstration by a consultant of the physical sign of **visible peristalsis**: 'At first you don't know what you're looking for. With that patient, for example, I saw a movement. Whether that was **visible peristalsis**, I don't know. Later, you see exactly the same as them [doctors].' Learning to see, hear and feel in this way is not always easy: the sounds of **heart murmurs**, for example, are notoriously hard for novices to identify. But here again, there is a prescribed formulaic series of techniques to be gone through, in the examination of the various 'systems' – the **cardiovascular system**, the **respiratory system** and so on; within the examination of each system, there is another sequence, that of **inspection, palpation, percussion and auscultation**, which involves, respectively, sight, sight + touch, sight + touch + hearing, sight + touch + hearing through a stethoscope. These four historical modes of examination, in which the predominance of sight is obvious but not exclusive, also implicitly involve the sequential use of students' own sensory modalities that they were taught about preclinically: they confirm their Neurophysiology lecturers' description of the 'information-processing' functions of the **central nervous system**, thus reinforcing this definition's limited approach to human sensitivity and its teleology.

Experience, being specialised information about someone else's body, is therefore (unlike communally available Knowledge) only available through the apprenticeship of medical training. Students were told, 'Don't listen to your own heart; it's confusing!' And so it is; students need to know how to hear the sounds and rhythm of other people's normal hearts so as to distinguish those of **heart failure**, for example. Like the information from the history, the information gained from physical examination is predominantly of a Yes or No sort; occasionally ambiguous results or 'soft' signs are mentioned, but usually findings are either present or absent. So students are told not to say, 'I think I can feel the liver', for example, but 'The liver is enlarged.' The former may be entirely true, but is more a reflection of the student's lack of Experience than of the patient's objective state; the latter statement indicates the student's confidence in his own capacity and, if wrong, it can be shown to be wrong by a doctor with more Experience. While the student may be uncertain about his own skill, there is no real doubt about the presence or absence of signs, even though students may be told that at their level they wouldn't be expected to 'get' a difficult sign.

The Ways that Experience Differs from Knowledge

The differences between Experience and Knowledge are again as found in the DR: Experience is personal, involving senses other than vision, taught orally, and gained not from occasional access to books or lectures but from regular access to patients. These

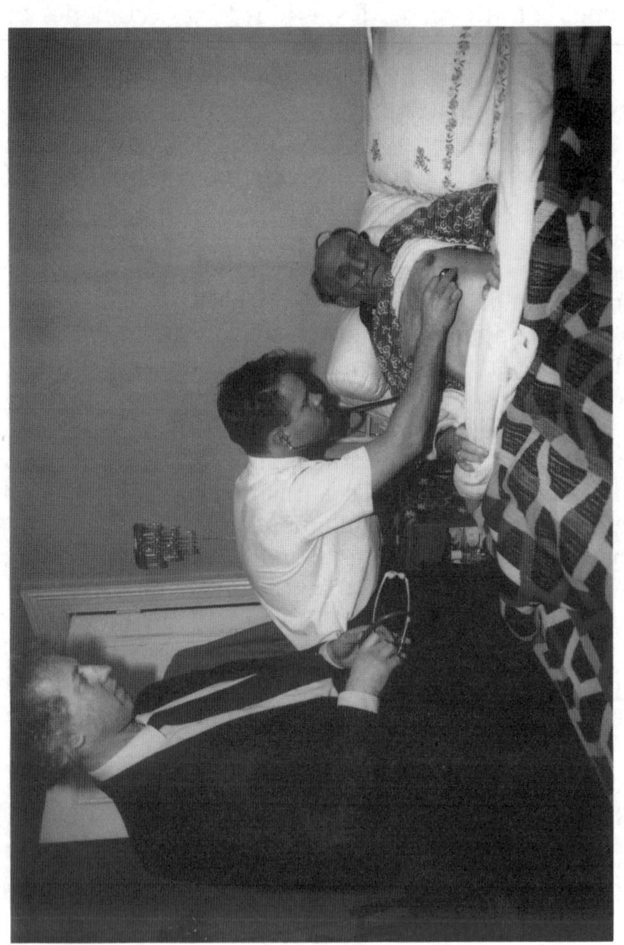

Figure 17. Experience: physical examination. An individual student learns the official body techniques of Experience under supervision; 'taking a history' is generally not supervised. (This photo was clearly taken at a patient's home, perhaps because of the novelty of such teaching there; UCL had no photographs of the same configuration of doctor, student and patient in the overwhelmingly more common setting of the hospital.) [UCL]

differences are often stated: 'You need to practise examining patients over and over again, so that when it comes to the real thing in the exam [*sic*], you know what you're doing and what comes next, and you're not trying to remember page 2 in the book!' Teachers also often mention the difference of clinical reality from written accounts, saying, 'The books don't describe this [physical sign] well' and 'You won't find this in the books!' But perhaps the most frequent way in which the difference is referred to is in the frequent use of the word 'classic' or 'classically' – in a rarely explicit gloss on the meaning of the word, an SR asked a student, 'Come on, what are the classic signs associated with **rheumatoid arthritis**? If you were going to write a book about it, what would you say?'

Knowledge is certified through Experience, students often being told to 'hang' what they know about a particular condition on to a named patient they have seen (as 'Remember Mr Leeming and you won't forget anything about **duodenal ulcers**') and, indeed, one student described each patient he saw as 'a tiny overhead [projection]'. Knowledge is also certified by 'good' clinical examples (as in, 'She gives a really good history of **acute pancreatitis**' or 'He's got a good chest [to examine]'). The force of 'good' here is 'good or typical example of' the symptoms or signs of a pathological condition; 'good' is to be contrasted with the adjective 'interesting', which implies atypical (that is, abnormally abnormal) symptoms and signs. Though not necessarily clinically relevant, such 'interesting' features might be the basis for a written paper in the disposition of Knowledge. The extreme forms of these different adjectives are 'beautiful' or 'wonderful' (from 'good') and 'fascinating' (from 'interesting').

Students learn, often originally to their dismay, that there is not always a commonly agreed way of gaining Experience, though there may be commonly acceptable ones within certain professional segments – a rheumatologist examines the hip joint in a different way from an orthopaedic surgeon. But even within professional segments, individual doctors also perform physical examinations in different ways, and may insist that students learn a particular method while on their firm. In the context of Experience, such personal methods may be thought of as 'quasi-normative' practices (using the same word as Bosk does to describe junior surgeons' transgressions of consultants' personal practice of Responsibility). The individual teachers' personal techniques demonstrate their art, encompassing accuracy, grace and Economy, and sometimes the authority of history too:

> The consultant Dr Atkins had been telling students how to **take the pulse**, describing it as a 'dying art'. He then said, 'This is how I **take the pulse**', using a student to demonstrate on. Dr Atkins held the student's right elbow with his left hand and felt the **brachial pulse**, while he felt the **radial pulse** at the student's wrist, which he held with his right hand in such a way that he could see the wristwatch on his left wrist. 'This is how I was taught by Professor [name indistinguishable]. This way you support the arm, feel the **brachial pulse** [in addition to the **radial pulse**] and can time it all at once.'

And, indeed, as Dr Atkins implied, there are strong suggestions that the personal arts of Experience may be disappearing. Given the personal method of transmission of these specific body techniques, they may easily be lost within a generation of teachers, and also, perhaps, 'deskill' doctors who now increasingly rely on technological results rather than personal findings. The current lack of attention paid to the traditional methods of examination may partly be because students' clinical exposure to patients is now less than it was (I. McManus *et al.* 1993: 941–4), but also because of the hugely increased use of all sorts of investigations with visual outputs, from biochemical results to X-rays and ultrasounds and all the electronic wizardry of CT and MRI scans. These all provide images that have much in common with communally visible and available Knowledge, and that can sometimes show up an individual doctor's Experience as wrong. Evidence of the decreasing importance attached to Experience was found, for example, in the reference in one lecture handout (the setting for the teaching of Knowledge) to 'The Black Art of **Auscultation**', now superseded by the **electrocardiogram** and **echocardiogram**. And round the bed of a patient in **keto-acidotic coma**, the powerful and clinically highly relevant smell of **ketones** was not mentioned by the doctor taking the ward round, though the printed biochemical results were discussed at length.

Pathologising the World

It is important to remember what Becker seemed almost to forget, that clinical students also continue 'book learning'. Again, they are taught Knowledge in lectures, now mostly about pathological conditions and their treatment. As preclinically, Knowledge is projected on to the world; but, whereas then their world was scientised, now it is pathologised. So they were told that the black mould growing on the wall of the student accommodation bathroom was **Aspergillus niger** and, in a surprising inversion of lay understanding, that '*Domestos* [a household disinfectant] is a good **culture medium**. It's used as a selective ingredient for growing **Pseudomonas**, as it brings out the pigment of the bacteria.' While clinical students may again pathologise themselves (again resulting in 'medical students' disease'), they are now officially encouraged to consider not themselves but other people in this way; a lecturer said, 'If you go into any pub and you see the old men in the corner with their pint and their cigarette, they've all lost weight because of this extra work of breathing [due to **chronic obstructive airways disease**].' Lecturers often mimic the sort of visible pathology that patients may display, the **Parkinsonian gait**, for example, making this easier for students to recognise immediately on **inspection**, the first stage in physical examination, whether of patient in hospital or man in the street.

The aids to pathologising the world are very similar to those described in scientising it. Students are provided with mnemonics of varying sorts, again giving lay words clinical associations: the causes of a **distended abdomen** were given as 'The Five Fs' (Fat, Fluid, **Flatus**, **Faeces** and **Foetus**); 'DANISH' is what they are advised to remember for **cerebellar lesions** (**Dysdiadochokinesia, Ataxia, Nystagmus, Intention tremor, Scanning or Staccato speech, Hypotonia**). Like preclinical students, clinical students also make up mnemonics for themselves, like a Greek Cypriot student's mnemonic for **aortic stenosis**: 'As Ed Screws, Abdul Comes Again' [**Aortic Stenosis** (has an) **Ejection Systolic** (murmur, heard in the) **Aortic area** (radiating to the) **Carotids** (and) **Apex**]. Lecturers also use famous people to 'hang diseases on': Freddie Mercury's death from **AIDS** was used to demonstrate the **immune changes** in this condition, in that he was never **HIV positive** because the test was done so late that he had lost his **seroconversion**; and I lost count of the number of times that Mrs Thatcher's **Dupuytren's contracture** was mentioned. Combinations of facts are also used when teaching Knowledge; here a lecturer is pathologising others, mentioning a famous patient and giving an embryological account of a symptom of a disease, as well as its treatment and prognosis, in the usual method of teaching Experience by Question and Answer (though his Questions here are mostly rhetorical):

> When someone's voice is hoarse, what do we as respiratory physicians think of as a knee-jerk reaction? Involvement of the **recurrent laryngeal nerve**. What's the **course** of this nerve? The **left recurrent laryngeal nerve** is brought down into the chest by the **ligamentum arteriosum** developmentally, and may be involved if there is a cancer . . . Involvement of the **recurrent laryngeal nerve** means that the cancer has spread outside the lung into the **mediastinum**, which means that it's **inoperable** except in special circumstances; what would they be? It's a historical question, I'm afraid. Well, if your name happens to be George VI. An operation was done, but you'll remember he didn't happen to do terribly well.

Groups of people as well as individuals are associated with disease: by occupation (the 'occupational diseases', such as **Farmer's Lung**); by race ('The Mediterranean races tend to have **Beta Thalassaemia**'); and by nationality (the only thing that some clinical students may ever know about Finland is that the fish tapeworm, **Diphyllobothrium latum**, is prevalent there because of the Finns' habit of eating raw fish).

But there are problems with applying some pathological conditions to other people, particularly those which depend for their explanation on forms of Knowledge, such as Neuroanatomy (see Chapter 6), which are difficult to apply to oneself, mainly because of the difficulty of looking at one's own brain. Neurology is thus found to be the most difficult clinical specialty, just as Neuroanatomy was the most difficult preclinical subject. A remarkable example of the difficult dual process of learning the Knowledge of normal Neuroanatomy on the self and transferring pathological Knowledge of Neurology on to others was provided by a consultant trying to explain the nature of **nystagmus**, in which the normal movements of the eye are deranged; he asked the students to remember the **midbrain centres for lateral gaze** and the **frontal centres** by a pair of most unusual images:

> Medical students always get confused by **nystagmus**. I'm going to explain it to you in a way you'll never make a mistake ever again. You need to visualise the system. Do you read *Biggles*? [*The students, surprised, shook their heads.*] Imagine there are magnets on the side of

> your head like the earphones Biggles wore; these draw the eyes to the side, like the **midbrain centres for lateral gaze**. Did you see the film 'The Ten Commandments'? You had Kirk Douglas [*sic*] as Moses, standing there, looking over the Israelites as they went on to where was it? The Red Sea . . . no, that wasn't it, was it? Canaan. I don't know, but the image of him standing there [*The consultant mimicked this.*] with the wind in his hair is like the way the **frontal lobes** work – the **right frontal lobe** drives **gaze** to the left, which is corrected to the right . . .

When the students, some clearly more puzzled than before by his highly personal way of remembering the **neural mechanisms of gaze**, asked the consultant questions about its clinical application to **nystagmus**, he did not answer immediately, as this involved converting an explanation formed primarily on himself, into the effect that a disturbance of this system would have on someone else. As he put it, 'You may have noticed I took my time about answering some of your questions; the Moses thing allows me time to think about it.'

Clinical students are told to see other people differently; in doing this, and learning the associated facts, the world becomes (to coin another word) a 'nosophany', a representation of disease. When they can, students also practise the other sensory modalities used in physical examination, **percussing** out the supports of a table for example, but, away from patients whom they can fully examine, it is the vision of **inspection** that predominates. Clinical students will sometimes reveal this individual though collective process of pathologising the world, despite the cultural disapproval of Idealism, in unofficial settings. When I was walking down the street with Delia, for example, she pointed out to me the **peripheral cyanosis** evident in the face of the old man coming towards us; Tim said, 'I was sitting opposite someone on the tube and I wished he'd just move his head a bit to the side so that I could see whether his **JVP [jugular venous pressure]** was raised or not.' Sometimes, evidence of this process is found within the official teams of students: one student held up the remains of an apple she'd been eating and asked the others, 'What's this?'; they quickly replied, '**Cancer of the oesophagus** [because of the **apple-coring** seen on a **Barium swallow** X-ray].' The implications of this particular episode cover the whole area of the well-known 'Food School' of pathologists, with their descriptions of **redcurrant jelly**

stools, coffee ground vomit and so on, terms brought in from the lay world to describe the pathological conditions revealed by Experience; the pathological meanings are now projected back on to the lay world. And, while pathologising the world is seen as a preliminary to gaining Experience on proper patients, there is no doubt that this second cognitive process is an important part of the aggregation of students towards the professional world of medicine.

The Language of Experience: Its Scientific and Oral Nature

As with preclinical students acquiring Knowledge, in acquiring Experience clinical students are taught a further vocabulary: a clinical one. Doctors are more or less insistent on students' using it – lay English was referred to by a consultant as 'NCOs' [Non-Commissioned Officers'] language' – even though they by no means always use it themselves. After one student had replied to an SHO's question about the treatment for a **pneumothorax** by saying, 'Stick a tube in and take the air out', the SHO responded by repeating this lay account sarcastically, '"Stick a tube in and take the air out, doctor sir"? Is that what you're going to say in the exam? [*Here he changed his tone to a more didactic one, saying:*] You've got to speak the lingo! [*And then, providing the correct use of clinical language expected in official frontstage settings:*] "**Insert an underwater chest drain**, sir doctor professor!"' So students learn from ward rounds, lectures and books a huge clinical vocabulary, which is used both to describe patients' experience (as gained from the history) and to describe findings on examination; as with preclinical languages, words are directly related to things, and the new words used to describe symptoms objectify the patient's experience. And as with the preclinical languages, the words may be new, usually of Latin or Greek derivation: **anorexia**, for example, describes the symptom of loss of appetite, while **crepitus** describes the creaking of a joint, both heard and felt, on physical examination. But, again, a large number of lay words acquire clinical and materially referent meanings: **acute** now refers to a sudden onset, **attachment** to the physical fixation of a **mass** (or **lump**), and **power** to the function of muscles, graded from **total paralysis** to **normal movement against resistance** as offered by the examiner. **Heal** is now always used intransitively (for example,

'How's the [surgical] **wound healing?**'); **tender** and **sensitive** mean painful on pressure, rather then displaying tenderness and sensitivity. Students must also be aware of the context in which words are used: **shock**, for example, can either mean **circulatory collapse** or the use of electricity as part of **cardio-pulmonary resuscitation**. They learn a new range of eponyms, all male, just like the eponyms learnt preclinically (for example, **Bell's palsy, Cushing's disease, Kerley B lines, Sims' speculum**); the clinical world, like the preclinical worlds of hard science, was discovered by men. And students also have to learn the vast range of drugs, whether by generic names or brand names, and the large numbers of acronyms referring to drugs and to other aspects of medical life.

The preclinical student learning Knowledge had to hear new words only to be able to read and learn them; the clinical student has to speak them too. Linguistically, Experience is mostly an oral culture and, though closely related to the literate culture of Knowledge, it is (as I have shown) easily distinguished from it. Students were often reminded of this fact on the wards, frequently by being told, usually by consultants, not to write things down; one student was told, 'If you turn up on the wards with a clipboard, they'll think you're a time-and-motion man!' This general attitude obviously limited to a considerable degree the extent to which I could take notes and remain unidentified, but was quite adequately offset by features of the oral culture that aid memorisation. As Ong's account of oral cultures indicates, some of the features of Experience already described are explicable on this basis: the rigid sequential formulaic form of questions, examination, and presentation is necessary for organisation and memorisation, and the conservatism of these methods preserves, through constant repetition, these forms of knowledge that are hard to come by (Ong 1991: 33–6, 41–2). While the processes of scientising and pathologising the world make Knowledge most unusual among written cultures in not separating 'the knower from the known' (1991: 44), Experience has other features common to oral cultures: the total engagement of the person, including the body, and the agonistic manner of interpersonal communication (1991: 43–5, 67) I describe later. But there are some other specifically linguistic features to be mentioned first, some of which are atypical for oral cultures.

Using the same pronunciation is clearly not atypical. Speaking clinical language involves the Club Spirit; deviations from the common medical pronunciation are extremely rare, only then drawing attention to an otherwise astonishing uniformity. When deviations are found within the profession, they can be attributed to ignorance in students, foreignness in doctors, and not being open to correction in consultants (who here may be thought of as using another 'quasi-normative' practice). Patients, though, not uncommonly speak clinical words without using the accepted pronunciation; their deviation does not provoke correction as students' would, but irritation, doctors often wincing when a patient pronounces a clinical word incorrectly. The patient may have had access to communally available Knowledge by reading it in a book, but has not had the privileged access to the oral medical culture of Experience.

The command of a common language and its common pronunciation is an important factor that allies students to superordinates in the profession. Patients in teaching hospitals, sited in metropolitan cities, come from all over the world; doctors and students do too (from Ireland, and other countries in the EU, India, Pakistan, Iraq, Iran, Sudan, Cyprus, Nigeria and so on). So a Portuguese patient may be clerked in Out-Patients by a Kenyan student and presented to a Pakistani doctor in clinical language correctly pronounced. But though students are sometimes encouraged to use the patient's own words when they describe the 'Presenting Complaint' and its 'History', they may also be criticised for doing so (by a doctor saying, for example, 'That doesn't sound very scientific'). What seasoned students often end up doing is giving an account in lay language, not in the patient's own words but in terms that are easily translatable into clinical language: 'She occasionally wakes up short of breath in the night', for example, is immediately translatable by a medical audience into the symptom of **paroxysmal nocturnal dyspnoea**. This is obviously the point at which much verbal miscommunication takes place between doctors and patients, doctors failing to understand the words that patients use (as when a consultant failed to appreciate that a patient using the lay word 'gathering' meant a **local infection**). Equally patients may not understand the words that students use to ask questions (doctors have usually developed the unusual clinical lay language that I describe in Chapter 9). Netta, talking backstage, said she had asked one elderly patient whether he was on any **medication**. 'He said, "Speak English, girl!" So I asked him if he was taking any drugs and he was most affronted [saying]: "What do you take me for? Taking drugs? Never!"' Patients may also find incorrect reasons for the incomprehensibility of students' questions in clinical language: Raj, a student born in the UK of Sri Lankan parents, having asked a patient a question on a ward round, was loudly told by the patient to 'Say it in English, can't you!'; the patient had assumed that the clinical language was indeed a foreign language.

But the volubility and redundancy that characterises oral expression is not found. Speech that is not so redundant – sparsely linear or analytic speech – is, as Ong (1991: 40–1) points out, structured by the technology of writing; and it is scientific writing that has made oral clinical language so unusual. In fact, clinical language contains all the features found in Ziman's description of scientific language: formalised statements, in which rigorously defined terms are used in unambiguous syntactical arrangements designed to produce perfect precision and overwhelming certitude. Words that do not have such implications are rejected: a student was asked what shapes **lumps** could be described as being and answered that they might be oval. 'Oval?', the consultant replied, 'You mean ovoid, rugger ball-shaped. Who ever made a meaningful deduction from the fact that a **lump** was ovoid? No! You want shapes that *mean* something!' Logical necessity is also found: an **opening snap** heard on **auscultation** necessarily leads to a diagnosis of **mitral stenosis**, for example. Students are frequently reminded of the implications of clinical words: when a student said that a patient was **clammy**, the SR asked him, 'What does **clammy** imply?'; the student's reply that the patient was cold was brushed aside. 'He's **clammy**, he's **shut down** [his **cardiovascular system** is **shut down**], he's got a rotten urine output. What's the key word? **Shock**!'

The logical necessity of such statements is further extended to the whole narrative, so that students learn to provide a condensed, non-repetitive and internally coherent account; they also learn not to repeat all the answers to the extensive questions they have asked their patients, but to select only the 'important negatives' that might cast doubt on a diagnosis, and not to mention a positive symptom or finding without following its implications further; if they don't, they may be asked, 'How do you fit that in?' Practice in removing the information superfluous to reaching the diagnosis is given by the frequent exercise of asking students to provide a concise summary of two or three sentences at the end of a presentation. In fact, it seems entirely likely that the scientific qualities of the spoken clinical language may actually emphasise some common features of oral cultures: the need for personal mnemonics and collectively formalised patterns, the conservativeness of the type of knowledge learnt and the agonistic nature of verbal exchanges.

But there is one very important consequence of the insistence in official settings on speaking the deliberately and precisely referential scientific language: the increasing reliance on non-verbal methods for communicating anything else. On ward rounds, therefore, while students are learning explicit body techniques for physical examination, they are also learning to become aware of physical gesture, other students' and doctors', and how to react to it with their own physical expressions. This is generally obvious in the unorchestrated but close physical co-ordination involved when a ward round moves on; students have to turn around without incommoding their colleagues and keep up with the group, forming the crocodile trailing after the doctor down wards and passages. I describe the acquisition of the 'hexis' of the medical habitus in more detail below.

Ward Rounds: Presentations on the Theatrical Stage

While teaching, learning and assessing Knowledge all take place in different settings, in the disposition of Experience they all take place on the wards and in some variant of the ward round, which is still by far the commonest setting for these purposes, by the traditional Question and Answer method. I have indicated how important theatrical settings are in medical training and how these allow students to learn the roles particularly associated with the three qualitative dispositions of Knowledge, Experience and Responsibility. Preclinically, students have learnt the disposition of Knowledge and, with it, the role of acting as an audience reacting to a performance. In the next chapter, I shall show how housemen learn the disposition of Responsibility and, with it, the role of being an actor the whole time they are on duty, on the official front- and backstage. Clinical students are at the intermediate level, where, as they learn the disposition of Experience on the official frontstage that ward rounds create, they play roles as both audience and actors.

The typical ward round takes place within the curtains drawn around a patient's bed, in the same configuration as a *viva* in the DR, so creating the same form of temporary dramatic space. Many other settings clinical students find themselves in can be seen as transformed ward rounds: students group themselves round an X-ray box in similar fashion, and, in Out-Patient clinics, it is patients that move in and out of the room where the doctor and students stay put, rather than the doctor and students moving round the beds where their patients are. On ward rounds, then, students 'present' their patients, standing to the left of the head of the patient's bed, and repeating out loud their formulaic narrative of both parts of the clerking to an audience that includes their fellow-students, as well as a doctor, and usually the patient too. The doctor also stands at the head of the bed; if on the left, to one side of the presenting student, who is closer to the bed. The other students form a rough semicircular standing audience round the bed so that they can all see and can all be seen (see Figure 18). While one student is presenting the patient, the others look and listen; when they are called upon to examine the patient themselves, they move round in order, occupying the presenter's original position. Students may already have been made aware of these features not only in popular depictions on films and TV but also in the dramatic representations of them at medical school revues and plays, and they have practised them themselves in the DR.

So now, on ward rounds, they are still involved as audience, but may also become the protagonist; students therefore become skilled at assessing others' performances as well as performing themselves. While ward rounds swiftly become taken for granted as the way of teaching and learning, some students (those with experience of acting) are not unaware of their theatricality:

> Two first-year clinical students, both MDs (see Chapter 5) were discussing this, unofficially backstage. Joe, who liked the 'old-world staginess' of some consultants (though he added that most of the teaching was done by junior doctors), was describing his presentation of an X-ray on a ward round. He had been in ebullient mood, and fully expected to be shot down for his exaggeratedly dramatic presentation. 'I started off, "This is a Chest X-ray [that is, according to the ritual formula with which students are taught to present X-rays, similar to that used to present patients]", but I soon abandoned the [formalaic] system. I said [*miming pointing to the X-ray, and now speaking deliberately portentously*], "This draws our attention to the most

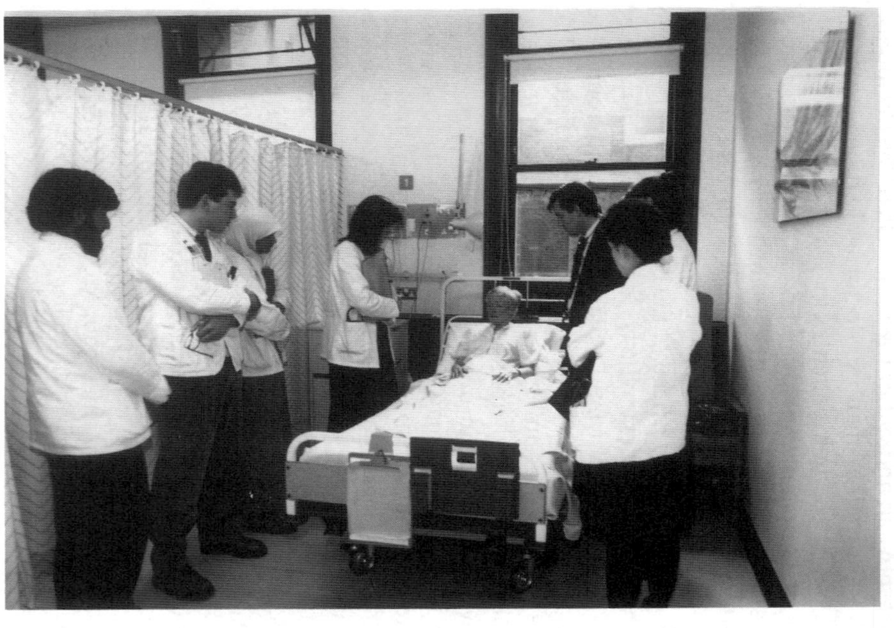

Figure 18. The ward round. The woman student to the left of the bed is clearly in the 'hot seat'; atypically, the doctor stands on the right. Note the circular configuration of the round (the curtain has not been drawn and a gap has been left for the photographer to 'see' as well), looking down and in on the patient, and the way students tend to hold their arms across the chest (some tucking away their writing-pads in this way). [UCL]

> dramatic feature . . .".' Joe was astonished that, instead of being criticised, his presentation was received with rather awed praise by the junior doctor taking the round, who said, 'You're rather good at this, aren't you!' As Joe recounted this, he laughed again and again. Although he identified a particular phrase ('This draws our attention to the most dramatic feature') as a key one, he reckoned it was generally important to be confident and to ham it up. But his friend Matt, a noted MD, had been having a very hard time on the wards, needing help and support from his friends. He found the kind of extempore response required on ward rounds very difficult and quite different from a performance on stage; on the wards, he had not yet found definite lines to be spoken.

Further evidence for the theatricality of presenting patients on ward rounds is found in the occasional use of lecture theatres for the teaching of Experience in clinical demonstrations (such demonstrations are given at the beginning of the clinical years, in the Introductory Course, and at the end, in the Revision Course). On one of these occasions, a consultant played something like a television panel game, guessing the diagnoses of patients he had never seen before, and then checking his answers with the correct one from a sealed envelope. But both during the Introductory Course and the Revision Course, the overt theatricality of these events was marked by the audience of students applauding when patients left the theatre.

In the taken-for-granted, but nevertheless theatrical, ward round, where disbelief is not just willingly suspended but is almost impossible, the very notion of disease in general and the nature of specific diseases in particular may be validated. Atkinson describes the pedagogy of bedside teaching as 'transparent'; by this he means that the social mechanism of knowledge production and transmission are not themselves made apparent and explicit. The questions about the symptoms and signs of diseases, their causes, treatment and prognosis all obviously emphasise the 'preconstituted nature of illness as an ontological entity, while the social production of disease categories remains invisible' (Atkinson 1981: 120). A further aspect of the power of this affirmation is that of the theatre. I have alluded to the way students learn to present patients; this starts with patients' own 'presentation' to hospital, and continues with the 'Presenting Complaint' and its own 'History'. The word 'present', then, is used to apply to disease, patient and student. Unpacking this notion of presentation leads to the following implicit, unspoken series of theatrical presentations: the disease presents to the patient, in what may be an unusual or 'dramatic' presentation; the patient presents to the hospital, where the student clerks him and takes a history, starting with the 'Presenting Complaint'; the student then presents the patient to the doctor. I am suggesting that the theatrical setting of ward rounds in which students learn to present their patients is the last in a series of past presentations; both the formal language learnt and the dramatic setting confirm the active physical nature of the disease, first unfolded in this way before the audience's ears and eyes, and then personally verified when each student examines the patient in turn.

There are several reasons for the different dramatic qualities of Casualty, where students find 'hot' medicine and where so many television series are based. First, students' presence only in twos or threes, the presence of junior doctors (housemen, SHOs and registrars) and the almost complete absence of consultants, and the presence of other professionals, particularly nurses, means both that the cast of the dramatic setting of the ward round cannot be mustered, and that outsiders are present. Second, the setting is very fluid in Casualty; there are people coming and going, trolleys needing gangway; and even round the patient's temporary bed in a cubicle, interruptions are frequent (nurses checking how the patient is, for example). There is no chance of staging the static and formal set of a ward round – everyone is too busy for that. Third, the smaller difference in Status between junior doctors and students than between consultants and students is further lessened by the real Co-operative contribution of Responsible action that students may make in Casualty, and their close association with the junior doctors on the firm over a period of hours; a significant difference in Status is necessary for the Question and Answer series to continue. Fourth, the situation in Casualty is that diagnoses are in reality often only provisional, whereas on ward rounds the diagnosis is usually already known; the certainty that can be taught in ward rounds is not available in Casualty. Teaching in Casualty then, for these reasons, is not characterised by the sort of relationships involved in Question and Answer series on ward rounds, and is marked by the relative ease with which students can ask questions and expect to have them answered and not reversed. It will be recalled that Casualty was the only setting where Becker did not find his Academic perspective (see Chapter 2).

Teaching on Ward Rounds: Question and Answer

The elements of the Question and Answer method of teaching Experience, still discernible in the DR, were described in Chapter 7. While questions naturally tend to concentrate on the 'cold' patients centre-stage, two alternative and hypothetical stages, those of Casualty and the Final clinical exams, are often set, both by and for such questions. The first, 'What are you going to do in Casualty?', is referred to by Becker (1961: 228) as '"the emergency room" or "the patient comes into your office with . . . What are you going to do?" gambit'; in Atkinson's terms, it is the artificial recreation of 'hot' medicine. It sets the scene for anticipatory thought and hypothetical action about medical Responsibility in Casualty, the main area where students can expect to have some real Responsibility (taking blood, **suturing lacerations**, putting up **intravenous lines**, talking to **relatives**, and writing notes that will form part of the legal record). Students' ability to answer this question depends, to some extent, on whether they actually were in Casualty; considerable importance is attached by consultants to students' attendance there, another point that draws attention to Responsibility, despite its prevalent institutional absence for students. A similar question about Responsibility, in a setting corresponding to Becker's 'your office', used to be asked twenty years ago, along the lines of, 'You're a single-handed GP in Cornwall; what are you going to do for this patient?' This is now rarely if ever asked, no doubt because, since then, all prospective GPs have been obliged to spend an extra two years working in hospitals after their house jobs.

The second setting is made clear in the common question, 'What are you going to say in the exam?' Although exams are stylised events, this stylisation is only an accentuation of features found in ordinary ward round settings. In exams, of course, students are also likely to be asked the first question, 'What are you going to do in Casualty?', to judge their capacity for acting Responsibly in an emergency. 'Nice pass/fail questions' is how questions about emergencies were described by one registrar, as she encouraged a final-year clinical student to learn that **Flumenezil** was the **specific antagonist** for **Benzodiazepines** by asking her what **antidote** she would give to a patient who had taken an overdose of **Diazepam**.

In other words, just as one aspect of Responsibility, ownership, is delegated by consultants to students, who now have 'their' patients over whom they exercise hypothetical Responsibility, so the other aspect of the disposition, action, is also hypothetical, in the hypothetical situations evoked by Question and Answer series. Such encouragement to students to think in ways directed by questions is expanded by instructions on how to feel: students were told about investigating one patient's symptoms, 'You'd be obliged to exclude a **carcinoma of the colon**', for example, but these instructions are more concerned with management and the mature judgement of Responsibility: 'You'd be worried about putting them into **ventricular tachycardia**', 'You'd be reluctant to **anti-coagulate** them' and 'You'd be hesitant to operate.' The hypothetical nature both of students' Responsibility for patients and the questions about treatment echo Bourdieu's games of 'let's pretend', and his 'structural exercises' testing the sense of ritual language.

All Question and Answer series can be used as assessments as well as for teaching and learning. It is partly the sum of these daily assessments that leads to the 'firm grade' given to each student at the end of their six-week attachment; even if a separate assessment is made, this will be of the form of clerking and presenting a patient, followed by a Question and Answer series. But it should be noted that students will be questioned on their own questioning of patients: 'In both cases, question-and-answer formats are used to elicit and structure "information": the discourse itself inscribes the asymmetry in status and power of the respective parties' (Atkinson 1994: 136–7). The form that many medical interviews with patients take, with their frequent 'closed' questions, is homologous with, but secondary to, the questioning that students (and junior doctors) are subjected to by senior doctors.

This is perhaps the place to mention the relatively recent introduction of courses in 'Doctor–Patient Communication' or 'Communication Skills', in which students are taught other methods of listening and talking to patients. These take place away from the wards of the teaching hospital and are always run either by Departments of General Practice or Psychiatry, both among the very-lowest-Status segments of medicine as seen from the teaching hospital (as described at the end of this chapter). Such courses are not held on medical or surgical wards, for example, and there students and housemen are both taught and assessed by Question and Answer, the method also used in Final clinical exams. For these reasons, the different approaches to patients advocated in 'Communication Skills' courses, or found by students in their attachments to General Practice, have little significant influence on hospital practice. Indeed, such courses may even, perhaps, only serve to provide students with a way of talking and listening to patients that conflicts with their own use of Question and Answer sequences with patients. Further, the other methods of interaction advocated in courses on 'Communication Skills' may be even converted into the traditional methods of gaining Experience; one consultant told students, 'Patients think they're being listened to more if you look them in the eye, did you know that? So you have the opportunity to examine their **iris** closely while you take a history.' But some of the common techniques in such courses (the use of actors paid to take the role of patients, and of video-recordings of interactions) may actually exaggerate the existing theatrical aspect of 'seeing patients'. While these theatrical aspects may, in some courses, be explicitly concentrated on to understand doctors' roles in order, in turn, to understand their patients', it seems entirely likely that the ultimate effect is only to emphasise the general dramatic qualities of medical training.

The Certainty of the Answers to the Questions

As with questions asked in the DR, there is no doubt that the questioners know the answer; indeed, their questioning and their knowledge of the answers form part of their authority. Given the way the questions are phrased, the answers are also definite and, in the language of sociology, certain. For, as with Knowledge, in Experience too it is certainty and not uncertainty that is promoted. The nature of the history and examination, with the definite presence or absence of symptoms and signs, shows this, as does the Question and Answer method of teaching itself. The sociological suggestion of uncertainty has however found favour among doctors, who may use it to show the overwhelming difficulties they face.

Uncertainty was in fact cited to me by a senior consultant when describing the problems faced by new clinical students: 'Some of them find the uncertainty of clinical medicine very difficult to cope with. One very clever girl came to me [privately] and told me this; for example, she said, "Why is the rash of measles so different from the rash of German measles?"' My own response to this statement at the time was to express admiration for the student;

but in fact the consultant's example demonstrates exactly the reverse of the point he thought it did. The clinical Question and Answer method (unlike this question about the different rashes) does not use questions to which the answers are unknown or uncertain (except to individually ignorant students). So the clever student's question was one that she first put to herself before asking it in private of the consultant; it is not one that is asked by doctors in official frontstage settings, as the answer is not known. If such a question were asked, the doctor's and the students' shared ignorance would give them equivalent Status; but, in fact, the doctor's higher Status is not compromised in this way, and he asks questions to which he knows the answers.

In other words, whatever it may seem like to some outsiders and indeed some students, these questions promote certainty and not uncertainty; I suggest below that medical practice is based on such certain knowledge, both gained and tested in this way. But it is also quite understandable that during their training students should be taught a minimum level of commonly accepted and certain knowledge to become a competent and safe member of the profession. This is obviously the reason for the way in which students (as well as being asked, and told, what they should say in the exam) are told what not to say in the exam, not because it is wrong, but because (being new Knowledge) it contravenes the generally accepted doctrine. So, for example, in Out-patients, after an SR had been explaining some recent research evidence that **beta-blockers** might be helpful in some cases of **heart failure**, he concluded his explanation by saying, 'But whatever you do, don't say that you treat **heart failure** with **beta-blockers** in the exam!' In fact, it seems entirely likely that the 'clinical mentality', which has been described by some (Atkinson 1984; Freidson 1970) as characterised much more by certainty than uncertainty, is itself based on the method of teaching and learning by Question and Answer.

Question and Answer: The Formation of the Clinical Mentality?

During fieldwork as a clinical student, I was sometimes asked questions on subjects I had not had anything to do with for nearly twenty years (about the **management** of **post-operative** patients, for example, by a consultant who did not know of my identity); I was amazed to be able to answer these questions correctly. Oral answers learnt in response to oral questions seem to persist in a way that written answers to written questions do not. It is partly for this reason that I now suggest the 'Socratic' Question and Answer method gives rise to an early form of the clinical mentality, based on the questions that are likely to be asked by a teacher or superordinate and their certain answers: the interlocutor, necessary for sustained thought in oral cultures (Ong 1991: 34), is first present in the flesh, and then becomes internalised.

Students are often, quite explicitly, told that they must learn how to think in a medical way, that preclinical teaching has stopped them being able to think, and so on. Here, in fact, the 'Socratic' allusion may hold more weight, with reference to the notion of *anamnesis*, of remembering what is unwittingly known. A consultant surgeon, having first asked a question that no one could answer, then, by asking a series of other questions, managed to extract the answer to the first; he concluded, almost triumphantly, 'You see! You knew the answer all along! It's just a question of organising what you know!' And that medical thought involves asking questions is sometimes also quite explicit:

> Mr Masters, a consultant obstetrician, was giving a clinical lecture: 'So why should some babies present as a **breech**? "Why is this baby a **breech**?" is the first question I should ask myself. I always ask myself, "Why is the baby upside down? Isn't there room to be the right side down?" There's one thing that takes up room . . .' [*As he said this, he looked around the theatre encouragingly, for the answer to the now implicit question.*]
>
> Student [*who had judged that it is safe to volunteer information to this consultant and who might also, Competitively, want to show he knew the answer*]: '**Placenta praevia**.'
>
> Mr Masters [*consideringly*]: 'Yes, that's one thing. It produces a very high **breech presentation**. I was thinking of another abnormality. [*Here he paused, again expectantly, before giving the answer himself, saying:*] A **bicornuate uterus**.'

Mr Masters had clearly described his own method of questioning himself, and he had in effect asked his audience the precise questions he was asking himself ('What are the causes of **breech presentations**?', and, more specifically, 'What are the **obstructive causes**?'). The student's answer to his question was normatively correct ('Yes, that's one thing'); but Mr Masters also used another common practice by suggesting that he had something else in mind ('I was thinking of another abnormality').

Correct answers may be rejected because of the often-quoted truism that 'Common things commonly occur'; so answers to questions about causes (like the one Mr Masters asked) should be ordered. The first answers should be causes that Experience has shown to be clinically more likely (and a common disparaging remark about rare causes given as answers, 'That's small print stuff!', also disparages Knowledge). So, when an SR had asked for causes of **cardiac arrhythmias** and Fiona had given a list, he asked, 'What else would you mention? [*Fiona was silent.*] **Chest infection** is a very common precipitant of **AF** [**atrial fibrillation**]; it's a mechanism that ought to be part of your thought processes. You see it again and again and again!' But even apparently unobjectionable answers may be met by the doctor's saying, 'That's not what I'm thinking of.' Students then have to produce another normatively equally correct answer that also satisfies this new, personally idiosyncratic condition. This tendency provides further evidence of the personal certainties of medicine, and the way in which particular Questions and Answers have special importance for the thought of individual doctors.

There is other evidence that internalised questions are crucial to clinical practice. Doctors, when demonstrating the techniques of Experience to students, often give a spontaneous running commentary not just on what they are doing (and why) but also what they are thinking (and why). This allows students to understand the doctors' reasons for doing as they are, and provides them with examples of the sort of questions they may be asked when they themselves are performing a physical examination in an official setting, and a model for answering them. After or during either a presented clerking or one being performed there and then, doctors may ask students, 'What [symptom, condition] are you thinking of?', or 'What possibilities are going through your mind?', or tell them, 'You should be thinking of . . .'. So students are taught to be able to say out loud both what they are doing and what they are thinking, and in both cases their actions and their thoughts are directed by questions within questions. They are also taught that this thought (that is, the answers to questions) should (and eventually will) carry on while the history-taking and examination proceed 'on automatic pilot' or 'at **brainstem level** [without conscious thought]'. A first-year student explained how he tried to practise this when taking a history: 'You have to think ahead of what question to ask [the patient], but try not to let this influence your current attention.'

Question and Answer on the Official Backstage

Students transfer the methods of Question and Answer that they have learnt on the official frontstage to the official backstage. Here, Co-operatively but also clearly Competitively, they continually question each other in a similar manner, particularly before ward rounds or firm assessments. Sometimes their backstage use of Question and Answer demonstrably involves learning the questions as well as the answers. I was attached to one spectacularly 'bad' official team of students on a surgical firm, only a few of whom had turned up one day for the ward round with Mr Rodney, the consultant. He took us to see a patient with **cirrhosis** (whom nobody had clerked) and asked students questions in all the ways described above. At the end of the round, he gave them a moral homily about turning up to rounds and clerking patients, ending by saying, 'When the others come, you'll have to demonstrate the physical signs for them.' Some of the other students came in the next day for another timetabled ward round, which was then cancelled at short notice. While they were wondering what to do, Giles, one of the students present on both days, offered to take them to see the previous day's patient. Giles then played the part Mr Rodney had taken the previous day, asking his colleagues almost exactly the same questions he had himself been asked the day before in almost exactly the same order. Giles had internalised the answers and the questions too; he had also learnt the reciprocal relationship to his normal role of learning student, that of teaching doctor.

In students' continual questioning of each other on the official backstage, they often use 'you' in a way they hear doctors using it when describing and explaining clinical events to them, for example: 'You get **portal-systemic encephalopathy** because you've wrecked your **intrahepatic circulation**.' This use of 'you' is ambiguous as regards Status, potentially referring to the student either as doctor or as patient; such ambiguity is also found in the frequent statements by doctors about normality, such as 'You're allowed a **Q wave** in **AVF**' [a **Q wave** in this section of the **ECG** is not abnormal]. In their backstage questioning of each other, students often use 'you' in this ambiguous way ('What do you get with **nephrotic syndrome**? I know you get **peripheral oedema**, but do you get **oedema** anywhere else?'). But students must beware of using 'you' like this with doctors, whose medical Status is unambiguous:

> In a clinical lecture, a surgical SR was teaching a group of students, using a Question and Answer series.
>
> SR: 'What are **varices**?'
>
> Debbie: 'When you've got **portal hypertension** . . .'
>
> SR [*interrupting, affronted*]: 'When *I've* got **portal hypertension**! When *one's* got **portal hypertension**! But what are they?'

No doubt there are other factors (such as their increasing clinical vocabulary and decreasing lay vocabulary on the official frontstage, and the process of pathologising the world), but it is likely that the adoption of the Question and Answer method by students backstage goes a long way to explaining the general observation that, whereas preclinical students hardly talk about medicine at all, clinical students talk about almost nothing else.

Punning and Irony Again Distinguish Institutional Areas

Another contributory factor is clinical students' increasing segregation from others and aggregation to the profession. The nature of preclinical students' work meant they could absent themselves from official teaching in lectures with impunity, perhaps in order to perform as members of representative teams on the unofficial frontstage. But clinical students' absence from clinical work is not excused on these grounds (the UCL rule of keeping Wednesday afternoons free for games no longer applies, for example) and they need to be visible on ward rounds; further, the regular assessments of Knowledge and other commitments (such as part-time work, or their own family) means that, for clinical students, their institutional areas shrink to three; the unofficial frontstage has almost gone. Whereas preclinical students used puns that showed their ambiguous Status and medicalised the world, clinical students are more closely aggregated to the medical world. They now use puns to indicate a different distinction, between their official and their unofficial life, in terms that are not now so recognisable to laymen (see Figure 19).

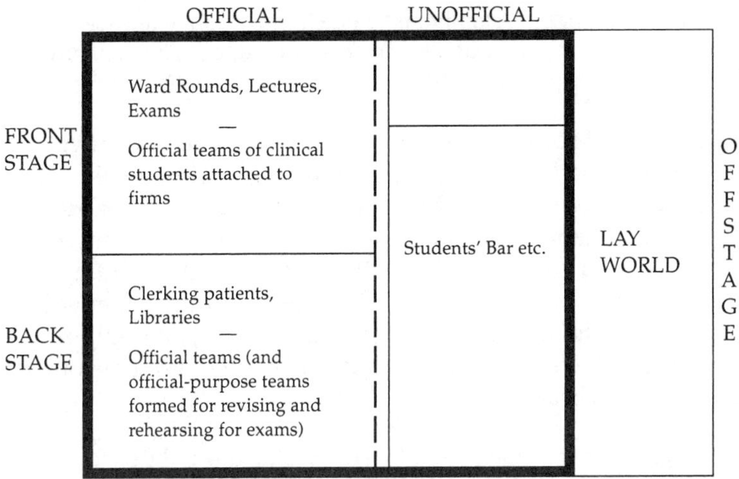

Figure 19. Clinical students' institution. The unofficial frontstage has shrunk (as has the lay world) and the most significant distinction alluded to by clinical students is now between the official and unofficial stages.

Unofficially backstage, they talk of consultants and patients as **benign** or **malignant**, like tumours; people are described as **ectopic**, like a pregnancy in a **Fallopian tube**, rather than out of place; and the student who said of himself, 'I've had a **radical** rug**ectomy**' was referring to a severe haircut rather than a major operation. The use of irony to make the same distinction also becomes more obvious. If the listener does not 'get' the ironic comments and stories, this implies the surer medical Status of the teller, who know both meanings. My own Status among students was sometimes ambiguous (not really being a student, not even really being a doctor); and on this occasion I was found wanting:

> A firm group had just been on a ward round with Mr Gurney, a consultant, who, at the beginning of the round, pointed out one male student's failure to wear a white coat by simply saying, 'White coat, Tim!' [Consultants, of course, rarely wear white coats.] While some members of the firm group and I were sitting unofficially backstage, I mentioned this episode and Tim asked me if it was going in my thesis. 'Oh yes', I said. Tim then told me that in fact things did not end after the round:
>
> Tim: 'He [Mr Gurney] asked me, "Why aren't you wearing a white coat?"; "Why aren't *you*?", I said.'
>
> SS [*naively*]: 'Really?'
>
> Tim [*continuing*]: '"A fair point", said Gurney, "and, while we're here, why don't you take my daughter; she's only twelve years old!"'

At this point I realised that I had fallen for it. The irony involved the contrast between the official frontstage nature of the ward round with my unofficial backstage understanding that matters might have changed so much since I trained, that a student might now answer a consultant back like that, an understanding that was shown to be ludicrous. Students may also find themselves educated in the next level of irony (described more fully in the next chapter), which relies on the distinction between the official front- and backstage:

> A registrar, two students and I were walking down the street on our way from the Middlesex to UCH, to see patients there. The registrar said, 'I love hospitals! The smell of them! It's the patients that I hate!' Both students were taken aback, saying, 'You can't mean that!', 'How can you say that!' The registrar simply repeated what he had just said, smiling.

Even though most clinical students are by now well aware of the need to show professional Idealism on their official frontstage of the ward round, this forthright denial of personal Idealism disconcerted these two considerably.

The Ward Round: Displaying Professional Idealism

Oral Question and Answer series between high-Status doctors and low-Status students start on students' first day on the wards, when they are astonished to be asked questions that they could not possibly know the answer to; they also find the method of Question and Answer now used in lecture theatres. These are therefore instantly transformed from the preclinical setting, where they could relax as an audience, to one that is, in effect, a ward round, where they may singled out for questioning and perforce become a most unwilling actor. The change between preclinical and clinical students' physical carriage in the same setting of the lecture theatre from preclinical to clinical is striking; one cannot relax when likely to be asked a question publicly. This was clearly shown in one of a course of revision lectures given just before students' Experience was tested in clinical Finals; the consultant-lecturer said to the students who were spread out at the back of the theatre: 'I want you closer [to me at the front]!' The students did not move; it was only when he said, 'Come on, I'm not asking questions!', that they moved forward. In another such lecture, students were jocularly reminded of one of the rules of Question and Answer series, that questions asked the wrong way round may simply be reversed: at the end of his lecture, another consultant asked, 'Any questions?' One student put up his hand, but the consultant said, 'Quickly! Put your hand down there!', and, as the student did so, applauded him, saying, 'Smart move, smart move!' But it is in the much more personal ward round that students learn the precise 'hexis' of the medical habitus:

> Dr Vickers, a consultant, was on a ward round and had stopped by a patient's bed.
>
> Dr Vickers [*looking at Yusuf, a student*]: 'Look at her eye and tell me what's the matter.'
>
> Yusuf [*having moved towards the patient and looked briefly at her eye*]: 'She's got a sore eye.'
>
> Dr Vickers [*derisively*]: 'The *gardener* could have told us that, the *gardener*! What are you going to tell the patient? "You've got a sore eye; there's a lot of it about, a *great deal* of it about"? How are you going to *do* anything about it if you don't know what it is? Look at her eye!'
>
> Yusuf [*now looking more closely*]: 'There's **conjunctivitis**.'
>
> Dr Vickers: 'Is there? [*He himself examined the eye, holding down the lower eyelid for*

Yusuf to look as well.] *Is* there?' [*The patient started talking as Yusuf was looking.*]

Yusuf [*now standing back*]: 'No.'

Dr Vickers [*still holding down the eyelid and smiling, not altogether pleasantly*]: 'The patient's just given you the diagnosis. It's lucky you don't listen to the patient or you'd know the answer! [*More firmly*:] Look at this lower lid! Is it red?'

Yusuf [*now again leaning forward to look*]: 'No.'

Dr Vickers [*excitedly and forcefully*]: 'Yes it is red! Look at it! Is it red?'

Yusuf: 'Yes.'

Dr Vickers [*more quietly, almost resignedly*]: 'And what do we call an inflamed eyelid?'

Yusuf: '**Blepharitis**.'

In this exchange between a consultant and a student, several important features of the disposition of Experience are found: the official importance attached to 'listening to the patient', the learning of techniques of examination with the particular stress on visual **inspection** (and of knowing what to look for), and the oral description of definite examination findings in precise clinical language. But also evident here is the explicit purpose of gaining Experience, which is the action found in the disposition of Responsibility, action which is both moral and instrumental. Yusuf, however, has hardly displayed his spontaneous practice of these features; indeed, his originally cursory examination of the patient's eye with his use of lay language to describe his findings evoked Dr Vickers' contempt. On ward rounds, the attitude most looked for in students by doctors is that of professional Idealism in the pursuit of Experience, clearly not shown by Yusuf. In other words, it is less in lecture theatres and more on ward rounds (with their much closer personal contact) that surveillance by the teacher is exercised; and what Goffman calls 'role distance' (here, the student indicating his rejection of the professionally Idealistic role) is minimised by the use of 'teaching by humiliation'.

Students may indeed be coached in displaying such Idealism, as when, during a ward round in preparation for a firm assessment, a student performing physical examination was told, only half-jokingly, by a consultant, 'Now James, you take over and do it as if this was the thing you *most* wanted to be doing!' or when, during a Question and Answer series, a consultant said, 'Come on, Giselle, is the information bubbling out of you, or am I having to drag it out of you?' Students may show such Idealism in various ways: their visible presence on ward rounds and at out-patients and presenting 'their' patients all clearly provide evidence that Experience has been vigorously pursued. Verbally, Idealism for Experience is assumed in the frequent instructions to students phrased as, 'Do you want to . . .?'; while theoretically possible to answer negatively, it is practically impossible to refuse such a demand, a refusal demonstrating beyond doubt the absence of the expected Idealistic 'wanting' to do what they are instructed to do. The singular circumstances surrounding the only time I ever heard of student refusing an instruction phrased like this indicate their prevailing obedience to this norm: a consultant's bleep had gone off, and she had asked a female student, 'Do you want to answer that?' The student said, 'No', to the incredulous laughter of her colleagues. The obvious circumstances were that she was considerably older than most students and foreign (and was therefore often picked out by doctors); but, unknown to the other students and to the consultant, she was also medically qualified in her own country and had, for her own purposes, recently attended an 'Assertiveness Course'. But the commonly expected professional Idealism on the official frontstage may be rejected backstage: Zahida expressed her distaste for it, saying, 'I can't be bothered to play games: to look really worried if you don't know the answer, to say, "Oh yes, of course!", when you're told it – they [doctors] love that!'

The Manifestation of Dispositions in Physical Deportment

On ward rounds, students also show their understanding of other non-verbal methods of communication (which I have suggested above is a consequence of the use of clinical language) and, in particular, of the physical manifestation of dispositions. On ward rounds, the presenter's own physical position may sometimes be referred to as the 'hot seat' (a term that is also transferred to any questioned student, as it was in the DR); all eyes are now on him.

After the presentation, the Question and Answer series starts with him, before moving to the student standing next to him. Generally, a position in the middle of the semicircle is favoured by students; here vision is unimpaired but, if the doctor follows the usual form, the student will not be the first to answer a question (with no time to think about it) nor the last (when the commonly known answers will already have been given). When describing the rules of Question and Answer series in Chapter 7, I suggested that they promoted both Co-operation and Competition, as directed by the higher-Status doctor. The favoured position in the middle of the semicircle represents any student's best compromise to the dilemma of Co-operating and Competing with his fellows. But clearly not everyone can take such a position. In the position at the other end of the circle, the student is vulnerable to the chance that the questioner will start that end 'for a change' or a chance of a different sort; for example, students on a ward round arranged themselves round the bed of a patient they hadn't seen before, who turned out to be unconscious and lying in the **left lateral position** (that is, facing the right of the bed). The student who had deliberately placed himself at the extreme right of the semicircle round the bed was, to his annoyed surprise, the first and not the last to be asked about the **examination of the unconscious patient**. And students' failure to show professional Idealism (by not paying attention or even, unusually, whispering to each other) may bring chance questions their way, as may its demonstration, when questions can be a reward for keen or knowledgeable students.

Ward rounds may be cramped affairs, and, though this may involve students touching each other, this is avoided when possible. Arms are therefore less likely to be held by the side or in jacket pockets than in one of three other positions, behind the back 'at ease', held across the chest or together in front. The first is the mode often used when students are told to **inspect** a patient in the practice of Experience; arms held behind the back then signify that **inspection** is all the student has in mind. The last is piously Idealistic and submissive. Standing with hands clasped together in front of the chest is the way that students are told to stand in operating theatres but, more commonly, students fold their arms across the chest; this implies colleagueship or Co-operation, the detachment of Experience but preparedness to act Responsibly – and, instrumentally, it keeps the hands out of the way (see Figure

18 above). The only time I saw students with hands in their trouser pockets was among a small group of MB/Ph.D. students, separated from other students by their commitment to Knowledge. The use of the elbow, with arms akimbo, was used only by male doctors of superordinate Status with a subordinate audience. The doctor's Status in the face-to-face ward round means that no student can leave a round (unlike a lecture) without having made an earlier arrangement, although the doctor may be bleeped away; at the end (unlike lectures), way is made for the doctor, who leaves first.

But in students' presentation of self, both verbally and non-verbally, in the theatrical ward round, it is undoubtedly the case that the emotional detachment from patients found in Experience is most emphatically not associated with an emotional detachment from other members of the profession, either doctors and fellow-students. And, while students are frequently instructed to be polite to patients, this is not a quality that characterises intra-professional relations, informed as they are by the disposition of Co-operation.

Teaching by Humiliation

Whatever the attitude to displaying professional Idealism, a student's failure to get the main points of the history, to pick up major clinical signs, to state the likely diagnoses or the fundamental principles of management may be felt as deeply wounding to his own personal sense of identity and moral purpose. So some students are hard on themselves (as well as being treated hardly by their teachers) for failing to 'get' a clinical sign; one woman student was in tears because, despite repeated instruction, she could not 'see' the raised **jugular venous pressure** in a patient's neck. And in a clinical lecture, I was told, another student had failed to give the correct answer to a question about the **management of diabetic keto-acidosis**. The consultant asked the audience of other students: 'Would you want this person to be *your* doctor?', to that student's immense personal and public discomfiture. Such failures may not just reflect on students' own inadequacies, but sometimes also even carry implications of letting down their families. Small wonder, then, that students may try, successfully or not, to 'bullshit' when asked questions, answering confidently even when they are less than confident about the answer, or even lying confidently.

'Teaching by humiliation' can only work if the failure to give the right answer is seen as a personal (or group) moral failing; it is used in teaching variably, some consultants favouring it and being known for it; they may indeed be regarded quite affectionately by students as a consequence, but may also evoke great dislike and even fear, much more than other consultants who do not use this style. I should note that my own fieldwork involved attachment only to firms whose consultants were prepared to accept me; this undoubtedly meant that my own experience was confined to fairly humane uses of this style, though I heard of several female students who were in tears after this kind of discourse.

> Liz [*in the coffee room, to a student on another firm*]: 'I've just had the most unbelievable hour and a half of my life! This surgeon was amazing! So sarcastic! As we left, he said, "There goes the future of Urology!"'
> Dave: 'Was he a consultant?'
> Liz [*dismissing his question as over-obvious*]: 'Oh yes.'

Liz was not in tears, but she was extremely angry. Some doctors make their efforts to treat women students the same as men very clear, while others are explicit about the differences. A senior consultant on the staff of the medical school told me that if female clinical students ever came to him about difficulties they were having, he would console them, telling them not to take it to heart; if male students came, saying the same thing, he would be much rougher, telling them that, 'if they couldn't stand the heat they should get out of the kitchen'. The way he explained this difference was that, 'I'm an old stag; they're young stags.' It is generally accepted that good-looking female students will be treated best (in terms of not being humiliated) and that women in general can often manage to get the better of the predominantly male consultants, although this may well be at the price of not being taken seriously as a future doctor.

Certainly the oral language confirms other impressionistic evidence that men are both taken more seriously and treated more harshly: the term 'chaps' is commonly used for a mixed group of students, with no female equivalent, but more importantly there is no female equivalent for a 'bollocking'. And the profession was widely perceived by students as being sexist and racist; some women students found this outside the profession too, hairdressers especially (I was told) being quite unwilling to consider the possibility that female students might become doctors rather than nurses. Certainly too, women seem to do worse in studies of 'Medical Student Abuse' – all of these seem to be from the US (for example, Sheehan *et al.* 1990; Silver and Glicken 1990) – because of the extra category of sexual harassment or abuse; but this should not hide the extent to which the majority of clinical students, both male and female, describe their experience of mistreatment from many sources (including nurses and patients), but mostly from their clinical teachers, whether faculty members or house staff.

Dealing with Experience

So far I have mostly described the official frontstage teaching and learning of Experience. What happens on clinical students' official backstage? Do they manage this work in the same way they did as preclinical students, by practising Co-operation and Economy? Simply, the answer is Yes, and I have already mentioned the Co-operative (but implicitly Competitive) practice of students asking each other questions on the official backstage; Competition becomes increasingly important in the practice of Co-operation, and the vehicle for this is the display of professional Idealism.

Co-operation and Economy

Co-operation between students is originally held to be the best form of existence, as it was for preclinical students. In a clinical lecture, Andy had volunteered the correct answer to a question put by the lecturer at large, and had then answered two further questions put to him. When students were leaving the theatre afterwards, a friend approached him, saying in disgusted reference to the answers Andy had given, 'What's this? **Marfan's Syndrome**? **Connective Tissue Disorders**?', and putting his finger down his throat to suggest his nausea at Andy's keenness and Competitive stepping out of line. But for learning Experience, students find themselves attached to firms in official teams; it is the medical school rather than they themselves that decides the teams' membership. It will be recalled that the clinical environment was the setting for Becker's derivation of his perspective of Student Co-operation, which indicates how strong this general disposition is for clinical students. They must Co-operate, on the one hand, because they are told to (and arrange for two of their number to be at Out-Patients every week, for example) and because they need to, to help each other out (for example, by covering up for one another's absence, as they are held to be Responsible for each other). Students' need to Co-operate is well understood by doctors: 'Don't worry! They covered up for you well!', I was jokingly told by a consultant after I had been away for a few days. Co-operation may be practised between individual students on ward rounds. In this example, the method of doing so between a pair of students who were close friends further stresses the theatrical qualities of ward rounds, which were also appreciated by the consultant:

> On a Post-Take ward round, Nick had presented a patient admitted through Casualty and was being questioned by the consultant.
> Dr Cooper: 'What makes you think of an **atypical pneumonia**?'
> Nick: '**Systemic signs** . . . [something inaudible]'.
> Dr Cooper: 'No.'
> Nick [*quickly*]: 'That's what *he* [*indicating Sasha, another student*] said!'
> Dr Cooper [*laughing*]: 'He's been feeding you lines, has he?'

The frontstage Co-operation between the pair of friends was also associated with Competition (in Nick's exposure of Sasha). On another round, Competition between them was expressed backstage afterwards, again with reference to the theatre. When Sasha was presenting the results of his examination of a patient to another consultant, Dr Livingstone, Sasha mentioned a 'significant negative' finding:

> Sasha: 'There were no signs of **testicular atrophy**.'
> Dr Livingstone: 'Did you examine them [the **testes**]?'
> Sasha [*unhesitatingly*]: 'Yes.'
> Dr Livingstone: 'There's no need to examine the **gonads**.'
> Sasha [*answering what he understood as a criticism*]: 'When I asked if I could examine his **abdomen**, he uncovered them, so I did.'
> After the round, Nick mocked Sasha about his performance, mimicking Sasha, saying sarcastically, '"Yes, I examined them!" [*Now*

> *expostulating*:] When you pointed out the scar from the **fem-pop [femoro-popliteal] bypass**, you were surprised – you never examined him!'
> Sasha [*smiling*]: 'You need to be a good actor!'

Sasha then in turn teased Nick for his 'stagey' delivery and unusually loud voice when presenting a patient on the same round. This pair of friends also occasionally tried, Competitively, to make each other burst out laughing (or 'corpse', in theatrical terms) on the ward round stage. But more general Co-operation between students on a firm is also expected; this next episode also draws attention to a way non-verbal communication may be used to help other students on ward rounds:

> When a surgical SR asked Anna [by looking at her and saying], 'Where else does the pain [from **cholecystitis**] **radiate**?', she was silent. I looked at her, putting my left hand on my right shoulder. Taking this non-verbal cue, Anna was then able to answer the SR's question, saying, 'The shoulder.' Afterwards she said to me: 'Thank you for that, making the firm not look too hopeless!', emphasising the Co-operation expected within a firm group.

Deviations from the Co-operative rule are possible, either as a cause or a consequence of enmity or real friendship; 'getting on' is important, though the general need to Co-operate may also exacerbate inter-personal disharmony. But Co-operation is usually generally maintained.

Students find real difficulties in fulfilling their official frontstage obligations, difficulties increased by recent changes in health care delivery (increased throughput of patients, shorter hospital stays, superspecialisation in teaching hospital firms, and the dwindling local populations (see Towle 1992: 39)). So during their shorter stay, patients may be difficult to find: they are often moved from ward to ward, especially with the split site of UCH and the Middlesex; they may be off the ward for investigations or treatment, having lunch, or seeing relatives. Patients themselves are increasingly unwilling to be seen by students, but nurses may also tell students not to clerk patients: on CCU, for example, a student had just started to take his patient's blood pressure, an action that caught the Ward Sister's eye; she called over, 'What are you doing to my patient? He's in **sinus rhythm** now! Leave him alone!' Difficulties in finding patients to clerk are compounded by the other demands made on students' time: these may be official (there are an increasing number of lectures, for example, Knowledge again appearing to score over Experience) or unofficial (in the form of part-time jobs and domestic commitments); and junior doctors often encourage students to take time off now, telling them they won't be able to later. Clerking can become a chore; as one student put it, 'I found myself clerking a patient after everyone [else on the firm] had gone home and thought to myself, "What am I doing here? I'm not being paid!"' That students also Co-operate to use Economy to deal with these practicalities is sometimes quite explicit: after the first day on a new firm, Mike said backstage to the rest of the official team, 'They said "Clerk every patient"; we'll just have to see what we can get away with.' The forms that Economy takes are various: before ward rounds, students may establish who has patients clerked and on this basis decide who will answer when the doctor says, 'Who's got a patient for us to see?'; the same patient may be presented to different doctors; students may only 'clerk the notes' and not actually clerk the patient, though they will briefly introduce themselves to the patient before the round, to avoid potential embarrassment during it; students will turn up to those firm events where both their presence and their absence would be most noticeable (often consultant's rounds), and particularly to ward rounds towards the end of the firm, because it is thought that the doctors giving grades will only attend to this matter at the end of the firm, and their notice can be most efficiently attracted at this stage.

Increasing Competition

Despite the Co-operation expected by both doctors and students, Competition is also looked for by both, students because of their interest in getting a good firm grade, and doctors on the lookout for outstanding students. The tension between Co-operation and Competition starts to increase throughout the first clinical year and can lead to quite severe criticism by students of each other:

> Rashid was talking unofficially backstage about the other members of the official team, describing the ways Oliver could be seen to be deliberately flouting the rules of Co-operation between students:

> 'Oliver's getting really annoying! He butts in [during a Question and Answer series] with extra stuff – "Oh, you mean like **Dressler's syndrome**?" [thus demonstrating his own possession of the answer to what might be the next question, and so preventing the next student from giving it, as well as committing a serious breach of convention by asking a question to which he knows the answer]. If someone [another student] asks a question, you know, rather uncertainly, he turns round and answers the question, and then if he's asked what he's doing he says, "I was just explaining something he didn't know" [thus placing himself in Status above his ignorant fellow-student]. If he doesn't know the answer, he puts his head on one side, and frowns . . . It's all so *obvious*!'

Oliver's presentation of himself, including his transparent adoption on a ward round of an appearance conventionally indicating a professionally Idealistic worry about his ignorance, was despised by Rashid as evidence of his increasing Competitiveness instead of the expected Co-operation. So the student on a ward round may find himself drawn three ways: by his own Idealism to be a good doctor (which partly involves the acquisition of Experience), by the Competitive need to display to doctors professional Idealism for Experience, and by the need to maintain Co-operative links with the other students. This internal and external conflict (or 'role-conflict' in Goffman's terms) is due to students' ambiguous Status as 'student-physicians' and as 'boys in white' – a conflict noted by Shuval (1975) – but also involves their own private Idealistic purposes. The conflict can clearly be resolved in more than one way; for example, the student may decide that his acquisition of Experience and the need to impress doctors is, at that time, less important than retaining links with the other students in the firm group, as he will need their help for some other matter. But whichever way it is immediately resolved, it will be in a way that, once again, reinforces the power of intra-professional relationships over those with patients.

The tension between Co-operation and Competition continues for the remainder of the clinical years. Clinical students become increasingly segregated from the lay world, as they are drawn more closely into the exclusively medical environment, and the pressure of work has resulted in the gradual loss of their membership of representative teams, in which the more familiar forms of internal Co-operation and externally directed Competition exist. In a backstage discussion, Liz, now a second-year clinical student, described fellow members of the official team rehearsing before firm assessments, which had never happened before with that group; and when they were told that anyone who presented a patient for a seminar would get an A as a firm grade, an appeal for volunteers was met by several students responding, whereas similar appeals in the past had been ignored. Alf, who preclinically had been a prominent member of several representative teams and was now in his final clinical year, dressed in a suit for house job interviews, agreed: 'I've given up reassuring people [other students who are worried about their Final clinical exams by saying] "You'll pass." You're in it for yourself!'

The sense of Competitive isolation from each other is exacerbated by the Competition for house jobs (see Chapter 9), but is also experienced as distance from the medical school itself. Contact with the medical school is, by and large, through notices pinned up or with secretaries, and in the recently introduced regular 'academic reviews'. With the large number of brief firm attachments, the unceasing exams and assessments, and with the increasing awareness among students of the financial benefits that students bring to UCLMS, some conclude that the medical school is only interested in as many of them as possible passing the exams; students' impersonal relationship with the medical school often turns into a form of hostility. The only time I experienced any real hostility from any students was on my attachment to a firm where there were only two final-year students. Because they thought I was employed by the medical school, for two weeks these two students addressed no remarks to me, answering my remarks and questions with monosyllables if at all, not eating at the same table, and using postural forms of exclusion to cut me out physically from standing near them in the semicircle of ward rounds. And, as students approach Finals, they describe the way they feel they have been let down by the medical school. They are worried that their diagnostic skills are not as advanced as they should be; and so ill-prepared do they judge themselves for these exams that many enrol at non-teaching hospitals for short courses on 'How to Pass Finals', for which they pay themselves, a remarkable comment on their three years' clinical teaching. Clinical Finals, of course, principally assess not their diagnostic skills but their capacity to practise Experience by clerking patients and act Responsibly in emergencies (in other words, to be a competent, safe houseman); and most of them pass the exams.

Putting it all Together: Clinical Finals

The use of Economy is especially evident as Finals approach. The hospital is scoured for patients with 'good' histories, but especially with 'good' signs, and students line up to practise taking a history from them or to improve their examination technique, with no concern for which consultant the patients belong to; acquiring as much Experience in as short a time as possible is now paramount. First-year students may help at clinical Finals, thereby acquiring Experience of 'exam cases', patients often chosen for their physical signs; after the exam, a registrar ran down the list of Short Cases for the benefit of the first-year students: 'He won't mind [if you examine him] . . . this one's a spot diagnosis – ask him to take his shirt off . . . he's got good hands . . . very interesting eyes . . . a great abdomen to feel . . . he's dead . . . he's barking mad [a psychiatric patient, with no physical signs].' For students preparing for Finals, the lottery of the sort of patient they may get for their 'long case' is a great source of worry. In general they hope for a patient with 'good' symptoms and signs (and so a surgical or medical patient, rather than a psychiatric one); but even more important is whether the patient is Co-operative or not; as one Finalist put it, reversing the usual ranking of specialties that I discuss below, 'I'd rather have a co-operative psyche [psychiatric] patient than an unco-operative surgical one; some patients have really **malignant** personalities!'

The Final clinical exam is of the same form as ward rounds and firm assessments, with all elements exaggerated. Overall, it is the importance of students' being able to examine and present patients professionally (that is, as if they have done it many times before) while being examined themselves that is stressed, as is the consequent confidence; Finalists are often told that their confidence may be judged by an examiner from across the room, and they are therefore now told to show this even if they don't feel it (by, for example, not saying they've forgotten something even if they know they have). Students are told above all not to be rude to patients or to hurt them, and that this evidence that they are unfit to assume the Status of doctor is the only thing that may fail them outright. With the official accentuation of these dramatic elements of Experience, all students notice it, complaining unofficially, 'It's all so theatrical!'; 'Be slick at this! Be slick at that!'; 'We need acting lessons!'

These dramatic aspects were stressed in an official film shown just before clinical Finals, with now explicit advice about the successful student's verbal and physical presentation of self: 'Look smart; look the examiner in the eye and say, "Good Morning"; memorise the first part of the history; change what the patient said into medical language; list the important symptoms, using medical terms to describe the symptoms; do not use your body to indicate their localisation; mention only important negatives; go straight through the clerking, without any unnecessary summary; stop after giving the symptoms and signs; beware being told the diagnosis by the patient; [when the examiners talk to you] never answer a question with a question; just answer the question asked; say decisively what you would do for management.' This advice is repeated in a short book *Final MB: A Guide to Success in Clinical Medicine* (Dalton 1991); summing up, in a simple mnemonic, the successful candidate's approach as a mixture of Competence (and Common Sense), Caring and Conventionality, the crucial point about the candidate's relations with the patient is repeated: 'Never hurt the patient. *Always* ask the patient if he is comfortable' and with the examining doctors: '*On no account must you argue with the examiner – even if you know you are right*. Examiners regard this as insulting' (1991: 20, 21; original emphasis).

Students prepare for clinical exams in an entirely different way from the written exams of Knowledge; for the latter they revise together, while for the former, they rehearse together (often again forming official-purpose teams to hear and criticise each other's performances). And it is this highly dramatic representation (presenting oneself presenting one's patient, and being examined on one's examination) that leads to the high anxiety that pervades the weeks, days, hours and minutes before clinical Finals; it is stage fright, heightened by the unknown nature of the patients to be seen and the knowledge that your performance on stage is a short one, of an hour or so. The audience is a critical one and, if your performance does not measure up to that of a safe and competent practitioner, the earliest repeat presentation is at the retakes months later.

Combining Professional Segments

In Chapter 6, I described a major part of preclinical students' work as integrating the Knowledge taught by distinct academic departments, which are paid in terms of time spent teaching students. Clinical students do the same, only now they have to integrate the Experience taught by different segments of the profession in the teaching hospital. In their rotation round the different specialties, which are paid for teaching on the same basis as preclinical departments, clinical students are benefiting the specialties financially as well as having to combine these different branches of medicine cognitively and practically (in terms of having to work hard enough to pass exams, written and clinical, in Surgery as well as Psychiatry, for example). Students often see their rotation as a privileged glimpse of different specialties, to allow them to see which branch of medicine they might choose; the idea that it might be a form of subordinating exploitation does not occur to them. And, just as preclinical students rank academic disciplines, so clinical students rank segments of the profession, now more confidently, in terms of dispositional categories, which, as well as being practised, are again found 'good to think with'. As Bourdieu (1977: 165) puts it, the taxonomies of the system 'at once divide and unify, legitimating unity in division, that is to say, hierarchy'.

Dingwall (1977) has described the use of 'atrocity stories' by members of a profession to create taxonomies with categories that define which occupations can be included and which excluded; this method of categorisation by disparagement is used by the medical profession to define both non-professionals and intra-professional segments, and consultants show clinical students the way. As doctors, they disparage non-doctors, such as administrators and managers, about whom adverse comments are frequent; the main point doctors make is that their lack of medical Status means they have no medical Responsibility for patients (although it may also be relevant that, in clinical language, doctors **administer** drugs or treatments to patients, having discussed their **management**; some of the contempt doctors have for these employees may be based on their lay and abstract names). As clinicians, consultants disparage preclinical teachers; as hospital doctors, they disparage GPs; and as specialists, they disparage other specialties.

So, for example, a consultant ENT surgeon made a remark in the course of a clinical lecture (often the setting for such comments, presumably because of the absence of members of any other professional segments) about the **management** of a child with

croup: 'The paediatrician may say "Do a Chest X-ray"; and down the cold corridor they [such patients] go, put on the cold lead shield. The kid'll die in X-ray [in the X-ray room]! And if you think radiographers are good at resuscitating children, you're wrong! A lot of children die each year out of ignorance!' The point being made by the ENT surgeon was that paediatricians (in a branch of Medicine) and radiographers (not doctors at all) don't know what they're doing – the paediatrician here was not basing the request for an X-ray on adequate personal Experience (but perhaps on published Knowledge), and consequently did not take the correct Responsible action. Here again we have the elements of the basic professional stereotypes: Surgery scores higher on Responsibility, perhaps higher on Experience, and less on Knowledge than Medicine. Some surgical specialities culturally require even less Knowledge than others, as an orthopaedic surgeon implied in a lecture, asking the audience, 'Why do orthopaedic surgeons have hunched shoulders and flat foreheads?', answering his own question, 'Because when you ask them a question, they go [*He shrugged his shoulders to indicate ignorance.*] and when you tell them the answer, they go [striking his forehead with his right palm to indicate their recognition of the obviousness of the answer]!' In teaching hospitals, Medicine and Surgery previously shared the highest Status, though probably through different routes, the greater Responsibility of Surgery being matched by the greater Knowledge in Medicine; now Medicine has overtaken Surgery, no doubt because of the increasing value attached to Knowledge. At any rate, it is possible to go through each of the specialties in turn, and the sub-specialties, arranging them according to these dispositional categories, giving a cultural judgement which very much accords with my analysis of Becker's students' attitudes (see Chapter 2).

One specialty is of particular interest here. Obstetrics is, for some students, the high point of their clinical years. The reasons for this are not hard to find in terms of the practice of dispositions. On Obstetric wards, where students are attached for a period when they do not have to attend any conflicting lectures of Knowledge, their patients (clearly 'hot') are individual women, whom they may stay with throughout their labour. During their attachment, at first they are closely supervised by midwives (but not doctors), but later it is only the delivery that is supervised, the midwife sometimes simply being present with a few words of advice or help. Students' medical Status is therefore less ambiguous than it normally is on the wards; their patients provide not only Experience but, much more importantly, the opportunity for the practice of the action of Responsibility. During the hours spent with the patient, a close relationship may be established in the practice of a less exclusively medical Co-operation than usual, in that the aims of the student (in whom, for once, personal and professional Idealism closely overlap) and the woman in labour are effectively identical, and usually realised in a safe delivery. Moreover, the powerfully physical process of labour allows students full range for the verbal and indeed physical encouragement of Co-operation, as they strain and breathe in sympathy with their patients.

But it is essential to appreciate that, just as preclinically Psychology and Sociology were accorded least respect, the lowest-Status professional specialty is Psychiatry, a stereotype first provided to preclinical students by medically qualified Anatomy demonstrators, who tend to be surgeons, but affirmed by hospital consultants; for example, one physician said vehemently, speaking of patients with **enuresis**, 'It's a tragedy when patients like this fall into the hands of the psychiatrists.' Such low Status is confirmed for students by several dispositional factors. Psychiatric patients tend to score low on the category of Co-operation, just as Becker's students found. As with Psychology and Sociology preclinically, words are used by psychiatrists that do not have any concrete physical referent, and are therefore no doubt hard to understand for many clinical students; and, of course, many words (like 'depression', 'anxiety' and 'schizophrenic') are in regular lay use. The psychiatric 'literature' contains different approaches taken towards patients' problems (based on the varieties of assumption made about the origins of psychiatric symptoms), and is thus short of proper Knowledge. Further, in Psychiatry, the patient's history is not just a straightforward account from the patient, but itself becomes part of the equivalent of the physical examination, although this yields no proper Experience in the form of definite evidence of concrete pathology. And students find that psychiatrists lack Responsibility for their patients in terms of both ownership and action: not only are there 'multidisciplinary teams', including many non-doctors, but nearly all psychiatric treatment is negotiated, and much treatment is talking, hardly action at all. Rather perversely, the lack of Responsibility that psychiatrists are held to have for their patients may be confirmed for clinical students by the fact that psychiatric patients are the only ones for whom they themselves can have real and continuing Responsibility, by getting on the supervised scheme to meet a patient once a week for psychotherapy. That consultant psychiatrists should hand over Responsibility in this way to untrained students may further emphasise the lack of Responsibility in Psychiatry; to put this another way, no cardiac surgeon would ever hand over complete Responsibility for one of his patients to a student. For all these reasons, then, Psychiatry is the lowest-Status specialty in general medical culture. This is confirmed elsewhere by students' answers to a questionnaire about medical specialties (Furnham 1986). The unscientific nature and the ineffectiveness of Psychiatry clearly refer to the relative absence of Knowledge and Experience on the one hand, and of the successful practice of Responsibility on the other.

That students themselves actually use dispositional categories in this way is quite clear from the example of Abdul (both of whose parents and one of whose sisters were doctors, thus giving him closer access to the medical mentality and confidence to express it) describing Rheumatology as 'the housewife's specialty'; in explanation, he said, 'It's all out-patients, all women and children, all tablets and aches and pains.' In other words, not only is the ownership of Responsibility limited to out-patients, and the action of Responsibility to giving tablets, but the patients' problems are seen to be 'aches and pains', not providing any Experience in the form of real pathological findings, and the patients themselves are women and children; this combination makes Rheumatology a low-Status specialty, suitable for women doctors, who may well work part-time, making it 'the housewife's specialty'.

The association implied by Abdul between low-Status specialties and women doctors is in fact quite a strong one: the lowest proportion of women consultants is found in Surgery (4.3 per cent) and Medicine (8.6 per cent) (Medicine here has been created by lumping together the six highest-Status subspecialties of General Medicine, Cardiology, Diabetes and Endocrinology, Gastroenterology, Nephrology and Thoracic Medicine); in Rheumatology it is 16.2 per cent, while in Psychiatry it is 29.8 per cent (DOH 1996: Table 7A). The highest proportion of women consultants is actually now in Paediatrics (33.6 per cent), which appears to be thought the subsegment of Medicine particularly suitable for women, perhaps because of the greater personal Idealism identified by Becker's students as needed for this specialty. Abdul's point about women tending to work part-time in low-Status specialties is demonstrated by the proportion of all SRs who are women training part-time: 0.02 per cent in Surgery, 3.3 per cent in Medicine and 12.7 per cent in Psychiatry (DOH 1996: Table 7D). It would be hard to determine cause and effect in terms of low Status and ease of part-time training; but these figures lend further force to my description of all professional dispositions as being historically male and derived from Surgery.

Chapter 9

Responsibility: Ownership and Action at Last

Of all 'is five years' schoolin' they don't remember much
Excep' the not retreatin', the step an' keepin' touch.
It looks like teachin' wasted when they duck an' spread
  and 'op –
But if 'e 'adn't learned 'em they'd be all about the shop.

Rudyard Kipling

House jobs are the work of the compulsory pre-registration year; housemen must be supervised, and these jobs must be approved by the university as educationally suitable (GMC 1992b). Over the years, teaching hospitals have accrued housemen's posts at various hospitals (at the teaching hospital itself, at those nearby and at some quite far off) for inclusion in the Pre-Registration House Officer Appointment Scheme (the 'matching scheme'); at UCLMS, this has some 150 posts in Medicine and 150 posts in Surgery for the 200 or so graduates each year, though students are not obliged to join the scheme and some prefer to arrange their own house jobs. All house jobs in the country now start on 1 August and 1 February, and most students who pass their Finals in July will start the pre-registration training a month later. Currently, applications for house jobs must be made some time before the posts are to be taken up, towards the end of clinical students' second year.

Applying for House Jobs

The application form that students fill in has sections for recording their achievements in the practice of the professional dispositions that they will have learnt at the medical school; there is a space for prizes and distinctions (that is, for evidence of Competitive excellence in Knowledge) and for university or medical school activities (recording Co-operation, usually in representative teams). On the reverse of the form is the list of the grades given to students after their attendance on the firms they were attached to (the assessments of Experience acquired), with the percentages scored in written assessments of Knowledge. Some candidates have extremely impressive records, with papers published and some even with books written, along with a cluster of prizes. There is also a space for recording 'student assistantships': in their second and third clinical years, students may do such 'locums' and for a few days do the work of a houseman on leave to practise the disposition of Responsibility in Medicine and Surgery, which they otherwise only find in Casualty. New housemen who have worked as locums say that locums are very protected: while they work for these few days, they are not allowed to sign their names or to write up drugs, and are looked after in a way that they do not find as housemen. But doing locums is fairly generally known to be a help when applying for house jobs, because of the Responsibility exercised during those few days.

Students' applications for particular house jobs depend on several factors: their own assessment of their chances of success and practicalities like location, but particularly the personal value they place on the sorts of job available. The cultural value attached to a 'good' or 'busy' job (providing plenty of Experience and Responsibility) is matched by that attaching to jobs of high Status (within the teaching hospital); both of these will attract applicants who reckon that these are the highways to professional advancement, practising the Economic disposition just as Becker's students did when considering their future career. But Economy may also be personally practised in a counter-cultural way (perhaps especially by some women) who look for 'soft' or 'easy' house jobs, with less arduous conditions and consequently less scope for speedy advance.

The medical school circulates students' applications to consultants, who return a list of shortlisted candidates for interview. The more general Competitiveness that is increasingly found during the clinical years is added to by this specific Competition. A peculiar atmosphere, characterised by rumour and suspicion, is generated: one student has been definitely promised a job by a consultant, it is said, or another well-known student, or perhaps two, are said to be applying for an attractive job – so there's no point in anyone else applying for it; some hospitals are rumoured to have unwritten conditions, such as only interviewing students who have put them as first choice. The spirit of Co-operation, so strong in the preclinical years both officially and unofficially, and weakened by Competition on the firms, is now found in a very uneasy yoke with Competition.

A week or so was timetabled for interviews for these posts, when candidates were seen individually by a panel of consultants whose house jobs they had applied to do; for the UCH/Middlesex house jobs both in Medicine and Surgery, all the consultants were men. The consultants who asked questions of the candidates were usually the two consultants whose jobs the candidates had put as their first and second preference. Perhaps the commonest general question was along the lines of, 'I know it's early to say, but what are your career plans?' (equivalent to the question, 'Why do you want to do medicine?' at the interviews for medical school); the answers, now as then, need to show unqualified commitment and a definite personal statement of intent: 'Surgery is something I've always wanted to do', or, 'Oh, definitely Medicine, but I'm not sure which branch yet.' The commonest specific question (equivalent to the question, 'Why do you want to come to *this* medical school?') was, 'Why have you applied to do Respiratory Medicine [or Orthopaedic Surgery, or whatever segment was involved in the post]?'. In answering this, candidates tried to show their interest ('I'm very serious about Vascular Surgery', or even, 'Kidneys fascinate me!') and their positive enjoyment of it ('I've always enjoyed the practical aspects of Surgery', or, 'I enjoyed Oncology – it was very interesting'). When candidates, uncommonly, said they thought General Practice was their future career, the second question about the specific jobs was usually not asked. In answering these questions, students (just under half of whom will still end up as GPs) have learnt to state firmly in this official frontstage scene what they may be much less sure about unofficially.

In other words, as in interviews for medical school, it is important to demonstrate obvious Idealism in the pursuit of Status. To do so, clinical students rely on their experience of presenting their patients (and therefore to that extent themselves) and their awareness of the need to demonstrate their enthusiasm. Some of them are very good at it, though the interest and indeed fascination they usually expressed at interview contrasted with the attitudes expressed unofficially elsewhere. Most students prepare for these interviews by rehearsing them, just as they are likely to have rehearsed for their interviews to get into medical school years before. It is not that medical interviews are unusual in being concerned with personal presentation – all interviews are – but that the dramatic qualities looked for in a good presentation by the candidate echo features from other dramatic settings found in medicine, especially the ward round. For example, the same spatial configuration is found in most interviews, with the single candidate facing, sometimes almost being surrounded by, the interviewers; interviews for house jobs are no different, but the configuration echoes that of the ward round, with the candidate now presenting not a patient but himself to a surrounding audience of experienced doctors, who are alert for slips or inconsistencies. And, like a patient with a 'good' history, the candidate should aim to give a concise and consistent personal history that ties in their past with their plans for their future career in terms that make sense to their audience. So the candidate for house jobs, like the candidate for a place in medical school, must demonstrate to the interviewers that, for most purposes, he is already suitable for membership of their official teams; as was said about the medical school interviews, these are interviews to join a particular sort of club as judged by demonstration of existing qualities, now especially Responsibility, rather than interviews to determine anything else (such as candidates' individual need for training).

The Importance of Responsibility

Consultants were especially concerned to assess candidates' Responsibility: a surgeon told the other members of the panel that he asked himself the following questions about candidates, 'Are they bright? Have they done well? Do they give you confidence that they'd get things done?' [Have they shown possession of Knowledge? Have they shown interest in acquiring Experience on their firms? Do they appear to be Responsible?]. A physician put the same question in more general terms about candidates who had done well academically and on their firms: 'Does it translate?' [Does their good performance as regards Knowledge and Experience translate into Responsibility?]. Given that only doing locums could give evidence of Responsibility, candidates who have not done locums found themselves at a disadvantage. One said, 'I can't wait to start working!', but her admission that she had not done any locums rather undermined her professed Idealistic enthusiasm for Status and Responsibility. Questions about doing locums may also be asked when candidates have said they are unsure about their future careers: 'Have you done any assistantships to help you make up your mind?', in much the same way that candidates for entry to medical school are asked if they have gained any experience of their future careers; here again, not having done so is evidence of not having taken the available opportunities to practise Responsibility. While there are, of course, other questions asked at interviews, it is the applicants' ability to demonstrate their capacity for Responsible action that matters most, despite their paradoxical institutional deprivation of it during their training so far.

After each candidate had been interviewed, the consultants ranked them and indicated which they would like to have as their houseman. In addition to references to Responsibility and to other dispositions, comments were also made on candidates' presentation, not this time on their presentation of a patient, but of themselves: confidence but not cockiness (even confidence about when to hesitate), concision but not too much abbreviation, consistency but with a distinctive quirk. The interviewers were sometimes moved to comment how well a candidate had interviewed (how they had – like a patient giving a 'good' history – led the audience along to the obvious conclusion). So, just as the candidates competed among themselves for the consultants' jobs, so the owners of the jobs competed among themselves for the candidates; the reverse side of patronage is that a good client gives the patron a good name.

The Nature of Responsibility

There is no ceremony about new housemen going to the laundry and getting their first long white coat, a change of dress indicating their new Status with their assumption of Responsibility, which is much more significant than the academic robes hired for the graduation ceremony. It is official policy in most hospitals for all staff, including doctors, to wear badges; the only doctors who rarely wear either white coats or name-badges are consultants (and, to a lesser extent, SRs). Housemen carry in their coats very much what students do, with one most important additional attribute of Responsibility, a 'bleep'. These machines, only carried by students when On Take, go off whatever housemen are doing; someone (as they quickly learn) is almost certainly going to ask them to do something else. When housemen are absent from the hospital during normal hours, they usually ask a colleague to 'hold' or 'carry' their bleep; that is, to answer it, and deal with any really pressing request but otherwise to note who called and why, so that the proper holder can deal with the matter on return.

Housemen have to learn their way about the hospital, and even the relatively few housemen working in their teaching hospital need to relearn its geography for their new role. Most firms have a particular ward on which they try to place most of their patients and whose nursing and secretarial staff housemen therefore come to know better. But the greater 'consultant bed scatter' means that most housemen have to work on any ward where their firm's patients are, and therefore to have a working knowledge of different wards' arrangements and routines, matters that were of only occasional concern to them as students: the whereabouts on the ward of the medical notes, patients' X-rays, paper for notes, request forms, various sorts of apparatus (**sphygmomanometers**, equipment for taking blood, for putting up **Venflons**, for performing **rectal examinations**), which trays for specimens the porters clear and when. Each ward is different, even when they have exactly the same design; arrangements and appearances, especially around the nurses' station, are different, chronologically layered and organic; lists of telephone numbers, of bleep numbers, timetables, doctors' duty rosters, notices from management and notices about visiting hours are stuck up on and around the desk. Housemen also have to discover other parts of the hospital that were equally irrelevant to them as students: the various departments where investigations take place (X-ray, ultrasonography and so on), the mortuary (where they must go to identify dead patients), Medical Records, the Pharmacy, and where the administrative offices are (for their contracts, for example). Housemen's necessary movement about the hospital causes them many problems at first: they leave their own equipment (pens, stethoscopes, tourniquets) behind on these different wards; they forget their notebooks, or odd bits of paper on which results have been written down; their absence from one ward means the nurses bleep them on another ward to remind them of something they may or may not have forgotten to do.

Responsibility: Ownership and Action

The first aspect of Responsibility, ownership, has been understood by housemen since their first day on the wards as clinical students. It is the case, as everyone knows, that every hospital patient belongs to a named consultant. It is not just in oral use that this is the case; every sheet of paper in the notes and every investigation request form has a space for the patient's consultant's name and, on the wards, the consultant's name over or at the end of the patient's bed may be larger than the patient's own. This ownership was alluded to by the registrar On Take, saying of a patient he had just seen in Casualty, 'He must belong to somebody; he's had recent treatment.' The relationship of the first aspect, ownership, to the second, action, is not always as clearly expressed as it was on a ward round by Mr Hunter, a surgical SR, to Zak, the new houseman, as they talked about the patients for the next day's **operating list**:

> Zak: 'There are out-lying patients on other firms, mostly for **Hickman lines**.'
> Mr Hunter: 'Have they been clerked?'
> Zak: 'Yes.'
> Mr Hunter: 'And **worked up**? What about the **clotting**? [Are the results of these blood tests back?]'
> Zak: 'I'll check.'
> Mr Hunter [*feeling the need to explain his questions*]: 'Even though in this case we're only technicians, we need to make sure they've got all the results, otherwise they could bleed to death on the [operating] table.' [Making sure 'they've got all the results' I take to mean here 'the patients have all their results with them' in their notes which go with them to theatres.]

Mr Hunter's explanation indicates that, while he and his firm are very definitely going to take action directed at these patients, in the form of an operation, the patients belong to other firms; his firm's absence of ownership for them means his firm is not fully Responsible for them, and he and the other surgeons on his firm are therefore 'only technicians'. But all the work preparatory to the operation has been delegated to Zak, to do himself or to ensure that it has been done by someone else. Despite the pervasive and powerful disposition of Responsibility in practice, the twin aspects of ownership and action may be dissimulated in speech. So when a consultant asks a student, 'Now, what are we going to do for him [the patient]? Remember doctors only advise or suggest. What are we going to advise this patient?', the verbal reminder to observe in speech what is hardly observed in practice, appears to apply just as much to the consultant himself as to the students he is teaching. It should also be noted that, in this question, the Idealistic moral aspect of action, doing something 'for' a patient, is preferred to the instrumental aspect of Responsibility, that of doing something 'to' someone.

Though housemen are familiar with some of their duties (clerking patients and attending ward rounds), the action that they take is at first a great surprise to them; it has no equivalent in their previous five years of training, and even doing locums is little preparation for it. This remarkable discovery parallels the ways in which preclinical students find the world of medical school quite unlike anything else, and clinical students find that their preclinical years have hardly prepared them at all for their new situation. Just as Knowledge and Experience are distinct medical dispositions, so is Responsibility; and Responsibility, like Experience, is anticipated with both excitement and apprehension.

Housemen and Consultants' Responsibility: An Ambiguity

Before they started work, at the newly instituted Induction Day on their first day of employment, housemen were told a bit about their work; a biochemist said, 'You'll find the buck stops with the houseman, now. You do it [take the blood] if it's not [been] done!' and a haematologist, 'If the patient gets cancelled [for an operation, because an investigation hasn't been done], the shit hits the fan and the person that gets it in the back of the neck is you!' This was expanded on later, by an SR to the two new housemen on the firm:

> You're the filter; no one has the same handle on the patient as you . . . I can't explain it; if you haven't clerked a patient in, you never really get the same handle on someone, even if you spend an hour with

> them at the side of their bed – I'm not saying you shouldn't spend an hour with them . . . No one ever tells you about being a House Officer – it's your responsibility to get things done. How you work it out between you is up to you both, but you're equally responsible!

From the SR's account of the housemen's Responsibility, it would appear that nearly everything to do with a patient, except perhaps doing a surgical operation, could fall into their remit. Of course, for housemen, their Responsible action is mainly administrative (that is, action that is not directed specifically at patients but that, though specifically concerned with patients, is directed at other employees in the hospital), taking endless blood samples, and arranging tests, investigations and referrals for their patients. The slowness of the internal post for returning the results of these means that housemen spend a lot of time on the telephone to various departments and laboratories, 'chasing' results (even though, in the teaching hospital, blood results are now put on a computer, the houseman still has to consult this). The time spent with patients is relatively small and the time spent doing things to patients (apart from taking blood) is tiny; but giving intravenous drugs, sometimes highly dangerous ones, does normally fall within their duties. Surgical housemen, certainly in the teaching hospital, seldom find themselves in operating theatres, though some housemen may learn specialised techniques (putting in a **chest drain** or draining fluid from the abdomen by **paracentesis**, for example). Doing these for the first time may be nerve-racking, especially if what I heard referred to as the 'Guy's Rule' was followed: 'See one, do one, teach one'. But housemen often refer ironically to their general lack of the archetypal action of Responsibility as they greet each other in the hospital: 'Hello Sarah! Saved many lives today?' And one houseman talked of the embarrassment she felt when explaining to patients each time she saw them that nothing had happened since the last time she saw them, adding, 'You can't *do* anything!'

But even given housemen's mainly administrative Responsibilities, there is a theoretical problem; for, as everyone knows, each hospital patient is placed under a consultant, who is 'ultimately responsible' for their care and treatment. It might therefore appear that there are two sorts of Responsibility: the houseman's (to do whatever it is that he has to do in the course of doing the job), and the consultant's (which is due to his rank).

This ambiguity is not discussed, perhaps because the materially referential language makes this difficult. But the nature of medical 'responsibility' is, in fact, easily understood by consideration of the two aspects of Responsibility, ownership and action; the former is ascriptive, attributed to those who hold the office of consultant, while the latter is descriptive, applying to those who actually take Responsible action, and who may or may not be consultants. Medical 'responsibility' recalls Gellner's fictional concept of 'bobility' (1970: 38–9), which may be used both of those who hold a certain office and of others on the basis of their conduct. The former privileged group therefore acquires the prestige of this virtue without the need to practise it, in a socially functional and systemically stabilising way. The medical concept of 'responsibility' (that its practice is not the same as its attribution) is identical, and equally socially functional, in its preservation of privilege and power with high Status and delegation of action and its consequences to subordinates. These differences are found very clearly in law: consultants' 'clinical responsibility' for patients (their ownership of them) is quite different from any 'legal liability' (as a consequence of medical action) for patients, which, with the major exception of surgical action, is more likely to be taken by housemen and junior doctors. As some recent legal cases show, the consequences of housemen's and junior doctors' action falls on them alone, without 'their' consultants, who are still 'clinically responsible' for patients treated by their juniors, necessarily being personally involved at all (see Brazier (1992) for a general discussion, and Childs (1995) for a review of some recent cases concerning 'gross negligence manslaughter' by junior doctors). The origins of this problem (as it certainly is for housemen) may once again be derived historically, in that the disposition of Responsibility (like all others) arose from surgical practice; the individual surgeon, visibly taking action directed at the patient, is also entitled to be attributed with the patient's ownership.

Responsibility and Certainty

In the context of the sociological discussion about the uncertainty and certainty of the medical knowledge that doctors learn and base their actions on, I have indicated that certainty is looked for and found by preclinical students in their acquisition of

Knowledge, and that Experience is also certain, both in its unquestionable (because physical) nature and the form of the Question and Answer method of clinical teaching (in which only questions to which the answer is known are asked). Now housemen learn, through action, the personal certainty of Responsibility; they learn the effects of what they do. In other words, it is only after they have been asked the question about their own real Responsible action, 'What have you done?', rather than the question about their hypothetical Responsible action, 'What would you do?', that this new form of certainty arises. Clinical students will almost certainly have come across such certainty expressed; here Dr Stock, an SHO, was stung by a student's question to stress the certainty resulting from personal action:

> An official team of students was being taught by Dr Stock on a teaching ward round; he had shown them the **ECG** of a patient who had been having episodes of **sudden loss of consciousness**:
>
> Dr Stock [*summarising the findings*]: 'So she's got **second degree heart block, Mobitz Type II**. Is it significant?' [*He went round the semicircle of students in turn, directing the question simply by looking at them; the first four of the six students did not answer, and he then looked at me.*]
>
> SS [*motivated to answer by the Co-operation expected, in order to avoid the firm group collectively seem totally ignorant, and, perhaps rather perversely in the circumstances, by its inverse, Competition, to show that I still remembered some medicine, but qualifying my answer because of my Status, unknown to the doctor*]: 'If she's having blackouts, it presumably is.'
>
> Dr Stock: 'Yes! [*looking at my name badge, to remember this now "visible" student*]: And the treatment is to put a **pacemaker** in.'

Roxanne, another student [*to Dr Stock*]: 'But how do you know that's what's causing her blackouts?'

Dr Stock [*vehemently*]: 'Look, I *know* that's what they've got; I *know* that's what you do; I *know* they get better and I *know* they leave hospital!'

Here Dr Stock was clearly reasoning backwards; his own knowledge that such patients leave hospital, having got better from this form of treatment (or action directed at such patients), led to his confidence that this form of action was indicated for this particular patient. The same sort of reasoning was shown, though with less outward confidence, by another SHO, here in Casualty. Her equal certainty was based on a kind of action that housemen are rather more personally familiar with, administrative action, and was concerned with the results of investigations:

The firm was On Take, and we were in Casualty. Dr Todd had asked the two students On Take, Charlie and myself, what investigations we would do on a patient (a Greek Cypriot in her seventies with **asthma**) whom we had just seen.

Charlie: '**MSU** [a **mid-stream urine**].'

Dr Todd: 'For what?' [*Charlie was silent, as was she; his answer, not leading to any further catechism but only to this dead-end, was now ignored by both students and doctor.*]

SS [*taking a turn at the question*]: '**E's and U's** [**Electrolytes and Urea**]'.

Dr Todd [*agreeing with my answer by asking a further question*]: 'Anything else? [*We were silent; she hesitated, before saying:*] I'd do a **blood sugar**.'

SS [*able to ask this question because we were in Casualty*]: 'Why?'

Dr Todd [*blushing*]: 'It may be erroneous and it's not in the books as far as I know; but it's my experience that elderly Greek ladies tend to have **Type II diabetes**.'

It was her experience of her past exercise of Responsibility in doing investigations on her patients that led Dr Todd to this idiosyncratic plan; her blushing and her apology that it might be erroneous was explained by the absence of published Knowledge on this subject or her ignorance of its presence – Responsibility differs from Knowledge in the same way that Experience does. But even when such Knowledge exists, it may be publicly discounted, as it was by this SR addressing new housemen: 'Because it's printed in a journal, it doesn't necessarily mean it's true! Now you're qualified, you've realised that the dogma you learnt as students isn't the case; it's not question of black or white – it's a question of experience!' The SR has thus used the word 'experience' to cover the dispositions of Experience and Responsibility and to contrast them, and their superiority, to written Knowledge.

This accords with the view taken by several sociologists. Freidson (1970: 170) describes 'a kind of ontological and epistemological individualism' as characteristic of the clinical mentality; Bosk (1979: 91–4) describes the trumping of academic knowledge by 'clinical acumen' or 'clinical expertise'; in the same way, Atkinson (1984: 953) emphasises the 'training for dogmatism' and the way in which clinicians work in a state of certainty based on their 'personal knowledge and experience'. While I consider that these analyses would be improved by a distinction between clinicians' knowledge of a certain presentation (that is, their Experience) and their knowledge of what to do about it (their Responsibility), it is clear that something very interesting has happened. Written Knowledge, learnt as certain by preclinical and clinical students, is now for housemen being referred to as uncertain, with certainty now limited to 'experience' (which should be expanded as above to Experience and Responsibility). Only what has been personally experienced, whether the Experience of 'seeing' patients or the Responsibility of action directed at them, is now certain, while written Knowledge is now itself debatable and uncertain: the scientific base of medicine, needed for the profession's successful emergence, gives way to the personal authority of its practitioners, which both maintains the profession's exclusive cognitive base and the system's own internal authority. The written Knowledge that doctors (rather than students) read is often in the form of statistical results of clinical trials. But Statistics was never accorded full medical Status, partly because of its very uncertainty (as I discussed in Chapter 6). This may in turn account for what one statistician has called, in a recent leading article in the *BMJ*, the 'scandal of poor medical research' (Altman 1994). While the publication of such Knowledge is crucial to professional advancement in the Competitive 'publish or perish' climate, 'huge sums of money are spent on [medical] research which is seriously flawed', mainly owing to doctors' inadequate grasp of the methods of both science in general and Statistics in particular. 'Amazingly, it is widely considered acceptable for medical researchers [that is, doctors] to be ignorant of statistics. Many are not ashamed (and some seem proud) to admit that they "don't know anything about statistics"' (1994: 283). This finding is perhaps not so amazing when preclinical students' attitude to Statistics is recalled.

There is clearly a continuing tension between the personal certainty of Responsibility and Experience and the published probability of Knowledge, recently increased by the new trend emphasising '[published] Evidence-Based Medicine'; doctors do change their views about some things very quickly, about others never. Instances of the influence of the previous exercise of Responsibility in relation to the absence of specific Knowledge are common: 'We haven't done the trials but I'm sufficiently impressed to prescribe it [Aspirin] even without a previous **myocardial infarction**', said one SR. Doctors, though, often dissimulate their reliance on their past exercise of Responsibility by saying, 'It's only anecdotal evidence, but . . .', and so apparently conceding the primacy of the authority of scientific evidence. But, as one surgeon put it, when being consulted on the telephone about whether another surgeon was well suited to performing a particular operation, 'Does he believe in it? You can't do *any* operation unless you believe in it!'; and any such belief comes much more easily from the personal practice of Responsibility. Housemen, too, accord more importance to one patient they have personally treated – not just 'seen' (and gained Experience from, as they may have as students), but 'had' (and exercised Responsibility over) – than a published study involving many patients; they may apply, ironically, the nature of scientific clinical trials expressed in written Knowledge to the results of their own personal Experience and Responsibility by saying, 'In my own **controlled double-blind cross-over series** of two [this figure would be in the tens or hundreds in such a published trial], I've found . . .'.

It is the personal certainty that arises from past action that gives rise to what Bosk calls 'quasi-normative' errors, when junior surgeons have failed to accommodate to different consultant surgeons' idiosyncratic practices of Responsibility, even when treating patients with exactly the same conditions. Housemen on both surgical and medical firms quickly get to know what these rules are, as must any newcomer to the firm, even the SR, and the idiosyncrasies of each of the firm's consultants must be catered to; not doing so leaves the junior doctor guilty of transgressing not just the normative rules of Status (implying that those with the rank of junior doctor are more than equal to the consultant in terms of Knowledge, Experience and Responsibility, which is manifestly absurd) but also the quasi-normative rules of personal Status (implying that this particular junior doctor is superior in those terms to his own consultant, which is a personal insult). While these rules are usually concerned with the action of Responsibility (always prescribing patients with **fistulas** a **high-fibre diet**, for example, or never using the drug **Septrin**), they may also be connected to ownership: all the doctors on Mr Cope's firm will learn, for example, that Mr Cope doesn't like any of his patients being discharged from hospital on Friday, because that way he keeps the bed till Monday; he can then admit another of his patients into it, rather than risk its occupation by another firm's patient admitted over the weekend.

Speech and Non-verbal Communication; Writing and Legality

All the features of clinical language that housemen learnt as students continue to be emphasised on their official frontstage of the firm's ward rounds, which have now become 'business rounds': the precise and referential vocabulary, the internal consistency and specific implications of words, phrases and sentences, and most importantly in this half-oral, half-literate disposition of Responsibility, the correct pronunciation of words. The Club Spirit in the medical disposition of Responsibility assumes real importance; the instrumental implication of a common pronunciation is the reduction of the dangers of confusion (between the names of drugs, for example), which might have serious consequences for the patient. Housemen continue to enlarge their vocabulary, perhaps especially of names of drugs and abbreviations and acronyms, which may be of almost anything (a pathological condition, a drug, an investigation, a hospital, or a consultant's initials).

The formidably precise clinical language again promotes non-verbal aspects of communication between doctors. Just as the presenting student or the patient is the focus for other students' gaze on teaching rounds, so doctors on business rounds may look either at the patient or at the houseman who is presenting the patient. But if results of tests are being asked about or looked for in the notes, then all eyes are on the houseman holding the notes in which he is Responsible for writing up results; the direction of doctors' eyes means he cannot avoid this duty. Equally, when the consultant says, 'We must chase that result', the Responsibility for doing so can be delegated to the houseman by the SR's simply catching his eye, raising his eyebrows and nodding. Senior doctors' surprise at or disapproval of action taken is conveyed by facial expression; doctors acknowledge complicit understanding by their eyes meeting, when a patient changes their story on a ward round, for example, or when a significant result (indicating a serious condition, for example) is spoken out loud in a patient's presence but not explained. Housemen's sensitivity to these non-verbal reactions becomes greater. The combination of the shared pronunciation of clinical language (which means that doctors close to each other can talk quietly, whether or not in this language, and can be understood by other doctors and not by patients) and the close grouping on a ward round means that it is quite possible, for example, for two adjacent doctors to talk to each other so quietly that no one else on the round, let alone the patient, can hear what they are saying.

The oral aspect of Responsibility is therefore much as described for Experience; writing is different. Students in Casualty and doing locums may write in patients' official notes, but this becomes part of the legal record only after it is countersigned by a superordinate doctor; what housemen write needs no countersigning, as they are now Responsible for what they write in the notes. Housemen become aware of their legal liability on their first day, when they are asked to provide specimen signatures for the pharmacy, as when opening an account at a bank. Some housemen are very aware of being potentially legally responsible for what they write; others may need to be reminded of this, as Mark was by a Staff Nurse's saying:

> I've been looking at your notes on that patient you discharged yesterday. [*She showed the notes to Mark, indicating where he had written that referrals to a gynaecologist and to a chest physician had been asked for by his consultant, but that nothing had been written after that entry.*] You're not protected, that's why I'm hounding you. You can just imagine if in six months' time she comes in with **stage III Ca Cervix**! She's had an abnormal [**cervical**] **smear**. Or if she had an **apnoeic attack** in the street. It wouldn't look good [for you in court]!

The nurse reminded Mark of the need to protect or 'cover' himself by writing up the notes fully; the legal record is in writing, and the houseman does most of the writing. In patients' notes, they write up both their clerking and decisions made on ward rounds of action to be taken; they may also write discharge summaries, where correct clinical language must be employed, a fact that was used to correct a houseman's improper spoken clinical language: when, at an academic session, Roger explained that a patient's kidneys had 'packed up through contaminants' the SR rejoined sarcastically, 'That's going to look jolly good on the discharge summary!' Housemen also write drug charts and fluid charts; they write request forms for investigations and record the results of investigations; they learn the need to look at charts recording measurements (temperature, blood pressure, and fluid balance charts). They are the scribes of the firm, whether standing deferentially with pen in hand on ward rounds, or sitting at desks on the ward and writing as quickly as they can.

Transferring Responsibility: Making the Patient the Agent

When originally discussing Ziman's description of scientific language, I suggested that such a self-consciously precise and materially referential language only obscures from scientists (and doctors themselves) the metaphors so obviously found in it. I have referred to the 'Food school' of pathologists in the context of Experience; the large number of military metaphors to be found are equally obviously associated with Responsible action directed at patients' diseases. There is, though, a form of speech that contradicts the definition of medical Responsibility (that of ownership of and action towards patients) by 'blaming the victim' and Making the Patient the Agent. For example, a consultant said to students about a patient they had just seen, 'He's clobbered his **pyramidal tract**', and an SHO presented a patient to his registrar on a round, saying, 'He **perforated** his **sigmoid colon** when on holiday.' This form of speech, which makes the patient responsible for his problems, is frequently used for explanatory accounts of individual patients' situations, as well as of results of investigations and of making decisions ('She's **retaining** water; we'll get her to increase her [urine] output [by giving her a **diuretic**]'). Such remarks are not confined backstage, but are almost entirely made by doctors of the Status of SHO and above.

In her analysis of medical accounts of women's reproductive systems, Martin (1987) finds two main metaphors: those of body as machine (with the doctor therefore as technician) and body as productive organ (with the doctor as supervisor of labourers or even as the owner of a factory). But these metaphors are not confined to Obstetrics and Gynaecology. The first metaphor, concerning the 'machine' of the body, is employed when doctors describe psychological problems as **functional** [using the ancient Anatomical Method to indicate that there is a **functional** deficit in the machine's working, unaccompanied by any discernible **structural** derangement]; the site of such problems is sometimes localised by the equivalent word **supratentorial** [above the **tentorium cerebri**, an anatomical **structure**, below which lies the **mid-brain** and its **autonomic functions** and above which are the **cerebral hemispheres**, which deal with **higher functions**, and where preclinical students have been taught 'personality' is somehow located]. And the second metaphor is clearly seen above in **retention** and the management decision to 'increase the output'. In the practice of hospital medicine, then, the implication of these two metaphors is that all patients are workers at their machine, which (when in hospital, at least) is owned by another, the consultant, the head of the firm. The role of the houseman, then, is, on the one hand, in the surveillance of production (one main duty of housemen in producing results of tests) and, on the other, being the lowest-Status member of the firm, the main medical intermediary between higher management and the occasionally recalcitrant worker (for in their role of supervisors of results, housemen may find that these results may apparently give the lie to what patients have told them). It is in this context that the question of Responsibility arises. While no doubt many housemen and doctors see patients as hapless victims, and treat them with great concern, Making the Patient the Agent puts a contrasting view, seeing patients as at fault for their problems; and it is then a matter of deciding who is in charge, the doctor or the patient. There is no doubt that doctors find some patients' problems morally less easy to deal with, those of patients whom they see as Luddites, deliberate wreckers of the machines of their bodies, like 'the despised alcoholic's esophageal bleed' (Good 1994: 83), for example. It might be worth noting, though, that surgeons seemed to use these metaphors less than physicians; physicians are more concerned with **function** than **structure**, while surgeons' concern is pre-eminently with the mechanical **structure** of the body. To this extent, it would follow that surgeons' technical work, by specifically excluding the psychological, at least makes allowance by default for its existence.

The Firm

Housemen now have the Status of doctors: their long hours during the day and their duties On Take or On Cover in the hospital overnight make their segregation from the rest of the world very clear, a segregation matched by their aggregation to the profession in general (now being called 'Doctor' by patients) and to one element of it, the official team of their firm (where they are 'Dr Finn's houseman'). For housemen have a role ready and waiting for them to fill; although they themselves may at first be quite unclear about what their Responsibility involves, simply being present ensures that others will tell them what to do. They are now full but junior members of an organisation with two very different cultural components, in Handy's terms (1993: 180–216), those of a Power culture and a Role culture. Power culture of 'small entrepreneurial organisations' is obviously seen in the firm itself, with its historical origins of honorary doctors charging students and junior doctors for training; firms are still based around the central figures of the two or three consultants, whose authority gives the firm their own names, and whose personalities give any firm its own distinct atmosphere. But although housemen (and indeed any junior doctors) describe themselves as 'working for' a particular consultant as if employed by the consultant, all the junior members of a firm are in fact individual employees in the bureaucratic Role culture of the huge National Health Service, with terms and conditions of employment for junior doctors still (at the time of writing) set nationally. All firms that housemen work on are identical in terms of some aspects of social organisation, with consultants and junior doctors, and all are ranked equivalently for official purposes, with payment at the same rate (even though some jobs have longer official hours). But firms differ from each other in many significant ways: for example, the degree to which housemen are helped and supervised by more senior doctors, the turnover of patients and the amount of paperwork (like writing discharge summaries) are factors that contribute to the general atmosphere of each firm. So despite housemen's posts' equivalence in the Role culture of the NHS, they differ considerably because of the Power culture that each firm represents, and students know this when they apply for house jobs.

The Changed Nature of Co-operation Within and Between Firms

Whereas students in their six-week attachment to firms only had a passing loyalty to the firm's doctors, and preferentially maintained the Co-operation between themselves, housemen's only loyalty is now to their firm, a coherent group implicitly indicated by the collective first person plural. 'We may just want to tail off the **diuretics**' and 'We need to speak to the physio about Mrs Savage's **mobilisation**' are in fact instructions by a registrar or SHO to a houseman couched as the wishes of the collective 'we' of the firm. Co-operation with the other members of the firm's team is expected and unquestioned. On one firm where the two housemen were antipathetic to each other, they tried to submerge their personal differences (quite unrecognised by the consultants) by generally 'getting on' with each other. Although Co-operation is often conjured by using the sporting metaphor of 'the team' that is so frequently used of the firm (in, for example, the commonly found disparaging description of another firm as 'the B team'), this hides the important change in the nature of Co-operation that has occurred with students' appointment to house jobs: as students, Co-operation was horizontal, between equals; now housemen find themselves in a vertical hierarchy, where different Status is all-important, and calling the firm a 'team' to some extent hides this reality. And because the firm is now the most important social unit, previous associations with other housemen become affected by the distinctive and often antagonistic Competitive attitude of different firms to each other, again partly because of the 'team' metaphor.

For, although housemen's further aggregation to the profession might be assumed to be accompanied by increased Co-operation with other doctors, housemen's incorporation into a firm – a social unit integral to the hierarchical segmentation of the profession and maintained by the individual differences of the consultants heading the firm – effectively separates them from each other along the lines of specialty and consultant. And even the hierarchical firm does not offer the solidarity it once did: now that housemen actually leave the hospital (rather than staying there every night as they used to, doing a so-called 1-in-1), doctors on firms 'cover' other firms' patients at night, so taking temporary Responsibility for them. Housemen may easily find themselves On Cover for all the patients in the hospital, with only a doctor they have never seen before as the Resident Medical (or Surgical) Officer, whom they can call upon for help. Firms do usually (but not always) stay together, though, for the 24 hours On Take, when one firm from each major specialty (Medicine and Surgery) assesses and admits patients who are referred or present as emergencies in Casualty.

Intra-professional hostility is highest when the title of ownership of patients is ambiguous, such as at night when one firm 'covers' another's patients, and when patients are transferred from one firm to another (in the US, the process of transferring patients is known as 'turfing', in an obvious reference to ownership). Transfers occur as planned changes of Responsibility for patients between consultants, usually when it becomes apparent that for the two main reasons of condition or age the receiving firm is better suited to treat that patient. When doctors 'refer' patients to another firm, requesting their transfer, patients are in a sort of limbo in which the doctors on the original firm no longer feel full Responsibility for them; when the patient has been accepted by the second firm but cannot be transferred, often because there is no bed, such ambiguous ownership may lead to marked intra-professional hostility. In the following two episodes, the senior doctor of the firm On Take makes clear both the hostility resulting from ambiguous ownership and the need to dissimulate it under assumed general professional Co-operation:

> The Lloyd/Jenkins firm was On Take one night; Dr Ahmed the registrar (as Resident Medical Officer) had been called to see one of Dr Rodgers' patients as an emergency, which he dealt with. Tim, one of the Lloyd/Jenkins housemen, also On Take, had been talking to the nurses on the ward and now told Dr Ahmed: 'Rodgers told them [the nurses] to take the [**urinary**] **catheter** out; what's he going to say tomorrow when he finds he's [the patient has been] **recatheterised**, with a **CVP line [Central Venous Pressure cannula**]?'
>
> Dr Ahmed: '*We* say [*giving a V sign*] *that* to what he thinks! [*Muttering disgustedly*:] Tidying up after other firms . . .'.
>
> Later, at about midnight, when Tim and Dr Ahmed were going over what remained to be done before they went to bed, the latter said, 'We've got to go and see someone on the Obstetric ward who's delivered a diabetic [baby]. [*Complainingly*:] Why can't they refer routinely in the morning [when this patient will no longer be an emergency Responsibility of the Lloyd/Jenkins firm]?'
>
> Tim: 'Why not leave it, then?'
>
> Dr Ahmed: 'You don't want to be seen as unhelpful!'

Firms On Take do their best not to admit patients who could be redirected to another firm; as one SR put it, vigorously moving his head as if heading a football, 'The best patients are the ones you can volley straight from Casualty without touching the ground!' Casualty can in fact still be used in the same way that it was in the last century, for doctors to admit the patients they want to, and this use of Casualty may also exacerbate hostility between firms:

> The Lloyd/Jenkins firm had again been On Take, and I had gone over to Casualty with the registrar, who was taking the two new housemen to take over from the retiring houseman. While we went through the patients that were being admitted, the registrar commented, 'There's a lot of Thorne patients coming in [patients ordinarily under Dr Thorne being admitted as emergencies through Casualty under Drs Lloyd and Jenkins], which is good as they go back tomorrow [to Dr Thorne's firm]'. The registrar paused before wondering, 'Is something going on? Can't he get his elective patients in?'

The registrar was suspicious that Dr Thorne might have told his patients to come to Casualty for admission, because Dr Thorne did not have any beds he could admit them to routinely as the hospital was full. The registrar's original pleasure at only having temporary Responsibility for these patients turned to the hostile suspicion that his firm was doing Dr Thorne's firm's work for them.

Such hostility may also be evident when the firm that has just been On Take tries to 'hand back', or transfer, another firm's patient whom they admitted. The way 'handbacks' are arranged differs between hospitals; in the following account, a new houseman, Anna, was learning the formalities that surround such transfers of Responsibility:

> It was after lunch on a medical ward. Anna, Dr Finn's houseman, had bleeped her ex-fellow student Natasha, now the houseman on another medical firm, the MacIntosh firm, in order to hand back a patient. Natasha had answered her bleep by ringing the ward phone, which Anna had just answered.
>
> Anna: 'Is that Natasha? I just want to tell you about a MacIntosh patient we admitted last night.' [*Natasha replied, presumably, that Anna's registrar would have to talk to her registrar about this.*] I'll get him to talk to your registrar, shall I? Or can I talk to your registrar myself? Oh, he's there . . . [*Anna now briefly presented the patient to Natasha's registrar on the phone; then she listened before saying, rather taken aback:*] 'Oh! Not today, then, tomorrow. [*As she put the phone down, she said angrily:*] Cunt! He was really rude! You can only transfer patients between 9 and 10 [a.m.]! [*To SS:*] Have you heard of that?'
>
> SS: 'No.'
>
> Anna: 'I feel really bad now; that's my bad etiquette. [*She paused, with a suspicion that she might have been "set up" by a member of her own firm, the registrar.*] But we talked about this at lunchtime with Hassan; he knew I was going to refer her this afternoon – he didn't say anything!'
>
> Later, however, she said: 'I should have known that [about when to hand over patients]; it's common sense really.'

What had happened was that Anna had learnt the rules (no doubt written down somewhere but usually learnt by customary practice) about the transfer of Responsibility for patients between consultants. This learning took place officially but backstage, despite being in the middle of the ward, seen and heard by a group of nurses at the nursing station, itself only a few yards away from the nearest patient's bed. Anna expressed her opinion of the registrar of the other firm quite clearly ['Cunt!'], showing the externally-directed hostility of masculine Competition. But even though the earlier Co-operation between her and Natasha had clearly evaporated, Co-operation within her own firm was by no means as sure as Anna would like; she had a suspicion that the registrar on her own firm might have undermined her attempt to transfer the patient. But later she saw the whole episode as her ignorance of the practice of common sense, rather than one of a million such consequences of singular historical developments.

Housemen were indeed officially encouraged to Co-operate with each other, when they were covering each other's patients, by writing a note for the houseman On Cover about patients that needed seeing or bloods that needed taking over night or over the weekend. But housemen on Cover are highly unlikely to do this work unless it forms part of their emergency Responsibilities: Anne, discussing the houseman On Cover the previous night with Roger, the other houseman on the firm, said, 'They don't do what we ask. I left a list, one blood, one consent [for an operation]; the next day, none of it had been done!' Roger explained, 'They don't get into any trouble if they don't do it; nobody takes responsibility for other firms' patients. [*Only half-jokingly:*] I don't know what they do all day!' And even when housemen do try to Co-operate with each other, this may be thwarted. For example, on one occasion the group of housemen tried to use Co-operation for the same purposes of Economy that they did as clinical students: they agreed that, for the new weekly teaching sessions, none of them would use acetates for overhead projection, to maintain a common front and prevent any individual Competitive demonstration of professional Idealism. When the SR taking the session said that acetates would be helpful (indicating the importance of a visual component for any medical lecture), Ray said, 'I thought we'd agreed not to, otherwise you get [through such Competition] to computer print-outs on overheads!' The SR replied, 'You may have decided that, but it may improve the presentation to have acetates!'

This particular attempt at mutual Co-operation was officially prevented.

More generally, though, Co-operation between housemen is prevented principally by the structure of the profession, and intra-professional Co-operation, based on real and metaphorical teams, is limited to firms and there dependent on recognition of Status; sometimes it seems it has almost evaporated. Further, as I have indicated above, Co-operation within the firm is adversely affected by the legal aspects of Responsibility: the medical firm is quite unlike a commercial firm, where, on the principle of vicarious liability, the employer is responsible for his employees' actions. 'You're on your own' is the way many housemen may describe their position – from a member of a group of two hundred preclinical students, to one of the official team of eight clinical students, to one often isolated houseman, the process of medical training is one of socialisation through individualisation. And the changes that have been introduced into housemen's terms of employment (shorter hours, fewer nights On Cover and On Take, and shift work) mean that Co-operation on the firm between housemen themselves and between housemen and more senior doctors is further weakened. When they were all in it together, and Co-operation was greater, housemen could also exert combined pressure about their living and working conditions; though meetings about these matters have recently been instituted (called 'whinge sessions' by the consultant who chaired them), these are no more effective than preclinical staff–student meetings. Housemen are now even more isolated both individually and as a group, incapable of concerted action and easily ignored. The now bleak and unwelcoming Doctors' Mess, with a television but no beer (that great promoter of male Co-operation), is powerful evidence of this change, as it is of another change to housemen's institutional existence, also promoted by their shorter hours: their unofficial backstage life, at least in this teaching hospital, seemed to have almost completely disappeared. So housemen, because of their short appointments and their dependence on their consultant for a reference for their next job, and their difficulty in Co-operative organisation, are in no position to change the system they find themselves in – they simply work out the most efficient way of discharging their Responsibilities, making their own mistakes and learning from them how best to work the system; questioning it, even if possible, takes up time.

Dealing with Responsibility

And the practice of Responsibility itself is conducted, as it always was, on the official front- and backstage. In Dowling and Barrett's (1991) study of housemen, based on interviews of housemen and other hospital staff they worked with, twenty-one different areas of housemen's work were identified; these can mostly be easily divided up into direct and indirect patient care (and so into some aspect or other of Responsibility), with only two areas ('to learn' and 'to promote direction of future career') not falling into these two categories. 'Learning' here refers to Knowledge, which, despite the recent introduction of an hour's meeting for 'formal education' every week, is (as for Miller's interns) not a priority; it is Experience and Responsibility that are important. And, given housemen's other work, the fact that failure to attend these meetings may jeopardise their satisfactory completion of the year (and hence their GMC registration) makes them often seem to housemen just another unwelcome burden. The other nineteen areas of work identified do not represent aspects of a rational and consciously thought-out job description of the sort often found in Role Cultures; it is much more likely that they are the consequence of needing to perform well at consultant ward rounds, based on the original houseman's role in the Power Culture of the nineteenth-century teaching hospital firm headed by a consultant. Although 'preparing and organising for consultant ward rounds' is listed as one area of housemen's work, ward rounds themselves, very oddly, are not mentioned. This is even odder because consultant ward rounds were identified both by housemen and consultants (Dowling and Barrett 1991: 16, 51–2) as being the one regular occasion when they meet each other; only here did housemen's work become 'visible' to consultants, who report that it was often on housemen's performance on ward rounds that they based their assessment of them (and hence the reference they gave them when applying for their next jobs). As I have already stated, such 'business' ward rounds form the official frontstage for housemen (prominent among the settings which, it will be recalled, Bosk studied), while the rest of their time is spent on the official backstage (where Miller studied). Before describing the official backstage work, where housemen co-ordinate the hospital's different functions and practise Economy in doing so, I first describe the official frontstage of the ward round, where professional Idealism should again be presented.

The Ward Round: The Official Frontstage

Housemen go on many rounds; those taken by SRs, registrars or SHOs are preparatory to, and in effect rehearsals for, the traditional weekly (or sometimes twice weekly) consultant rounds that are the main arena for review and planning management (that is, for generating the houseman's work), and housemen's performance also reflects on the other junior doctors on the firm who have been coaching them. Consultant ward rounds for housemen are homologous to teaching ward rounds for students: the spatial arrangements are very similar except, now, the smaller number of doctors tends to cluster round the foot of the bed and the presenter (the houseman) no longer stands to the left of the patient's bed, but tends to stand to the right of the small group, so allowing senior doctors easier access to the left of the bed, to speak to or examine their patient. The round starts with the same preliminaries if there is more than one houseman on a firm; the consultant asks which of them has Responsibility for his patients – 'Who's looking after her?' or, 'Whose patient is she?' – just as he asks students attached to his firm which of them has hypothetical Responsibility for his patients in the same words.

But there is no longer any suggestion that the method of Question and Answer, found on these just as on teaching rounds, is related to the Socratic method; it is now used not to test clinical students' hypothetical Responsibility (by asking 'What would you do?'), but to test the houseman's real Responsibility (by asking 'What have you done?'), though this is often couched in the collective 'we' of the team ('What have we done?'). And, in answering, housemen have the opportunity to demonstrate an exhaustive knowledge of their patients as evidence of their professionally Idealistic commitment to their care. While SHOs and other superordinate doctors may add to the houseman's presentation, extending and sometimes superseding it, the majority of the consultant's questions are addressed to the houseman. But consultants may ask the patient questions too; an inconsistency with or departure from a patient's previous account as presented by the houseman is now of serious import, implying that the houseman has failed to take an accurate history from the patient. Housemen are keen to demonstrate their Idealistically intimate acquaintance with patients' welfare, sometimes to the ludicrous extent of competing with the patients themselves: when a consultant asked a post-operative patient, 'Are you eating and drinking?', before the patient could reply, both the houseman and the Staff Nurse simultaneously answered, 'She's drinking but not eating!'

For the most impressive effect, housemen's answers should be remembered without recourse to written notes or records, though there are dangers in trying to carry off a display of such an extensive memorised knowledge of patients:

> On a ward round, Mr Edmonds the consultant, Mr Oliver the SR and Zak the houseman had stopped by a patient's bed.
> Mr Edmonds [*looking at Zak*]: 'What's his [this patient's] **albumen**?'
> Zak [*confidently, without looking at the notes he was holding*]: '42.'
> Mr Edmonds and Mr Oliver [*together, incredulously*]: '42!'
> Mr Edmonds [*again to Zak*]: 'Are you sure? I doubt it! Isn't it 32? [*Jokingly:*] Mr Oliver here only runs on an **albumen** of just over 41!' [*Zak was forced to look at the notes and, embarrassed, agreed that the* ***albumen concentration*** *was indeed 32 g/L.*]

This episode was referred to twice by Mr Edmonds over the next few days, on both occasions to Zak's disadvantage. So the answers to questions about the results of Responsible action should be both certain and accurate, the houseman's aim being to demonstrate a watertight case to the consultant, as regards covering all possibilities in pursuit of a diagnosis and as a result of treatment.

In their wish to demonstrate professional Idealism in their activities, unaffected by Economy, housemen may try to make it clear with circumstantial details how much work they have personally done by saying, for example, 'I managed to get the old X-rays out of the department', or 'The cardiologists were very busy, but they said they could see her later on today.' Consultants are not, however, interested in how this official backstage work has been managed, or what compromises with housemen's own ethical purposes have been involved in their necessary practice of Economy. Even though consultants presumably know what is involved, they are only concerned with the answers to their questions, however unusual or unfair these may seem: there is only ignorance (and lack of Responsibility) or knowledge (and Responsibility). As Bosk (1979: 76) puts it, 'attendings [consultants] do not believe that housestaff can be asked unfair questions about actions taken on the service [firm]. A response that denies responsibility or knowledge is unacceptable for it communicates to attendings a disinterest in clinical care', or, in my terms, a lack of professional Idealism for Responsibility.

Idealism is evident in forms of words that doctors use, always from super- to subordinate; as clinical students, housemen were familiar with the words, 'Do you want to . . .?', which assumed their presumptive Idealistic wish for Experience. Such Implied Idealism is now supplemented by the Unanswerable Question ('Why don't you . . .?') and the Unfulfilled Condition (of which a remarkable example was this instruction from an SHO to a houseman: 'I think tomorrow for the [consultant's] ward round, if you can put all the results in, so that we know this is what they were and when they were, if you see what I mean', to which the houseman answered 'Yes'). Housemen also start to use forms of speech, heard as students, to demonstrate their wholehearted concern for their (and their consultant's) patients by referring to their emotional commitment to the patient's welfare. For example, the commonest manner in which housemen ask for help from a superordinate is to say that they are 'worried' by a patient (and, by implication, that this worry has superseded the worry about calling a superordinate unnecessarily). They may also sometimes say they are 'unhappy' with a patient, though this is less likely, as it implies a state of contentment dependent on a level of Responsibility they do not yet have; anxiety is a more appropriate mood. And the word used to describe the opposite state of mind is 'happy'; so, 'Are you happy with that [course of action]?' may be asked by superordinates of junior doctors, and by them of patients. The common use of these simple lay words brings out the emotional aspect of the practice of Responsibility, that of mature judgement, stressing housemen's professionally Idealistic concern about or satisfaction with their patients' physical condition; but the range of words for describing doctors' own mental states on official occasions is further limited.

Questions are asked on rounds by the most senior doctor present, who, when given the answers, makes decisions; other subordinate doctors (who may therefore ask the houseman questions on preparatory rounds) are bound by the official frontstage nature of consultant rounds. The combination of observance of the consultant's superior Status and the Co-operation expected in the team are almost impossible to deny anyway (for example by disagreeing with a course of action), but especially in front of a patient:

> The round (consultant, registrar, SHO, houseman, two students and I) was at the end of the bed of a patient whose provisional diagnosis was of a **transient ischaemic attack**, a temporary form of stroke. Dr Gayforth, the consultant, had tested her **reflexes**, which were consonant with this diagnosis, but did not preclude a more serious disorder, including a **cerebrovascular accident**, a major stroke.
>
> Dr Gayforth: 'She should be on some Aspirin, shouldn't she?'
>
> Registrar [*nodding, indicating that she was*]: 'Yes. What about other investigations?'
>
> Dr Gayforth, not answering, looked at the patient and held out his hand till someone put a stethoscope in it. He then listened with it to the patient's **carotid arteries** for **bruits**, and looked briefly at the registrar, saying, 'I don't think we need that', before turning and making his way towards the door of the ward, as a clear indication that there was no more to be said. While he was doing this, the registrar turned in the opposite direction, to the others on the round, who are all junior to her.
>
> Registrar [*disagreeing with Dr Gayforth in an explosive whisper*]: 'She needs **carotid angiograms**! She needs **carotid Dopplers** at least!' [*And she quoted a research finding.*]

The only sure way of getting these investigations done would have been simply by arranging them before the round. Another possible way might have been by preliminary discussion before the patient was seen, perhaps with reference to these research findings of Knowledge (along the lines of 'Evidence-Based Medicine'). But the registrar recognised that she had blown it; to challenge Dr Gayforth's Experience and Responsibility combined in his Status on the official frontstage setting of the ward round was impossible.

I stress this because of the effect of consultants' use of the Question and Answer series on housemen; it can expose a houseman's knowledge or ignorance of what he has done or left undone, and therefore not only the houseman's Idealism for

Responsibility (or lack of it) but his Responsibility (or lack of it) itself. In line with my suggestion that the Question and Answer method provides the basis for the clinical mentality for clinical students, I now suggest that the same method at the next level of training provides the next layer of this mentality, where it concerns Responsibility. On one round, for example, the consultant asked the houseman several questions about her patients that she could not answer:

- 'What's her urine output?': she had only told the nurses that morning to put the patient on a fluid balance chart.
- 'Why's she on **Warfarin**?': the houseman hadn't looked through the patient's notes thoroughly enough to find that she had had a **venous thrombosis** the previous year.
- 'What's this **Maalox**?': the houseman had simply written this previously prescribed drug up on the drug chart, without checking its nature or the reason for giving it.
- 'What are his **hip movements** like?': the houseman had not done a full examination of the **musculo-skeletal system** of this patient, who had again been admitted for a **chest infection**.
- 'Where are his X-rays?': the houseman had not checked before the round that the X-rays had come over with the patient when he was transferred from a different ward.

At the end of the round, the houseman said to me, 'I hate looking stupid! It pisses me off!', clearly showing that she had felt humiliated by her public inability to answer these questions. My suggestion, then, is that housemen come to know the questions they are likely to be asked and, in anticipation of them, ask these questions of themselves ('Does this patient need a fluid balance chart?'; 'Why is this patient on **Warfarin**?'; 'What is **Maalox** and why has it been prescribed for this patient?'; 'Have I examined this patient fully?', or the more advanced question 'What are the other **systems** relevant to **chronic chest infections**?'; and 'Have I got all the results ready for the round?'). To put this another way, such consultant ward rounds have the following features: housemen have been coached in the questions and answers likely to be asked on preparatory rounds taken by junior doctors on the firm; clinical decisions are based on the answers to such questions; housemen here can demonstrate to themselves their own personal Idealism for their Responsible care for their patients; and zealous professional Idealism for Responsibility is looked for by consultants who use housemen's performance to form their assessment of them. In view of these features, and given that failure to answer questions will therefore have several adverse consequences and, in any event, will provoke intensely felt public exposure of ignorance, the power of the setting of the business round indicates that it would be extremely odd if housemen did not anticipate and internalise such likely questions.

But the same features (excepting only personal Idealism) also suggest that it would also be extremely odd if housemen, like clinical students, were not at least tempted to 'bullshit' and answer confidently as if they know the answer to questions, sometimes even making them up. Indeed, new housemen are warned about the dangers of bullshitting:

> An SHO, Mr Shah, was talking to the two new housemen on the firm about the previous housemen (Chris and Roger) and warning them about not bullshitting the SR (Jason) because of the impression that would be given to the consultant (Mr Rodney):
> 'Jason got really cross because the **INR [International Normalized Ratio]** wasn't done. He'd ask, "What is it today?", and Roger said, "It's OK." [*Mr Shah mimicked Jason asking Roger the same question again.*] "What *is* it?" So Roger said he'd go and check on the computer and there was only yesterday's results [Roger had tried to bullshit his way out of the fact that he hadn't taken blood that day to check the **INR**]; this happened every day. Jason said, "Look, it's dangerous," and told the other houseman to do it and told Roger he'd report him to Mr Rodney. I told Roger just to do it himself and not say anything. Chris was excellent; you knew if he was told to go and check if a patient was **pyrexial** he'd go and do it.'

This encouragement to the virtue of truthfulness was rather undermined by the same SHO, on a ward round soon after, on which both the housemen were present. He was being asked by Jason about a patient he had admitted with **abdominal pain**:

> Jason: 'His **U's and E's** and **amylase** were OK?'
> Mr Shah: 'Yes, his **U's and E's** were normal.'

Mr Shah took refuge in the precision of clinical language to avoid answering the question about the result of testing the patient's **serum amylase**. This test had not in fact been done, because the firm's junior doctors On Take (Mr Shah and one of the housemen) had the usual problem with getting this investigation done, in that the duty Biochemistry technician did not think the test warranted. The junior doctors had not even been able to use Economy backstage to get the test done, and Mr Shah bullshitted Jason to conceal this.

The Official Backstage and the Practice of Economy

Housemen are the continuity men of the whole production, working hard behind the scenes to try to ensure that, for the dramatic settings of the ward round, everything is in place; if, despite their best efforts, it is not, they may try to ad lib their way out. Most of their time in hospital is in fact spent on the official backstage, without any superordinate doctor present. But here their role is now that of actor; they are no longer an audience (as they were in lectures and ward rounds), but actors in the public eye for most of their working day, thrown into the performance of a highly conspicuous professional role. Isobel, a new houseman, put it like this: 'You've got to appear confident, just like in Finals. You have to answer questions from patients, from **relatives**, nurses sometimes. You don't know the answers; you have to bluff. The other doctors know what you're doing; it's a bit of a farce really.' Isobel was quite aware that her performance on the official backstage was continually evaluated by nurses and patients alike.

Housemen's work on the official backstage is informed by the practice of the same disposition that informed preclinical and clinical students' work there: Economy. It will be recalled that Miller, studying interns in the same setting, described them dealing with similar work by developing what he called the Operating perspective, similar in all respects to Becker's Final perspective from which I derived my Economic disposition. At first inefficient and forgetful, housemen find their work very tiring, both physically (especially in their feet) and mentally. One houseman said of her first weekend On Cover, 'I didn't feel human! I've never felt like that before. I had three hours' sleep the first night, five hours' the second. The wards were so busy!' It is possible to watch housemen progressively slowing up as the day and then the evening go on; subjectively, it is like being stuck in a slow-moving film without any outside reference, where time passes in surges.

Things they should do get forgotten, even when written down, and are remembered on the way home or even when there. Housemen soon become more efficient at using their note-books and organising their time, but they also start to practise Economy in other ways, some of which I describe here more fully.

Economy is Found in Several Ways

Housemen's main practice of Responsibility is arranging for blood tests and other investigations to be done and ensuring the results come back in time for one round or another. The tests they are told to arrange, however, are not always agreed to by those technicians or doctors who perform them. As Jason's question and Mr Shah's limited answer showed, the blood test for **serum amylase** is often asked for by senior doctors, but Biochemistry technicians usually need to be persuaded that this test is **indicated**. Persuasion is usually not enough in circumstances like this and housemen learn that they must sometimes use Economy with the truth (or lying) to get tests done by providing convincing (if inaccurate) reasons on the telephone or the written request form:

> Mary, a new houseman, had been told by her registrar to get a chest X-ray done in Casualty; she wrote up the form (requesting a **CXR**) and took it down the passage to the radiographers; she came back, telling me, 'They [the radiographers] say it's not **indicated**. I'll have to think of a reason which will satisfy them', and then wrote **SOB ?MI** [the patient is **short of breath** and may possibly have had a **myocardial infarction**, a heart attack], though there was no evidence either from the history or the examination for either of these. The radiographers now accepted the form and did the X-ray.

Many investigation forms therefore have such inaccurate but necessary information on them, often with the ubiquitous question mark preceding a condition (**?Sarcoid**), which is as much as the houseman can do to guarantee the investigation will be done. But for some investigations, particularly specialised radiological ones, the departments insist that the houseman goes in person to give details about the patient and explain why the test has been requested, and often be questioned in the process. So, when Felix had been told on a ward round to arrange for an **abdominal ultrasound scan**, he went to the department and was questioned about the reasons for the request. He evaded these with a double lie, 'I wasn't on the ward round so I can't tell you much; but I think it may have been a **[pancreatic] pseudocyst** they were worried about.' In fact he was on the round and it was not the possibility of a **pseudocyst** that was at issue, but his request for the ultrasound scan was now accepted unquestioningly. The specific difficulty that housemen have with such radiological investigations may be because the radiologists whom they have to talk to are also medically qualified.

The pressure that housemen are under to fulfil their multifarious Responsibility also promotes their Economical development of a personal and efficient system for clerking patients. Taking the history now takes the form of a brisk series of questions, personally formulated on the basis of the teaching of Experience and listening to other doctors, to minimise misunderstanding of the question by the patient and to ensure unequivocal answers (often simply of Yes or No), which can then be followed up if necessary. Questions of this sort can be heard in Casualty the whole time, often shouted to an elderly patient to avoid repetition: 'Do you have a cough? Is it every day? Do you cough anything up? What? How are your bowels – regular? How often do you open them – once a day? What about the waterworks? Do you have any dizzy spells? Or fits? What about faints, or funny turns?' In this case, learning the medical lay language – in what circumstances other than talking to doctors (or nurses) does anyone talk about their 'waterworks'? – minimises patients' misunderstanding of doctors' questions and therefore maximises Economy from the doctors' point of view. In the same way, housemen develop a method of physical examination which is now a co-ordinated and fluent Economical process, far removed from the disjointed and halting examination of most clinical students. So, for example, the examination of the **respiratory** and **cardiovascular systems** becomes merged, housemen learning to **percuss** and then **auscultate** the front of the chest with a series of personally standardised movements. And just as they adopt unambiguous questions for the first part of the clerking, so they also develop a similar series of unambiguous instructions to patients when examining them: 'Look up at the ceiling! Now sit up for me! Take a deep breath in and hold it! Now breathe away again! Blow your tummy up to meet my hand! Cock your wrists; don't let me push them down! Keep your heels on the bed; don't let me lift them up! Now let me take the weight of your legs; you let them relax; I'll do the work!'

Economy in Language

It is no doubt the case that the clinical language doctors learn is part of their professional identity, enabling efficient communication with other doctors and, purposefully or not, mystifying patients. Doctors may also use the clinical language when talking to the few patients whose lay status they may judge equivalent to their own, and who may then find themselves being talked to as if they were a promising medical student. But the usual form of language employed when talking to patients is the distinctive lay clinical language. This sometimes takes rather startling forms, as when Dr Burns, a consultant, told one patient, 'Your ticker's [heart's] not working to scratch!' and another, 'We're going to do some special X-rays of your nut [head]!' It could be argued that such lay clinical language is a vehicle for conveying doctors' medical Status and their privileged access to the forms of medical knowledge (it perhaps being their idea of how consultants should talk, learnt from their days as students and junior doctors) or, through its rather jovial tone, as promoting Co-operation (perhaps in their own distant memory of lay language for medical matters). While I have no doubt that Status and Co-operation are important dispositions at work in these exchanges, I shall try and show that Economy is also an influence, perhaps the most powerful.

When doctors use clinical language in front of patients, its nature can make it quite incomprehensibly foreign. But there is also potential for some understanding, and hence for misunderstanding, by patients, partly because of the use of words which have both lay and medical meanings (see Chapters 6 and 8). But simpler misunderstandings may occur, as when an SR said on a surgical ward round: 'That [**wound discharge**] looks very **serous**' and the look on the patient's face strongly suggested he had heard this as 'serious'. I suggest that it is partly to avoid the Economic consequences of misunderstanding (and so having to take time to repeat what they say or to provide a further explanation) that doctors translate their clinical language into lay words so simple and unambiguous that patients find it hard to answer back, without running the risk of appearing either to be wasting doctors' time or to be incorrigibly stupid. So, for example, the form of words frequently used by Dr Gayforth, a consultant, to explain a particular course of investigative action to patients was, 'We're going to put a torch down and have a look at the food-pipe.' Though this was usually accepted by patients unquestioningly, on one occasion a patient replied, 'You mean a **gastroscopy**?', at which Dr Gayforth had to agree and expand on the procedure. In another example, the same consultant's use of medical lay language was Economically entirely successful:

> The full firm was on a ward round and, in between seeing patients, Dr Gayforth had approached a patient's husband, who had been waiting in the corridor to see him. Dr Gayforth's words were quite audible to the rest of the ward round, as we stood in a group four yards away clearly waiting for this interruption to end. He spoke rather ponderously but not unkindly: 'I'm afraid we've reached the end of the line. The cancer's catching up with her and the indications are it's spread to the bone. There's really nothing more to do except to keep her comfortable.' After a brief pause, he said, 'Have you any questions?' The patient's husband was silent. Dr Gayforth rejoined us, while the husband turned further away from us, removed his glasses and took out his handkerchief.

Here, in addition to the setting and the timing of the interview, the almost brutally simple nature of the consultant's explanation made it impossible for the patient's husband to ask questions (even though there were things that he wanted to express, emotional and psychological matters that again the lay clinical language protects doctors from); the round moved on without much of a pause. It is no doubt in imitation of this sort of oral communication to patients that housemen start to use it themselves, sometimes with a more demotic accent, when talking to patients and **relatives**. Jack did this when talking to a patient's **relatives**: 'Her gall-bladder got a bit infected and she got a bit dry. We weren't very happy with this; it wasn't getting better. So we're going to be a little more aggressive about finding out what's going on.'

The use of Economy in the literate aspect of Responsibility is rather more obvious. Students have, of course, developed their personal methods of Economic writing when learning Knowledge. While clinical students copy doctors' shorthand notes for clerking, it is only with continued practice that these collective Economical abbreviations become immediately understandable, practice really only found when students become housemen and have to write so much so quickly. Abbreviations are found in drug charts, several of them Latin: for example, **nocte** [at night], **b.d.** [*bis die*, twice a day], **p.r.n.** [*pro re nata*, as required], and **p.r.** [*per rectum*, rectally], with the old apothecaries' abbreviations Ṫ, ṪṪ and ṪṪṪ for one, two and three tablets. When housemen write in the notes, they consolidate what they learnt as students, coding the clerking as they saw housemen had, to save time in the formulaic recording of this frequently repeated act. The patient's complaint is headed by **c/o** [complains of] and the history headed by **Hx**, in a similar neo-traditional form to **Rx**, the Latin abbreviation for making up a prescription [*recipe*]. Symptoms are often abbreviated (**SOB** for **shortness of breath**, for example) and, if relevant but absent, abbreviated too (so **PND°** means 'no symptoms of **paroxysmal nocturnal dyspnoea**'). Diagrams take the place of verbal description, resulting in both Economy and accuracy. The abbreviation found in writing is particularly striking when applied to the summary at the end of the clerking: '**47 yrs ♂ c̄ 2 yrs Hx bladder Ca. Rx c̄ prostatectomy, urethrectomy + RTh. Self-catheterising. Presenting with constipation & radiation proctitis. Nil of note on examination. Hx of Rheumatic Fever**' [This patient is a forty-seven year old man, who has had cancer of the bladder for two years. This has been treated surgically by its removal, together with that of the prostate and the urethra, and also with radiotherapy. The patient now has an artificial bladder, surgically constructed out of bowel, which he drains himself with suprapubic catheters. His current problems are constipation and symptoms arising from chronic inflammation of the lowermost part of the gastro-intestinal tract, which was caused by the radiotherapy. There is nothing, apart from the results of these treatments, to be noted on physical examination; he has a past history of Rheumatic Fever, which is noted because of possible consequent damage to heart valves].

In housemen's general use of Economy on the official backstage, there is a recapitulation of what they had established preclinically and clinically; in the acquisition of all three dispositions of Knowledge, Experience and Responsibility, personal Idealism gives way to Economy; but, for clinical students and housemen, on the official frontstage of ward rounds, Economy must be dissimulated and professional Idealism presented. The difference for housemen is that, owing to the process of socialisation through individualisation, they are now on their own; their learning of Economy for the third time is a thoroughly personal re-acquisition of this general professional disposition.

Contrasting Idealism and Economy: Irony

Housemen's Institutional world has effectively shrunk to two areas, the official frontstage of professional Idealism and official backstage of Economy. Whereas preclinical students used punning to show the difference between the professional institution and the lay world, and clinical students used a more medical form of punning and irony to show the difference between official and unofficial areas, housemen and other doctors use humour and irony to draw the distinction between the official front- and backstage (Figure 20). Again, the users of irony tend to be those of surer medical Status in the higher ranks of junior doctors (registrars and SRs), rather than the still probationary housemen. So a male SHO's ignorance of the serious implications of the abnormal **ECG** of a patient in Casualty was mocked by the female registrar; she suggested, apparently agreeing with his opinion that the **ECG** showed no change from a previous one, that he was going to treat the patient by arranging for a Social Worker's visit and Meals on Wheels, in a parody of some 'holistic' care that might be presented on a ward round. It was only when she started to make telephone calls to the ward about the patient's admission that the SHO realised his ignorance and her irony, which involved contrasting the reality of official backstage work to the Idealism found on the frontstage. The same contrast is found in another example, which also shows the 'corporate corporality' I have described:

> A ward round was in progress and the team (SR, registrar, two housemen – a woman and a man – and I) were just approaching the lifts to the wards. The female houseman and the SR had been discussing the average length of penis found in patients of different races, a discussion in which her authority was finally granted because she had done a Urology house job. The registrar had interceded to express his disagreement with what one of them had just said by saying, 'Bollocks'. 'No', said the SR, 'That's tomorrow afternoon's clinic, the Impotence Clinic. [*He paused*.] I must say I find some of the work there frankly unacceptable, testing the quality of people's

erections, for example . . .' [*After a further pause, he smiled, having kept a straight face until then.*]

The point here is that 'testing the quality of people's erections' by implication involves manipulation of patients' erect penises, which can just be envisaged as possible medical action. There are, after all, medical scales for measuring almost everything (the **level of unconsciousness**, the spread of **metastatic** cancer, of **retinopathy**, of **depression** and so on), as well as the machinery for measuring erections (in the form of the **penile plethysmograph**). There is therefore nothing intrinsically impossible in there being a scale to measure erections, which might form part of some absurd professional Ideal of patient treatment, but which, of course, does not exist in routine clinical reality.

It is in this context, that of contrast between the two different settings, that the crudity and cruelty of some medical humour must be understood. When a consultant, showing slides of patients in a lecture, told clinical students that one patient's prognosis was that 'he shouldn't put on a long-playing record', so poor was it, or that 'you could play "The Bluebells of Scotland"' on another's ribs, so **cachectic** and emaciated was he, the doctor's use of lay language

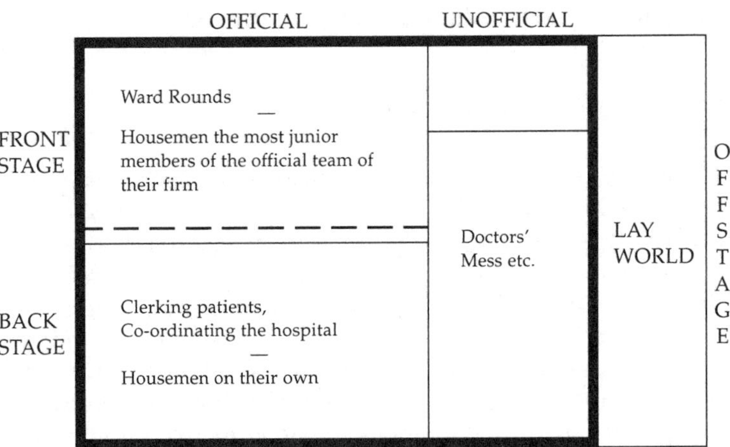

Figure 20. Housemen's institution. The unofficial backstage has now also shrunk (as has the lay world even further), while the official stages have expanded. The distinction is now between official front- and backstage.

and his cruelty is to be compared to the official frontstage of the ward round, where such words would never be used. It appears that the routine use of such irony is more highly developed in the US, if Konner's account of his clinical training is anything to go by. Among his glossary of House Officer Slang (1987: 379–90), he records 'crispy critturs' and 'toasted toddlers' (referring to chronically hospitalised children with **full-thickness burns** over most of their bodies, whom Konner describes as some of the saddest cases in medicine), while the apparently medical acronyms BFI stands for 'Big Fucking Infarct' (indicating a **massive myocardial** or **cerebrovascular infarction**) and CTD for 'Circling The Drain' (referring to someone who is dying).

I am not, of course, suggesting that the use of such gallows humour is only a reflection of different social settings, perhaps with the effect (like DR stories) of promoting social solidarity; it no doubt also provides doctors with cathartic relief from heart-rending situations. But the irony also protects them, and prevents (as do the social settings that it derives from) acceptance of other realities of these situations, just as doctors' and students' preference for the language of hard science makes it difficult for them to describe, either sociologically or psychologically, the position in which they find themselves. And the irony may become their reality, leading to boredom, contempt or despair.

Co-ordinating the Hospital

The need to develop Economy backstage again comes, partly, simply from the volume of work, though this may be actually surprisingly small. The greater pressure arises from housemen's need again to do something that they have also done twice before, which is the practical and cognitive work of holding together the disparate elements of the institution: preclinically, it was academic departments; clinically, it was clinical specialties; now it is the disparate functions of the hospital provided both by medical and other professions and occupations that housemen co-ordinate. This time, it is not payments made on housemen's behalf that benefit the segmented institution financially, but their relatively cheap labour.

Housemen's work is, in the words of one SR, 'to be all things to all people'; what this description leaves out is that it is over patients that housemen take this polymorphous action. All hospital patients have consultants, and nearly all consultants in Medicine and Surgery have housemen. Any patient, therefore, has both a consultant and a houseman, and anyone who has anything to do with any patient will contact the houseman (and, conversely, the houseman may have to contact them). The range of such contacts is huge: with nurses, physiotherapists, phlebotomists and ward clerks; with technicians from Biochemistry, Haematology, Microbiology, Nuclear Medicine and other departments, such as those involved in the imaging investigations of X-ray, ultrasonography, CT and MRI scanning, and those for ECG, EEG and medical photography; notably for surgical housemen, with the staff of different wards and of operating theatres, as well as with anaesthetists; for general administration, with secretaries, medical records, porters, hospital administration, and mortuary attendants.

Housemen's work of co-ordinating the disparate work of the many different departments of the hospital, most of which are bound by various restrictive practices, means that housemen have to compromise themselves and resolve conflicts between the different instructions that may be given by different functioning units in the hospital:

> Rick had been bleeped by the Microbiology lab about the dosage of a drug he had prescribed. Afterwards he explained to me: 'The microbiologist said that recent research suggested a higher dose of **Teicoplanin** was better, so I've put it [back] up to 800 mg – that's a lot! [*He paused, briefly.*] I originally wrote up 800 mg; the nurses looked it up in the **BNF** [the British National Formulary] and said the dose was too high. So I put it back down to 400 mg, and now the microbiologists have rung to say that's too low!'

Again, the mortuary attendant goes home at 3 p.m., so when the mortuary rings the houseman to sign a cremation form, the houseman has to drop everything and rush down there before the mortuary is shut for the day. The houseman must resolve the internal contradictions of the increasingly complicated hospital and the restrictive practices of its different branches; this conspicuous role serves to define the medical identity of housemen. As well as such disparate elements of hospital function, housemen may also have to co-ordinate other medical segments too: for example, when housemen are told to arrange a referral for an opinion from a doctor on a different firm. After a consultant's or registrar's instruction to 'Get the **orthopods** to come and see her', the houseman phones the Orthopaedic Department, but finds that the duty registrar is in theatres, that no one else is answering their bleep, that the secretaries have gone home, and that this task will have to wait for the next day. When housemen have to contact more senior doctors from another segment of the profession in pursuit of acting Responsibly for the patients on their own firm, this can prove extremely difficult.

Housemen's frequent Responsibility for taking blood often causes problems in co-ordination:

> Pat, a houseman, was filling out a blood form when her SHO told her not to write 'High Risk' on it, because one of the nurses had complained that all the other patients would see this stigmatising information as the form lay in the tray for collection. Pat expostulated, 'But we've got to tell the [Haematology] lab [to warn the technicians of the dangers of handling the specimen]!' The SHO shrugged and turned away, leaving it to Pat to resolve this herself; this she did by simply leaving the form upside-down in the tray.

Understanding, and then complementing, the practice of phlebotomists is therefore vital. One houseman had filled in a blood form and left it for the phlebotomist to take, but when she returned the blood had not been taken; when she asked why not, the phlebotomist told her that phlebotomists would only take blood if the patient was easily located when they came round, which they only did once in the day, and they would not try to persuade any patient who at first refused to have blood taken. So if the patient was off the ward for any reason or was not keen to have blood taken, it was again the houseman's work to take it. Sometimes phlebotomists' practice is even more exclusive: on one surgical ward, none of the bloods had been taken, and, when the houseman again asked why not, it was explained that phlebotomists would never take blood from the arm on the same side as a surgical operation (for no good medical reason) nor (medically, correctly) from the arm where a drip was sited. The consequence of these rules was that the houseman on this ward and not the phlebotomist would always have to take blood from the many patients who were in for breast operations: anaesthetists routinely put drips in the arm opposite the side operated on, to allow the surgeons easy access. The frequency with which housemen have to take blood leads to another small way in which the world is seen differently (as I have described in Chapters 6 and 8) – it is now this aspect of Responsibility that skews housemen's perception, as they start to look at patients with taking blood in mind; 'bad' veins are a real problem for them, and patients with big ('good') veins are seen with relieved approval. Konner (1987: 366) also recounts this: 'On a bus, I noticed the veins on a woman's hands – how easily they could be punctured for the insertion of a line – before noticing she happened to be beautiful.'

So, in their practice of firm-centred Co-operation, housemen usually have to bargain or negotiate with others, in whom the presence or absence of the lay reciprocal relationship to professional Co-operation (that is, of lay co-operation with medical practice) is commonly used by housemen to categorise them as Co-operative or not. To promote such wider Co-operative relationships is important for housemen because of their need to get things done quickly; maintaining good relations is important because they will almost certainly be involved in them again; such relationships are usually the means to an end. There is both great scope for putting other people's backs up, especially by relying on Status (and using too peremptory a tone, for example, when housemen are often in effect suppliants) and for creating special relationships, by cheerfulness and joking or flirting, with other hospital staff; the fact that most nurses and secretaries are women perhaps leads both to make male housemen more likely to be accepted by them and to make such relationships mutually satisfactory.

Nurses

Of all the other professionals that housemen now have to work with, it is nurses that housemen find themselves in most contact with. On the Induction Day, an outgoing houseman advised the new ones, 'Nurses can make your life very easy. I should stress that it's important to be friendly: listen to them – you're going to spend a lot of time with them. Listen to them, but don't necessarily do what they say!', adding a warning about the way that nurses might use their own official records (the **Kardex**) as evidence that housemen did not respond to nursing requests. So 'getting on with' the nurses is usually accorded a high priority by housemen. For example, if the telephone rings while a houseman is sitting at the desk at the nurses' station, it is open to him to answer it or not; if he does, this means that a nurse does not have to leave whatever she is doing to answer it; if he doesn't, it means he doesn't have to interrupt whatever he is doing and then tell a nurse the message he has taken. A houseman who, unusually, ignores a telephone ringing by him will annoy nurses, who may then reciprocate by not telling him relevant information (such as warning him of the timing of a patient's absence from the ward for an investigation, or whatever it might be). As Miller's study of interns indicates, housemen and nurses can make each other's work easier or more difficult, and they negotiate the terms on which they relate. Dowling and Barrett (1991: 54–7) have drawn attention to the way in which nursing staff actually supervise housemen, especially when they are new – a supervisory role that is, officially, and certainly legally, completely ignored. Nurses provide practical information about ward procedures, both clinical (how to connect the **limb leads** to the ECG machine) and administrative (how to get hold of old notes), and about medication, as well as about the patients themselves. They also act as a source of information about their own ward policy and about consultants' idiosyncratic 'quasi-normative' practices; further, to some extent at least, they provide information of a personal nature about other housemen, now they are separated into ones and twos on different firms, and undoubtedly some emotional support. This, though, depends on a degree of closeness to the nurses on 'their' ward, which these days may be greatly limited by the 'consultant bed scatter'. And, anyway, nurses are different: they work shifts and have days off (and days 'off sick') in a way quite foreign to housemen.

The price of this help for housemen is 'keeping the nurses happy': doing what they ask (for example, to make a change in medication, or to examine an elderly patient who has fallen), or at least taking the time to give a reason why not, and abiding by the different ward rules and routines (not interrupting nursing **handovers**, for example). 'Other wards are awful for doing Cover [on]; you can't find anything!', said one houseman; if they don't know where things are kept, they have to ask or be shown, which means that they are dependent on a free nurse to answer or show them, which both uses up time and puts them under an obligation to a whole new group of nurses.

It is nearly always nurses who ask housemen to 'see the **relatives**' – often something of a nuisance. Relatives can hold things up (ward rounds or housemen's individual work) because they have to be asked to leave the patient's bedside or, if they don't, because their questions too have to be answered. They may add information about the patient, which may be repetitive, confusing, or the cause of extra work for the houseman. For housemen on duty, visiting relatives are the cause of a reversal of the usual outnumbering of the patient by doctors: the single houseman may be surrounded by the questioning group of patient and relatives. Relatives have to be seen when a patient is dying or has died, and nurses may remind the houseman to do this, which may be more upsetting than the actual death of the patient. However deeply felt by the houseman (feeling failure, guilt, or simply the loss of someone they had come to know), the death of a patient means that, while there may be more administrative work to be done as a consequence, this is limited; relatives, on the other hand, may still need to be seen, representing more work, which is often of an uncongenial emotional nature.

For a few housemen, the necessary negotiation with nurses and the consequent compromising of their Status is deeply wounding; when they achieve higher Status, they will not countenance any repetition. With the gradual loss of the medical profession's prestige relative to others', and the reduction in numbers of nurses on the wards (with the consequence, for example, unthinkable twenty years ago, that no nurse may accompany a consultant's round), housemen find they may, rather apologetically, have to fall back on their consultants' Status rather than being able to rely on nurses' unquestioning acquiescence to the instructions housemen relay from their superordinates. Perhaps because of this, perhaps because of housemen's need to get on with nurses, disagreements between housemen and nurses are very rare; housemen are usually compliant and, if there is disagreement, they refer to their superordinates. It is SHOs and registrars who are more likely to find themselves confronting nurses when nursing and medical views conflict.

Patients

Housemen, like clinical students, also tend to dichotomise patients according to whether they are found Co-operative or not, valuing those patients who do not affect the Economic execution of their work. While housemen, like nurses, are subject to open hostility from patients, particularly in Casualty, this is not common. Co-operation is more likely to be compromised by patients refusing (or only reluctantly agreeing) to physical examination, admission or having blood taken, expressing doubts about tests' value or complaints about treatment or side-effects of drugs, and asking questions housemen find difficult to answer, or evincing any other tendency to slow housemen's work; being a 'poor historian' is particularly exasperating (notably in relation to deaf people and foreigners). So the houseman's job is to try and secure patient Co-operation at almost any cost; the price may be encouragement, cajoling or even pleading, while patients who apparently withhold it for no good reason may be criticised:

> Mary had clearly met with some resistance from a patient when she had taken blood from him. She was carrying away the equipment for taking blood and had just shut the door of his room when she told me: 'He's a bit of a wimp! He said, "I thought all this [blood-taking] would be over!"' For the purposes of taking blood, she had apparently forgotten that the patient had had bladder cancer, for which he had been **surgically castrated**, had an artificial bladder that he drained himself with a catheter four times a day, and had **radiation stenosis** of his **rectum**; and that his wife had just divorced him.

Housemen quite often thank patients after seeing them (to examine them, for example, or to take blood), as clinical students often do after clerking them; these thanks are, in effect, for their Co-operation. Thanks expressed by patients (the only sort of thanks housemen are ever likely to get) are brushed aside, with 'We're only doing our job' or 'It's our job [to get you better]'; even when thanks are specifically directed at the individual houseman, this collective disclaimer is made. One houseman responded to a departing patient's thanks by using a not uncommon phrase, saying, 'I'm glad you're better! I hope we don't see you again!', a real enough expression of good wishes in one way, but definitely also a hope that the patient does not return via Casualty later on.

The nature of the Co-operation looked for among patients is straightforward, not involving any psychological appreciation of their position, but encouraged rather by an incessantly cheerful physical reassurance, patting patients on the back or holding their hands. This is no doubt one contributory reason for the absence of housemen's interest in the sometimes glaringly obvious psychological problems of their patients. There are no doubt many others: their own lack of interest in and awareness of low-Status Psychology and Psychiatry and the corresponding emphasis on real (that is, visible and tangible) pathology, which is reinforced by the resolutely physical nature of the problems that are identified by their superordinates. Non-psychiatrists only refer their patients to psychiatrists after exhaustive efforts to find somatic causes for patients' problems, so in effect somatising their patients' distress (see Padgett and Johnson 1990).

But a sizeable proportion of both medical and surgical housemen's work concerns psychiatric patients who are temporarily their Responsibility. These are the large numbers of patients admitted to hospital as **Overdoses** (those who have taken deliberate overdoses of medicinal drugs) and clerked by medical housemen, and as **Head Injuries** (those who have lost consciousness for a significant period, overwhelmingly the result of drunkenness), clerked by surgical housemen. Though there is sometimes some useful Experience to be gained from examining them (and occasionally Responsibility, in putting up a **Parvolex** drip on someone who has taken an overdose of Paracetamol, for example), this is usually not the case, and these patients are referred the next morning to the psychiatrists whose Responsibility they properly are. But such patients (as well as those who are dependent on illegal drugs and who are **HIV positive**) have clearly been the Agents of their condition, and housemen's (and medical and surgical consultants') Responsibility for them is thus doubly doubtful. Seen under housemen's centrally important dispositions of Economy and Co-operation, such patients are especially provoking: they are likely to be poor historians (this being another reason why housemen usually don't concern themselves with taking a **psychiatric history**); despite such patients' frequent resistance, all have to be physically examined (sometimes particularly carefully, if there is the possibility of missing an **organic** cause for their symptoms, though there is usually nothing to be found); and they may well be argumentative and not Co-operative in other ways, not unusually discharging themselves 'against medical advice'. For all these reasons, it is not surprising that housemen may end up sharing the view of the registrar who said, when he had heard that an **Overdose** had discharged himself, 'Good riddance to bad rubbish!' Housemen usually find that the culturally low Status of Psychiatry is fully deserved in practice.

Chapter 10

The Medical Habitus and Mental Illness

> Some – there are losses in every trade –
> Will break their hearts ere bitted and made,
> Will fight like fiends as the rope cuts hard,
> And die dumb-mad in the breaking-yard.
>
> Rudyard Kipling

The Basic Medical Habitus

By the end of their year as housemen, medical graduates have learnt through practice the general professional dispositions of medicine and what might be called the basic medical habitus. In my ethnography I have no doubt succumbed to a tendency to reify these professional dispositions. This tendency may be offset by considering the practice of Status, for example, by the anthropological *homo hierarchicus*, of Economy by *homo economicus* and so on, but all by any one person. Among the consequent conflicts, possibly the most important is that between the *homo quasi-religiosus* of personal Idealism and the *homo quasi-quasi-religiosus* of professional Idealism. At any rate, it should be borne in mind that every student is transformed in the ways described in the following brief summary of medical training, which results in some variation of the basic medical habitus.

In their serial acquisition of Knowledge, Experience and Responsibility at the three main levels of training, the disjunction of these professional dispositions both from lay equivalents and from each other means that students are obliged to learn them all from scratch; the settings of the DR, where atypically for preclinical students, Experience may be gained, and Casualty, where atypically for clinical students Responsibility may be practised, may tend to mask the disjunction of dispositions from each other. Incessant assessment has made them aware of the need for institutional conformity in answering questions, rather than asking them or arguing with them – in fact the whole of my account could be recast as describing the sorts of questions that can be asked of whom by whom.

In official frontstage settings, students' role has moved from that of audience in lectures, through combined audience and actors on ward rounds, to full-time actors as housemen. In the last two periods of training, surveillance and potential humiliation (justified by the moral aims of the profession) promote the professionally Idealistic and confident performance necessary for professional advancement.

In this process, the personal Idealism of helping people (that forms a motive for so many students) gives way both to Economy and to professional Idealism. Co-operation, so strong preclinically in unofficial frontstage and official backstage teams, becomes more and more associated with its inverse, Competition, in clinical official frontstage teams; for housemen, Co-operation is only found within the firm, where it depends on observance of Status and the 'quasi-normative' rules that are to be found on each firm. Responsibility, only found preclinically in its inverse of public licence, is usually only hypothesised for clinical students; housemen find that their sudden access of delegated Responsibility for everything does not apparently deny the continuing overall Responsibility of their consultants. But the disjunction of Knowledge, Experience and Responsibility and the conflicts between dispositions inherent in the institutional structure are left to students to work out for themselves. Further, in another form of social control, the social meaning of dispositions changes at the three different levels: their original Idealism can only be retained personally, with no place officially; Co-operation has changed from a horizontally operating egalitarian practice to a vertical one; Knowledge, the certain foundation of preclinical work, has been replaced by the certainty of Experience for clinical students and of Responsibility for housemen.

In addition to trying to resolve these difficulties, students have also learnt, first through its scientising and then its pathologising, a new way of seeing the world; this major cognitive shift in their aggregation to the profession (which I have called a 'corporate corporality') in turn results in the formation of a new relationship between themselves and others. This cognitive shift is promoted, certainly by the nature of the knowledge on which they are tested, but also by the new language they have learnt; the precise clinical language with material referents prevents discussion, at least in official settings, of matters without such referents, while also engendering untaught bodily positions and an acute sensitivity to other doctors' non-verbal communication.

With this comes an awareness of the differential Status not just of individuals within any segmented professional hierarchy, but also of the professional segments themselves and those segments' patients, in terms of trainees' own practice of professional dispositions. In addition to the personal work of dealing with dispositional conflicts, students' institutional work is to integrate widely different segments, the preclinical disciplines from Anatomy to Sociology and the clinical departments from Surgery to Psychiatry; this is matched by the houseman's need to co-ordinate the disparate functions of the branches of the hospital itself.

Medical students' initial separation from the lay world in medical school originally hardly seems matched to their professional aggregation; preclinical students are not treated as an integral part of the professional world they aspire to. With their progress through the clinical years, separation becomes more pronounced and, with their practice of professional dispositions, so does aggregation. But it is during their year as housemen that they learn proper professional allegiance. This is the period when they come to appreciate the importance of doing what they have been told to do (and acting in anticipation of what they will be asked about) by their professional superordinates. As part of this process, they come to see others, whether patients and their relatives or other health professionals, through the dispositional category of Co-operation – do these others comply or not with their own professionally purposeful actions? Housemen's professional allegiance is also certified by the practice of Economy on the official backstage in their dealings with others, while presenting professional Idealism on the official frontstage. Housemen, as newly qualified professional practitioners, therefore come, individually, through practice to have the same characteristics as Freidson has identified in the profession itself (see Chapter 1): a basis in specialised medical knowledge (of the three sorts I have described); an ethical commitment certainly, but primarily to the profession itself; accountability certainly, but overwhelmingly to the profession in the shape of their professional superordinates; and a lack of control over their colleagues, separated from them by specialist segmentation but joined by the common knowledge of what is involved in the practice of professional dispositions.

But within this apparently uniform institutional processing, medical graduates have also become highly individualistic. This is for several reasons: despite the omnipresent metaphor of the Co-operative team, the process of socialisation is through individualisation; Knowledge is checked and memorised by the use of each individual's own body; the nature of Experience and Responsibility leads to a personally certain epistemological base (however little housemen themselves can give evidence of this), dependent on each individual's different biography; and the value they place on the culturally stereotyped professional segments when they consider their subsequent career is, of course, a matter for their own judgement. So, even in their practice of the basic medical habitus, housemen can, in Bourdieu's word, impart their own 'style' to it.

The Advanced Medical Habitus

This has not been an account of those who teach students and junior doctors, but of the way students and junior doctors are taught and what they learn. However Hahn's (1985) detailed descriptive 'portrait' of an individual attending [consultant], 'Barry Siegler', shows the accomplished practice of medical dispositions by an expert stylist of the advanced medical habitus.

Dr Siegler's pragmatic certainty about his own practice of Medicine, based on his own practice of Experience and Responsibility and derived from his patients, is to be compared to his attitude to 'academic' medicine ('the literature' of Knowledge): 'The stuff you read in the literature is bullshit, 90% is bullshit, maybe 95%, maybe even 98% . . . you can quote me.' While he relies on undisputed scientific fact for his practice, the indeterminacy of science (and he is often clear about the absence of scientific answers) provides him with both distaste for academic doctors (who exercise no Responsibility) and a mandate for using his own, non-scientific, judgement.

Dr Siegler keeps a close watch over his subordinate apprentices, both students and junior doctors, whom 'he questions, socratically, but he also corrects them definitively'; his corrections are either based on his own, quasi-normative, judgements or the absence of choice about treatment. His biographer's report that, 'The constitution of pathology and the impulse to treat pathology are so strong, so ingrained in his thought and conduct, that they are no longer thought of as choice', strongly suggests that the clinical mentality based on Question and Answer is at work. The certainty, institutional and personal, that he relies on determines his relations with other doctors: with the other attendings in his service [firm], these are generally amicable (in professional Co-operation), except when they make different judgements from him about treatment; then he is irritated (and tells his juniors so), but does not criticise them face-to-face. His relations with doctors from other services are less cordial: he says of another doctor who (in a transfer of the ownership of Responsibility) referred him a troublesome patient years ago, 'I've never gotten even with him'; while of another doctor in a different professional segment, to whom he has referred a patient for advice, he says, 'Fuck the anesthesiologist.'

The nature of these official backstage remarks differs from those he makes to patients and other doctors, frontstage, when he 'presents a gentle manner, speaking softly and smiling frequently', except when he finds cause to criticise a junior doctor. At the same time (in the delegation of Responsibility and its ambiguous nature that I have described), he 'tells the residents [his junior doctors], that the patients are not his, but theirs: "You are the attending on all these. I'm just a bystander."' The consequences for medical Responsibility of the linguistic form of Making the Patient the Agent are also found in his attitude to patients; he objects morally to patients 'who seem to be the principal agent in their own disease', such as alcoholics and patients on welfare, sometimes finding their relatives even worse: of one patient's daughter, he says, 'Bitch, I'd like to wring her tits off, honest to God.' As Dr Siegler's official backstage comments indicate, he 'lives in a corporeal universe, as it lives in him'; his frequent, and barely veiled misogynist, 'sexual and scatological references are not simple metaphors. Literal reference remains close by. A crude sexuality underlines his condemning urges to "screw" this or that.' His own corporeal universe (or corporate corporality) is most clearly found in his attitude to patients with psychological problems, the 'Pandora's box', as he puts it, of 'functional' non-somatic (and therefore non-medical) problems: 'The black and white certainty which haunts his medical practice is absent here.'

Now I am not suggesting that Dr Siegler's presentation of himself is anything more than one particular American specialist doctor's personal 'style', which displays his own advanced medical habitus and his own personal command of the general professional dispositions of medicine. Certainly, one might expect the manifestations of high medical Status to be rather more gentlemanly in England, with rather more oblique and less obviously violent language, and that a consultant in a London teaching hospital would practise the disposition of Knowledge much less antagonistically than Dr Siegler does. But these are personal differences of emphasis, and there is no reason to think that Dr Siegler's habitus is not composed of the general professional dispositions.

The Medical Habitus and Internal Events

In this section, I consider some of the implications of the acquisition of the basic medical habitus. In relation to the original debate about the change from idealism to cynicism among students, I have shown that there is an institutional development of cynicism found in the different forms of irony demonstrated verbally. This develops as a consequence, first, of students' segregation from the lay world, then of students' different official and unofficial existence, and then of housemen's frontstage Idealistic presentation compared to their backstage Economical work. But there is also a real transition to cynicism, with consequences evident in the studies, referred to in Chapter 1, which show high rates of mental illness among students and junior members of the profession; that mental illness is not simply an occupational hazard, but a professional probability caused by training, is strongly suggested by the equally high rates among doctors qualified for some years.

This problem has been described in non-psychiatric terms as the 'disabling' effect on students of the 'dual discourse' between caring and competence, between students' nature as ordinarily caring individuals and the way students, in their professional transition, learn to relate to patients officially (Good and Good 1989 and 1993). This well-known problem would be rephrased in my terms as the outcome of the conflict between the personal

Idealism that students enter medical training with (in effect, a lay form of Idealism) and their acquisition of the basic medical habitus, which results from the central professional enterprise of producing safe and competent doctors, rather than 'good' or caring ones. No doubt there are major consequences of this for patients. I am not, however, concerned with patients in this account (except peripherally as the source of knowledge of different forms), but with the effect on medical students and doctors of the 'symbolic violence' – this phrase is used by Bourdieu (1977: 237 n47) to describe the domination exerted through the communication in which it is disguised – of such conflicts; for this 'dual discourse', though perhaps the most significant, is only one of many structural contradictions that I have shown exist in medical training.

In Chapter 2, I explicitly criticised Becker's perspectives, with their concrete nature and their precise allocation to specific periods of training, and derived equivalent general dispositions. I then showed that dispositions have elements in common with the schemas of cognitive psychologists, which makes it possible to analyse dispositional conflicts in psychological terms. For, when psychological schemas compete or conflict, they are held to give rise to cognitive dissonance; this then results in a disagreeable internal emotional state. Those who experience this emotional state attempt to minimise it by changing whatever they can, usually by altering their situation or by giving less importance to one or other of the schemas.

Students' Unawareness of Internal Conflict

The use of psychological schemas in anthropological studies has recently been discussed by Holland (1992), but then dismissed as being unhelpful for understanding people's actions 'in messy situations' or for understanding the complicated pathways to censorship and inaction. This dismissal is based on a rather crudely deterministic definition of schemas, and leads to the apparently unacceptable conclusion that such 'schema-driven' people are strangely unable to attend to social and political relationships, are oddly untouched by social constraints and struggles and particularly immune to psychic distress (1992: 75–6). There is, of course, the rather obvious objection to this conclusion that cognitive psychologists do actually use schema theory in 'messy situations' for both understanding and treating psychic distress in real patients. The way this is done is by elucidating the schemas that may explain individual people's problems, by providing them with this understanding and then, on this basis, by helping them to do things differently. But such criticisms of the application of schema theory have particular relevance for medical students; although not immune from psychic distress, many students may indeed be unable to attend to social and political aspects of relationships, and be untouched by social constraints and struggles and, generally, unaware of the reasons for their distress. It is not just that students are fixed in a situation that they cannot alter (one of the ways of reducing cognitive dissonance), except by leaving and sacrificing the role associated with whatever stage of medical Status the student is at. There is also within the profession the pervasive cultural aversion to investigating social and psychological matters, except in the low-Status disciplines of Psychology, Sociology and Psychiatry.

A recent criticism (S. Turner 1994: 14–27) of the notion of shared 'practices' itself makes a very similar assumption to that quoted above of 'schema-driven' people. Practices are again defined as causative in a deterministic way; this assumption is then easy to dismiss, and the analytic concept of 'practices' is replaced by those of public performances and individual habits. This, intriguingly, may again be very similar to medical students' own view of their situation, with their comments that 'You've got to say the right things' and 'It's all a game', and their general description or explanation of events in immediately concrete and personal terms, with their reservation on more private matters. By and large, they are not disposed to do otherwise because of their wish and need to surmount the incessant hurdles of exams and assessments, which test their acquisition of facts, the certainty of which is not in doubt, and, conversely, because of the doubt or uncertainty that is associated with the personal knowledge of any internal events and experiences.

So, by and large, medical students are not characterised by 'existential *angst*' in relation to their transformation, and even less so because of any uncertainties they face in the forms of knowledge they have to learn. Some of them are, of course, aware of the personal changes that take place during their training: they may describe themselves as becoming disillusioned, harder and more cynical; and, as their comments about the need to present a particular facet of themselves to doctors on ward rounds indicate, they have an understanding of the particular roles they must learn. But it would be a mistake, in my view, to use the evidence that students can be encouraged to talk in greater detail about the effect their training has on them to conclude that they often do so by themselves. There is, for example, such evidence from Harvard provided by Good (1994: 65–87). It may, of course, be that this is the result of differences between students at Harvard and at UCLMS: the former are likely to be older, from wider intellectual backgrounds, perhaps more psychologically minded, and might be assumed to have a greater interest in their training in that they are often paying for it themselves. Even so, the fact that Good is actually on the staff of the medical school and the likelihood that his interests are known to students should be remembered (and may explain students' perhaps rather pious accounts recorded in what may be a form of official frontstage settings). But, certainly in London, the combination of the pervasive antagonism of medical culture to psychological and social forms of analysis, the general use of materially referential language, and the gradual loss of unofficial settings all mean that discussions of this sort between students are rare: a clinical student who had done a Sociology B.Sc. said of this now unusable knowledge and experience framed in a different language, 'I have to keep it all in a cupboard [in my head].' Further evidence of the cultural antagonism to psychological methods was provided by clinical students' attitudes to a questionnaire study in progress during my fieldwork (referred to in Chapter 1). The researcher from the Psychology Department who was organising these questionnaires into personality and logical ability, now timetabled in for every clinical student, described to me the constant hostility from the students who did attend (something like 60 per cent), which was profoundly personally upsetting. No doubt there was a combination of factors here: the researcher's position (her lay Status, and her separation from the teaching staff, yet her association nonetheless with the medical school); the examination-like and yet psychological nature of the questions; their intrusiveness; the students' suspicion that their answers were not anonymous; the time taken off clinical work; and the manner in which the reason for their absence from their firms was received by consultants. But, whereas previously, when the questionnaires were voluntary, a large number of students had taken up the offer of feedback and being told the results of these tests, not one student had asked for this now that they were official.

For such reasons, then, students' cognitive awareness of cognitive dissonance itself may therefore be absent – an outcome made more likely by the common knowledge that medical training and medicine are stressful. Students, long before they start at medical school, are aware of the stress (the term here is used in its lay sense) in terms of hard work and long hours needed to become a doctor, and the hard work and long hours that will be expected of them when they qualify. As I have described, even at their interview for medical school coping with that stress is understood to be part of the proceedings by both candidates and interviewers; I have also described how the pressure exerted by exams and assessments is seen by some as a deliberate official prefiguring of the stress of being a doctor. Medical students, then, are well accustomed to the idea of stress within the profession. The anticipated stresses of exams are in fact accompanied by what students describe as evidence of this: sleeplessness, diarrhoea, vomiting and other physical manifestations of anxiety are common before exams, and at clinical Finals some candidates are almost paralysed by anxiety.

For students, then, stress results in mainly physical problems, explicable in terms of the physiological functions they have been taught about. Indeed, the tendency of students to see some of their problems (in passing exams, for example) as deliberately engineered by the medical school may be usefully thought of as a way of reducing the cognitive awareness of any conflict between dispositions. Such an attribution of deliberate and consistent policy to a traditional and historically unplanned form of training may in turn be contributed to by the principle of consistency so important in scientific method (which, when applied to the self, may also minimise any inconsistency, or conflict, found).

Further, as I discussed in Chapter 2, the different settings in which conflicting dispositions are learnt may serve to reduce any conflict experienced; an example of this may show what I mean:

> Steve, a clinical student on a surgical firm, was On Take one night, and had spent six hours, mostly in Casualty, with Michelle, the houseman, helping her in many ways (filling out forms, taking blood

and so on). The morning after, Michelle, Steve and I were waiting on **CCU** for the Post-Take ward round with the consultant and the other doctors on the firm. The Staff Nurse at the nursing station called over to Steve: 'Do you want to put a **Venflon** in? He's a medical patient but you could do it!' Steve checked with Michelle that it was all right for him to do this and went to find the equipment in the cupboard – but there was no **Venflon** of the right size there. Steve then looked through his pockets and found one. He then set things up, arranging the equipment on the patient's bed, and put a tourniquet on the patient's arm, while he prepared the needle. All this took some time. A few minutes before the ward round was due to start, Mr Bridges, the consultant surgeon, appeared on the ward for the round and looking round the ward, saw Steve and asked him: 'What are you doing?'

Steve [*looking over to Michelle for support*]: 'Putting up a drip, aren't I, Michelle?' [*She didn't look back at him and didn't answer.*]

Mr Bridges: 'Well, you're supposed to be coming on a ward round with me. Come on!'

Steve [*still hoping for some help from the houseman whom he was helping in Casualty only a few hours before*]: 'Michelle, what shall I do?' [*But again, Michelle averted her eyes and did not answer.*]

Steve looked at me, shrugged, undid the tourniquet, apologised to the patient and joined the consultant.

The point here is that there was a conflict at work between Steve's practice of Responsibility (first in the relatively egalitarian practice of Co-operation in Casualty and then carried over to the ward when he prepared to take blood) and his frontstage role as a student learning Experience and merely hypothetical Responsibility in the hierarchical setting of the incipient ward round; this conflict he tried to resolve by appealing to the common factor in these settings, Michelle. But her appreciation of the great difference between the two settings (and the presence of the consultant on the ward) led her, in effect, to ignore Steve's appeal to their earlier shared practice of Co-operative Responsibility in Casualty and, in doing so, to confirm the different dispositions that tend to be practised by students in these different settings. Michelle's lack of support was discouraging to Steve, but he did not comment on his own ambiguous position, both as a team-member and subordinate student. I suggest that, in the corporate corporality of training, where the mental and emotional are so disregarded, the dissonance experienced by Steve was limited by these different settings: while, for the remaining few weeks of this firm attachment, he distrusted Michelle, having attributed his difficulties to her personally, he was not likely to make the same mistake again. His own personal integrity would henceforward be ensured and his experience of dissonance limited by the embodied practice of dispositions appropriate to their settings.

More empirical evidence for the general professional lack of introspection is found in the small but intensive study of SHOs by Hale and Hudson (1992). The majority of these found access to the more personal aspects of their own experience very hard; when asked to relate an episode of whatever sort about each of five significant people in their life (their present consultant, some other member of the medical profession – a previous consultant was often chosen – father, mother, and spouse, partner or close friend), 'many experienced difficulty. Yet more found the task virtually impossible to perform, the familiar pattern of response in these cases being embarrassed laughter and stalling, followed by resort to generalities, or to episodes of obvious triviality' (1992: 456–7). The authors of the study were alarmed at the number of these SHOs going into general practice, often from a recognition that they would not get on in hospital medicine, for whom 'the personal is a "no-go area" – in some cases *terra incognita*'. This lack of interest in themselves was no different from the way in which these junior doctors, particularly those from overseas, were treated by their consultants; one SHO reported 'that, to the best of his understanding, his consultant did not even know his name – neither his first name nor his surname' (1992: 460).

The foregoing section shows that there were good reasons for my own unwillingness to undertake any psychological questionnaires during my fieldwork, quite apart from the business of decoding and analysing data involved in such studies. For, in summary, while anxiety and unpleasant internal experiences consequent on cognitive dissonance may be common among students and junior doctors, these are likely to be attributed to the individual's immediately identifiable concrete experience, rather than to any personally psychological or broader social and political aspects of training.

Psychological Findings in Terms of Dispositions

This summary is very much an echo of what Young (1980) has called the scientific 'discourse on stress', in which stress is seen as the result of physiological activity, which is in turn caused by an individual's awareness of particular events; it is the relation between these two that the scientist, often a psychologist, seeks to establish in the production of this form of written scientific Knowledge. This literature is based on a series of assumptions, chiefly concerned with the empiricist nature of its methods (including the use of a value-free language), its exclusion of social determinants and its concentration on individuals' apparently easily ascertainable psychological determinants.

Scientific culture, in the context of which investigators make these assumptions in their psychological studies of stress and depression among students and junior doctors, is very similar to the medical culture in which students and doctors find themselves; investigators and subjects share the same assumptions. Stress, depression and so on, both as perceived by those studied and as indicated by empiricist quantification (from individual subjects' scores on questionnaires, scientifically acceptable to psychologists and psychiatrists) are then correlated with self-reported accounts of subjective experience; and these, for reasons that I have described earlier, are likely to be the subjects' individual appreciations of their concrete practice of dispositions, rather than their attribution to any more psychological and social considerations, such as dispositions themselves.

What I now propose to do is to interpret some such psychological studies in the light of dispositions. But before doing so, I should emphasise that I am not attempting to explain all such findings of emotional distress in terms of the practice of, and conflict between, dispositions that I have described in my ethnography. It is no doubt the case that there are conflicts that I have not described (such as that between personal Idealism and Responsibility in the infliction of pain on patients), and that there are other factors as well. Further, while quantification of psychological findings is essential for the academic purposes of the discipline of Psychology, this approach is not likely to get at either the precise nature or the cause of mental events (if only because of the nature of the questions asked). There are many other difficulties that I will not discuss (return rates of questionnaires, for example, as well as, even in psychological terms, the problematic nature of concepts like 'stress' and 'burnout').

But, despite the problems with interpreting such studies, there are two points that should be made. First, it is highly likely that measured 'stress' (for example) does bear some positive relation to unpleasant internal events; and, second, whether it does or not, measurements of 'stress' are held to do so by the profession itself – the BMA, for example, recently published a small book on *Stress and the Medical Profession* (BMA 1992), which depends on just the sort of studies I now discuss. These are psychological studies of medical students and junior doctors, mostly those conducted in England by Firth-Cozens and referred to in Chapter 1. They are based on following up large cohorts of students through their years in training, using various questionnaires, including the standard General Health Questionnaire, to provide scores of overall emotional distress. I shall confine myself to their main findings, which I shall recast in terms of dispositions.

The Study of Clinical Students

The first study (Firth 1986) of students in their second clinical year found an estimated prevalence of emotional disturbance of 31.2 per cent (compared to 9.7 per cent found in young unemployed people), with no difference between men and women. There is no suggestion that these high rates are associated with similar proportions of students receiving help by becoming patients; we may assume that the distress is somehow 'coped' with.

Students reported that what they disliked most about their roles was not overwork; as I have discussed above, this is expected by all students. Rather, 'feeling useless' was the commonest response, evidence of their lack of Responsibility. While one of the main reported sources of stress was talking to patients, the author points out that talking to patients was the activity students reported as most generally liked (although it may not be over-cynical to detect professional Idealism at work in this avowal); she considers that their report that this also caused stress was because they were about to start their psychiatric attachment, emphasising the difficulties that students (and doctors) have with Psychiatry.

Other stressors were the effect that training was having on their personal life, anxieties about ward rounds ('both of which may be unchangeable aspects of training') and dealing with death and suffering. But the category that most strongly aroused feelings was 'relationships with consultants', a category that was also reported as particularly stressful by the largest proportion of students; they usually described occasions when they had been humiliated before their fellows. Now 'relationships with consultants' and ward rounds should be seen together, remembering that consultants in a teaching hospital are highly likely to be all men. The stress experienced is due to the Question and Answer method of teaching Experience and learning, in the dramatic frontstage setting of ward rounds; students need to demonstrate professional Idealism, often in conflict with their own personal Idealism, but promoted by the moral humiliation of 'Student Abuse'. The growing separation from other aspects of life that students experience is related to their increasing segregation; dealing with death and suffering is simply not part of what they are taught, but is something students have to deal with on their own.

The Study of Housemen

In the second study (Firth-Cozens 1987), which 'was encouraged by the reactions of staff to the suicides of two junior house officers', these students, now housemen, were tested in much the same way, with the addition of a measure for depression. Now emotional strain was found to be higher than among students, at 50 per cent (compared to 36 per cent among male and 34 per cent among female executive civil servants); overall, depression at a level that indicated treatment was found in 28 per cent – housemen in teaching hospitals were significantly more stressed than those in non-teaching hospitals. Here again, clinical levels of depression were not accompanied by details of rates of housemen becoming actual patients. Now they reported the most stressful aspect of their jobs as 'overwork', followed by 'talking to distressed relatives', 'effects on personal life' and 'serious treatment failures'. Empirically, stress and depression were highly correlated between 'relations with consultants', 'effects on personal life', 'overwork' and 'making decisions'. The sudden access of hitherto unfamiliar Responsibility for housemen, and their need to co-ordinate, backstage, the divergent workings of the hospital is added to their pre-existing conflicts. A more recent study (Humphris *et al.* 1994) found housemen reporting similar stressors: long working hours were ranked highest, with insufficient staff, on-call duties and 'morale and institutional climate' following. Fifth came the implications of mistakes 'e.g. litigation, humiliation or patient deterioration', showing an increasing awareness of the legal liability of junior doctors and the fact that little protection is likely to be forthcoming from their consultants; and sixth came their uncertainty about their next post.

It is important to note that there was no relation between stress or depression and the number of hours actually worked, despite 'overwork' being reported as stressful. In a later study, Firth-Cozens (1992) again found that, though teaching hospitals were again found to be more stressful to work in than non-teaching hospitals, objective measurements of work done (such as the number of patients cared for or of hours worked) did not predict the stress experienced by housemen or their attitudes to their jobs. This at first surprising finding is mirrored in the study of SHOs mentioned above (Hale and Hudson 1992: 455), where the SHOs who were coping best worked the longest hours, and vice versa. But if housemen spend their whole life on stage in the hospital (as their consultants may tell them that *they* had to as housemen), not only will they experience a greater sense of Co-operation but also, spending their whole life in the hospital, they would be a force to be reckoned with, having scope for more possibility of improving their living conditions; conversely, they would not experience any conflict arising from 'effects on personal life', where 'personal' means on the non-medical offstage. 'Overwork' might be more accurately seen in terms of the need of housemen, while having Responsibility for patients, to integrate the different, and often conflicting, workings of the hospital. The stressful nature of this major aspect of housemen's work is again given support by Humphris's study, where a striking distribution of the psychological measure of 'burnout' among junior doctors was found: overall, 18 per cent of the doctors were burnt out, but the differential distribution by Status was 32 per cent of housemen, 23 per cent of SHOs, 5 per cent of registrars and 0 per cent of SRs. This strongly suggests that increasing Status in any professional segment corresponds to a decreasing amount of stress caused by the work involved in co-ordinating with other such segments.

Once again, relationships with consultants feature strongly as stressors; but, again, Firth-Cozens does not point out that most consultants in teaching hospitals are male, a fact perhaps highly significant in the differences in psychiatric morbidity found between housemen in those and in other hospitals, as well as the others she suggests (in my terms, increased Competitiveness and awareness of Status, there also associated with Knowledge). Relationships with consultants are almost exclusively found on ward rounds, when housemen's inability to answer consultants' questions about what they have done is taken as evidence of lack of Responsibility. This is combined with the inverse difficulty of asking questions, disagreeing or explaining their difficulties, and with the need to accommodate to consultants' idiosyncrasies – references, vital for the next job, have assumed more significance. In the light of my attribution of emotional distress to dispositional conflict, it is hardly surprising that the most depressed and stressed housemen scored highest on empathy, self-criticism and disillusionment; such doctors' own greater personal Idealism causes greater conflict both with the need to practise Economy backstage and to present professional Idealism on ward rounds.

The Study of Women Housemen

The third study (Firth-Cozens 1990) was to investigate the position of female housemen, in the light of their generally higher levels of depression than both other women professionals and male doctors, and because women doctors' suicide rates had been reported to be up to four times their age-mates'. In this study, 46 per cent of female housemen were depressed at a level indicating treatment (compared to 14.9 per cent of a community sample of women in London). While the levels of stress were related to much the same stressors as reported in the previous study of housemen, for these women the conflict between career and personal life was most strongly related to depression; also strongly related were sexual discrimination by senior doctors and sexual prejudice from patients; these women housemen also noted prejudice from nurses and from other departments (like ECG and X-ray, which I have noted are particularly tricky for housemen, as they are run by doctors too).

So, while women found themselves in a predominantly masculine cultural environment throughout medical school, they were able to cope with this (perhaps by forming mutually supportive groups). Working as housemen, however, very much on their own, they now find that the professional segments they work in as housemen, Surgery and Medicine, really are masculine; not only senior members of the profession and those working in other departments, but also nurses and patients, see these segments of hospital medicine as a man's job. The conflict between medical and personal life is expressed here in terms of conflicts between career and marriage or children; no figures are given for numbers of married female housemen, but I guess they are relatively small. An additional source of stress for women may be the loss, through the geographical displacement of new housemen, of the system of personal supports used by women through their training up to this point; as discussed in Chapter 5, the masculine sort of Cooperative camaraderie found in teams, even scratch teams like firms, is more easily available to men. In other words, only with their full integration into the institutional family do women now appreciate the real difficulty of combining a successful career in medicine with family life. Forcible socialisation without much possibility of advancement to higher positions leads to demoralisation consequent on marginalisation, as Musgrove (1964: 142–7) shows, contrasting the astonishingly stable success of the forcible training of young Christian slaves in the Ottoman Empire with the pathetic failure of the equally ruthless re-education of indigenous Indians in the US. The key feature in the creation of Janissaries was the openness of the highest positions in the Empire to these foreigners, while the Americans offered young Indians 'only life as marginal men and second-class citizens on the reserves'. Seen from the teaching hospital, General Practice, where so many women graduates end up, is certainly marginal, as are the low-Status segments of medicine, like Psychiatry, which are more open to women.

How Do They Cope With It All?

There is no doubt that some students and housemen find the medical institution congenial and get on well, either unaware of its structural contradictions or (highly unlikely in my view) aware of but accepting them. It is possible that men may find it easier to avoid the sort of internal conflict between dispositions by practising a sort of cognitive Economy which simply aligns them, so that Experience, Responsibility and Knowledge, as well as Co-operation, form a single cognitive schema closely united with Status, with male consultants acting as models. This solution may be accompanied by a rather strange form of control within the profession. I have described the culturally masculine aspects of emotion associated with the three dispositions acquired during training (scientific objectivity in Knowledge, emotional detachment in Experience, and mature judgement in the ownership and action of Responsibility); in this upward-looking hierarchy, where professional relationships are more important than any others, clinical students and junior doctors discuss consultants' individual attitudes and quasi-normative preferences in personal terms, perhaps especially because of their dependence on their seniors (rather than their patients) for references for future jobs. In doing so, junior doctors attribute their seniors with emotions other than those associated with the dispositions that they embody, and therefore treat them as fuller people, in a way that they do not treat themselves. Consultants can be nice or nasty, **benign** or **malignant**; it seems to be a matter of choice. Their emotional diversity then leads to a powerful charismatic ambiguity to consultants' Status: they have reached the pinnacle of all these dispositions, and act as models for them all, and yet may contravene the dominant emotional aspect associated with each of them.

Other students and housemen simply leave the profession, a matter I discuss in the next chapter. But the high rates of alcoholism and cirrhosis in the profession, noted in Chapter 1, may, like the professional probability of mental illness, be consequent on the acquisition of medical dispositions during training. In the study on students, 17 per cent reported drinking 'a lot occasionally' and 4 per cent 'a lot often', with no difference between men and women, and with emotionally distressed students drinking most; half the students reported an increase in their intake of alcohol over the past two years. This is almost certainly a serious underestimate (given that many of the 21 per cent of non-responders to the questionnaire were likely to be antipathetic to psychological enquiries of this sort, being, let me suggest, of the Rugby Club Sort). This finding emphasises the part that alcohol plays in the formation of Co-operation, particularly preclinically. It also suggests that alcohol is used as a way of dissolving the conflicts experienced by clinical students in the absence of a verbal understanding of these internal events.

Among housemen, 19 per cent reported drinking 'a lot occasionally' or 'a lot often', with many of these reporting similar levels two years previously. The use of drugs for recreation was 7 per cent. A quarter were taking drugs for physical illness, though very few for anxiety, depression or sleep. There was no relation between stress and depression and use of alcohol. Firth-Cozens suggests that for some housemen alcohol was a way of maintaining psychological health in the short term (no doubt, as in the past, by promoting Co-operation and resolving conflicts); it may now also be used for night sedation. For, hardly surprisingly (given the presence of questions about sleep and eating in the questionnaires about stress and depression, because disturbed sleep and eating patterns are both results and causes of depression and anxiety) both depression and stress were related to problems with sleeping patterns and diet. But drinking on duty has now become an offence for which doctors may be dismissed, limiting its use and therefore perhaps increasing the manifestation of mental illness in other ways. The use of sleeping tablets (as of any other psychotropic medication) at this stage is small, no doubt because of the continuing distaste for even self-medication as a psychiatric patient. This may explain the surprisingly high rate of medication for physical illness among housemen, who may attribute physical expression of psychological distress to physical causes and treat themselves with medication now more freely available to them.

The Effect of Such Studies

There is thus evidence, as scientific as it could be, of serious and widespread problems in the high rates of depression, anxiety, stress and burnout (terms used by the profession about patients) among both students and housemen. The conclusion of one of these papers is the (perhaps rather confusingly stated) one that 'physicians should try less to heal themselves and more to heal each other' (Firth-Cozens 1987: 535). But these studies that show the pathogenic (iatrogenic, indeed) effect of medical training appear to have been effectively ignored by the institutions that provide it.

The reason for this lies in the very nature of such evidence; this is to 'blame the victim' rather than the system of training itself. And blaming the victim takes a particularly powerful professional form; students' and doctors' collective medical Status is not only reversed by pathologising them into individual patients, but they are made patients of the lowest-Status medical segment, Psychiatry. Just as there are attempts to use psychological tests to predict which students will fail in the system of examinations in medical training – a rather pointless project, one might think, in view of the standard use of norm-marking of these tests, in which, say, 5 per cent will always fail – so there have also been attempts to establish precisely which students and doctors may be classified into this professionally most uncongenial category of psychiatric patient.

In the studies I have interpreted, though, the rates of those depressed enough to warrant treatment are not illuminated by associated rates of those actually receiving such treatment; my guess would be that very few indeed actually are. They are far more likely to ignore the possibility that they may need help; this is not because, as the recent BMA report (1994/5: 19) states, 'Sadly, medical school culture does not yet encourage students to admit to either physical or psychological problems and to seek help.' As I have argued throughout, student culture is based on the acquisition of general professional dispositions; it is a great disservice unwittingly done by Becker's great study to have identified student culture as autonomous.

But this view is held so strongly that, while there is plenty of evidence about students' and housemen's mental illness, there is very little about senior doctors in hospitals. It is only the junior members of the profession that are stigmatised wholesale in this way; the relative lack of information about consultants apparently preserves their sanity among their vulnerable and feeble juniors, as well as some degree of mystery about them. An interesting example of this is the 1992 study by Firth-Cozens referred to above, which related stress experienced by students and housemen to their experience of their own families; the fascinating conclusion is that students' and housemen's perception of their own families strongly predicted their experience of their relationship with consultants (itself a major predictor, as usual, of stress). The relationships within and between students' and doctors' own families and the institutional 'family' in which they work are of great interest (see also, for example, Johnson 1991 and Vaillant *et al.* 1972), but, once again, only one side of the relationship is given; if consultants evoke fathers to students, it is more than possible that students evoke children to consultants, who treat them accordingly. But there is no information about this reciprocal relationship; consultants are not the subject of this sort of enquiry. It is therefore only students' and junior doctors' families that can be described and treated as pathogenic, in giving rise to the sorts of problems described, and not the senior doctors', whose families might in some way have protected their children from the stresses that they now appear to contribute to. It is equally possible, of course, that the process of transference works in other ways: that women doctors, for example, who are known to have a particularly high rate of divorce, transfer to their husbands the qualities that they have found in their male superordinates, finding them impossible to live with. But, once again, it is the victims (and in this case the victim's families) that are blamed and pathologised in the way so powerfully degrading within the profession, by making them, in effect, psychiatric patients.

There seems little doubt that if a series of papers were published, showing similar rates of illness among another group, not organised in the way that professions are, there would be some reaction from the medical profession calling for funds not just for further research but for intervention. This is not the case among the senior members of the profession; they have no medical Responsibility for students or junior doctors. The reaction is of a rather different but historically familiar sort, to bargain with the State for improved terms; the State is pressed to improve the working hours of junior doctors, even though the published evidence seems clear that long hours in themselves are not related to the problems described, and may even reduce the rates. Medical schools themselves react, if at all, by setting up, on an individual basis, student counselling services, which are often not used for the reasons described above.

Psychological Illness in Longer-qualified Doctors

My interpretation of these studies clearly assumes the social origins of emotional distress manifested in anxiety and depression, in that I have related anxiety and depression to the practice of professional dispositions. Lastly, I suggest that the relatively high prevalence of mental illness among longer-qualified doctors may be associated with more general features of the medical habitus.

The high rates of mental illness in the medical profession have been known for some time. Information has been available about mortality (which, related to age, provides some measure of health) among different occupations since 1841, after the first Marriage and Registration Act of 1836, one of a series of Benthamite measures for surveying the population. The usual way that this information is presented, therefore, is in the numbers of each occupation dying from a registered disease, numbers that can be used comparatively against the number expected if the members of that occupation died in the same proportion as the whole working population of the country; given that the latter is always 100, figures greater than 100 for an occupation and disease mean that the Standardised Mortality Ratio (SMR) in those circumstances is higher than would be expected.

While there are difficulties associated with the method (the working population is healthier than the unemployed, higher social classes are healthier, women may be classified by their husbands' class rather than their own), the results from these and other studies indicate that doctors, both male and female, generally have a low mortality from the common physical diseases, like heart disease, up to their 60s (see BMA 1993: 15–28); these figures and those that follow are for the period 1979–83. On the other hand, SMRs in the same age group from causes that, while perhaps immediately attributable to physical disease, may be considered to have a significant psychological aetiology, are higher in doctors; examples of such categories are cirrhosis (almost always due to excessive alcohol consumption), poisoning and suicide. Male doctors' SMR for deaths from cirrhosis of the liver is 115, the same as for lawyers and a little less than dentists' 117; these indices are not statistically significantly different from the norm (those which are, I shall indicate with an asterisk). The SMR for external injury and poisoning among male doctors, however, is 182* and for suicide 172* (male lawyers 92 and 128, male dentists 113 and 222*) and for female doctors these SMRs are 182* and 371 (female lawyers 47 and unreported, female dentists 184 and 284); the high suicide rate for women doctors is confirmed by other studies.

While doctors, like members of other professions, are physically healthier than the norm, therefore, there are indications (from the rates of cirrhosis, external injury and poisoning, and suicide) that they, like dentists but not like other professionals, are mentally less so. If these SMRs are taken as indicators of the mental health of the profession, then this may have improved; in 1970–2, for example, the SMR for cirrhosis among doctors in England and Wales was 311, for accidental poisoning 818, and for suicide 335 (Whitefield 1981: 724). But SMRs by themselves cannot be taken as an index of mental health: it might be, for example, that doctors are now, rather than actually killing themselves, simply leaving the profession; or that, rather than drinking themselves to death (perhaps because of doctors' increasing recognition of the physical consequences of drinking too much alcohol), they are simply becoming psychiatrically ill without dying. Certainly, other studies seem to confirm the high rates of psychological morbidity among doctors, both here and in the US (see, for example, Firth-Cozens 1987: 533; Rucinski and Cybulska 1985). All the studies using official data share the problems that doctors treat themselves, receive informal help from colleagues, or may delay looking for treatment until their illness has reached an advanced stage, with the consequence that all these figures are likely to be considerable underestimates of the rates that would be found among doctors if they were less able to avoid the usual methods of survey. But, even using these methods, figures for admission of male doctors to psychiatric hospitals in Scotland were more than twice as high as those of a socially comparable group, with rates for drug dependence, alcoholism and affective disorders (mainly depression) all significantly higher among doctors than non-doctors (Murray 1976); and treatment for doctors with problems with alcohol and drugs is often delayed for years (Brooke *et al.* 1991).

Clearly, only more general interpretations of these figures are possible; there are no grounds for doing more than simply suggesting that several features of the medical habitus may be at work to account for such high rates of many sorts of mental illness (whatever their immediate social origins) among members of the profession that itself treats illness. Most of these features have already been mentioned: the underlying importance of not complaining or 'whinging', in the shared practice of medical Co-operation; the distaste for the low-Status segment of Psychiatry; unwillingness to examine, or unawareness of, internal mental events; the lack of a conventionally acceptable scientific language to use; and, equally, unfamiliarity with, or unwillingness to use, lay expressions of distress. But perhaps the most important feature (as found in the delay in doctors' being treated) is the great difficulty doctors have in reversing their medical Status and becoming a patient. In addition to the loss of central personal identity in this way (and, if known to their colleagues or superordinates, its potentially damaging effects on their careers), doctors know how they may regard their patients on the official backstage, with feelings that range from ironic amusement to frank distaste; the possibility that they themselves might put themselves in a position to be regarded in such ways by other doctors may be unthinkable.

Chapter 11

Concluding Remarks

> So many books are crying out loud 'Unfair!',
> see themselves Brontë-wise, wronged governesses
> who could tell the world a thing or two. Injustice.
> Novels are written to prove the world's a cad,
> and every morning someone wakes up to the fact
> that he/she is married to an unpleasant person.
> There's something in it. But what were you expecting?
> No justice can turn back the springing tiger.
>
> Gavin Ewart

In this book I have given an account of basic medical training and the social and psychological construction of doctors in terms of the formation of the basic medical habitus, itself created through the practice of historically and socially developed dispositions, and incorporating an 'exclusive professional identity'. While the rather pessimistic implications of the previous chapter might indicate that there is a need for the radical revision of training, if only to improve the mental health of the profession, alternative products of a different medical training would therefore rely on the historical and social creation of different dispositions. It is inherently unlikely that this is either an easy or a welcome task for those expert practitioners of the advanced medical habitus like Dr Siegler, who are more likely to see very good reasons why they should train others as they have themselves been trained.

The psychological problems encountered by those in training are in part due to the acquisition of a specialist language that is utterly unsuited to dealing with internal mental events, let alone altering social aspects of doctors' practice. But this also has its great advantages. For without this language, and its associated emotions of objectivity, detachment and judgement in such dramatic settings, it is difficult to see how some doctors could do the work they do. No one would want, I imagine, to be operated on by a surgeon who could not distance himself from his patients' experience; this is the value of a training that is itself, I have suggested, historically based on surgical training. It is, however, by no means clear that all medical students should be taught this, particularly those who will become general practitioners (the specialist training for which appears to involve 'unlearning' so much of what is taught in medical school). Equally, few people finding themselves patients would wish to be denied the most effective treatment available, based presumably on the most up-to-date scientific evidence. But again, it is by no means clear that most medical consultations require this, though they would all seem to require an understanding of patients' problems.

And there are other reasons why fundamental changes are unlikely to be made. The profession has, in effect, contracted with the State to produce what the profession regards as safe and competent medical practitioners; this, in turn, implies the mass-production of doctors by some sort of standard transformation, based on precedent, of those who have enlisted for training. As I have indicated in Chapter 3, the formation of the profession was due to a great extent to the intervention of the State, with the Apothecaries' Act, the Anatomy Act and the Medical Act. But within this contract, the profession maintains its own autonomous right to train doctors as it thinks fit. The State does not appear to wish to interfere with the profession. The very recent radical reorganisation of higher medical training (that is, within professional segments) was certainly the result of pressure from the State rather than the GMC. But the State-appointed Chief Medical Officer was only instructed to produce his recommendations, in the 'Calman Report' (DOH 1993), following the threat of legal action by the European Commission against the UK for failing to comply with the terms of the Medical Directive concerned with the transferability of higher medical qualifications between member states: the UK had agreed to this in 1975.

And the profession has negotiated with the State highly favourable financial terms for training medical students, the overwhelming number of whom are paid for by the State (from local government and from the Department for Education and Employment). This money is usually distributed within the institution according to the teaching time allotted to the different disciplines and departments, in terms of the equivalent numbers of full-time students in each segment. The likelihood is that these considerable financial rewards to the segmented institution function as a powerful factor for its stability. The separate disciplines and departments teaching Knowledge and Experience benefit from teaching medical students, without much evidence of these sums of money being directed specifically to teaching them. Teaching hospitals also receive substantial sums from the Department of Health for each clinical student in the form of SIFT (Service Increment for Teaching). The history of medical schools' reform without change (which makes Becker's account of 1961 still familiar to medical students) may itself be due to, rather than despite, the rapid developments of biomedical science and medical technology. It has been suggested that such scientific activity (and the associated production of Knowledge, which forms the written base of medicine) has itself become the prime function of medical schools, though masked by the profession's stated Idealistic aims: 'medical education's manifest humanistic mission is little more than a screen for the research mission which is the major concern of the institution's social structure' (Bloom 1988: 295). And many medical schools do tend to act as administrative bureaux for sorting out the allocation of tasks and funds to disciplines and departments, rather than as central directorates with their own funds that can organise research into and plan their own function of training.

So, at the same time as State-funded students maintain the disparate preclinical disciplines and clinical departments, they also have to co-ordinate them cognitively and practically. This I have shown to result in students' ranking them hierarchically, along the lines that they are ranked in the general culture of medicine, with the social sciences ranked lowest preclinically and Psychiatry clinically. This ranking is confirmed for housemen, whose work also involves co-ordination, this time of the fragmented hospital, while supporting the two traditionally strongest segments of Medicine and Surgery; in doing this co-ordinating work, housemen no longer bring money into the institution, but their short tenure and low pay (with overtime still paid at substantially below the normal rate) again shore up the existing institutional structure.

The idea that these junior members of the profession should be responsible for altering the system is, however surprisingly, promoted: 'Ultimately the strongest driving force for change must be the students and young doctors themselves', writes Lowry (1993: 83), in *Medical Education* published by the *BMJ*. In fact, of course, students and housemen have minimal power of this sort; they must pass exams and gain good references. There is, however, good evidence of their dissatisfaction with their training, expressed as their regret at having decided to become doctors at all. This appears to be increasing: the overall figures found in 1986 for those qualifying in 1966, 1976 and 1981 were 16 per cent, 28 per cent and 48 per cent, with little difference between rates for men and women (Allen 1988: 291–2); in 1991, of those qualifying in 1986, 58 per cent of men and 76 per cent of women expressed such regret (Allen 1994: 229). These rates are not accompanied by any accurate figures about those who turn their regret into action and leave the profession: it appears to be no one's responsibility to establish this. Certainly, junior doctors' subsequent careers are of no interest to the medical school after their year as a houseman is completed, unless they achieve eminence and can be claimed as an illustrious example of the school's work. If housemen do go on to be SHOs (from whom the demoralised group studied by Hale and Hudson came), they then compete in the *laissez-faire* market for medical posts, where, with short tenure, long hours and continuing dependence on their consultants for references, it is not surprising that patronage prospers (Allen 1988: 153–68) and also appears to be increasing (Allen 1994: 116–28). Further, the apparently still unceasing supply of doctors from overseas, particularly from the countries of the old British Empire (to which the system of medical training was exported wholesale) but now increasingly from the countries of the European Union, means that they can make up for any loss in numbers of doctors trained in England. The GMC has recently speeded up its processing of applications for registration for overseas doctors, previously often a long and tortuous business. Whatever the wastage in terms either of potential doctors untrained and money spent training those who do not practise, such losses to the profession are not experienced by those who train them. Medical schools' function is to train students, not to follow them up in the way that clinicians would follow up their patients after a course of treatment; and they are paid for doing this and are not penalised for any problems that the training causes. It is the State (or rather the taxpayer) that bears the cost of any such wastage.

Of course, my account of the process of training deals with the way it was at the time I studied it and, to that extent, is no doubt in some respects already out of date. I have indicated that some changes had indeed been introduced to basic medical training at UCLMS; other changes were shortly to be introduced, and in fact already have been in some medical schools. I obviously have not studied the effect of such changes, but it seems entirely likely that such alterations are of three sorts. First, they introduce more efficient and explicit teaching of what is already taught in traditional training. An example of this is the attention to the problem of the loss of clinical students' Experience (mentioned in Chapter 8) by methods such as the Objective Structured Clinical Examination (see Lowry 1993: 45–58). Second, they graft on changes foreign to the traditional training, which are likely to be rejected in practice. Examples of this are the attachments in General Practice and courses in 'Doctor–Patient Communication' (also mentioned in Chapter 8), which for the reasons given there are unlikely to have any effect on what happens in hospital. Third, there are changes that simply realign existing elements in the traditional training. This is probably the case with the introduction of 'Problem-Based Learning', which, though it may enable more facility with the manipulation of Knowledge – certainly no bad thing – still takes place in medical schools within the paramount disposition of professional Co-operation. And, while Problem-Based Learning may accomplish some degree of integration between the preclinical and clinical levels, the 'clinical experience' would appear to remain relatively unaltered. Further, even in such new systems of training, 'social and behavioral issues are always a tiny part of medical curricula, and in the clerkship [clinical] years, these so-called "psycho-social" dimensions of medicine are always marginalized, absorbed within the standard work-up, set aside for exceptional cases, or discounted entirely' (Good 1994: 84). Beyond these undergraduate years, there does not appear to be any further integration with the third level of training, the 'national disgrace' of the pre-registration year (Weatherall 1993: x). I suggest, in fact, that both existing and envisaged reforms are unlikely to exert any major effect on the basic form of medical training in terms of the dispositions I have described.

Freidson's criticisms of the profession (as described in Chapter 1) are mainly connected to its autonomy. This is based to a large extent on the profession's specialist knowledge and its expressed ethical commitments; such professional Idealism, however, lacks congruence with its actual practice in providing services to the public. It will be recalled that Freidson's proposals for realigning them are: a wider range of recruitment, dismantling self-sufficient institutions, greater interaction between hospital doctors and general practitioners, and both professional and lay review of medical practice. To have most force these should be applied in the formative years of training and they could, in fact, all be very simply accomplished by reverting to a more personal and less institutional apprenticeship, with the overwhelming bulk of basic medical training taking place in General Practice and not in medical schools and teaching hospitals. A brief outline of the possible form of such a training follows. First, in attachments to general practices, students would gain an early and intimate acquaintance with the scope and nature of patients' problems and of the practice of medicine in these settings: familiarity with the work of other professions (if not a fully 'cross-professional' training) would result in a less medical Co-operation, and personal Idealism would become firmly rooted in reality. At this level, students would analyse their experience through the social sciences, which are currently lost without trace. Later would come learning both Knowledge (possible in these different settings by the use of new technology) and Experience, both in general practices and in specialist Out-Patient clinics (perhaps assessed by more objective methods described above). Throughout these periods, a gradually increasing share in the care of patients would lead to a new disposition, formed by an amalgamation of some aspects of Co-operation and Responsibility, in which sharing responsibility with patients and others became the primary form of relationship. Satisfactory completion of such basic training would result from success in national examinations, which would give the public the assurance of safety and competence as well as preventing the development of 'second-class' forms of qualification. At the next level, the question of specialisation would arise, help here being provided both by the now more organised higher training and, dare I suggest, by some more psychological approach to individual doctors' own aptitudes. This would tie in with the earlier assessment along these lines as part of the application for medical training, where 'impression management' would give way to a more thorough appraisal of individual capacities for such a career.

But I have argued that the existing dispositions acquired during training actually give rise to the existing structure. Changes as fundamental as those sketched out above are consequently highly unlikely to be the product of the profession's own reforms, especially when the financial implications of any such changes are considered. For medical training does not lead to an autonomous student culture, or even to a dependent subculture, but should be thought of as an integral part of medical culture, its own maintenance crucial to the survival of the traditional structure of the profession. In view of the legal and financial insistence any such major changes would depend on, it is only the State that could accomplish them; but the novel intervention of this sort by the State would also depend on the involvement of the general public in these matters. We are paying for all this and, to some extent at least, we get the doctors we deserve.

Bibliography

Abel-Smith, Brian (1964) *The Hospitals 1800–1948: A Study in Social Administration in England and Wales*, London: Heinemann.

Allen, Isobel (1988) *Doctors and their Careers*, London: Policy Studies Institute.

—— (1994) *Doctors and their Careers: A New Generation*, London: Policy Studies Institute.

Altman, Douglas G. (1994) 'The scandal of poor medical research', *British Medical Journal* **308** 283–4.

Anonymous (1948) 'Selected seed', *Lancet* **2** 333–4.

Atkinson, Paul (1981) *The Clinical Experience: The Construction and Reconstruction of Medical Reality*, Farnborough: Gower.

—— (1983) 'The Reproduction of the Professional Community', in Robert Dingwall and Philip Lewis (eds), *The Sociology of the Professions: Lawyers, Doctors and Others*, London and Basingstoke: Macmillan.

—— (1984) 'Training for certainty', *Social Science and Medicine* **19** 949–56.

—— (1988) 'Discourse, Descriptions and Diagnoses: Reproducing Normal Medicine', in Lock and Gordon (1988).

—— (1994) *Medical Talk and Medical Work: The Liturgy of the Clinic*, London: Sage.

Ballard, J. G. (1991) *The Kindness Of Women*, London: HarperCollins.

Barker-Benfield, G. J. (1992) *The Culture of Sensibility: Sex and Society in Eighteenth-Century Britain*, Chicago: University of Chicago Press.

Beck, Aaron T., Arthur Freeman and Associates (1990) *Cognitive Therapy of Personality Disorders*, New York and London: Guilford Press.

Becker, Howard S., Blanche Geer, Everett C. Hughes and Anselm L. Strauss (1961) *Boys In White: Student Culture in Medical School*, Chicago and London: University of Chicago Press.

Bentham, Jeremy (1983) [1815–17] *Chrestomathia: Being A Collection Of Papers Explanatory Of The Design Of An Institution Proposed To Be Set On Foot Under The Name Of The Chrestomathic Day School Or Chrestomathic School For The Extension Of The New System Of Instruction To The Higher Branches Of Learning, For The Use Of The Middling And Higher Ranks Of Life*, ed. M. J. Smith and W. H. Burston, Oxford: Clarendon Press.

Bloom, Samuel W. (1971) 'The medical school as social system', *Milbank Memorial Fund Quarterly* **49, 2: Part 2**.

—— (1988) 'Structure and ideology in medical education: an analysis of resistance to change', *Journal of Health and Social Behaviour* **29** 294–306.

BMA (British Medical Association) (Scientific Division) (1992) *Stress and the Medical Profession*, London: BMA.

BMA (British Medical Association) (Board of Science and Education) (1993) *The Morbidity and Mortality of the Medical Profession: A Literature Review and Suggestions for Future Research*, London: BMA.

BMA (British Medical Association) (Working Party on Medical Education) (1994/95) *Report C41*, London: BMA.

Bosk, Charles L. (1979) *Forgive and Remember: Managing Medical Failure*, Chicago and London: University of Chicago Press.

Boud, David and Grahame Feletti (eds) (1991) *The Challenge of Problem Based Learning*, London: Kogan Page.

Bourdieu, Pierre (1977) *Outline of a Theory of Practice*, trans. Richard Nice, Cambridge: Cambridge University Press.

—— (1992) *The Logic of Practice*, trans. Richard Nice, Oxford: Polity.

Bourdieu, Pierre and Loïc J. D. Wacquant (1992) *An Invitation to Reflexive Sociology*, Cambridge: Polity.

Brazier, Margaret (1992) *Medicine, Patients and the Law*, Harmondsworth: Penguin.

Brieger, Gert (1993) 'Sense and Sensibility in Late Nineteenth-century Surgery in America', in W. F. Bynum and Roy Porter (eds), *Medicine and the Five Senses*, Cambridge: Cambridge University Press.

Broadhead, R. S. (1983) *The Private Lives and Professional Identity of Medical Students*, New Brunswick: Transaction.

Brooke, Deborah, Griffiths Edwards and Colin Taylor (1991) 'Addiction as an occupational hazard: 144 doctors with drug and alcohol problems', *British Journal of Addiction* **86** 1011–16.

Burns, Tom (1992) *Erving Goffman*, London: Routledge.

Bynum, W. F. (1973) 'The anatomical method, natural theology, and the functions of the brain', *Isis* **64** 445–68.

—— (1994) *Science and the Practice of Medicine in the Nineteenth Century*, Cambridge: Cambridge University Press.

Bynum, W. F. and Roy Porter (eds) (1985) *William Hunter and the Eighteenth-century Medical World*, Cambridge: Cambridge University Press.

Carr-Saunders, A. M. and P. A. Wilson (1964) [1933] *The Professions*, London: Frank Cass.

Childs, Mary (1995) 'Medicine and the law of manslaughter', *Journal of the Medical and Dental Defence Union* **11** 54–7.

Cooter, Roger (1984) *The Cultural Meaning of Popular Science: Phrenology and the Organization of Consent in Nineteenth-century Britain*, Cambridge: Cambridge University Press.

Dalton, H. R. (1991) *Final MB: A Guide to Success in Clinical Medicine*, Edinburgh: Churchill Livingstone.

Desmond, Adrian (1989) *The Politics of Evolution: Morphology, Medicine and Reform in Radical London*, Chicago and London: University of Chicago Press.

Dingwall, Robert (1977) '"Atrocity stories" and professional relationships', *Sociology of Work and Occupations* **4** 371–96.

DOH (Department of Health) (The Report of the Working Group on Specialist Medical Training) (1993) *Hospital Doctors: Training for the Future*, London: HMSO.

DOH (Department of Health) (NHS Executive, Statistics (Workforce) Branch) (1996) *Hospital Medical Staff – England and Wales: National Tables*, London: HMSO.

Dowling, Sue and Sue Barrett (1991) *Doctors In The Making: The Experience Of The Pre-Registration Year*, Bristol: School For Advanced Urban Studies.

Druce, Maralyn and Martin H. Johnson (1994) 'Human dissection and attitudes of preclinical students to death and bereavement', *Clinical Anatomy* **7** 42–9.

Eliade, Mircea (1959) *The Sacred and the Profane: the Nature of Religion*, trans. Willard R. Trask, San Diego, New York and London: Harcourt Brace Jovanovich.

Esmail, Aneez, Paul Nelson, Dawn Primarolo and Tudor Toma (1995) 'Acceptance into medical school and racial discrimination', *British Medical Journal* **310** 501–2.

Figlio, K. M. (1976) 'The metaphor of organisation', *History of Science* **14** 17–53.

Firth, Jenny (1986) 'Levels and sources of stress in medical students', *British Medical Journal* **292** 1177–80.

Firth-Cozens, Jenny (1987) 'Emotional distress in junior house officers', *British Medical Journal* **295** 533–5.

—— (1990) 'Sources of stress in women junior house officers', *British Medical Journal* **301** 89–91.

—— (1992) 'The role of early family experiences in the perception of organizational stress; fusing clinical and organizational perspectives', *Journal of Occupational and Organizational Psychology* **65** 61–75.

Fissell, Mary E. (1991) 'The Disappearance of the Patient's Narrative and the Invention of Hospital Medicine', in Roger French and Andrew Wear (eds), *British Medicine in an Age of Reform*, London: Routledge.

Foucault, Michel (1989) [1973] *The Birth of the Clinic*, trans. A. M. Sheridan, London: Routledge.

—— (1991) [1977] *Discipline and Punish: The Birth of the Prison*, trans. Alan Sheridan, Harmondsworth: Penguin.

Fox, Renée C. (1957) 'Training for Uncertainty', in Robert K. Merton *et al.* (1957).

Freidson, E. (1970) *Profession of Medicine: A Study of the Sociology of Applied Knowledge*, New York: Dodd, Mead.

Furnham, A. F. (1986) 'Medical students' beliefs about nine different specialties', *British Medical Journal* **293** 1607–10.

Fussell, Paul (1990) *Wartime: Understanding and Behaviour in the Second World War*, Oxford: Oxford University Press.

Geison, G. (1972) 'Social and institutional factors in the stagnancy of English physiology, 1840–70', *Bulletin of the History of Medicine* **46** 30–58.

Gelfand, Toby (1985) '"Invite the Philosopher, As Well As the Charitable": Hospital Teaching as Private Enterprise in Hunterian London', in Bynum and Porter (1985).

Gellner, Ernest (1970) 'Concepts and Society', in D. Emmet and A. MacIntyre (eds), *Sociological Theory and Philosophical Analysis*, London: Macmillan.

Gilbert, G. Nigel and Michael Mulkay (1984) *Opening Pandora's Box: A Sociological Analysis of Scientists' Discourse*, Cambridge: Cambridge University Press.

GMC (General Medical Council) (Education Committee) (1992a) *Commentary On The Second Survey Of Medical Education Practices In United Kingdom Medical Schools*, London: GMC.

—— (1992b) *Recommendations on General Clinical Training*, London: GMC.

—— (1993) *Tomorrow's Doctors: Recommendations On Undergraduate Medical Education*, London: GMC.

Goffman, Erving (1961) *Encounters: Two Studies in the Sociology of Interaction*, Indianapolis: Bobs-Merill.

—— (1974) *Frame Analysis: An Essay on the Organization of Experience*, New York: Harper and Row.

—— (1990) [1959] *The Presentation Of Self In Everyday Life*, Harmondsworth: Penguin.

—— (1991) [1961] *Asylums: Essays on the Social Situation of Mental Patients and Other Inmates*, Harmondsworth: Penguin.

Good, Byron J. (1994) *Medicine, Rationality and Experience: An Anthropological Perspective*, Cambridge: Cambridge University Press.

Good, Byron J. and Mary-Jo DelVecchio Good (1993) '"Learning Medicine": The Constructing of Medical Knowledge at Harvard Medical School', in Shirley Lindenbaum and Margaret Lock (eds), *Knowledge, Power and Practice: The Anthropology of Medicine and Everyday Life*, Berkeley and Los Angeles: University of California Press.

Good, Mary-Jo DelVecchio and Byron J. Good (1989) 'Disabling practitioners: hazards of learning to be a doctor in American medical education', *Journal of Orthopsychiatry* **59** 303–9.

Gordon, Deborah R. (1988) 'Tenacious Assumptions in Western Medicine', in Lock and Gordon (1988).

Gordon, Richard (1955) *Doctor in the House*, London: The Reprint Society.

Gumperz, John J. and Jenny Cook-Gumperz (1982) 'Introduction: Language and the Communication of Social Identity', in John J. Gumperz (ed.), *Language and Social Identity: Studies in Interactional Linguistics*, Cambridge: Cambridge University Press.

Hafferty, Frederic W. (1991) *Into The Valley: Death and the Socialization of Medical Students*, New Haven and London: Yale University Press.

Hahn, Robert A. (1985) 'A World of Internal Medicine: Portrait of an Internist', in Hahn and Gaines (1985).

Hahn, Robert A. and Atwood D. Gaines (1985) *Physicians of Western Medicine: Anthropological Approaches to Theory and Practice*, Dordrecht: Kluwer Academic Publishers.

Hale, Robert and Liam Hudson (1992) 'The Tavistock Study of Young Doctors: report of the pilot phase', *British Journal of Hospital Medicine* **47** 452–64.

Handy, Charles (1993) *Understanding Organizations*, Harmondsworth: Penguin.

Harris, A. D. (1948) 'The selection of medical students', *Lancet* **2** 317–21.

Harte, Negley and John North (1991) *The World of UCL 1828–1990*, London: UCL.

Heckshер, W. (1958) *Rembrandt's Anatomy of Dr. Nicolaas Tulp*, New York: Washington Square Press.

Hellman, Cecil (1991) *Body Myths*, London: Chatto and Windus.

Hertz, Robert (1960) [1909] *The Pre-eminence of the Right Hand: A Study in Religious Polarity*, trans. Rodney and Caroline Needham, London: Cohen and West.

Holland, Dorothy (1992) 'The Woman Who Climbed up the House: Some Limitations of Schema Theory', in Theodore Schwartz, Geoffrey M. White and Catherine A. Lutz (eds), *New Directions in Psychological Anthropology*. Cambridge: Cambridge University Press.

Hudson, Liam (1970) *Frames of Mind: Ability, Perception and Self-perception in the Arts and Sciences*, Harmondsworth: Penguin.

—— (1974) *Contrary Imaginations: A Psychological Study of the English Schoolboy*, Harmondsworth: Penguin.

Hughes, Everett (1984) [1971] *The Sociological Eye*, New Brunswick: Transaction.

Humphris, G., S. Kaney, D. Broomfield, T. Bayley and J. Lilley (1994) *Stress in Junior Hospital Medical and Dental Staff*, Liverpool: University of Liverpool.

Hunter, Kathryn Montgomery (1991) *Doctors' Stories: The Narrative Structure of Medical Knowledge*, Princeton: Princeton University Press.

Jenkins, Richard (1992) *Pierre Bourdieu*, London and New York: Routledge.

Jewson, N. D. (1976) 'The disappearance of the sick-man from medical cosmology, 1770–1870', *Sociology* **10** 225–44.

Johnson, Mark (1987) *The Body In The Mind: The Bodily Basis of Meaning, Imagination and Reason*, Chicago: University of Chicago Press.

Johnson, W. D. K. (1991) 'Predisposition to emotional distress and psychiatric illness among doctors: the role of unconscious and experiential factors', *British Journal of Medical Psychology* **64** 317–29.

Jordanova, J. L. (1985) 'Gender, Generation and Science: William Hunter's Obstetrical Atlas', in Bynum and Porter (1985).

Kelly, George (1955) *The Psychology of Personal Constructs*, New York: Norton.

Klass, Perri (1987) *A Not Entirely Benign Procedure: Four Years as a Medical Student*, New York: G. P. Putnam's.

Konner, Melvin (1987) *Becoming A Doctor: A Journey of Initiation in Medical School*, New York: Viking.

Lane, Joan (1985) 'The Role of Apprenticeship in Eighteenth-century Medical Education in England', in Bynum and Porter (1985).

Laqueur, Thomas (1987) 'Orgasm, Generation, and the Politics of Reproductive Biology', in Catherine Gallagher and Thomas Laqueur (eds), *The Making of the Modern Body: Sexuality and Society in the Nineteenth Century*, Berkeley, Los Angeles and London: University of California Press.

Larson, Magali Sarfatti (1977) *The Rise of Professionalism: A Sociological Analysis*, Berkeley: University of California Press.

Latour, Bruno (1987) *Science In Action: How to Follow Scientists and Engineers through Society*, Cambridge, Mass.: Harvard University Press.

Lawrence, Susan C. (1991) 'Private Enterprise and Public Interests: Medical Education and the Apothecaries' Act, 1780–1825', in Roger French and Andrew Wear (eds), *British Medicine in an Age of Reform*, London: Routledge.

—— (1995) 'Anatomy and Address: Creating Medical Gentlemen in Eighteenth-Century London', in Vivian Nutter and Roy Porter (eds), *The History of Medical Education in Britain*, Amsterdam and Atlanta, Ga.: Rodopi.

LeBaron, Charles (1981) *Gentle Vengeance: An Account of the First Year at Harvard Medical School*, New York: Penguin.

Lella, Joseph W. and Dorothy Pawluch (1988) 'Medical Students and the Cadaver in Social and Cultural Context', in Lock and Gordon (1988).

Lock, Margaret and Deborah R. Gordon (eds) (1988) *Biomedicine Examined*, Dordrecht: Kluwer Academic Publications.

Lowry, Stella (1993) *Medical Education*, London: BMJ.

McManus, I. C. (1995) 'Examining the educated and the trained', *Lancet* **345** 1151–3.

McManus, Chris [I. C.] and Diana Lockwood (1992) 'Medical Education, Training and Research', in Eric Beck, Susan Lonsdale, Stanton Newman and David Patterson (eds), *In the Best of Health?: The Status and Future of Health Care in the UK*, London: Chapman and Hall.

McManus, I. C. and P. Richards (1984) 'Audit of admission to medical school: I – Acceptances and rejects', *British Medical Journal* **289** 1201–4.

—— (1986) 'Prospective survey of performance of medical students during preclinical years', *British Medical Journal* **293** 124–7.

McManus, I. C., P. Richards, B. C. Winder, K. A. Sproston and C. A. Vincent (1993) 'The changing clinical experience of British medical students', *Lancet* **341** 941–4.

McManus, I. C., P. Richards, B. C. Winder, K. A. Sproston, V. Styles (1995) 'Medical school applicants from ethnic minority groups: identifying if and when they are disadvantaged', *British Medical Journal* **310** 496–500.

Maltz, Daniel L. and Ruth A. Borker (1982) 'A Cultural Approach to Male–Female Miscommunication', in John J. Gumperz (ed.), *Language and Social Identity: Studies in Interactional Sociolinguistics*, Cambridge: Cambridge University Press.

Martin, Emily (1987) *The Woman in the Body: a Cultural Analysis of Reproduction*, Boston: Beacon.

—— (1992) 'Body Narratives, Body Boundaries', in Lawrence Grossberg, Cary Nelson and Paula Treichler (eds), *Cultural Studies*, New York and London: Routledge.

—— (1994) *Flexible Bodies: Tracking Immunity in American Culture – From the Days of Polio to the Age of AIDS*, Boston: Beacon.

Maulitz, Russel C. (1987) *Morbid Appearances: The Anatomy of Pathology in the Early Nineteenth Century*, Cambridge: Cambridge University Press.

Merton, Robert K., George G. Reader and Patricia L. Kendall (eds) (1957) *The Student-Physician: Introductory Studies in the Sociology of Medical Education*, Cambridge, Mass.: Harvard University Press.

Millar, W. M. (1948) 'Personality studies of medical students', *Lancet* **2** 327–31.

Miller, S. J. (1970) *Prescription for Leadership: Training for the Medical Elite*, Chicago: Aldine.

Moss, F. and I. C. McManus (1992) 'The anxieties of new clinical students', *Medical Education* **26** 17–20.

Mumford, Emily (1970) *Interns: From Students to Physicians*, Cambridge, Mass.: Harvard University Press.

Murray, Robin M. (1976) 'Alcoholism amongst male doctors in Scotland', *Lancet* **2** 729–31.

Musgrove, F. (1964) *Youth And The Social Order*, London: Routledge and Kegan Paul.

Newman, Charles (1957) *The Evolution of Medical Education in the Nineteenth Century*, London: Oxford University Press.

Ogden, C. K. (1932) *Bentham's Theory of Fictions*, London: Kegan Paul, Trench, Trubner.

Ong, Walter J. (1991) [1982] *Orality and Literacy: The Technologizing of the Word*, London: Routledge.

Padgett, Deborah and Thomas M. Johnson (1990) 'Somatizing distress: hospital treatment of psychiatric co-morbidity and the limitations of biomedicine', *Social Science and Medicine* **30** 205–9.

Palmer, Roy (1990) *'What A Lovely War': British Soldiers' Songs from the Boer War to the Present Day*, London: Michael Joseph.

Peterson, M. Jeanne (1978) *The Medical Profession in Mid-Victorian London*, Berkeley: University of California Press.

Porter, Roy (1989) *Health for Sale: Quackery in England 1660–1850*, Manchester: Manchester University Press.

Reilly, Philip (1987) *To Do No Harm: A Journey Through Medical School*, Dover, Mass.: Auburn House.

Reiser, Stanley Joel (1978) *Medicine and the Reign of Technology*, Cambridge: Cambridge University Press.

Richards, I. A. (1965) [1936] *The Philosophy of Rhetoric*, New York: Oxford University Press.

Richards, Peter (1993) *Learning Medicine 1994: An Informal Guide To A Career in Medicine*, London: BMJ.

Richardson, Ruth (1989) *Death, Dissection and the Destitute*, Harmondsworth: Penguin.

Rogoff, Natalie (1957) 'The Decision To Do Medicine', in Merton *et al.* (1957).

Romanyshyn, Robert D. (1989) *Technology as Symptom and Dream*, London and New York: Routledge.

Rucinski, Jacek and Eva Cybulska (1985) 'Mentally ill doctors', *British Journal of Hospital Medicine* **33** 90–4.

Ruston, Joe (1993) *Getting Into Medical School*, Richmond: Trotman.

Ryle, Anthony (1990) *Cognitive–Analytic Therapy: Active Participation in Change: A New Integration in Brief Psychotherapy*, Chichester: Wiley.

Schwartz, A. H., M. Swartzburg, J. Lieb and A. E. Slaby (1978) 'Medical school and the process of disillusionment', *Medical Education* **12** 182–5.

Segal, Daniel A. (1987) 'A patient so dead: American medical students and their cadavers', *Anthropology Quarterly* **61** 17–25.

Sheehan, K. Harnett, David V. Sheehan, Kim White, Alan Leibowitz and DeWitt C. Baldwin (1990) 'A pilot study of medical student "abuse":

student perceptions of mistreatment and misconduct in Medical School', *Journal of the American Medical Association* **263** 533–7.

Shuval, J. (1975) 'From "boy" to "colleague": processes of role transformation in professional socialization', *Social Science and Medicine* **9** 413–20.

Silver, Henry K. and Anita Duhl Glicken (1990) 'Medical student abuse: incidence, severity, and significance', *Journal of the American Medical Association* **263** 527–32.

Singer, Charles (1959) 'The strange histories of some anatomical terms', *Medical History* **3** 1–7.

Smollett, Tobias (1930) [1748] *The Adventures of Roderick Random*, London: Oxford University Press.

Smyth, D. H. (1946) 'Some principles in the selection of medical students', *British Medical Journal* **2** 357–67.

Sperber, Dan (1979) 'Claude Lévi-Strauss', in John Sturrock (ed.), *Structuralism and Since*, Oxford: Oxford University Press.

Spindler, Susan (1992) *Doctors To Be* (accompanies the BBC TV series), London: BBC Books.

Stevens, Rosemary (1966) *Medical Practice in Modern England: The Impact of Specialization and State Medicine*, New Haven and London: Yale University Press.

Tomlinson Report (1992) *Report of the Inquiry into London's Health Service, Medical Education and Research*, London: HMSO.

Tosteson, D. (1994) 'Problem-based learning', in Henry Walton (ed.), *Proceedings of the World Summit on Medical Education, Medical Education* **28, Supplement 1** 108–11.

Towle, Angela (1992) *Undergraduate Medical Education: London and the Future*, London: King's Fund.

Turner, Bryan S. (1987) *Medical Power and Social Knowledge*, London: Sage.

Turner, Stephen (1994) *The Social Theory of Practices: Tradition, Tacit Knowledge and Presuppositions*, Oxford: Polity.

Turner, Victor W. (1967) *The Forest of Symbols: Aspects of Ndembu Ritual*, Ithaca and London: Cornell University Press.

—— (1974) *The Ritual Process: Structure and Anti-Structure*, Harmondsworth: Pelican.

Vaillant, George E., Nancy Corbin Sobowale and Charles McArthur (1972) 'Some psychologic vulnerabilities of physicians', *New England Journal of Medicine* **287** 372–5.

Vickers, Brian (1988) *In Defence of Rhetoric*, Oxford: Clarendon Press.

Weatherall, D. J. (1993) 'Introduction' to Lowry (1993).

Westall, W. Graham (1987) *How to Obtain a Place in Medical School*, London: Chapman and Hall.

Whitefield, A. G. W. (1981) 'Illness among doctors', *Journal of the Royal College of General Practitioners* **31** 723–5.

Whorf, Benjamin Lee (1956) 'Science and Linguistics', in John B. Carroll (ed.), *Language, Thought and Reality: Selected Writings of Benjamin Lee Whorf*, Cambridge, Mass.: MIT Press.

Witz, Anne (1992) *Professions and Patriarchy*, London and New York: Routledge.

Young, Allan (1980) 'The discourse on stress and the reproduction of conventional knowledge', *Social Science and Medicine* **14B** 133–46.

Youngson, A. J. (1979) *The Scientific Revolution in Victorian Medicine*, London: Croom Helm.

Ziman, John (1991) [1978] *Reliable Knowledge: An Exploration of the Grounds for Belief in Science*, Cambridge: Cambridge University Press.

Index